The Age of Mozart and Beethoven

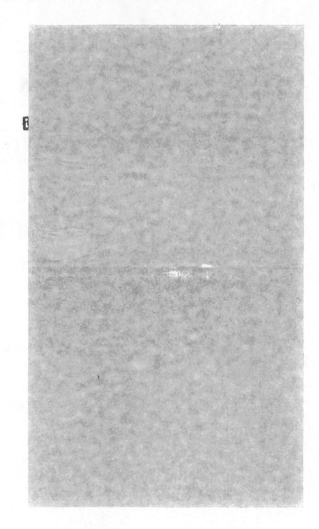

THE AGE OF
MOZART AND BEETHOVEN

GIORGIO PESTELLI

TRANSLATED BY ERIC CROSS

CAMBRIDGE
UNIVERSITY PRESS

ie University of Cambridge
t, Cambridge CB2 1RP
10011-4211, USA
ne 3166, Australia

a di Mozart e di Beethoven
by Edizioni di Torino, Turin, 1979 and © 1979 E.D.T.
English translation © Cambridge University Press 1984

First published in English by Cambridge University Press 1984
as *The Age of Mozart and Beethoven*
Reprinted 1985, 1987, 1988, 1990, 1991, 1995

Printed in Great Britain by
Athenaeum Press Ltd, Gateshead, Tyne and Wear

Library of Congress catalogue card number: 83-14256

British Library Cataloguing in Publication Data

Pestelli, Giorgio
The age of Mozart and Beethoven.
1. Music-Europe-History and criticism-18th century
2. Music-Europe-History and criticism-19th century
I. Title
II. L'età di Mozart e di Beethoven. *English*
780'.903'3   ML 240.3

ISBN 0 521 24149 9 hardback
ISBN 0 521 28479 1 paperback

CE

Contents

Contents

Contents

Author's note

The present volume contains more *and* less than the title suggests. More because the account starts from the death of Bach (1750) and therefore includes phenomena and composers that were born and grew up before Mozart, like the *galant* style, Gluck, C. P. E. Bach and Haydn. Less because there are only passing references here to figures such as Weber, Rossini and Schubert, whose activity, within a year or two, would strictly have to be included in the chronological confines of a 'Beethovenian age'. The presence of these 'contemporaries of Beethoven' within the following pages, however, apart from removing their names from books devoted to nineteenth-century Germany and Italy, would have meant an intolerable size for a volume which, as it is already, has greatly exceeded its original plan.

I have not used the terms 'classical', 'classical style' or 'classicism', although they are frequently used to describe the period dealt with here (what would the gap left unfilled between Bukofzer's 'Baroque Era' and Einstein's 'Romantic Era' in Norton's famous history be called, if not the 'Classical Era'?); and it is certainly not out of lack of interest in the historiographical and stylistic concepts and all the problems that their definition carries with it, but rather because I considered that those terms were not very useful for an approach that intended to be essentially historical. Indeed, to call a period (or a work) 'classical' does not say much about the period itself; if anything, it explains something about the person who considers it as such.

Apart from these omissions, I have tried to include in the book, above all, what is logical to find in a book of this kind, written from a general viewpoint, without the specialized assistance of notes and musical examples. In this matter I have made much use of ideas resulting from my ten years of contact with the students of the

Author's note

University of Turin, where a considerable part of this material became more clearly defined by passing through courses, seminars, examinations and dissertations.

I dedicate this book to Massimo Mila, remembering the twenty years of our acquaintance.

Florence, 26 May 1979   G. P.

AUTHOR'S NOTE TO THE ENGLISH EDITION

In introducing the English edition of *The Age of Mozart and Beethoven*, I should warn new readers that the limitations of the subject are partly a result of the book's origin – as the sixth of a ten-volume history of music by various authors, published under the auspices of the Italian Musicological Society. The main problem is, of course, that of limiting the period to be covered, something which is, as always, the result of practical compromises. Nevertheless, given that the subject was meant to be, above all, an 'age', with its own intellectual character and vitality, I felt that it was legitimate to suggest an independent volume separate from the complete series for which it was conceived.

I am very grateful to Dr Eric Cross, who has produced the translation. In the course of preparing the notes he has given me the opportunity to check and revise sources to which I had given insufficient consideration, and I am indebted to him for suggestions on many passages which were not very clear in the Italian edition and which are corrected in the present version.

Turin, October 1982   G. P.

Translator's note

For the English translation the original form of the book, written from a general viewpoint without musical examples, has been followed, but notes have been added to provide details of sources. I am most grateful to the author for supplying much of this information. I would also like to thank Professor Philip Yarrow for providing the translations of Readings 2 and 9 and Elizabeth Skinner for that of parts of Reading 11, Hugh Shankland for his invaluable advice on linguistic problems, and Ian Rumbold for suggesting countless ways of correcting and improving the text.

Newcastle upon Tyne, June 1982   E. C.

I

INSTRUMENTAL MUSIC

1 The geography of music in the middle of the eighteenth century

A great change was about to take place in the musical geography of
Europe in the second half of the eighteenth century. Italy, 'the true
academy of music' as Schütz had called it as early as 1648,[1] the
country that from the end of the Thirty Years' War had dominated
almost the whole of Europe and become the land of singing and
playing *par excellence*, was on the point of losing its supremacy and
was about to enter a period of eclipse that was to affect its whole
future history. This was clearly apparent at the end of the century:
the most important musicians were not Italian, and the leading
Italians were abroad, adopting styles different from those of their
native country. While foreign musicians became established in Italy,
instrumental music became the leading genre, the centre of new
developments and changes – but Italy had exhausted its age-old
reserves in this field.

This, of course, is an evaluation by posterity; for contemporaries
Italy continued to be the home of music. Naples was still a brilliant
centre of the first magnitude, with its conservatoires and internationally renowned Teatro San Carlo. Rome, under Benedict XIV,
an intelligent man, receptive to contemporary European culture,
enjoyed a period of theatrical success and was still the centre of
sacred music with its Sistine and Julian chapels in St Peter's, St John
Lateran and Santa Maria Maggiore. Bologna was also a lively
environment: in 1750 a group of noblemen decided to construct a
large new publicly owned theatre, the Teatro Comunale, inaugurated in 1763; and living in Bologna was a Franciscan priest,
Giovanni Battista Martini, regarded by all musically knowledgeable
Europeans as an indisputable authority. Tuscany, well governed by
the Lorraines, passed through a flourishing cultural period: Diderot

I

and D'Alembert's great *Encyclopédie* was printed at Lucca and Leghorn between 1758 and 1775. Not only was there a thriving theatrical life in Florence and Leghorn, but Tuscany also led the rest of Italy in the field of instrumental music, especially chamber music. Instrumental music was also important in Modena, while Parma, under Philip of Bourbon, saw intense theatrical activity, thanks to the minister du Tillot. Milan, an Austrian province, had all sorts of trading links with Vienna, and halfway through the century its theatrical life centred on the Teatro Regio Ducale. The Teatro Regio served the same function in the Turin of Charles Emmanuel III, but Lombardy and Piedmont were even more important for instrumental music – the Turinese school of violinists was also well known in Paris, and great numbers of Sammartini's symphonies took the road from Milan to Paris and Vienna. A horizontal axis along the Po stretching to Tuscany was the equivalent for instrumental music of the theatrical axis between Naples and Venice. And finally there was Venice, with (like Naples) four conservatoires, as well as the basilica of St Mark's, and many small theatres, named after the parishes in which they were situated (e.g. San Benedetto, San Salvator, and San Moisè). La Serenissima, in its golden decline, continued to offer hospitality to all kinds of music, to cultivate the publishing trade, and to encourage contact with the Austro-German world; and on its stages the début of the librettist Goldoni gave a new look to the theatrical life of Italy and Europe.[2]

Italy's political isolation in the second half of the eighteenth century, apparent in the charter ratified by the Treaty of Aix-la-Chapelle (1748), was not clearly paralleled in musical life halfway through the century. The commercial success of music and the presence of Italian composers beyond the Alps continued, but other centres took on a leading role, and new situations gave rise to different lines of development. By this time France and England were at the centre of the political and intellectual life of Europe. The two great nations had many similarities: both were characterized by mercantile politics and a strong legal system, and they challenged each other in America and the Indian seas. France, badly governed by Louis XV, was deeply disturbed, but it had a population almost three times that of England, as well as a flourishing industrial development, and it claimed an indisputable cultural supremacy, as shown by the diffusion of the French language throughout all the European courts. Paris, with its theatres, its public concerts, its music publishers and its instrument makers, provided work for innumerable musicians. It became a unique pole of attraction, a catalytic centre: Pergolesi's *La serva padrona*, the symphonies of the Mannheim composers and Gluck's French operas are all Parisian phenomena that grew to European dimensions. Meanwhile an Académie Royale de Musique was also formed in Lyons, and in 1752 a similar institution was founded at Bordeaux – a sign of the affluence which this city had acquired from Atlantic trade.

Yet the supremacy of French culture was approached by that of England. England was highly regarded not only for its political institutions but also for its scientific and literary movements; London rivalled Paris as the centre of musical trade, and some cities in the west of England (such as Liverpool and Manchester) also saw the birth of a cultural life with the building of their first theatres. One aspect of the significance of Paris and London must be stressed: it was not, as in the past, a localized school, centred on an emerging personality, that was important, but the anonymous and industrious organizational fabric, the liveliness and development of a circulation of music and musicians on an international scale which was much less restricted than in other centres.

In central Europe the great event halfway through the century was the sudden leap to prominence of Prussia under Frederick the Great compared with the old, glorious Austria of Maria Theresa. The figure of King Frederick, broad-minded, cultured and a fine musician, was a symbol of energy, decisiveness and the spirit of adventure for the younger generation. By this time Prussia was regarded as the home of three revolutions: those of Copernicus, Kant and the politics of Frederick. Nevertheless the musical heart of central Europe was still Vienna, the imperial capital; faithful to its cosmopolitan mission, it attracted musicians from Italy (especially for the court theatre which remained a centre of Italian opera), the German states, Burgenland (eastern Austria) and Bohemia. The War of the Austrian Succession and the Seven Years' War provoked an emigration from Prague to Vienna, and Bohemians made a name for themselves with their great skill, especially as string players, following in the steps of Tartini, whose influence was strongly felt in that region. Salzburg was also an important centre, and the circulation of music in Austria was still fed by a group of monasteries (Mariazell, Lilienfeld, Melk and St Florian) where not only sacred vocal music but also symphonies and quartets composed at Vienna or Salzburg were copied and either kept or put on the market. To the north, in the young kingdom of Prussia, Berlin became more prominent with the palace at Potsdam. Here, where Frederick played the flute with Quantz and had C. P. E. Bach in his service, there was a concert every evening and an opera twice a week. Unlike the cosmopolitan character of Vienna, Berlin was more typically German, something which was to make it one of the future centres of romanticism.

But Vienna and Berlin certainly did not complete the picture, as the old political and cultural particularism of the empire had a positive side in the many independent centres where instrumental music competed on equal terms with that of the theatre. Bavaria was traditionally open to influences from the south, particularly Italy, through the centres of Munich and Nuremberg. Slightly further north the cheerful citizens of Bamberg and Würzburg were enjoying a splendid period under the Schönborn dynasty, which had its palaces decorated with frescoes by Tiepolo and maintained a rich musical chapel under the direction of the Italian Platti. In central Germany there was Leipzig, the little Paris, linked for some time with French culture, famous for its fair and rich in music printing and musical instruments. It had been the centre of J. S. Bach's activity for most of his last thirty years, and even if mid-century taste was looking well beyond his example, the city still retained an aura of supremacy in musical doctrine and a severe conception of music, nourished by erudition and intellect. Around the 1750s, Dresden's prestige was even greater: plenty of Vivaldi's concertos had made their way there thanks to the violinist Pisendel; Hasse's presence made it a centre of Italian opera and a draw for instrumentalists like Quantz and Veracini; and in 1756 the court theatre's orchestra, well stocked with Tartini's pupils, was the most famous in Europe, and it was not until after the Seven Years' War that it conceded this supremacy to the orchestra at Mannheim. Dresden and Leipzig, moreover, lay on an indispensable route to the east, attracting musicians from Italy and France who then set out for Poland and Russia.

In the German lands further centres were still worth attention: Stuttgart, invested with the musical passion of its sovereign Carl Eugen of Württemberg; the Rhine valley from Basle and Strasbourg to Düsseldorf via Mannheim, Mainz, Bonn and Cologne – a fertile furrow of cultural exchange whose fruits went mainly to Paris and Vienna; and finally, to the north, great commercial cities like Bremen and Hamburg, which kept traditional contacts with English culture. And these were only the main centres of the German states, all, even the smallest, furnished with chapels, theatres and musical societies. Thus music entered everyday life, even crossing social strata. In Vienna, it was said, even the cooks had to know how to play the viola, and Madame de Staël in her *De l'Allemagne* of 1810 was to report with indicative optimism that both in cities and in the country almost every soldier and peasant knew music, the prerogative at one time of those born at the foot of Vesuvius.[3] The Lutheran education in singing, the intensive cultivation (gained from the Italians) of every branch of music, and the interest in instrumental technique had by this time prepared a foundation of the broadest understanding on which the extraordinary success of German music in the eighteenth and nineteenth centuries was to be largely based.

Even though the main stage of action in the new era still comprised Italy, Austria–Germany, France and England, a few other places on the musical map of Europe should also be mentioned. Lisbon and Madrid, where numerous keyboard composers grew up in the wake of Domenico Scarlatti and where Boccherini had settled, stood out on the Iberian peninsula. After 1750 Holland, faced with the new powers, declined as a European commercial trading centre, but Amsterdam remained a great city and maintained its importance as a centre of music printing for a long time. In Poland the illustrious traditions of Krakow gave way to Warsaw, increased in influence by Stanislav Augustus Poniatowski, who re-established the previously disbanded court chapel, attracted famous violinists (such as Pugnani and Viotti from Piedmont) and had a new theatre built. Copenhagen and Stockholm welcomed German, French and Italian musicians for quite long periods. At the end of the 1750s a troupe originating from Prague and Dresden, under the direction of Giovanni Battista Locatelli, introduced Italian opera to St Petersburg and, encouraged by their success, went as far as Moscow. A few years later the Empress Catherine, who wrote to Grimm that she would reward anyone who could find a remedy for the insensitivity of her musical ear, nevertheless tried to attract the most famous musicians of the time to Russia, looking to Naples, Venice, Vienna and Dresden; and, though to a lesser extent, she also encouraged local elements and founded a Russian school for the study of singing and music.

Finally, the map of Europe was no longer sufficient: across the ocean in Boston, New York, Philadelphia and Charleston a concert life sprang up, music and instruments were imported from Paris and London, and societies dedicated to St Cecilia were founded. Not far from Philadelphia the Moravian community in Bethlehem, Pennsylvania, formed by German, Bohemian and Dutch emigrants, had from 1744 a 'Collegium Musicum' which later played works by the Mannheim symphonists, J. C. Bach, Haydn and Mozart, while these European composers were still alive. For the first time in musical history a piece of music could reach the public throughout the entire civilized world, and a work written in Vienna, Mannheim or Milan could be performed at once in London, Paris and America.

2   The *galant* style and the new sensibility

Johann Adolf Scheibe's hostile criticism of J. S. Bach in his journal *Der critische Musikus* (1737)[4] is one of the most famous sources dealing with the new musical style which was widespread in Europe between 1740 and 1760: it was too difficult; there were too many restrictions imposed by notating ornaments that should be left to the performer's instinct; and there was too much polyphony – so much that all the parts were equally important and the main melodic line became blurred. By reversing these censures one can extract some positive precepts of the new artistic code known as the *galant* style. In the broad context of European (above all French and German) culture, from manners to literature, from education to art and fashion, this adjective was associated with the qualities 'gay', 'pleasant', 'free' and 'spontaneous'. Wherever one can see the mark of a rationally refined sensibility, the adjective 'galant' appears with the variable frequency of fashionable words. The great misunderstanding that Bach was artificial, scholastic and rather unnatural was now in fact the symptom of a profound change. For the second edition of the *Art of fugue* (1752), no more than thirty people were found in about five years who were prepared to spend the four thalers that it cost; in Diderot and D'Alembert's *Encyclopédie ou Dictionnaire raisonné des sciences, des arts et des métiers* (1751–72), Rousseau allocated little more than twenty lines to the entry 'Contrepoint', and under the entry 'Fugue' he specified, after describing fugal technique, that it generally served to create 'du bruit' rather than beautiful melodies, and to show off the musician's learning rather than to fall pleasingly on the listener's ear.[5] As far as learning was concerned, then, it was self-evident that it no longer had anything to do with music. The process had been happening for decades, but, at least on the theoretical level, some people loved to preserve some vestige of the art of music's inclusion in the 'Quadrivium'.[6] This was not the case in Paris, however, and in the introductory table to the *Encyclopédie*, dealing with the categorizing of intelligence and its main subdivisions, music was by this time included under the section 'Imagination'.

Counterpoint was the thing to be avoided. The aim was a style of writing thinned down to two or three parts which clearly separated melody from accompaniment. Themes became shorter and more immediately appreciable, following the thematic models of Pergolesi's comic intermezzos even in the instrumental field. Phrases were constructed with greater concern for symmetry so as not to disappoint the listener's expectations. Rhythm tended towards absolute strophic regularity, with a uniform beat and no sudden outbursts, becoming closely related to dancing, while the forms of minuet, gavotte, polonaise and gigue were much more widespread and had rather more direct appeal to the vast public than courtly fugue subjects.

Melody had to be suggested by nature, but could be embellished by art. This coincided with the new popularity of investigating ornaments, classifying trills, mordents, turns, and upper and lower appoggiaturas; this concerned not only keyboard instruments with their short sound-duration, but also strings and wind, revealing an inclination towards detailed work (as in the precise inlaid work of contemporary architectural and artistic design) and the rococo side of composition. In the course of a few years treatises appeared by F. W. Marpurg: *Die Kunst das Klavier zu spielen* (1750; translated into French five years later), Quantz: *Versuch einer Anweisung die Flöte traversiere zu spielen* (1752), C. P. E. Bach: *Versuch über die wahre Art das Clavier zu spielen* (1753–62) and Leopold Mozart: *Versuch einer gründlichen Violinschule* (1756). All of them concentrate on minute details of performance, on style and expressive inflections, and all tend to regard the performing musician as a professional; but in practice, with their meticulousness and copious examples, they also address the amateur, placing the 'true art' of playing harpsichords, flutes and violins, on their own or along with other instruments, almost within his reach. In collections of sonatas and concertos, too, dedications were no longer addressed solely to the glory of the prince or cardinal, and 'amateurs and experts' were often mentioned together. The difficulty of a piece became an important qualification, and some publishers' catalogues indicated beside the titles the classifications 'easy', 'very easy' and 'fairly easy'; a few collections were generously described as being for 'skilled and non-skilled performers', but the latter were clearly favoured. A kind of 'sonata for women' grew up: Christoph Nichelmann published *Brevi sonate da cembalo ad uso di chi ama il cembalo massime delle dame* (Nuremberg,

1749 and 1760), G. A. Paganelli called his 6 *Sonatines pour le clavecin* (Amsterdam, 1757) 'Divertissement de le beau sexe', and C. P. E. Bach wrote various sonatas 'à l'usage des Dames'.

Another term that frequently recurs on increasingly charming title-pages is 'conversation' (e.g. Guillemain's *Six sonates en quatuors ou conversations galantes et amusantes* of 1743, Toeschi's *Six pièces dialoguées* of 1766 and Boccherini's *Sei conversazioni a tre* of 1770). Charles Avison also illustrated this principle in the preface to his op. 7 sonatas (1760), likening them to 'a Conversation among Friends, where Few are of one Mind, and propose their mutual Sentiments, only to give Variety, and enliven their select Company.[7] A tendency towards simplification is also present in composition treatises, and few things are more indicative of the changes of the times than certain passages from J. A. Hiller and J. Riepel's *Grundregeln der Tonordnung* of 1755, which teach the grammar of composition by means of the minuet instead of the fugue; they too are addressed to the amateur, rather like an encouraging 'do-it-yourself minuet kit', two bars at a time, with a modulation to the dominant and a repeat of the opening. What a difference in a few years from the familiar strict discipline imposed by Bach's *Well-tempered Clavier*! Now it was no longer a matter of individual performers or narrow circles of pupils, but of the anonymous public of amateurs, more and more numerous and in a better position to influence the production of music.

If simplicity of style and ease of performance were symptoms of a musical society that had enlarged its boundaries in comparison with those of the baroque era, the *galant* style also carried within it a theoretical tradition, with declarations of 'musical poetics' aimed at placing it within an evolutionary design of the art of music. Mattheson, in his *Das neu-eröffnete Orchestre* of 1713, was probably the first to discuss the adjective *galant*, later followed by Scheibe who defined the *galant* style as a 'middle style', in a Ciceronian sense, as distinct from a high and a low style.[8] But around the 1750s, the *galant* style became the centre of every discussion, especially in the work of the Berlin trio Marpurg, Quantz and C. P. E. Bach. Marpurg in particular, nourished by French culture (he lived in Paris from 1746 to 1749), and Rameau's intermediary in Germany, was the leader of the group and the author of a vast theoretical output: the idea of a *galant* as opposed to a *gearbeitet* (that is, elaborate and contrapuntal) style gained ground in his *Handbuch bey dem Generalbasse* (1755–60) and the *Kritische Briefe über die Tonkunst* (1760–4). Even in his *Abhandlung von der Fuge* (1753), an early monograph dealing with

fugue, Marpurg resorts to the term *galant* to describe fugal treatment which is freer than Bach's, with a variable number of parts and
a certain emphasis on the upper melodic line. Marpurg's attitude
was tolerant: this *galant* style definitely existed and even affected
fugal writing, but it was to be accepted only in moderation; it
certainly could not replace the strict style of Bach's fugues – at the
most it could make it more flexible and attractive. This tone of
legitimation continues in later treatises (e.g. those by Kirnberger
and Koch)[9] up to the end of the century, but their words echo like
distant and indistinct rumblings in the background of the new
middle-class public, who wanted to play music themselves, and busy
publishers ready to satisfy the demands of amateurs and experts.

The *galant* style did not produce any dominant musical figures. The
great composers of the first half of the century, J. S. Bach, Handel,
Domenico Scarlatti and Rameau, were foreign to it (Bach used the
word 'Galanterien' in Part I of his *Clavierübung*, but it was a concess-
ion to the popular term, not to the style of writing). A few, like
Telemann (especially with his fantasias for solo harpsichord) or
Hasse, were able to act as intermediaries, but certainly no composer
of the first rank involved himself in these poetics of pleasantry.
Nevertheless the widespread *galant* taste marked an essential period
in European musical history, and it would be a mistake to simplify
this style as a facile pandering to the demands of the new public. It
needs to be considered in a wider context of the general importance
of feeling compared with the logic of reason, an attitude which
emerged around the 1740s with previously unknown force. This
current of thought, which embraced every sector of human activity
with new warmth, originated in England; its cradle was the third
Earl of Shaftesbury's cult of sentiment, the perception of the world
as something beautiful, and the conviction that valued religion much
more as an exercise in benevolence than as a code of regulations. A
universal benevolence, reproduced on an intimate scale and similar
to German Pietism at the beginning of the century, pervaded John
Wesley's Methodism and the religious poetry of his brother Charles.
The novels of a lower-middle-class printer, Samuel Richardson,
gained European fame through their philosophy of sentiment,
enlightenment and observation of characters: *Pamela* (1741), which
through a libretto by Goldoni was to provide material for the first
comic opera of international importance, and *Clarissa* (1748), translated into French by Prévost in 1751 and imitated by Lessing in his
tragedy *Miss Sarah Sampson* (1755), the first play with a bourgeois

plot to be produced in Germany. Charles Avison, by the time of his *Essay on musical expression* (1752), placed melody, harmony and expression on the same level as foundations of perfection, while appeals to feeling and emotion for their own sake are continually found in Carl Philipp Emanuel Bach's treatise of 1753 (see Reading no. 1).

There were some areas of influence which were important in the history of European taste for a long time, preparing the ground for romanticism; recognizing the guiding values of feeling and nature rather than the logic of reason meant leaning towards England rather than France. This closer connection with England originated in Zurich in the Protestants' aversion to Louis XIV, who was threatening the Swiss borders: Beat Ludwig von Muralt's *Lettres sur les Anglois et les François* (1725) had presented for the first time a contrast between balanced French culture, standardized by reason, and English culture, inspired by nature, a contrast that was to prove very popular. Halfway through the century in Germany differing national standpoints appeared in the theatre: looking at Shakespeare in the same way as the periodical *Bremer Beiträge* meant arguing with the rationalism of Gottsched, a leading representative of rococo poetry between 1730 and 1740 and promoter of an imitation of French classical tragedy. In France itself new voices made themselves heard: from the other side of the Rhine came Gessner's *Idylls*, translated in 1762 and copied by other German poets whose pastoral and moralizing idylls paved the way for Mme de Staël's *De l'Allemagne* (1810). But here too England was considered the most significant influence, with Voltaire's *Lettres philosophiques* (1734) and the translation of Shaftesbury's *Inquiry concerning virtue* made by Diderot (1745); and it was a work by one of Diderot's friends, Jean-Jacques Rousseau, which summed up all the aspects of eighteenth-century sensibility, the epistolary novel *Julie ou la Nouvelle Héloïse* (1761), a vast and industrious monument to the power of sentiment. Sentiment was not regarded as pure, but it could elevate mortals to the threshold of divinity; class prejudice does not allow the noble Julie to marry her beloved Saint-Preux, and to the girl's father he is only a 'quidam', a representative of his class; but this class, supported by moral strictness and learning, was by now getting ready to rule the world.

Rousseau, in *La Nouvelle Héloïse*, talks about music with far more warmth than in the dry words written for the *Encyclopédie* (see Reading no. 2). The emotional participation of the listener went far beyond the musical idea itself, and writers produced, for the first time in such a detailed way, a kind of 'music of the imagination' (which was to be popular up to Thomas Mann's *Doktor Faustus*), far more turbulent and advanced than 'real music', which was restricted by the problems of musical language. The success of the epistolary form that takes us back to the world of the French *précieux* (for example Vincent Voiture's *Lettres*) was very significant. Art at the middle of the eighteenth century was short-breathed; it tended towards precise detail, variation structure and documentary naturalism, and nothing met this requirement more than a story told through letters, each one complete within itself. When Marpurg urged the *galant* composers to study fugue, his aim was to help them to achieve a less 'jumpy' melodic style. Kirnberger was also concerned about the leaps of a *stile coupé*, of French origin, with its cadences in almost every bar, and Johann Christian Bach was to talk about writing 'in monosyllables' in order to be understood even by children.[10] But these are testimonies which bring to mind the style of the sentimental novel of the period, such as Johann M. Miller's *Siegwart, eine Klostergeschichte* (1776 – an early imitation of *Werther*), a style that Goethe defined as 'typically feminine, full of full stops and short phrases'.[11] The short-breathed style could certainly also have been the result of a desire to adhere directly to sentiment and to expression unfiltered by the art of literary composition. When Saint-Preux is compelled to leave his Julie, he can only write down these fragments: 'I am well ... I do not suffer ... I am still alive ... I am thinking of you ... I am thinking of the time I was dear to you ... my heart is a little oppressed ... the carriage makes me giddy ... I am depressed';[12] and when Rousseau found these expressions, or ones like them, set in short, sharp statements in Pergolesi's *La serva padrona*, he believed that he recognized in those notes nature in music, real life, for which to exchange the whole illustrious tradition of the *tragédie lyrique*.

The moving force of the *galant* style was based on this complex ideal, centred on subjective emotion and going beyond the ear-flattering banality, the formal insipidity and the dull simplicity of many of its concrete manifestations. This worthy origin really contained the germ of its replacement: a slight intensification of this sentiment was to be enough for the *galant* to become an old, frivolous world. In *La Nouvelle Héloïse* the adjective *galant* had already taken on a negative nuance: the city of Paris viewed for the first time, with the formality and scepticism of its inhabitants, was to be *galant* in the eyes of Saint-Preux, a Swiss citizen from the Vaud region who had read Plutarch. The danger of the *galant* was 'fadeur', insipidity, and the flowery *galant* speech was to seem the opposite of the language of sentiment. On the other hand, in order to get rid of the *galant* style in music it was necessary to consider it apart from the sentimental/expressive movement in an equally strong light of rational clarity, of conceptual courage beyond the bounds of good taste. Strong feeling and more broad-minded reason were to make the *galant* disappear, but both these had their origins there, in the decades of down-to-earth music between 1740 and 1760 which had nevertheless cleared away the remains of the baroque era, the supernatural, and a solemnity which no longer had any roots. Music was no longer a science, an art with limited frontiers, but was capable of social communication.

3 Sonata form as a basic form

If instrumental music was dominated in the first half of the eighteenth century, in the wake of Corelli and his European pupils, by the violin, the great event of the second half of the century was the slow but irresistible rise of the hammer piano (or 'forte-piano') at the expense of the harpsichord. The complete control of harmonic movement and the personal nature of keyboard music (only one performer was needed) caused some of the most important formal changes of the period to occur in music for this instrument. In the keyboard family only the organ was left in a secondary position, being confined to the forms brought to fruition by J. S. Bach. The harpsichord was much more attractive; it had been stripped of its responsibility for polyphony but was strong in the art of ornamentation, which was not only required from the inspired performer but carefully indicated by the composer himself to make every inflection more 'affected' and '*galant*'. Now, although the first fortepianos did not differ much from the harpsichord in intensity of sound and tone colour, it is easy to see how an instrument like the piano came about, with its opportunity for tonal shading (*forte* or *piano*, in fact) dependent on the accuracy of the performer's fingers, thus fulfilling the need for more and more expressive music.

In spite of this the harpsichord was not easily deposed. Bartolomeo Cristofori's invention of the piano ('gravicembalo col piano e col forte') was publicized in 1711; but the earliest sonatas, by Giustini da Pistoia, marked for 'cimbalo di piano e forte detto volgarmente di martelletti', date from 1732. The earliest public concerts for the piano, in Paris and London, took place at the beginning of the 1760s, but the harpsichord remained dominant until the decade 1770–80 (a few pianos at the court of Madrid were even demoted and converted into harpsichords). The editorial indication 'for harpsichord or piano' began to appear in 1763 and remained common until *c.* 1800, even though in sonatas by Mozart and Clementi, written in the mid-1770s for pianos with the first sustaining pedals, the indication 'for the harpsichord' was already in fact out of date. One other keyboard instrument, the clavichord, held in high esteem by C. P. E. Bach, still had a place: it allowed modifications of tone colour and also a characteristic effect, 'Bebung', a kind of vibrato obtained by varying the finger's pressure on the key. The clavichord encouraged the need for intimacy, domestic music and a kind of personal conversation with the instrument (C. P. E. Bach wrote a rondo in 1781 entitled 'Farewell to my Silbermann clavichord' after he had given the instrument to a friend); but because its faint sound was almost imperceptible to anyone further away than the player himself, it could not compete with the 'public' possibilities of the piano when the latter began to gain a hold.

A similar change to the one which led from the harpsichord, with its uncontrollable touch, to the piano, capable of the immediate translation of dynamic intentions, involved the concept of the orchestra as a unified body, more 'symphonic' than the concerto style of the baroque age. The baroque concerto, with its alternating or overlapping sections for 'concerto grosso' (or 'tutti') and 'concertino' (a variable group of soloists), could recall the colouristic play of the two manuals of a harpsichord; the 'terraced' style, with sudden increases or reductions in volume, echo effects, and successions of full and light scoring, could imitate the contrast of registrations on the organ. Now, however, the 'symphonic' orchestra tended to embrace the internal principle of dynamic arches, with crescendos and diminuendos, instead of building up blocks of sound, as in the baroque concerto. Pairs of sustaining wind instruments, at first horns, then oboes or flutes, reinforced the string group which was still dominant (first and second violins, violas, cellos and double basses); and the absorption of an ever-increasing and more varied number of wind instruments was to accelerate constantly until the multicoloured and diverse resources of the baroque concerto were replaced by a unified body, organized 'families' of instruments, whose treatment was nevertheless to involve careful blending, based on a common centre.

The parallel developments leading to the piano and the symphony orchestra were closely connected with, or perhaps rather motivated by, a fundamental form, a way of musical thinking that was perhaps the fulcrum of the whole historical period considered in the present volume: sonata form.

Like all formal classifications, the term 'sonata form' appeared long after the object it was meant to describe. Moreover it is important to remember that this term was intended to indicate a form, a structure, certainly typical of the sonata for one or more instruments (hence the name sonata form), but not exclusively for this medium; in fact it can be found also in other contexts – in the opera or concert overture, the concerto for solo instrument and orchestra, the quartet, the trio, etc. – all of which could employ sonata form; and even the vocal field was to be open to influence from the use of this structure which grew out of instrumental experience. Still on the subject of classification, it should be added that sonata form was typical of the *first movement* of a sonata, symphony, quartet, etc.

In itself, the sonata of the *galant* age seemed a simple composition, easily approachable, seeking above all to get away from the vertical combinations of counterpoint or from sudden whimsical diversions that were very dangerous from the point of view of communication and the work's sociability. For Lorenz Christoph Mizler, one of Bach's pupils writing around 1742 (*Neu eröffnete musikalische Bibliothek*), the only aim of the sonata was to be pleasant and attractive. To understand more about it, it will be useful to compare the average *galant* sonata with the general plan of an earlier type of sonata, that of Domenico Scarlatti. Scarlatti's type can be summarized thus:

First Part			Second Part	
A	B	C	B′	C′
Theme	Transitional episode to new key →	Cadential ideas	Diversionary episode →	Cadential ideas

In comparison with this structure, the sonata form of the *galant* age (in keyboard sonatas, symphonies, etc.) shows these modifications:

Section A, 'theme', which Scarlatti often left in the crude form of introductory arpeggios, a call to attention or an improvisatory opening, becomes in a certain sense more thematic, in fact a 'first theme', shorter and with more definite contours.

B, a transitional episode to a new key, remains but is shortened and above all regularized in direction: towards the dominant if the sonata is in a major key, and towards the relative major if the sonata is in a minor key.

C takes on a more regular appearance; before cadencing it tends to coalesce thematically, and in fact it often comprises a single 'second theme'.

B', the extravagant diversionary episode in which Scarlatti liked to make his most ambitious inventive experiments, either disappears to make way for the first theme in a new key, or is reduced to a few bars which prepare for the return of the first theme in its original key.

This recapitulation of the first theme in exactly the same form as its first appearance at the opening of the piece, often emphasized by a preceding bar which signals its arrival, stresses a clear division between sections B' and C' of Scarlatti's type of sonata, producing a third part of the structure called, in fact, 'recapitulation'. This is not restricted to repeating the final cadential ideas of the first part ('exposition'), but goes back over everything, including the second theme (if there is one) transposed into the home key. To sum up, the new scheme may be typified as follows:

First Part			Second Part	Third Part		
First theme $\longrightarrow$	Link	Second theme and cadential ideas	Diversionary episode	First theme $\longrightarrow$	Link	Second theme and cadential ideas
Exposition			Diversion	Recapitulation		

Still remembering that these plans are approximations, wide generalizations but useful for an overall view, let us again compare the two models. The progressive evolution from a bipartite form towards a tripartite one seems to be a complication; it is, however, the result of a tendency towards simplification and rationalization, according to the taste of the *galant* style mentioned above. It is significant that the changeable area of transition, indicated by the symbol $\longrightarrow$, is reduced both in length and in possible choices of harmonic schemes; the emergence of two themes provides the performer and listener with secure points of reference; the recapitulation, matching the exposition like a rhyming couplet, determines a strophic regularity that Domenico Scarlatti's surprises seemed to be trying to avoid at every step. If the 'melodic' presence of the two themes is the most obvious aspect of sonata form, in actual fact its true structural substance was a 'harmonic' one, anchored to precise, symmetrical, inter-related tonal areas. This structure has a tendency to emphasize the horizontal dimension, to exploit, although at this stage in a rudimentary way, the temporal scansion and the listener's memory. Basically the tension created by the relationships between certain degrees of the scale (I and V, I and VI, etc.) was already one of the fundamental principles of fugue: it exploited the complementary nature of the degrees I and V in an initial rotation of subject and answer. Sonata form extended the same complementary nature, increasing the distance in time between the area of the first theme (I, the tonic) and that of the second (V, the dominant). The tendency towards vertical build-ups in fugue (especially evident in strettos) is lessened on a horizontal level by a strophic regularity (exposition, linking episode, recapitulation) whose clarity is naturally emphasized by the intrinsic simplicity of the style and the fluency of its writing. One of the features of sonata form in the *galant* period was in fact the so-called 'Alberti bass', an accompanimental formula on the keyboard (named after Domenico Alberti, who had made much use of it) in which left-hand chords, instead of being, as they said then, 'marked', with all the notes together, were arpeggiated, played one note at a time, thus lightening the weight of the harmonies to the great advantage of the upper melodic line.

The overall structure of these multi-movement forms tended in a similar manner to achieve greater stability and regularity. The rather free order of fast and slow movements in the baroque trio sonata and concerto tended to organize itself into three movements, Allegro–Andante–Allegro. The pattern had already been established in the first half of the century by the majority of Vivaldi's concertos and by Alessandro Scarlatti's opera overtures, but halfway through the century the three movements also gained a specific internal organization: the first Allegro in the sonata form described above; the Andante (or Adagio or Largo) in a ternary ABA form, like a simple instrumental song; and the final movement in a dance (e.g. gigue or minuet) or rondo form, or, more rarely, sonata form like the first movement. Ending with a minuet was particularly popular in the symphony, where it took root; after the middle of the century, if a busier finale was preferred, the minuet, instead of disappearing, changed position. Thus the 'standard' form of a symphony (followed in this respect by the quartet) tended towards four movements (Allegro–Andante–Minuet–Allegro).

This well-articulated structure, easily transferable to every field of composition, must have made up for the loss of the formal unity of the baroque; toccata, fantasia, variation and suite somehow all combined in the sonata. In the orchestral field the symphony drew towards it the concerto in its various guises, the Italian operatic overture, the French *ouverture* and the sinfonia concertante, and it was gradually to absorb smaller genres, the divertimento, the serenade and the cassation. In chamber music, the harpsichord was still irreplaceable around the middle of the century, and there was a plentiful supply of duo and trio sonatas in which the violin (or flute) and cello doubled 'ad libitum' the right and left hands of the harpsichord or piano. But with the removal of the keyboard instrument the string quartet (two violins, viola and cello) was gradually developed – the most important result of the concept of the sonata. Sonata, symphony and quartet were thus to be the main channels of this unique current which, running into sonata form, was to unify late-eighteenth-century musical thought.

This brief glance at sonata form must end with a mention of the lively musicological debate entertained between the end of the nineteenth century and the first decades of the twentieth which aimed at establishing the priority of one composer or school in the invention and use of tripartite, bithematic sonata form. Although not so numerous as the places in Greece claiming to be the birthplace of Homer, German, Italian and French scholars tried, just as passionately, to demonstrate on the basis of chronological priorities that sonata form was the result of the activity of particular individuals who had lived in Mannheim, Venice, Vienna or Paris. This controversy, which, since it caused a considerable amount of music to be unearthed and studied, was very useful, was nevertheless based on a misunderstanding, the belated consequence of the romantic conception of the genius who would spontaneously invent for himself the forms that he needed. Sonata form was a syntactical, functional scheme which, like all formal designs, existed and had meaning only by virtue of how it was applied; all its elements (including the second theme, transitions and recapitulation) could already be found in their own right before 1750. The decisive catalyst was the current that unified them and slowly directed them into an organic whole; that is why suppositions and conjectures to establish the priority of a publication (sometimes resting on differences of a few years or even months) in which this or that element of the sonata appeared before it did elsewhere are no more than theoretical debate. Furthermore, the growing evidence uncovered in recent decades has shown that sonata form grew up simultaneously in all the nerve-centres of a Europe united in taste and cultural exchanges as at few other times in its history.

4 The Italian harpsichordists

Between Domenico Scarlatti and Mozart, Italy once again made its mark on instrumental music with a host of harpsichordists, almost all of whom originated in Venice or Naples but were active outside Italy. Although varying in importance, they had certain characteristics in common. They did not earn their living exclusively from the harpsichord: they played various instruments; they were singing teachers; they overran the theatres of Europe looking for success in the field of opera, but found it instead in a more modest area, publishing in London or Nuremberg keyboard sonatas (usually in groups of six) which were free and varied in their form – the scheme described in the preceding section was almost always avoided – in their style of writing and in their combination of movements, but all based on the *galant* ideals of simplicity and immediacy.

The most prominent figures were Giovanni Benedetto Platti, Pier Domenico Paradisi, Baldassare Galuppi and Giovanni Marco Rutini, all of whom had their first works published around the decade 1745–55. Platti, who was probably born in Venetian territory between 1690 and 1700, had already moved to Franconia by 1722 and until his death in 1763 remained in the service of the Schönborn family at or near Würzburg. He was the only one of the four not to write for the theatre; his first six *Sonates pour le clavessin sur le goût italien* were printed around 1742 in Nuremberg by Ulrich Haffner, a publisher who halfway through the century became an important producer of Italian sonatas, all of which were in four movements according to the old model of the *sonata da chiesa* (slow–fast–slow–fast). It is only in his later sonatas that the three-movement form gained a hold; and after the early works Platti adopted a transparent style of writing in two parts, with short, incisive phrases, while the Allegros in particular show the strophic grouping of the later sonata, with exposition and recapitulation separated by a balancing exploratory episode. Although he did not use a real second theme, one of this 'severe' *galant* composer's accomplishments was to create tension and fluency in the course of a piece by means of contrasting keys and very slight variations of the rhythmic 'tactus'.

Platti still lived like a composer of the old world, based at a court. Closer to the new type of artist was Pier Domenico Paradisi (1707–91), who, after an education in the Neapolitan conservatoires, made an early move to London to put on operas, established a name for himself as a teacher of harpsichord and singing in high society, and worked as an impresario, managing the King's Theatre in the Haymarket for a few years. Nevertheless it was not with opera that his name was to remain associated, but with the twelve *Sonate per Gravicembalo* published by Johnson in 1754 and reprinted five times in Paris and London up to 1791, something very unusual at this period. They are all in two movements, but the combination of groupings and rhythmic metres is carefully planned so that the same model is never repeated. In his allegro movements Paradisi exploited the discursive possibilities implicit in the interplay of first and second themes (the latter generally characterized by a different tonal area) and in the tripartite articulation of sonata form, but the reason for his pre-eminence lies in the elegance of his writing and the solidity of his harpsichord style, even though broken up into contrapuntal lines. The influence of Domenico Scarlatti, in particular of his *Trenta Essercizi* (published in London in 1738), was more important for Paradisi than anything else. On close examination he reveals a 'sonata language' which goes beyond the scheme of sonata form, concentrating rather on details, with pauses and subtle variations of ideas which, even when they do not have thematic significance, function as climaxes in the course of a piece. In slow movements – which are never Adagios, but rather Andantes, Larghettos and Moderatos – there is a comfortableness of proportions and pleasantness of sound which explains Paradisi's lasting success in a society as devoted to domestic pleasures as the English. The twelve sonatas are a mature, elaborate product: it is out of place to speak of 'primitivism' in connection with them; they are more concerned with autumnal conclusion than with beginning.

Baldassare Galuppi (1706–85) was one of Paradisi's contemporaries, a rather different, many-sided and prolific composer, famous throughout Europe for his comic operas on librettos by Goldoni, and tied to Venice by important appointments at St Mark's and the conservatoires. He wrote about ninety keyboard sonatas, and two collections of six sonatas each appeared in London in 1756 and 1759. No one appeared so little concerned with formal problems as Galuppi: the commonest scheme of his sonatas is Andante–Allegro–Allegro (the last two in different metres), but they could vary from two to four movements. A link with the suite is evident in the frequent gigue finales, and there are florid openings in toccata style, as well as strict fugues which are striking in their frequent distinction between elementary accompaniments and melodies. Galuppi, more than other composers, tended to make the keyboard sing, with a wider melodic range and a moderate use of ornamentation, relying on occasional help from the Alberti bass to keep the sound going. This last device was the corollary of opportunities for cantabile writing not only in Andantes but also sometimes in fast movements: the Allegro cantabile (or 'singende Allegro' as the Germans, recognizing it also in symphonic and operatic fields, called it) was to be one of the last Italian contributions to eighteenth-century European music, immediately identifiable as a feature of Italian musical style. Although his music is less controlled than that of Paradisi, Galuppi too showed interest in discursive details, repeating in the minor key an idea just presented in the major, for example, or recalling a theme and slightly varying its implied harmonies. These are aspects of style that established themselves firmly in the fabric of sonata form without any shadow of effort; indeed, with a certain fluent indolence that is also an indication of the limitations of Galuppi's style. Even well into his seventies he managed to write a collection of six sonatas under the title *Passatempo al cembalo*, apparently in homage to the Russian Grand Duke Paul who was visiting Venice; although dating from around 1780, these suave pieces seem to have been written thirty years earlier, in a peaceful lagoon unaware of the changes that were altering the face of European instrumental music.

Less talent for the 'singende Allegro' but greater instrumental awareness was shown by the sizeable output of the younger Giovanni Marco Rutini (1723–97), who was born in Florence but educated in Naples. He too tried for a theatrical career, which led to several journeys as a young man to Prague, Dresden and St Petersburg; but in Prague he published in 1748 his Sonatas op. 1, in St Petersburg he became harpsichord teacher to the future Catherine II, and in Nuremberg the publisher Haffner printed new collections of his sonatas every year from 1757 to 1760. In Rutini one senses an artist of a new generation. Although his early sonatas use successions of movements with the extemporary freedom of Galuppi, the regularity of the composition is often disturbed by sudden interruptions of diminished sevenths, by instrumental recitatives (as in the second sonata of op. 1) and by more weighty sections in the minor key. One sonata, op. 5 no. 5, has three movements in F minor, and a minuet in F major is provided as a trio section in the middle of the third movement, the rest of which is full of syncopations. The minuet is the only conventional passage, and keeps the emotional temperature of the whole work within limits. The sonatas from op. 2 to op. 6 are a significant link with the early works of Haydn and Mozart (a letter from Leopold Mozart of 1771 provides evidence of his son's famili-arity with Rutini's sonatas). [13] Later, with his return to Italy and the calm of the Grand Duchy of Tuscany, everything changed: the sonatas opp. 7, 8 and 9 rapidly developed into short, easy, pro-grammatic sonatinas; in the preface to the op. 7 sonatas (1770) Rutini acknowledged that he did not want to exceed the capabilities of a ten-year-old girl. The final sonata of op. 8 ends with an aria, 'Clori amabile', which the performer can sing if he or she so wishes while playing: a perfect return to Arcadia that has been accused of simplism and banality. Yet it is significant that his musical style did develop and that the remarkable change in his surroundings did leave its mark; in this receptivity Rutini again showed himself to be a more modern artist than the others.

If the musicians discussed above distinguished themselves to some extent by their personal traits, there were many other Italian composers of keyboard sonatas. It is necessary at least to note the names of the Paduan Giuseppe Antonio Paganelli (1710–62?), active in Bavaria and Madrid, and three composers all in varying degrees based in London – Domenico Alberti (born between 1710 and 1717), Giovanni Battista Pescetti (1704–66) and Mattia Vento (1735–76). It is also necessary to mention, as one of the most indicative sources of the Italian keyboard sonata midway through the century, the five anthologies by various authors which Haffner published in Nuremberg between 1756 and 1765 with the title of *Raccolta musicale* (opp. 1–5). Here, among others, all the names mentioned above can be found. The presence of long-winded fugues (one is part of a sonata by Antonio Gaetano Pampani) demonstrates that the composers did not intend to break links with the past, but the false attribution of the fifth sonata of op. 2 to Domenico Scarlatti shows what confused and vague ideas could be held about that great and unique harpsichordist by this time. One of the Haffner collec-tion's merits is that it is also the only source for three sonatas by another Italian, Giovanni Battista Serini, born in Cremona around 1710, a pupil of Galuppi, and in 1750 *Kapellmeister* at Bückeburg. While his orchestral pieces (*sinfonie a quattro*) sound conventional and inert, the keyboard sonatas were the most mature that the Italo-European *galant* world had produced. Serini had a tendency to make the central movement the core of the composition (e.g. the Lento in the first sonata); this can also be seen in the six concertos for harpsichord and strings, especially in the first concerto's Largo in G minor, where the orchestra is silent and the soloist seems to pursue the unpredictable path of a reverie. In these attitudes Serini was not being very Italian; he was approaching C. P. E. Bach and his circle, and blending into a north-European context.

5 C. P. E. Bach and the German harpsichordists

Of Bach's many sons, four stand out in the history of music: Wilhelm Friedemann, Carl Philipp Emanuel (sons of his first wife Maria Barbara), Johann Cristoph Friedrich and Johann Christian (sons of his second wife Anna Magdalena).

At first sight there does not seem to be any great difference between their lives as musicians and the patriarchal habits of their father: they were all church organists and *maestri di cappella*, and they all earned their living, with varying degrees of distinction, in the conservatism of the German states. Wilhelm Friedemann and above all Johann Christian made more daring choices, and the economic squalor of their last years and the debts which they left when they died warn of the difficulties that could be encountered on leaving the 'old circle' of German cities for the modern emporiums of European music.

No boy ever had a more distinguished musical education than Wilhelm Friedemann Bach (1710–84). His father wrote works for him that are still the basis of music teaching today, and his registration at Leipzig University, where he graduated in law in 1733, was one of the reasons for the family's move to that city. But Wilhelm Friedemann's character, changeable, discontented and prickly, proved unfavourable for his career; his relations with his father's granite-like personality were not easy, and he is one of many sons to be overshadowed by much greater fathers. He moved from Dresden to Halle as organist and *director musices*, but in 1764 he resigned from the post and in his last twenty years drifted without a fixed appointment, appreciated only as a performer and improviser, and getting by with private lessons and public concerts – two of the ways open to someone who had left the feudal position of the court musician.

Sacred cantatas, trio sonatas, concertos and fugues (a set of which appeared as late as 1778) show Friedemann as a musician of the baroque era, and the contrapuntal texture (even though reduced) and the principle of imitation were fundamental even in his keyboard sonatas and works such as polonaises and fantasias. Friedemann's sonatas, almost all in three movements, show within the individual movements a wide formal range: fugal sections, vestiges of the toccata, sonata form and other structures (including rondo and variations) all come into play without any one taking precedence over the others. The most valuable element is hidden in the peculiarities and sudden bursts of humour which draw Friedemann into the orbit of a style whose champion was to be his brother Emanuel: the so-called *empfindsam* ('sentimental' or 'sensitive') style, the impassioned nucleus of the *galant* style that appeared mainly in the north. (*Empfindsamkeit* and the French *sensiblerie* are terms to which the English 'sentimentality' does not do justice and which in music denote a manner characterized by restless irregularity and spontaneous emotion that is not impaired by formal limitations.)

Carl Philipp Emanuel Bach (1714–88) was the most familiar Bach to the public up to the 1830s; he, Emanuel, was the 'great Bach' until the rediscovery of his father which occurred within the romantic movement. His career was divided between Berlin, where he was court harpsichordist between 1740 and 1768, and Hamburg, where he succeeded Telemann as cantor of the Johanneum (the *Lateinschule*) and, in practice, as director of the city's musical life. The move from the strict life at court (where furthermore Frederick the Great was a firm admirer of Quantz – Emanuel was certainly not his favourite composer) to the freer climate of the big commercial city turned out happily, with even a degree of financial success. Emanuel, a different man from the old kind of *maestro di cappella*, was also an intellectual: he corresponded with Diderot and was a friend of Lessing and Klopstock, and in Berlin as in Hamburg his house became a lively centre for discussions and a meeting place for musical and literary figures and the first musical historians. The poetry chosen by him for collections of songs with texts by Gellert and Christoph Sturm also reveals his intellectual sensitivity, and was in the pietist tradition of the *geistliches Lied* (spiritual song).

Emanuel Bach is possibly the first musician from the middle of the eighteenth century whose keyboard works constitute a sizeable corpus, an area in which he showed a lasting personal interest, and not just compensation for lack of success in the theatre. There are approximately 170 sonatas for clavichord/harpsichord/fortepiano, and with various other pieces for these instruments the catalogue reaches a total of more than three hundred works. Almost all the principal collections date from the Berlin years (in Hamburg, following the city's traditions, he wrote many passions, cantatas and oratorios; only opera was excluded). The six 'Prussian' Sonatas (1742) began the series, followed by the 'Württemburg' Sonatas (1744) and 'Probestücke', six sonatas written as demonstration pieces for the *Versuch* (Essay) on the art of keyboard playing (1753). Between 1760 and 1763 three sets of *Sonaten für Clavier mit veränderten Reprisen* appeared in Berlin, followed by *Sechs leichte Klaviersonaten* (1766), *Six Sonates de Clavecin à l'usage des dames* (1770), and six collections (each with six pieces) of sonatas, fantasias and rondos 'for connoisseurs and amateurs', between 1779 and 1787.

Up to the 'Prussian' Sonatas, Emanuel's sonata adopted the scheme of three movements without a minuet; the first movement is in sonata form, and its thematic interest can be almost nil, being derived from the wanderings of the toccata (e.g. in no. 2 of the 'Prussian' Sonatas), or very distinct and open to the possibility, rare at this time, of two contrasting themes (e.g. in Sonata no. 6). The writing, as usual with Germans, is more in the traditional polyphonic style than *galant*; the Alberti bass never appears and the textural basis is that of the trio sonata transferred to the keyboard, two parts with imitative points in the right hand and one in the left. In spite of the discussions about form that have suggested it, Emanuel did not have a vocation for and possibly not even a deep interest in formal structure, or at least in sonata form; the forms that suited him most were the fantasia and the rondo, with its cyclical structure. Perception of the complete arch of sonata form was, for him, secondary to the possibilities offered in the way of independent details and meaningful interjections; even the introduction of a second theme in the more fluent late sonatas seems to be the result of this interest. The sixth sonata of the 'Probestücke' concludes (if one can really use this term) with a fantasia; the sonatas with 'altered repeats' explicitly contradict the sonata principle of the recapitulation that goes back over what has already been heard without changing it. The increase in rondos and fantasias in the late collections is another sign of the direction in which the composer's views on form were leading.

Emanuel, furthermore, was not an easily inspired musician; he had not inherited his father's fluent eloquence and lacked the persuasive conversational style typical of even the least inspired moments of the Italian *galant* composers. There is an element of laboriousness in Emanuel which combats a basic difficulty of expression, but it is an element that, far from being a defect (as his critics have suggested at various times), is his most fertile aspect, for it involves an effort of communication, of keeping, even in instrumental music, to a principle of speech ('redende Prinzip') of which instrumental recitative and the practice of rubato (the relationship between note-lengths is discussed in a section of the *Versuch*) are recurring manifestations.[14] With his continual sudden changes of direction and a style of writing full of parentheses and interpolated clauses, Emanuel showed himself to be the most complete embodiment of the *empfindsam* style, which broke away from the musical rococo of his Berlin colleagues Quantz, Marpurg and the Graun brothers. If we have to imagine the protagonists of *Siegwart* or *La Nouvelle Héloïse* playing something, it must be Emanuel's Adagios, and the poet Gerstenberg's application of the text of Hamlet's monologue to the Fantasia in C minor which ends the 'Probestücke' is also well justified in this context. Special importance is assumed in some works, especially in early collections, by the slow movement, as in nos. 1, 2, 5 and 6 of the 'Prussian' or no. 5 of the 'Württemberg' Sonatas, with its Adagio in E flat minor; and in his tendency towards the fantasia Emanuel shows the attraction of 'Schwärmerei', the swarming of thoughts in an atmosphere of excitement typical of the northern traditions. There is also evidence from the musical historian Burney on this point: a description of Emanuel at the clavichord as being inspired and 'possessed'.[15] Emanuel's fantasia was a passive one which seems to undergo fluctuations of feeling, often with fits of black humour which have been linked with the *Sturm und Drang* movement (see Chapter 22).

In fact Emanuel's 'sentimental' fantasia had firm roots in the work of his father Johann Sebastian rather than in the general characteristics of the *Sturm und Drang* movement. Like one of the wise virgins, Emanuel kept a little light burning to the cult of Bach, not only conserving papers and music which he had inherited, or writing concertos, cantatas and fugues with the undeniable stamp of his father, but also continuing (almost on his own) to remember another Bach, that of some of the minor-key preludes from the *Well-tempered Clavier* or the central section of the Chromatic Fantasia and Fugue BWV 903. This Bach, with his disturbing, immense expressiveness, was clearly even further removed from the sensibility of the second half of the eighteenth century than the contrapuntal Bach who, at least for teaching purposes, was always useful to have within reach.

The concept of the keyboard as a stimulus for experimentation, a testing ground, was firmly held by Emanuel Bach; the concertos for strings and one or more harpsichords and for strings and forte-piano are (like the symphonies) works of great skill, but they follow in the wake of Vivaldi, Handel and J. S. Bach without the usual problems of harpsichord works. Here instead harmonic pedals, sudden abrupt modulations and enharmonic procedures are used with an intensity unique for their time. They can of course be found in his father's music, but there it was as if they were inserted into an ordered universe, while Emanuel isolates them as elements of sur-prise and contrast in the new linguistic code of sonata form. With this intense activity one can begin to speak of 'development' in the sonata's central section, a view prompted by the realization that to vary a theme can mean to enrich it and not to ruin it.

Emanuel's importance as one of the main figures in instrumental music before Haydn is shown by his influence among contemporary German keyboard composers, especially those working in the north, all of whom were to some extent acquainted with the musical life of Berlin and Hamburg. In 1751 Johann Christoph Ritter (1715–67) published three sonatas with Haffner's firm which show at a glance the influence of the 'Prussian' Sonatas; with careful three-part writing, their emotional centre is the slow movement, and the G minor Adagio of the third sonata is almost a commentary on the Adagio in the same key of the second 'Prussian' Sonata. The imaginative climate of the *empfindsam* style is traceable in the sonatas by Jiři Antonín Benda (1722–95), even though they contain *galant* features and simplifications of writing such as the Alberti bass. Emanuel's mark is apparent in the few sonatas of Heinrich Rolle (1716–85), who was close to him at Frederick's court, and above all in those of Johann Gottfried Müthel (1728–88). Müthel was brought up as an organist but was so far removed from the old professional ethics of the northern organists that he confessed to Burney that he had not written very much because he could only write when he was particularly inspired[16] – a confession that indicates new paths of artistic sensibility, dangerous paths beyond the safe, regular crafts-manship of composition.

Not far from Berlin and Hamburg was Bückeburg, where Emanuel's half-brother Johann Christoph Friedrich Bach (1732–95) was firmly settled. In his early sonatas, along the lines of Serini and

Emanuel, the central movement is the most elaborate, but then, in later works following his journey to London in 1778 to visit his brother Johann Christian, the scale grows smaller, minuets appear as finales and an acquaintance with early pianos is apparent.

If Emanuel's influence was more notable in the Berlin circle, where even someone like Marpurg, who was little given to excessive expression, wrote 'sighing' and 'with tenderness' on certain slow movements, it was still felt by composers from central Germany who came to the fore in the same years as Haydn, such as Christian Gottlob Neefe (1748–98), Beethoven's teacher in Bonn, and Ernst Wilhelm Wolf (1735–92), keyboard player and theorist at Weimar. For them, and others like them, C. P. E. Bach was to be an appeal for seriousness and commitment, on the level of writing appropriate for the keyboard and above all on that of expression, in a mythology of 'northern' values that was to exist for a long time.

6   Schobert in Paris

The emotional intensification which appeared around the 1760s in the sonata from Rutini to Serini and Emanuel Bach, and which foreshadowed new expressive climates beyond the poetics of the *galant*, was paralleled in the instrumental output of Johann Schobert (1740?–67), a Silesian who worked in Paris. This composer has always been shrouded in mystery on account of his tragic death (he died along with his family as a result of eating poisonous fungi) and the scarcity of biographical information; and this mystery has to some extent affected the evaluation of his work.

The intellectual world of Paris was interested above all in theatre, but instrumental music was encouraged by a very active concert life, both public and private, and by a flourishing publishing industry. Unaffected by scholastic arguments, instrumental much more than vocal music broke with tradition. The art of harpsichord writing of composers such as François Couperin and Rameau became more and more distant. It was a forgotten heritage; it did not lead to imitations, however pedantic or limited, as happened with J. S. Bach in central and northern Germany or Domenico Scarlatti on the part of the Spaniard Antonio Soler. Music for the violin and other stringed instruments prevailed, encouraged to a considerable extent by the nearby Savoyard court of Turin, but Schobert moved on from the sonata for solo violin with basso continuo, derived from Corelli, to sonatas which still involve the violin, but sometimes *ad libitum* and always in a subordinate role. Only two sonatas (op. 4) are for keyboard solo; all the others (more than forty) are 'with violin accompaniment', or 'en trio' or 'en quatuor', yet keeping the main role for the harpsichord. This harpsichord, except in special cases, no longer has the miniaturistic sound of Couperin, but is given swift, dry lines, without ornamentation but with octaves, chords, arpeggios and even tremolos, full 'symphonic' textures which foreshadow the crescendos possible on the piano and sometimes give the impression of keyboard transcriptions of pieces conceived orchestrally.

Schobert worked as harpsichordist in the private orchestra of Prince Louis-François de Bourbon-Conti. The composer's innovations took shape in an old setting: the harpsichord was to some extent tied up with chamber music; the sonata, up to date in its first movement, was related to the suite in ending with polonaises and minuets. Sometimes Schobert realized the dynamism and the tension of the sonata movement, but he lacked themes (e.g. in the finale of the Sonata in D minor op. 14 no. 4). He often used the Alberti bass with Italianate melodies even in Allegros ('singende Allegro'); he sensed, more adventurously than C. P. E. Bach and in a more fluent style, that modulation and harmonic exploitation could be a gateway into unknown regions; he took only a few steps in this direction, however, and more frequently used series of symmetrical phrases. At times he wrote passages of bleak loneliness, such as the opening (for keyboard solo) of the Sonata in C minor op. 14 no. 3, unified by its driving rhythm with an air of baroque grandeur, or the trios of minuets which are sometimes full of melancholy (e.g. in op. 9 no. 2 or op. 14 no. 2), all passages which could express the passions of Julie and Saint-Preux, but are in any case a long way from the canons of clarity and reason.

Mozart as a child, invited in 1763 and 1766 to play in the house of the Princes de Conti, was influenced by Schobert (as is evident in his early sonatas for violin and keyboard published in Paris and London in 1764 and 1765); the predominance of minor tonality, moments of sudden seriousness and various melancholic features all reflect the influence of the Silesian musician in Mozart's early experiences. This serious aspect, running through C. P. E. Bach and Schobert, also applies to Johann Gottfried Eckardt (1735–1809), who was born at Augsburg and arrived in Paris along with Johann Andreas Stein, a great maker of organs and pianos. Eckardt taught himself from

C. P. E. Bach's *Versuch* and 'Probestücke', but ventured beyond the confines of the harpsichord; in the preface to the op. 1 sonatas (1763) he declared that he wanted to make the work 'equally appropriate to the harpsichord, clavichord and piano. It is for this reason that I have felt obliged to mark the softs and louds so often, which would have been useless if I had only the harpsichord in mind'.[17] Here too, even in the midst of a broad eclecticism of attitudes, one notices features of C. P. E. Bach: interrupted cadences, syncopations and little phrases from the *empfindsam* vocabulary.

7   Sammartini, Stamitz and the origins of the modern symphony

From around the 1740s the eighteenth century, this century of vocal music, saw a progressive increase in compositions called 'symphonies' (at least ten thousand have been counted between 1740 and 1810). The growth of the modern institution of the public concert certainly encouraged this flourishing, but so too did the unifying and summarizing character of this form of composition, whose attraction, with its broad adaptable formal framework, led to a restriction on the variety of the preceding era. For more than a century from around 1770, the symphony became established as the instrumental genre *par excellence*, or at least the one containing the greatest challenges and the grandest works. The structure, as stated in Chapter 3, was sonata form. The use of a large group of instruments also had an effect on musical form, in particular in the tendency towards a larger scale that, following primitive three-movement models with their final minuets, was to lead to a four-movement form, sometimes enlarged with a slow introduction prefixing the first movement. The nature of the themes, splitting up into two or more motives, was also to venture beyond the style of themes in contemporary piano music. Sonata form was to have more inertia in the symphony, where it continued with unwavering confidence although it was in time superseded in piano music.

Between 1740 and 1770, the symphony's main concern was in moving away from the baroque concerto. Sonata form, with its pre-established tonal areas, easily replaced the free play of ritornellos and tutti/concertino contrasts. Change in terms of sonority was also simple: the ripieno harpsichord which realized the continuo bass, so important in the concerto's orchestration for linking alternations of full and light scoring, lost importance; to compensate for this the string group, whose basses were often doubled by one or two bassoons, found a kind of solidity by means of sustained notes from a pair of horns. This instrument's limitations restricted the number of usable keys and the possibilities of modulation for some time, but this easily formed part of the tendency of the *galant* style towards simplification. Furthermore the timbre of the brass, and of other wind instruments which were gradually added, contributed a kind of sonorous cement which turned out to be productive in quite a different way from the harpsichord continuo.

If the changes were made easily, all things considered, and caught on rapidly between 1730 and 1740, the area in which the symphony advanced with slower steps than the harpsichord sonata was that of thematic material and the shape of principal or linking themes, which were to remain for a long time like those of the baroque concerto of Vivaldi or Handel, with numerous repetitions of the tonic note, built on scales or arpeggios from the underlying harmony. The internal texture also showed a certain reluctance to depart from the standard layout of the trio sonata, a reluctance that applied in Germany even to the harpsichordists; the first and second violins often overlap or make use of imitative phrases, the violas often follow the basses, and the writing as a whole tends towards three real parts. In getting away from the mould of the concerto and trio sonata, the overture (or 'sinfonia'), the instrumental piece played before the opera with the curtain lowered, had been very important. Here, in the tripartite Italian form established by Alessandro Scarlatti (Allegro–Andante–Allegro, with the last movement in triple time and easily transformed into a minuet), less restrained writing can sometimes be seen, almost as though being close to the theatre inspired a new approach, with richer instrumentation and a greater emphasis on individual themes than was usual in the primitive concert symphony.

The symphony before Haydn involved two particularly prominent figures, Sammartini and Stamitz, and a host of secondary composers, all of whom were united by formal affinities and common objectives.

Giovanni Battista Sammartini (1700?–75) differed from his Italian contemporaries in that he remained resident in his native land. He was born in Milan while it was under Spanish rule, and died there during the years of the periodical *Il Caffè* and the two Verri brothers; in 1725 he wrote Lenten cantatas for the Congregation of the SS Entierro, and when he died, half a century later, Clement XIV had been suppressing the Jesuits for two years. Although he himself did not move about very much, his music did travel: in January 1738 Vivaldi directed a Sammartini symphony in Amsterdam; Le Clerc in Paris and Walsh in London published his symphonies in 1742 and 1744; Count Harrach, governor of Milan between 1740 and 1750, introduced his name to Vienna; and in the decade 1760–70 he was famous throughout Europe, as manuscript collections, lightly scattered all over the place but particularly numerous in Prague, Paris and Karlsruhe, show today. The chronology of the seventy or so authentic symphonies is uncertain, but a continuous maturation up to the works attributable to the period 1760–74 is noticeable. His full realization of all the possible artistic means took place gradually on a personal level and without important influences from abroad, even after 1750, when the effect of Stamitz and the Mannheim school began to be felt, and after 1770, when Joseph Haydn's authority asserted itself.

Sammartini was a man of the first half of the eighteenth century, dominating the musical life of Milan and the province (Pavia and Cremona) from 1740. His predilection for the genre of the trio sonata (he wrote more trio sonatas than symphonies) itself revealed him as the composer of another instrumental culture, in a country which in this field held to the status quo and to the use of tried and tested forms. But his first group of symphonies, twenty or so up to around 1744, also show a Sammartini who only gradually broke loose from the baroque concerto; certain Graves or Largos lasting for a few bars in between the two fast movements are derived from it, as are cadential passages with all the parts in octaves and works which are symphonies in name but concertos in their structure of alternating tutti and concertino. The hand of an artist capable of evolution can be seen in certain details: a liking for unpredictable ideas, reserved for the coda, contrasts of shade achieved by juxtaposing statements of a short passage in the major and the minor, and a more unified sense of the overall shape of the symphony's three movements, with themes conceived no longer for the violin but for the whole orchestra. The central movement, apart from cases of simple decorated cadences, gained importance with Andantes and sicilianas in 12/8, often in the minor key, distinguished by a sensitive and expressive mood.

These early signs are fully borne out in the following symphonies. The outer movements become longer, while the slow one contains plenty of *galant* ornamentation with the frequent indication 'affettuoso', and, in the late works after 1760, seems to embody Sammartini's personality completely: the 'Sammartini Andante' in

Rousseau's *Dictionnaire de musique* of 1767 was the Andante *par excellence*.[18] The second theme becomes more and more important, achieving individuality by means of *buffo* characteristics and, later, through a more expansive cantabile style. The central exploratory section of sonata form becomes richer, exploiting and developing elements of the exposition, and the recapitulation itself varies and develops the exposition. This rational investigation came about through a very important dialogue style, a *new* counterpoint between the parts: new because it was no longer or not only imitative (where one voice imitates and repeats the same recognizable statement as another), but simply conversational, where every part, even the bass, takes part with motivic and rhythmic suggestions which, though different, nevertheless form an integral whole. Sammartini's importance as a symphonist lies in the gradual growth of this texture, and also in the static nature of certain general features, such as the three-movement structure, the lack of tonal variety (C, D and G major are his favourite keys), and the almost unvarying use of strings, two horns and two oboes. The frame remains the same while the outline and the light of the picture change.

Halfway through the century Milan was, thanks to Sammartini, the most progressive instrumental centre in Italy. Gluck came to study with Sammartini between 1737 and 1741, and both Leopold and Wolfgang Mozart met him in 1770; Johann Christian Bach, writing to Padre Martini in 1758, speaks of a 'Lombard manner of performing symphonies';[19] and the Bohemian Josef Mysliveček (1737–81), very well known in Italy around 1770, is credited with the description of Sammartini as 'Haydn's true predecessor'.[20] Haydn, asked about this by his first biographer, Griesinger, rejected this line of descent, dismissing Sammartini as a 'scribbler' ('Schmierer') and claiming C. P. E. Bach as his early model. But it is perhaps possible to recognize in this early-nineteenth-century assertion a sign of incipient nationalism; there is an artfulness in the use of form and a light-hearted fluency in Sammartini which make him a kindred spirit of Haydn. C. P. E. Bach was certainly an admirable and attractive model, but to Haydn the attraction was of someone different and unlike himself; the everyday elements of Haydn's work are found in Sammartini. In Sammartini lay another lesson, of which Haydn and Mozart were to be the world's masters: Haydn was concerned not only with ideas which revealed themselves in dissonant clashes, in angular passages and the sighs of C. P. E. Bach; these could be hidden under an agreeable surface and concentrated entirely in the concern to explore form and the search for suitable layouts and strict expression which, however crucial and premeditated, could leave the surface unruffled.

The other landmark for the symphony before Haydn was the Bohemian Johann Václav Antonín Stamitz (1717–57), who was a more striking innovator than Sammartini, not only because he made a name for himself in Paris, but also because of the nature of his musical ideas themselves, the product of a later generation than that of the Milanese composer. The son of a musician from Německý Brod, brought up in a cultured environment of artists and scholars, he was educated in the Jesuit college at Jihlava. By 1742 he was at Mannheim, the modern Mannheim where no building was more than a hundred years old, roughly at the same time as a jealous and ambitious sovereign appeared to rule the principality, the Elector Palatine Carl Theodor von Pfalz-Salzbach, who was to play his part in the development of German music after the 1770s. Educated at Heidelberg and a friend of Voltaire, Carl Theodor, like so many of his peers, wanted to make his court (at Mannheim and the summer residence at Schwetzingen) a new Versailles, and one of his most assiduous concerns was to improve the court orchestra, which was transformed in a few years into a perfect, efficient organism, much discussed by contemporary sources (see Reading no. 3). These accounts, dating from after 1770, are rather late, as is Schubart's famous description of 1784: 'No orchestra in the world ever excelled the Mannheim. Its *forte* is a thunderclap, its crescendo a cataract, its diminuendo a crystal stream babbling away into the distance, its *piano* a breath of spring.'[21] Nevertheless a few conclusions may be drawn: the cohesion and ensemble were the most striking aspects, worthy of astonished mention even in a small news item. Furthermore, such an insistence on the performance side shows the increased importance of a new public awareness of music, where the performance is important in itself, something to be judged apart from the music being played. The orchestra for which Bach had written the Brandenburg Concertos must indeed have been as good as that at Mannheim, but forty years earlier it was not news but a private matter for the court concerned, while by this time it was a fact for the public, the property of all the connoisseurs who discussed it in journals and memoirs.

Stamitz's activity seems to have been essential in giving the Mannheim orchestra this fame as a little symphonic machine; within a few months Carl Theodor was paying him the highest salary ever given to a musician at the Mannheim court. But this sovereign's modern mentality is even more apparent in the freedom he gave his *Konzertmeister* to go for a year (1754–5) to Paris, where Stamitz was already well known, his works already performed, and his figure even portrayed in a pamphlet by Melchior Grimm glorifying Italian opera, *Le Petit Prophète de Boemisch Broda* (1753). Stamitz was one of the first musicians to manage the leap from court to the free profession in a big city successfully. He made a name for himself at the Concert Spirituel, the first institution for public concerts in Paris, and he was given an opening by J. J. Le Riche de la Pouplinière, financier, music lover and Maecenas, once Rameau's disciple but now one of the firm admirers of Italian comic opera. Taking advantage of his presence, a new concert enterprise was founded in 1754, the Concert Italien ('Italien' implied 'new' or 'modern'), and in 1757 some of his symphonies were published. Stamitz, the violinist, composer and orchestral director, stood out against the background of a public thirsty for music and novelty.

This dynamic climate is reflected in the content of his seventy or so symphonies. Although he was performed a great deal in Paris, Stamitz was a less subtle and a less profound musician than Sammartini, but he was more forward-looking. The mature symphonies from op. 3 (1757) onwards are in four movements: the minuet comes third, providing light relief and a pleasant break, before a more substantial finale. The Parisian orchestras provided Stamitz with the possibility of introducing clarinets into the symphony; the viola takes on a more melodic function, and there is a rudimentary blending of woodwind and strings. In sonata form a stronger division appears between first and second themes, and a rhythmic first theme with brilliant wind fanfares is often followed by a second theme with soft string textures. Also typical of Stamitz is the use of a slower harmonic rhythm, that is, the use of longer sections without changes of harmony (the symphony op. 4 no. 6, for example, opens with twenty bars of tonic harmony in E flat), a convenient basis for orchestral crescendos, discursive simplifications which entirely favour a symphonic sound delighting in its own autonomy. The *galant* and rococo taste for inlaid work, scrupulously drawn detail and free ornamentation, from which Sammartini gradually broke away, were left behind by Stamitz's symphonies with their four-square lines and noisy bustle, showing that they are early examples of 'town' music, no longer born of courtly Arcadia. Leopold Mozart, writing to his son in 1778, described them as 'noisy' music, 'a hodge-podge, with here and there a good idea, but introduced very awkwardly and in quite the wrong place'.[22] Even though Stamitz has the aspect of thematic meditation along the lines shown by Sammartini, what struck his contemporaries most (and not always with the disgust shown by Leopold Mozart) was something of a different kind, a lively, 'noisy' style whose colours were deliberately exaggerated, leading to a new dimension of sound aimed at the wider public of the modern concert-hall. Public performance was a factor that seems to have influenced Stamitz's imagination *a priori*, and his music is perhaps the first to require the figure of the conductor on the rostrum.

A school, called in fact the 'Mannheim school' after the centre where both younger and older composers gathered around him, was based on Stamitz. It was a movement that soon crystallized into a true formalism of workmanship that never really surpassed its master. Among the earliest members of the school were František Xaver Richter (1709–89), Ignaz Holzbauer (1711–83), Antonín Fils (1733–60) and Carl Joseph Toeschi (1731–88). As their names suggest, they came from various backgrounds: Richter and Fils were Bohemians, Holzbauer was Viennese and Toeschi came from an Italian family. They were all drawn to Mannheim in the early years of the Duke Carl Theodor, and later all of them, particularly Toeschi, turned to follow the road to Paris. Holzbauer and Richter, who had studied with Fux in Vienna, appeared rather cautious in comparison with Stamitz's novelty; Holzbauer was an unusual figure, an intellectual musician who knew Horace from memory and who composed literary works on the meditations of Christ. One of his symphonies in E flat ends with a movement full of crescendos and diminuendos called *La tempesta di mare* (a title also used by Vivaldi). Toeschi and Fils, however, were more Stamitz's 'pupils' and already showed some of his mannerisms in their insistence on certain formulas. With this group of composers, to whom one can add two other Stamitz disciples who later settled in France, Franz Beck (1734–1809) and Valentin Roeser (1735–82?), German music (composed by non-Germans gathered together by Carl Theodor) took its first step at this period towards European fame. The Italian title which the French publishers gave their collections of symphonies, *La Melodia Germanica*, shows that something definite and clearly understood was beginning to be implied by the term 'German'.

The hospitality that Parisian concert-halls and publishers offered to foreign works surpassed their attention to local products. On the other hand, as stated earlier, a peculiarity of Paris (as also of London) was that it drew in from outside rather than creating things itself. The six *Symphonies dans le goût italien* (1740) of Louis-Gabriel Guillemain (1705–70) particularly recalled the deep roots that Corelli had spread into France; but the new directions of the symphony were apparent in François Joseph Gossec (1734–1829), whose extraordinarily long life made him a contemporary of both Rameau and Beethoven, and a witness of radically different artistic and social conditions. In his early collections of symphonies (opp. 3, 4 and 5, published between 1756 and 1761) he followed Stamitz's examples, adopting the four-movement form, enlarging the instrumentation by adding a pair of clarinets (in op. 5), and making a contrast between thematic groups. The appearance in op. 5 no. 2 of a movement entitled 'Romance' and the introduction of fugatos into the op. 6 symphonies show the tendency to experiment which was to develop in the course of Gossec's career. There were, however, no fundamental changes in his work, and his return to the three-movement symphony was to a certain extent symptomatic. Throughout the French symphony there was a rather static quality: the specific form of the preceding age, the Lullian overture with its slow–fast fugal–slow structure, left no trace, nor were any grafts attempted. After 1770 the output was channelled towards the symphonie concertante, which gained increasing popularity up to the first decades of the nineteenth century. The French symphony was becoming rather like a pool, separate from the historical river of its European counterpart.

Compared with Paris and Mannheim, with the sensation caused by the symphony and the formalism into which it resolved, Vienna stood at the opposite pole. The symphony began there from humble origins, with hundreds of links with tradition and the work of organists or pupils of Fux, in a calm cultural climate that was unaware of the modernistic scourge of a Carl Theodor or the competitive regime of the modern city. It progressed gradually to the great heights of Haydn and Mozart and then on to Beethoven and Schubert, so that the modern symphony was ultimately identified with the Viennese school. At the beginning of this process stand composers of the *galant* style such as Georg Christoph Wagenseil (1715–77), harpsichordist to Maria Theresa; he was active in every area, from *opera seria* to keyboard sonatas and concertos, from oratorio to the symphony (of which he wrote around a hundred examples in the three-movement form). He was the perfect 'little composer', a hard-working manufacturer of musical pieces in which, as in the inside of a watch, everything is in its place. In the next generation, before Haydn dominated Viennese circles, several composers appeared: Florian Leopold Gassmann (1729–74), whose opera overtures influenced the symphonic sphere; the violinist Carlos d'Ordonez (1734–86), of Spanish origin; and Leopold Hofmann (1738–93), who introduced the four-movement form (which was immediately imitated by Haydn) with a dozen symphonies before 1770, and who generally favoured adapting the rough Mannheim ways to the more refined and rather old-fashioned Viennese rococo.

The capital of the kingdom of Prussia, Berlin, although it had a very intense musical life, remained rather cut off from this symphonic current (which linked Milan, Vienna, Paris, Mannheim and London); neither its autocrat, Frederick the Great, with his passion for Hasse and Quantz, nor, for various reasons, his most important musician, C. P. E. Bach, could be the centre of modern symphonic interest. The Italian operatic overture gained considerable ground with Johann Gottlieb Graun (1703–71) and his brother Carl Heinrich (1704–59), but it did not interact with the strictly instrumental field. C. P. E. Bach's symphonic output, which dated almost entirely from his Hamburg years, was remarkable for its quantity, instrumental richness and fully discursive style, but it had something backward and old-fashioned, especially on account of the themes he used, which were in his father's mould and in the style of Corelli and Vivaldi, going back to the 'intricate' flights of fancy of the baroque concerto.

8 Johann Christian Bach: London and his meeting with Mozart

The life of Johann Christian Bach (1735–82) seems more like that of a son of Handel than of Bach. Scarcely fifteen years old when his father died, he spent a few years in Berlin, but at the outbreak of the Seven Years' War (1756) he went down to Milan, patronized by the illustrious Litta family, who also sent him to Bologna to study with Padre Martini. In Milan the 'amatissimo Giovannino' left his father's religion and became a Catholic; his sacred works were performed in the best-known churches, in 1760 he obtained the post of organist at the cathedral, and, attracted by the theatres, he wrote operas for the Regio at Turin and the San Carlo at Naples. Johann

Christian, then, learnt counterpoint not from his father but from Padre Martini; it was based on old vocal polyphony and not on the modern language of the *Well-tempered Clavier*, and in fact in the young man's experience counterpoint remained limited to church music and fugal movements in keyboard sonatas. The strongest influence that he absorbed in the Italian years was that of Sammartini, superficially evident in his use of the term 'allegrino', in his titles (*Six Sonatas or Notturnos* of 1763, which imitate Sammartini's *Sei sonate notturne* of 1760), and above all in his use of the 'Lombard' rhythm (a pair of notes, the first shorter than the second, with the accent on the first), common in Sammartini and a constant characteristic of Johann Christian. Nevertheless, as with Handel, England was to be his destination. In London, patronized to some extent by Queen Charlotte, a German by birth, Johann Christian in fact lived as a free professional, teaching the harpsichord, organizing public concerts together with C. F. Abel (the Bach–Abel Concerts, 1765), and above all trying his luck in the field of *opera seria*. He made such a name for himself in theatrical life that Carl Theodor wanted him at Mannheim in 1772, and in 1778 he was asked to write an opera for Paris; but his final years were spent in poverty and solitude – unlike Stamitz, he found the transition from the court to the modern city a bitter experience.

As an opera composer the 'London' Bach found himself at a disadvantage: in London, in comparison with the Italian tradition, he was overshadowed by 'original' composers imported from Naples or Venice, while beside the current of reform extending from Vienna to Paris he could not come out ahead of a contemporary like Gluck. It was exactly the opposite in instrumental music and the sonata: here Johann Christian picked the right moment and exploited the gap before Mozart, working in a centre which, like Paris, was extremely active in the instrumental field. To the Italians already mentioned, who came to London for operas but made a name for themselves as keyboard players, the name of the Turinese violinist Felice Giardini (1716–96) must be added. Germans became especially numerous in London towards the end of the 1750s when the devastation of the Seven Years' War drove musicians from the most affected cities (such as Dresden) to more suitable centres. One of these was Carl Friedrich Abel (1723–87), the son of Christian Ferdinand, viola da gamba player at Cöthen, that great pioneering centre of instrumental music during Bach's years there. Abel, the composer of about thirty symphonies and around a hundred sonatas (mainly trio sonatas), founded together with Johann Christian the

Bach–Abel Concerts in London, and this institution was an attraction for other German, Austrian and Bohemian instrumentalists.

The Englishmen active around 1760 showed that they were still following the immediate, clear model of Handel. Broad Handelian gestures, pointed French rhythms followed by fugatos, and the stately charm of Corelli were all familiar in concertos and overtures by Thomas Augustine Arne (1710–78), perhaps the leading English musician at the middle of the century (he is famous for 'Rule Britannia', the closing song of the masque *Alfred*). The influence of Handel's eight *Sonatas or Lessons* for harpsichord (1756) fades only in the face of another master of this previous age, Domenico Scarlatti, the object of a small cult in England. This is shown by, among other things, the concertos based on Scarlatti sonatas of the organist Charles Avison (1709–70), whose *Essay on musical expression* has already been mentioned. Also in the Handelian mould was William Boyce (1710–79) with his *Eight symphonys in eight parts* (1760), while the Mannheim stamp is just perceptible in the *Symphonies* (1764) by Thomas Erskine (1732–81), who had studied with Stamitz.

In short, Johann Christian Bach arrived in London after the experience of Sammartini in Milan with clear ideas on the *galant* style and the 'singende Allegro', and was writing by this time in an instrumental language that was at least twenty years ahead of that of the English composers. The six Sonatas op. 5 'for harpsichord or pianoforte' (1768) show this clearly; among the first to use the piano in public concerts, Johann Christian handled sonata form with a lucidity and an economy of execution that was unequalled in the 1760s. He played around with the form more than the Italian harpsichordists, using more irregular phrases and knowing how to differentiate them; and he had the gift of inventing melodic themes suitable for sonatas. In particular the nature of the second theme, as a lesser partner with a weaker character than the first, was sometimes drawn with unmistakable sureness (e.g. in the first movement of the second sonata). Even though the whole flowed unaffectedly, on a more detailed level his style was concerned with individual notes, and in this sense he was also influenced to some extent by Domenico Scarlatti (the Presto assai of the Sonata op. 17 no. 4 is the closest he comes to the Neapolitan composer's *Essercizi*). Unlike Carl Philipp Emanuel, he makes no great distinction between works for the keyboard and those for orchestra; Johann Christian affirms the principle of sonata form with absolutely equal results, regardless of the instruments involved, in sonatas and symphonies, the latter being in three movements like Sammartini's (op.

3 appeared in London in 1765 and op. 6 in Amsterdam at the end of the 1760s).

Mozart, at the age of eight, met Johann Christian in London in 1764 during the first grand tour with his father, and they became close friends. He turned three of the op. 5 sonatas into little concertos for harpsichord and orchestra, and many thematic suggestions from the same collection can be seen at a glance in Mozart's first piano sonatas (K 279 and K 280). After meeting Schobert in Paris the year before, Mozart discovered in Johann Christian an opposite pole of lightness and serenity, besides a more seductive 'singende Allegro' than he could find in Wagenseil. Also, this son of Bach, influenced by the Italians, had so little sympathy with minor keys that he hardly ever used them, but when he did he gave them a decisiveness as yet unknown, as in the Symphony in G minor op. 6 no. 6, whose tone anticipates the *Sturm und Drang* and constitutes the immediate predecessor for Mozart's Symphony K183 in the same key.

It is generally recognized that the young Mozart was much influenced between the ages of eight and sixteen by Johann Christian Bach; but, especially in German critical literature, there is a tendency to charge Johann Christian with squandering ideas and not being very clever at looking after the gifts that nature had given him, in an unspoken but obvious parallel with his half-brother Emanuel, who was always at loggerheads with his difficult disposition. But it is Johann Christian's facility that brings to an end this chapter on instrumental music 'after Bach' and 'before Haydn and Mozart', and concludes the historical process of breaking off from the baroque and all the remnants of the old world that still branched out into sonatas and symphonies. His artistic stature was not so high as Emanuel's. He had neither the inner richness of a Sammartini, nor the originality of a Stamitz or a Schobert, but whereas all of these tend to be spoken of as composers of a transitional period, Johann Christian is the first for whom this expression no longer comes to mind. He was not a great composer, but he was not a transitional artist; he was happily cut off from the past and showed no signs of progressing further. For him trio sonatas, the 'terraced style', Corelli, Handel and Vivaldi did not exist and perhaps had never existed; and he gave Mozart a vocabulary that was certainly simple and reduced, but already established, which his young pupil took over exactly.

II

VOCAL MUSIC

9 *Opera seria* and *opera buffa*

Following the main course of instrumental music halfway through the eighteenth century has taken us a long way from Italy, but this country returns to the centre of discussion as soon as the topic of vocal music, and especially stage music, is considered. Here the Italian language, traditions and artists provided an accepted basis, the starting point for any innovations, both in Italy and in the rest of Europe.

In vocal as in instrumental music, the 1750s saw the twilight of great figures. Handel ended his contribution to Italian opera in 1741, and up to his death in 1759 dedicated himself to oratorio. In Paris Rameau's *tragédie lyrique* dissolved after 1750 into pastorales and less ambitious works. Metastasio, who lived in Vienna from 1730, was admired and surrounded by the court's affection, and provided an inexhaustible source of Italian operas for all the European theatres. But in the decade 1730–40 the imperial court theatre in Vienna, with its tradition of splendour, was approaching exhaustion. The gap left by Caldara was felt, the court put off nominating a successor, and one has the impression that the great operatic spectacle no longer interested the Viennese ruling class. Hasse, the champion of Italian opera in the years 1730–40, was the arbiter of Dresden's musical life, but the Seven Years' War put an end to this happy period and the composer moved to Vienna, where Metastasio, many of whose librettos he had already set, was living. But it was rather late for the partnership between Hasse and Metastasio to bear new fruit: it was now 1764, and the Italian opera of the 1730s had been superseded both by a reformed *opera seria* (from which Gluck's *Orfeo* had already been born in 1762) and by the growing importance of comic opera, which was becoming increasingly popular with the European public just around 1760.

Vocal music

If *opera seria*, with its fundamental division of material into recitatives (simple or accompanied) and arias (mainly da capo), and with its heroic, noble subject-matter, expressed the element of continuity with the baroque age, *opera buffa* (comic opera) or semiserious opera was destined to represent the element of breaking away. In a certain sense one can regard the genre of comic opera as a theatrical equivalent of the *galant* instrumental style; as the latter moved away from counterpoint, so comic opera departed from an eloquent, turgid expressiveness given over to harsh harmonies, rhythmic tension and above all florid vocal writing of great difficulty. One meets the move towards the easy *galant* style again in the vocal field: the singers of comic opera, especially in its early days, were not required to have an exceptional performing ability; their vocal resources could be modest, and if anything lively acting was more important. The result was a simplified style of writing, a regularity or rhythm, a more rational harmonic planning, and a clear move towards natural dance-like melodies. There is no difference in musical thought between an aria from Pergolesi's *La serva padrona* and an Allegro by Galuppi, while nothing is further from mideighteenth-century feeling than the great arias from Steffani's or Giovanni Bononcini's operas.

There was also, of course, the difference in theatrical subjectmatter that in *opera seria* accentuated links with the old world, with the age of absolute or enlightened power, while comic opera, on the contrary, provided an easy way to reflect all the new cultural and social concepts that were transforming the civilized world.

Opera seria presented heroes from mythology or ancient history, as well as characters that had been made into legends, international allegories of the typical passions that transcend time, symbols of faith, courage, clemency and supreme sacrifice. The mysterious quality of the castrato voice accentuated the mythical and unreal component. The court continued to be the centre of life; opportunities for staging were dependent on the court calendar, and librettos were full of allusions to important persons. Comic opera, on the other hand, presented the middle classes or the people, with their varied surroundings, trades and languages; the events were commonplace and dealt largely with the family. Even here, apart from an openly farcical vein, the aim was to set examples (all theatre was basically educational), but of less exalted virtue, without the exclusion of all personal interests. Here, too, there was a happy ending, but not by means of the *deus ex machina* of the *tragédie lyrique*; it was in fact made to spring from the combined action of reason and nature, thus making the edification more persuasive. The two worlds, *opera seria* and *opera buffa*, were musically so different halfway through the century that they can almost be regarded as independent languages. This can be seen most clearly when comic opera approaches *opera seria*, following a liking for parody that it had had from its origins. It adopts the language of *opera seria* (e.g. vocal virtuosity, wide intervals between high and low registers and accompanied recitatives) to indicate someone who is not middle class – a nobleman or a high-ranking soldier, for example – or else, ironically, to characterize the other extreme of the social scale, a member of the common people or the middle class who foolishly aspires to higher positions. The artifice (i.e. the most consummate art) of vocal virtuosity was cultivated in this context as an infringement of the naturalness of behaviour and feeling.

So there were old distinctions and well-worn differences. Yet the great operatic phenomenon of the second half of the eighteenth century was to be a convergence of the two genres, serious and comic, which had become clearly apparent by the final decades of the century. It was the comic form that was more inclined to change its mould. The gentle vein of sensibility which has been discussed in connection with the *galant* style, the cult of sentiment and of tears as a sign of a lofty spirit, was to adjust itself spontaneously to the more flexible course of comic opera. Here, fluctuating between semi-serious, sentimental and *larmoyant* genres, the contamination grew up between tragedy and comedy that Voltaire had predicted in the preface to his play *Nanine* (1749) and that the 'bourgeois' theatre of Goldoni, Diderot (in *Le fils naturel* of 1757) and Lessing was beginning to show.

Still on the tactical ground of comic opera, the musical representation of 'action' took its first steps forward. If the regime of aria and recitative suited the heroes of *opera seria* with their continual alternation of reflection and action, the characters in comic opera, fundamentally, reflected little and acted a lot, thereby pushing the flow of action, albeit of a modest, everyday type, forward. The usual place for this was the finale of the act, a concerted piece in which all the characters came together, each with his or her own dramatic potential, thereby welding together a more or less continuous chain of musical items. The presence of bass voices (not much used in *opera seria*, in which high voices were preferred) guaranteed these concerted numbers balance of sound and completeness of the abstract musical piece. In this way late-eighteenth-century comic opera raised its social status with elaborate forms, complex architecture and vocal writing which was just as difficult as that of *opera seria*. *Opera seria*, for its part, became more flexible; the central sections of the arias gained importance with secondary themes and gentle ideas that had new life.

Its greater mobility and its orientation towards the future gave comic opera a special prestige; historical considerations seemed to favour it, leaving the defence of *opera seria* to rhetoric. In particular, the impressive development of comic opera in Italy throughout the second half of the century coincided with one of the least heroic moments in the history of the country: the years of peace but also of distrust and scepticism through which it passed between the peace of Aix-la-Chapelle (1748) and the wars at the end of the century. When the soldier Tagliaferro in Piccinni's *Cecchina* sings in his Germanicized Italian, 'Fenir, fenir con me,/ Che alla querra, contenti,/ Star tutte sorte de difertimenti',[1] he seems to be seeing the procession of noblewomen who used to accompany officers on their campaigns, in an Italy that was becoming less and less a military power and less and less a stage for decisive events (the Seven Years' War was by now taking place elsewhere, and was no longer concerned with the Italian regions). Here it was comic opera that seemed destined to reflect more honestly the climate of humble interests and real details which distinguished the true Italy of regional states from the one of imperial dreams. Yet it must be remembered that *opera seria* was to remain the most authoritative and accredited form of music in the theatre until the end of the century; every theatre and every operatic season opened with an *opera seria*. Its prestige was largely literary, and literary culture continued to take an interest in *opera seria* in order to improve it, but one must also add to this the public prestige conferred on it by the castratos (the 'virtuosi') and the prima donnas, whose art of singing was at the highest level of professionalism, and whose favourite sphere of action was this illustrious genre. Comic opera's greater accessibility to the modern sensibility (compared with the harder construction of *opera seria*) should not make us consider it more representative, more typical, or even *a priori* better than *opera seria*. Furthermore, there were at least two other factors turning this old-fashioned genre into something just as deeply rooted in the taste of the mid-eighteenth century: a new desire for reform, stronger or weaker depending on the place, but general and unanimous, and a deeper involvement with antiquity, which threw new light on historical and mythological material.

10 The European success of Italian comic opera

The European success of Italian comic opera is one of the salient facts in the musical and theatrical history of the decade 1750–60. The actual setting of this development could only have been Paris, a centre of incomparable importance, where the publicity ended up by giving the debate itself more emphasis than the subject under discussion.

In 1746 at the Hôtel de Bourgogne, the home of the Italian *commedia dell'arte*, Pergolesi's intermezzo *La serva padrona*, composed in 1733, was staged. The event passed unnoticed and there were only four performances; Pergolesi, who had already been dead for ten years, was described by the *Mercure de France* as 'a very young artist from the other side of the Alps'.[2] But six years later, in 1752, the picture changed: the same *La serva padrona*, put on by the modest company of Eustachio Bambini (the director of the Italian opera at Strasbourg), came by fortuitous circumstances to Paris's greatest theatre, the Opéra, which was dedicated to the *tragédie lyrique* of Lully and Rameau. The result was as sensational as it was unexpected, causing as it did a deep split in French musical culture which has passed into the annals as the *querelle des bouffons*, the old controversy about the merits of the French and the Italians brought up to date in terms of reasonableness and sensibility. In the two years 1753–4 around sixty pamphlets by men of letters, musicians and journalists appeared. The intellectuals, the Enlightenment circle – Rousseau, Diderot, d'Holbach and Grimm (a pupil of Gottsched who had been in Paris since 1749) – were all noisy supporters of Italian music as the only kind capable of inventing agreeable and natural melodies. French music, that is, the *tragédie lyrique* with its respect for verisimilitude in its declamation and passions, was defended by professional musicians and by the more traditional side of French theatrical culture. The latter, with Cazotte and the Abbé de Voisenon, sided in favour of Rameau (who also intervened personally with his *Observations sur notre instinct pour la musique*, 1754), above all in response to Rousseau's *Lettre sur la musique française* (1753) which had put forward the theory of the objective inferiority of the French on account of their dull and unmusical language.

Bambini's company, amazed that the antics of Serpina and Uberto had set so many famous minds buzzing, hurried to put on other comic works, all of them short and with two or three characters, by Pergolesi, Latilla, Rinaldo da Capua, Leo, Jommelli and others. The old Neapolitan intermezzo repertory was thrown onto the scales of European taste and taken as a model for a new kind of stage music. Rousseau, in fact, was not content just to contribute articles to the *querelle*, but in October of the same year, 1752, put on at Fontainebleau his 'intermède' *Le devin du village*, a skilful mixture of catchy little airs, now and again emphasizing sensitive minor keys, dance rhythms, and, for its 1753 revival at the Opéra, even simple recitatives. Within a few years the little work was performed throughout Europe (and in 1790 in New York), translated into Dutch, English and German. Other intermezzos in French versions put on by Bambini, like Rinaldo da Capua's *La zingara*, which became *La Bohémienne*, and especially Vincenzo Legrenzio Ciampi's *Bertoldo in corte*, a Goldoni subject dealing with a couple of virtuous peasants who prefer the country to corrupt city life, parodied by Favart in *Ninette à la cour* (1755), met with similar success.

The name of Carlo Goldoni appears at an important point in the development of comic opera; with around fifteen intermezzos and more than fifty *drammi giocosi* in Venice during the period 1749–62, Goldoni gave a decisive impetus to the humanization of comic opera beyond the stereotyped models of the intermezzo. To be sure, the comedy of errors and disguises was still the accepted basis for the dramatic structure, and the characterization in his librettos could scarcely attain the profundity achieved in his great comedies for the theatre. But if the action woven from the slender threads of the farce and the intermezzo could attain the breadth of musical comedy, it was because contemporary ideas entered more and more into his librettos: Nature as mother and guide; the various fashions of the Venetian partriciate and middle classes; the taste for the exotic, with explicit references to modern exploration and colonization of the world outside Europe; a certain maliciousness in the whole sphere of love; and a new attention to the arts and crafts and an interest in the working countryside. In short, a mirror, a tasteful allusion to the real life of the Venetians which can be extended to the whole of bourgeois Europe in its standardization of the opera libretto. The theme of trading and great international commerce resounded throughout the eighteenth century, from the Voltaire of the tenth of the *Lettres philosophiques* to the Goethe of *Wilhelm Meister*, who admired those 'crowds of bustling people who, like great rivers, cross the world, taking away and bringing back their goods'.[3] But *opera seria* was completely impermeable to this movement. Goldoni introduced something of it, though without any grand rhetoric, into comic opera; the emphasis in his librettos on the environment of middle-class merchants and the continual monetary metaphors remind one in a small way that beneath military and chivalrous pretences beats the true heart of modern society, 'the real war that the people of Europe wage with trade', as Pietro Verri had said.[4]

Before Goldoni no comic opera libretto had presented such precision of language in denoting every social type, such variety of metre, or so many opportunities for the musician to move from the canzonet to the serenade, the aria and the ensemble. If the development of the concerted act finale was bound up with the idea of involving the audience in the action, it is here that Goldoni contributes to this process in a definitive way, developing in his finales a type of dialogue on more varied levels and thus expanding on Metastasio's sharp distinction between quiet reflection and open declamation. The remarks of the characters who have been brought together on stage run on three levels here, being addressed to everyone, to some people (excluding a third party), or just to the person speaking himself (excluding everyone else). These three strata are indicated in the text by directions in parentheses; they interact continually and carry forward both the psychological and the stage action.

The first composer to be connected with Goldoni in Venice was Baldassare Galuppi. The partnership was inaugurated with three comic operas in 1749: *L'Arcadia in Brenta*, *Il conte Caramella* and *Arcifanfano, re dei matti*. There were another three in the following year – *Il mondo alla roversa, ossia Le donne che comandano*, *Il paese della cuccagna* and *Il mondo della luna* – and then an opera a year until 1754 when *Il filosofo di campagna* established itself on the leading Italian stages and was put on in the five years between 1755 and 1759 in Frankfurt, Dresden, Prague, Bratislava, Mannheim, Munich, Brussels, Barcelona and St Petersburg. *Il filosofo di campagna* already presented, albeit within narrow limits, a considerable repertoire of musical comedy. The basic elements of syllabic, easily understandable singing and short themes were the same as those of *La serva padrona*; but there was more variety of expression, from the maid Lesbina's canzonets about radishes or chicory to the little orphan Eugenia's melancholy, from the comic solemnity of Don Tritemio to the good nature of the philosopher Nardo, who announces himself by playing a pastoral tune on a small guitar and does not want to exchange his rural peace for a stormy marriage. There are more arias than in *La serva padrona*, and the finale of the second act is already a piece governed by autonomous musical laws, with changes of rhythm at every joint in the action, in which even the smallest idea, like the laughing 'ah ah ah', is used for a structural purpose.

Goldoni's encounter with the more fluent Neapolitan style had even more consistent results. Librettos from the second half of the 1750s, including *La ritornata di Londra*, *Il mercato di Malmantile*, *Il signor dottore* and *La fiera di Sinigaglia*, were set to music in Venice by Domenico Fischietti (1720?–1810?), a Neapolitan, who later moved to Dresden and Salzburg. But the sudden notable rise in quality came when *La buona figliola*, taken from Richardson's *Pamela* and adapted as a libretto in 1756, ended up four years later in the hands of Niccolò Piccinni, who came from Bari. For a non-serious opera, it achieved a previously unequalled success, something which could certainly not have been foreseen eight years before, when intermezzos and burlettas were causing such a stir in Paris. Piccinni (1728–1800) was a typical product of early-eighteenth-century Neapolitan musical culture, a student from the conservatoire of Sant'Onofrio and a pupil of Leo and Durante, and nobody was more suited than he, the man who had christened his daughters Giulia and Chiarella after the leading character and the cousin in *La Nouvelle Héloïse*, to receive the stream of sensibility that was softening the heart of eighteenth-century Europe.

Cecchina, an orphan and gardener at the country house of the Marchese di Conchiglia, is sketched with a consistent humanity that was to become widespread: the languid minor key, the anxiety of syncopated rhythms, the melodic caress and the rocking 6/8 are the musical elements of her self-pity ('Partirò . . . me ne andrò/ A cercar la carità,/ Poverina, la Cecchina, poverina la Cecchina'[5]). Her femininity is echoed in the peasant Sandrina (she finds herself in a similar position: 'Poverina, poverina, tutto il dì/ Faticar degg'io così'[6]), and the archetypal lonely woman, full of tenderness and ready to burst into tears, certainly makes her entrance into the history of stage music with Cecchina (in the instrumental field collections 'pour le beau sexe' for harpsichord or clavichord showed a similar interest). *La buona figliola* was not, however, just the portrayal of a character: it was a complete *dramma giocoso*. But at the same time there was an immediately obvious division: the characters of humble origin (or nobles endowed with worthy feelings) speak the language of the *galant* style with its more sensitive formulas; the noble characters, especially when they put on an air of arrogance, adopt the vocabulary of *opera seria*, with a great deal of difficult vocal display. This helps the early identification of wickedness (e.g. the Marchesa's aria 'Furie di donna irata') with melodic virtuosity, inhuman because of its mechanical nature, later taken as an example by Mozart in *Die Zauberflöte* with the Queen of Night. Action and music begin to show fruitful links: when Sandrina and Paoluccia come on and go off to report to their mistress what Cecchina is doing, their movement to and fro is emphasized each time by developing the same theme. Symmetry as a law of musical composition establishes itself at the same time as a vehicle for comedy. In the finale of the first act, slanders against Cecchina (in the major key, with rapid movement and syllabic, biting, staccato singing) are integrated with the lament of the Marchese, who is in love (in the minor key, with slower movement and expressive, legato singing). The finale's whole structure is based on this dual polarity, while the unified conception is still secured by the use of a rudimentary rondo form.

After its christening in Rome in 1760, *La buona figliola* remained in circulation for thirty years in the principal European theatres. *Il mondo della luna* and *Il filosofo di campagna* dominated London during the season 1760–1, and this success seemed to Burney to be a victory for the *galant* taste over Handelian seriousness. In 1758 Locatelli's travelling company introduced comic opera to St Petersburg, where, with works by Galuppi, Fischietti and Rutini, it found a popularity never achieved before with *opera seria*. At the beginning of the 1760s, comic opera, without reforms and programmes, simply growing from the intermezzo and the comic pastorale, had conquered all the countries of Europe as the other authoritative style beside its serious sister.

11 The rediscovery of classical antiquity

Opera seria had always chosen its settings and characters from classical antiquity, drawing on Greek mythology, the histories of Livy and Suetonius, the *Aeneid*, Plutarch's *Lives* and Ovid's *Metamorphoses*. In the second half of the eighteenth century, however, this world was given a new lease of life, separated from contemporary matters by an ever-decreasing division, across which it seemed almost possible for modern ideas to join hands with antiquity.

49

The first investigation into archaeological heritage, the birth of the modern 'dig' in the years following the end of the Seven Years' War in 1763, produced a confrontation with antiquity unknown to previous ages. In 1762 the 'English Society of Dilettantes' published the first precise description of Athenian architecture (*The antiquities of Athens measured and delineated*), and in 1764 it organized expeditions to Athens and the shores of Asia Minor. In Italy work was carried out for over a decade on the excavations at Pompeii, Herculaneum and Paestum, and from 1769 on those of Hadrian's Villa. In Paris in 1758 Le Roy published *Les ruines des plus beaux monuments de la Grèce*; in 1763 Galiani wrote to Tanucci that in Parisian houses 'all the furniture is now *à la grecque*',[7] and even the embroidery on clothing was based on an examination of Vitruvius. Rome was filled with connoisseurs; the discovery of antiquity was really aimed above all at Greece, but the calm, hospitable Italy of the second half of the eighteenth century ended up being a far more attractive place to stay; and in Rome two Germans, the archaeologist Johann Joachim Winckelmann (with his *Reflections on the painting and sculpture of the Greeks* of 1755) and the painter Rafael Mengs (with his *Inquiry into the beauties of painting* of 1762), founded the principles of a 'neoclassicism' that looked to antiquity not only as a source of inspiration but also as a model, the standard for contemporary works of art. In the autumn of 1764, sitting among the ruins of the Capitol while 'the barefooted fryars were chanting their litanies in the temple of Jupiter',[8] Edward Gibbon conceived the idea of his *History of the decline and fall of the Roman Empire* (1776–88). Never, from the time of the Renaissance, had the remains and documents from the 'morte stagioni', as Leopardi called them,[9] had such a strong voice, so capable of influencing the whole cultural life of modern man.

Winckelmann's greatest work, the *Geschichte der Kunst des Alterthums* (History of the art of the ancients, 1764), claimed 'noble simplicity and calm grandeur both in attitudes and expression'[10] as a principal characteristic of Greek art, the greatest art in history. It did not matter, for the time being, that the Greek art he was discussing was a Roman copy; it was really the capacity for extracting an ideal of beauty, superior in comparison with its individual products, that constituted his originality of thought and the reason for his influence in every area of art. In *opera seria* halfway through the 1760s, Metastasio's heroes began to seem too docile, surrounded by a *galant* lightness which contrasted with that 'noble simplicity and calm grandeur' which Winckelmann had described as the supreme goal of art. Compared with this ideal, taken up by the more cultured circles in Paris and Vienna, the traditional Metastasian and Neapolitan *opera seria* presented a set of internal rules, schemes and customs whose motives of abstract musical technique and craftsmanship should no longer have had any say in the matter where the goal of representing the ancient world in all its range was concerned. The artistic category of 'the Sublime', which Winckelmann assigned to Phidias and his circle, was due to return and to influence *opera seria*, driving out of it the sense of cheerful occasion and frivolity that had resulted from the professional independence of the individual 'virtuosi'.

The teaching and ethical appeal of the ancients was too important to leave opera in the hands of musicians; and greater knowledge of the ancient world in all its forms set up not only an air of severity, but also vibrations of fear and holy terror. We no longer see only a perpetual happy Arcadia, but also the barbarous face of gods who call for human sacrifice and who destroy man, wounding him where he is most vulnerable (the heart) and playing on his weakness, as happens to Orpheus, who is not allowed to turn round to look at Eurydice, to Alcestis, who can only save her husband's life by dying in his place, and to Agamemnon and Idomeneo, who have to kill their own children. Even if Metastasio's heroes died 'prendendosela con le stelle' ('cursing the stars') like Don Ferrante in Manzoni's *I promessi sposi*,[11] it always happened with an innate sense of mitigation, without straying too far from the rules of good behaviour. Now the clash with divinity, drawn from Greek theatre and from Sophocles in particular, was more integral and absolute, and librettos full of exclamations against 'barbari numi' (barbarous gods) and 'dei infidi e malvagi' (fickle and wicked gods) seem to call for a more austere pace of acting, and for direct expressions which do not balk at displays of anger and apocalyptic sonorities with direct significance.

This disturbing background, which removed any purely scholarly character from the rediscovery of antiquity in the second half of the eighteenth century, was not alone: there was a continual capacity for passing from the level of history to that of reality, for facing the present with new energy in the light of examples from the past. The greatest Greek art had flourished in the free republic of Athens, while tyranny suffocated the arts: this was a conviction of Tacitus and Pseudo-Longinus that was very popular with the more progressive middle classes in England and France. And a growing republic overseas, the United States, was covering its Protestant roots with continual references to virtue and the moral strictness of Greek and

Roman civilization. On the strictly private level a strong 'Greek nostalgia' grew up; many people, especially in the mists of the north, felt like strangers in their own home, and stood on the shore like Goethe's Iphigenia, 'searching with her soul for the land of the Greeks'.[12] For them Greece was not only the object of philological and archaeological studies, but an ideal home, a land of refuge from everyday misery and personal disappointments, and one could still fight, if not for ancient Hellas, for modern Greece oppressed by the Turks, like the young Greek in Hölderlin's *Hyperion*, or else seriously, a few years later, like an entire generation of romantics. This was the extreme manifestation of the aspect of real life which the late eighteenth century had embraced from the start in its rediscovery of the ancient world.

12 The discovery of the fabulous East

It was in the sphere of research into manners and customs that European sensibility in the eighteenth century first turned to Eastern culture, the influence of which can be traced in detail throughout the century in the history of European relations with the East. It was an encyclopaedic interest, but also involved a curiosity for *objets d'art* and oddities, almost as if it were a compensation for the regularity and balance of rationalism.

The vogue for China, stimulated in particular by the Jesuit missions, soon joined those for Turkey and Persia (the French translation of *The thousand and one nights* edited by the orientalist Antoine Galland came out in twelve volumes between 1704 and 1711). The rococo had been viewed directly as a cross between the baroque and oriental bizarreness, and in fact the mania for China penetrated European cultural taste and life from literature to fashion, from opera librettos to masquerades and ballets, from gardening to china factories. Towards the middle of the century the colonial war between England and France increased the attention paid to India, especially in religion and philosophy, while the intensification of voyages of discovery (James Cook made his third exploration, along the east coast of America, in 1776–9) completed the exotic picture with America and Oceania, imagined by European writers as paradises of purity and naivety, ideal places in which to set Rousseau's myth of the noble savage.

The oriental story and the 'Turkish tale' spread gradually, their main function being at first instructive and satirical. The contrivance of having Europeans judged by imaginary voyagers from the East had been re-used successfully in 1721 in Montesquieu's *Lettres persanes* (reprinted with additions in 1754). The tension between the old conception of the tolerant East on the one hand and the social and moral contradictions of 'civilized' Europeans on the other was resolved in favour of the East, and the natural purity of the primitive people usually triumphed over European wickedness. The position of women, through its exploitation in the theatre, was particularly important in this social conflict. Muslim women, who were kept segregated, had to use all the means at their disposal and all their cunning to get any happiness; the same applied to the European woman who had fallen into the hands of an oriental prince, to become reunited with her fiancé. To the oriental prince, moreover, the free European woman seemed a coquette, fickle and in the long run not easy to recommend as a wife. In other cases a magnanimous sultan could spontaneously renounce the woman and hand her over himself into the arms of her fiancé. The harem became a common place of intrigues, while jealousy, disguises and abductions dominated the action, along with dervishes and guards. Even the Muslim ban on drinking wine, with its predictable infringements and drunkenness, was to become a frequent source of comic situations.

If the wave of classical rediscovery was to affect *opera seria*, providing the current of reform with new plots, in the end the exotic mainly influenced the comic sector. The exotic nature of the various Tamerlanes, Montezumas and Genghis Khans of baroque *opera seria* did not go further than strange costumes and magnificent sets. Oriental material penetrated opera on a comic subject more easily, not only in the grotesque characterization of the harem's custodian or in the plentiful serenades prompted by the imprisoned women, but also in the music itself, where it produced a little repertoire of recurring features: augmented or diminished intervals, easily recognized in the regular context of major and minor scales; heavy chromatic progressions with all the parts moving together; the emphatic use of the Neapolitan sixth; quick, snappy acciaccaturas; mutterings in an imaginary Turkish language; and, above all, an immediately obvious timbre with the use of what was called quite simply 'Turkish music' – the picturesque quartet of bass drum, cymbals, triangle and piccolo. Since the Turks were, after the siege of Vienna in 1683, no longer a real danger for Europe, people began to look with curious interest at even their musical customs; the 'military music' of the janissaries, the sultan's bodyguards, found growing favour and later passed into the military bands of the revolutionary and Napoleonic armies. An instrument added to the 'Turkish' quartet of percussion and piccolo and even used by Berlioz was what the French called the *chapeau chinois*, known in England as the Turkish crescent or Jingling Johnny, a long pole with crescent-shaped brass plates fitted with bells. Similar noises, on the scale of a domestic toy, could be deafening even on harpsichords or fortepianos, which in the late eighteenth century were often provided with a 'janissary' stop ('Janitscharenzug').

This realistic copying of local styles, mostly adapted to the rapid rhythms of French *opéra-comique* (see Chapter 20), ballet or instrumental genre-pieces (Turkish marches), was to mix in the second half of the century with a new dimension of exoticism, less limited to practices and customs and more interested in extending the genre of the fairy-tale to fabulous lengths, involving mysterious initiations.

The fantastic element was prevalent in Naples in the librettos and comedies of Francesco Cerlone, many of which were based on *The thousand and one nights*. In Venice, the Italian city most naturally exposed to the East, the importance of the fairy-tale is shown by Carlo Gozzi, who later began a fruitful link with the north with the German translation of his works which appeared in Berne between 1777 and 1779. In Austria and the German lands the *Zauberstück* ('Zauber' means magic), an up-dating of the 'marvellous' theatre very popular with the Jesuits in the baroque era, was in fact experiencing great success. By virtue of the mutability of its material, the fabulous style found points of contact with other trends, downwards with the burlesque taste of popular comedy and upwards with a vein of secular education pervaded by mysticism and oriental, especially Egyptian, symbolism. In the same way, a novel by the abbé Jean Terrasson dealing with the education of a wise prince, *Séthos, histoire ou vie tirée des monuments anecdotes de l'ancienne Egypte* (1731) had rapidly been translated into German, English and Italian, and had already exerted a wide influence. Boehme and the mystics of the Reformation were re-read; in 1788 Emanuel Swedenborg's *Les merveilles du ciel et de l'enfer* appeared in a translation from the Swedish, and the exoticism of Jacques Cazotte, who became a follower of occult science, also reached mystical heights in his *Contes arabes* and *Feu de Bagdad*.

In 1786 Christoph Wieland published a collection of stories about spirits and fairies (*Dschinnistan*, the source of Mozart's *Die Zauber-flöte*) and drew the reader's attention to the ethical and cognitive value of the fairy-tale, which goes beyond its childish appearance. Goethe, too, frequently maintained the serious nature of the fairy-tale, and in 1784–85 he sketched a poem, *Die Geheimnisse* ('The mysteries'), which involved the esoteric initiation of a young man lost in an inaccessible place. In this direction of high-flown religious nobility, a general mixture of 'classical' and 'exotic' was eventually achieved, a combination of Greek and Eastern antiquity that seemed in some ways contradictory. On the other hand a greater knowledge of the Greek world revealed links with oriental styles, with Egypt and Persia; and the consecration to the mysteries of Isis of a young man struggling against evil forces which hold up his ascent to immortality had already been described in Apuleius's *Metamorphoses*. In the mid-eighteenth century the institution based on all these grounds, Freemasonry, reached its peak of conversion, turning to the intellectual and moral progress of humanity as a kind of official and hierarchical organization of the fabulous. Growing out of the secret societies of the English and Scottish Jacobites, it boasted very ancient origins going back to Solomon, builder of the temple of Jerusalem, and considered itself dedicated to building the temple to the great Architect of the Universe. From London Freemasonry spread its lodges to Paris, the Hague, Rome and Madrid, becoming most widespread around 1780, when it welcomed into its ranks people of every class, from the highest court dignitaries to the smallest trader, from Mozart, who presented it with *Die Zauberflöte*, to Cagliostro (Giuseppe Balsamo), the founder of an Egyptian sect at Lyons in 1782.

'Masonic music' was restricted to a few keys (especially E flat major, which was regarded as solemn), to wind instruments with dark, majestic timbres like basset horns and trombones, to certain figures (notes slurred in pairs, symbolizing fraternity, and chords repeated three times), and to a general atmosphere of a higher peace – all formulas which were used too generally to be significant. Exoticism, too, like the exploration of far-away places, did not allow itself to be localized as easily as the 'Turkish music': it was to have a sporadic effect in the transparent timbres and mystical atmosphere ascribable to individual instrumental sounds. Yet in new contexts even the old 'Turkish' devices could last for a long time: the theme of the 'March of the Dervishes' from Beethoven's *The ruins of Athens* and that of the satanic chorus 'Schwarzer Hauptmann, geh an's Land' ('Black captain, come ashore') from Wagner's *The Flying*

Dutchman come from a common root, the interval of the augmented fourth, one of the most widespread oriental features of eighteenth-century European music. The relationship between the two themes is an indication, on a linguistic level, of how one of the paths to romanticism passed through the exotic.

13 The 'literary' opera

There is certainly no shortage of appeals to rationality and coherence in the history of *opera seria*. They were mostly voiced by literary men, but also by cultivated musicians, such as Benedetto Marcello, who saw the musical theatre as a Babel of ridiculous and destructive habits, and who wanted a more 'literary' work, one in which the drama and words would have a weight equal to that of the music. This current was to grow and to gain new strength in the central decades of the eighteenth century, stimulated by Enlightenment culture which also demanded for opera the beneficial influences of nature and reason. Next to the composers at the table of reform, with a large, varied contribution of remarks and arguments, sat their librettists, like Ranieri de Calzabigi, Marco Coltellini and Mattia Verazi, all followers of Metastasio but, with varying degrees of determination, all aiming to progress further. Other people also took their seats: those who supervised performances and were able to intervene directly in the production, like Guillaume du Tillot at Parma or Giacomo Durazzo at Vienna; champions of a sister art, ballet (which became more important through Jean-Georges Noverre and Gasparo Angiolini); singers with a particular interpretive awareness like Gaetano Guadagni; and, naturally, a host of theorists and men of letters, among whom the names of Francesco Algarotti (with his *Saggio sopra l'opera in musica* of 1755, which was enlarged in 1762) and Antonio Planelli, Marmontel and Chabanon, Grimm and Sonnenfels immediately come to mind.

The mould of Metastasian opera had to be broken; not so much Metastasio in himself, who was never attacked directly even by those who considered that the picture of antiquity that his librettos provided was out of date. Even in the theatre foyers, on the level of professional competition, people moved against Metastasio with great respect. Even for Stefano Arteaga (*Le rivoluzioni del teatro musicale italiano dalla sua origine fino al presente*, 1786), Metastasian opera, consisting of aria, simple recitative and accompanied recitative, was the most perfect model of the *dramma per musica*. As a poet, then, his popularity seemed everlasting: for Voltaire (in the preface to *Sémiramis*, 1748) Metastasio's dramas were 'worthy of Corneille when he is not being rhetorical, and of Racine when he is not being insipid'.[13] There may be a slight flavour of scandal in the comparison, but even for the lovers of *La Nouvelle Héloïse*, Metastasio was, along with Petrarch, the most read and most quoted poet. The battle against Metastasio was indirect: it was conducted against opera performed 'in the Italian style' and against the theatrical customs accepted (involuntarily) from the succession of arias and recitatives.

Even this alternation between arias and recitatives was not in itself always unwanted. Chastellux (*Essai sur l'union de la poésie et de la musique*, 1765) felt 'inexpressible charm' in the moment at which the ear, 'after wandering through the irregular phrases and various modulations of the recitative, hears the musical period [of the aria] beginning, immediately sensing its plan and its structure'.[14] In fact the linguistic contrast between recitative and aria could be the source of emotion and stage movement, as even Arteaga was openly to claim, pointing accurately to the different functions of the two forms. But the day-to-day reality as far as performance was concerned was another matter: the aria was the only thing that counted, both for the performer who showed off his skill in it and for the public who talked during the recitatives without listening to them. The composition of a simple recitative (for voice over harmonies on the harpsichord) was completely disparaged, the job of an apprentice, infinitely reproducible. Conversely, the singer who dominated an aria technically and who enriched it with variations in the repeats ('da capo') ended up regarding it as his own, and he carried it around with him like his clothes, taking it from one opera to another and even inserting it in an unsuitable place just as though he were playing a trump card in his game with the public. It was difficult to say any longer who was the author of the libretto in operas performed in this way. Metastasio saw this corruption but was powerless; he referred in his letters to the dignity of tragedy with the same expressions as the 'official' reformers who, in the view of history, were to undermine his prestige. For his contemporaries there was no such clearly defined opposition, and reformers like Calzabigi, who published Metastasio's complete works (with an important introductory *Dissertazione*) in Paris in 1755, or like Noverre, who in the eighth of his *Lettres sur la danse* (1760) addressed an admiring eulogy to him, referred to him openly.

It is significant that these voices came from Paris; a vital feature of the whole question of reform opera in fact lay in its relations with France. Even though he saw Metastasio as the greatest among tragedians, ancient and modern, Calzabigi recognized in the *tragédie lyrique* an objectively richer and more articulate dramaturgical model than Italian opera; if only everything – poetry, music, mime, dance and painting – could be subordinated to a new force: the action. Algarotti was also steeped in French culture; he was a Venetian, spent about twenty years living in Paris, where he was in contact with Voltaire in the decade 1730–40, and then became chamberlain to Frederick the Great at Berlin, another centre of French culture. The fame achieved by his *Saggio*, echoed by D'Alembert in *La liberté de la musique* (1760) and translated into English (1767), German (1769) and French (1773), gained him the invitation to be adviser at Parma at a point when the city was an island of French taste and was trying to bring to life a type of French opera in the Italian language.

The whole movement of reform that ran through *opera seria* from 1750 to 1770 was in effect permeated by ideas debated in France and taken over by the whole of European culture. Above all came the demand, about which Algarotti was most insistent, for perfect illusion and the greatest scenic verisimilitude. To this end Diderot had already, in his *Discours sur la poésie dramatique* (1757), translated into German by Lessing (Berlin, 1760), called for the removal of the public from the stage, where it was common to have benches and seats. Noverre, too, was aiming at perfect illusion when he praised the actor Garrick, well known in London and a model of realism, who was no longer an actor but became each time the true, living character being portrayed. Another point was the organic unity of the whole, the just distribution of the many poetic, musical and symbolic elements that came together in opera: Algarotti declared that it was essential, but it remained a common topic for argument in all the discussions about reform. When Gluck's *Alceste* was due to be performed at Bologna in 1778, Calzabigi was worried about the balance of the various elements, the prerequisite of an advantage that disappeared 'if just one of these aspects is missing'.[15] Ideas on more crucial questions followed from these basic principles: the regime of aria and recitative, whose coupling delighted Chastellux, was regarded as a 'sharp contrast' by Gluck and Calzabigi,[16] and not very realistic in comparison with arioso, the dramatic declamation of Lully and Rameau, or recitative accompanied by a significant orchestral commentary. Algarotti regarded *recitativo accompagnato* as the most suitable place for dramatic realism, and other famous literary figures, such as Vittorio Alfieri and Vincenzo Monti, were later to repeat that the aria was an undue interruption of the organic progression of the passions. Another restriction was the da capo aria; passion did not fit into such rigid schemes, and in matters of stage action, as Noverre said, 'la symmétrie doit faire place à la nature'.[17] In Berlin Frederick the Great, who was anything but sympathetic towards the modernists in instrumental music, was, however, particularly ironic about the repetitions of the da capo aria and wrote (in French) the libretto for C. H. Graun's *Montezuma* with numerous bipartite cavatinas.

All these demands for alterations and modifications to Metastasian opera were widespread, but had no real systematic direction except in the most significant moments of the collaboration between Gluck and Calzabigi. On the other hand there are also plenty of ideas in Gluck which originated in France, so that his journey to Paris not long after 1770 was to seem like the return of reform opera to its mother's womb and the ideal home which it had left at the beginning of the 1750s.

14 Music and language; the melodrama

If artistic theory was abundant throughout the eighteenth century, its main intellectual concern in the field of music was the consideration of the analogy between music and language, a theme which continued until the first decades of the nineteenth century. All the discussions about operatic reforms started and ended up there, at the boundary between music and philosophy, further and further from practical music.

The interest in melodies that could be based on speech, the 'middle' form as it was known in the seventeenth century, was old and widespread; the concept of the word being master of the music had always been favoured by the humanist tradition, from the fathers of the church to the leaders of Florentine opera, and was still popular with the eighteenth-century reformers. Even instrumental music, however 'incomprehensible', gained a higher status when C. P. E. Bach made it 'sprechend' ('speaking'), and the greatest compliment that one could pay an instrumentalist was to say that he knew how to make his instrument 'speak'. There was a very widespread interest in the speech melodies of various countries among both travellers and experts, especially English ones, but the home of this trend, in the sphere of research into the origins of language, was France in the mid-eighteenth century.

The richest source is Condillac: the first chapters of the second part of his *Essai sur l'origine des connaissances humaines* (1746), taking ideas from English philosophy, Descartes and Du Bos, define a 'language of action', a complex of gestures and cries – the first stage of development. A 'language of articulate sounds' follows the first stage, but preserves traces of it in its variety of vocal intonation at different pitches and its abundance of syllables, later lost in the levelling out of tone in modern languages. From oriental languages to Greek, from Greek to Latin, and from Latin to modern languages, there was a gradual impoverishment of this 'musical' aspect of language. Few writings were as popular at this time as those of Cicero, who discussed prosaic rhythm ('numerus') and the 'quidam cantus obscurior', made up of metres and cadences and the deliberate rising and lowering of the voice that can be so useful to the professional orator.[18] In order to cultivate that hidden singing, Cicero had listened carefully to the actor Roscius, and in Greece the orators went to schools of music to learn 'phōnaskhia', the art of modulating the voice at will according to the appropriate expression. The ancient Greek language was envied for its variety of accents and metrical feet and its possibilities of different combinations. Dionysius of Halicarnassus had said that raising the voice to a high pitch or dropping it to a low one corresponded to the interval of a fifth; the wonderful effects of Greek melody, which are discussed in historical accounts, were certainly derived from the richness of language that was available to the Greek musician, with a metrical variety which he further extended and reinforced. To be sure, when Pierre-Jean Burette, a doctor and keen antiquarian, had transcribed some Greek fragments and had them performed at the Académie des Belles-lettres, the result had been modest, but, according to Rousseau, the fault lay with the listener, whose ear no longer had any idea of the variety of a sonorous, harmonious language.[19] Historical accounts, however, left no room for doubt: audiences had certainly been affected in ancient times. People were not, however, satisfied with looking at historical accounts; the question of the relationship between language and sounds was also current news, emerging from the increasingly frequent reports of travellers about the 'moeurs des sauvages' and primitive peoples. Here they had tangible proof of identical words which, spoken at different pitches, corresponded to different meanings; and Condillac too, remembering the 328 monosyllables of the Chinese, varying over five pitches, maintained that languages were originally 'pronounced with such clear inflections of the voice that a musician could have written down their pronunciation in notation'.[20] Now the modern musician, enlightened and aware of the possibilities of singing, had to face the task of climbing back up the slope of the civilized languages' 'musical impoverishment'.

The highest aim of music was, in fact, to make feelings perceptible, and in this capacity it became one of the imitative arts, and was understood as such. Painting and sculpture imitated objects and figures, music imitated the passions, but the passions had left their mark on language; therefore the more the musician, playing on the analogy between music and language, was to search for their common root, the more apparent that influence of the passions on language, stimulating new ideas, was to be.

Melody, being the most suited to the task, was to be the dominant aspect of music. Imitating the inflections of the voice, it 'expresses tears, cries of grief and joy, threats, groans; all the vocal signs of the passions are within its capabilities'.[21] If the painter or sculptor had had to make the effects of the passions visible (and a century earlier Le Brun's *Caractères des passions* had widely circulated a physiognomical grammar of the passions), the musician was concerned with making them audible with melodies containing the image of the passions. For G. A. Villoteau (*Recherches sur l'analogie de la musique avec les arts qui ont pour objet l'imitation du langage*, 1807) only expressive music was beautiful, but there was no expressive music that was not imitative, and no imitative music that was not declamatory: beyond this was arbitrariness, vocal display which was an end in itself, instrumental music without direction, and harmonic procedures that signified nothing, a physical system without a human coefficient.

The musician with a poetic text to set therefore had to examine closely the words and the verse structure in order to draw out the melody hidden within in an embryonic state. Cicero's 'cantus obscurior' was to be the philosopher's stone for the reformed musician to seek out. It became fashionable to refer to Lully's recitative as a model of adherence to language: Voltaire guaranteed to move listeners with the declamation of Lully's recitative 'following its notes and only softening its intonation'.[22] A particularly popular passage from Batteaux (*Les beaux-arts réduits à un seul principe*, 1746) concerned Lully, who, before setting verses to music, had them recited by an actress from the Comédie Française and quickly noted down certain sounds and inflections which he could then turn into singing with the help of his art.[23] French was not Greek, but the professional actor's skill set the musician off on the right track.

It is easy to guess how much this whole aesthetic development – these critical and philosophical interests and the belief that they were following nature – could move away from the concept of music as a trade. There were also internal satires, like the novel by Giacomo Casanova of 1787, *Icosameron ou Histoire d'Édouard et d'Élisabeth qui passèrent quatre vingt ans chez les Mégamicres* (the Mégamicres had a language solely of vowel sounds pronounced at different pitches), which defended music's autonomy without the encumbrance of a pre-existent language which had to be considered. The boundaries between the arts and the ideality (or uselessness) of their fusion are a recurring theme in Arteaga's writing, yet without doubt few eighteenth-century musicians put into practice the principle of drawing out the melody from the text: it remained an ideal at which to aim, a subject of great intellectual prestige on which, nevertheless, everyone drew. Calzabigi repeated the common position in a letter to the *Mercure de France* of 1784 claiming that declamation is 'an imperfect kind of music' and music 'a clever kind of declamation'.[24] Even Grétry, whose melodic inspiration was more naive than anybody's, often talked of the possibility of notating all the inflections of speech and amused himself by writing down in musical notation the phrase 'bonjour, monsieur', said to him in an affected manner by a friend. The size of speech intervals still interested Antonin Reicha in his Paris period (*Traité de haute composition musicale*, 1826), and the whole concept also skirted German romanticism (with Weber) and nineteenth-century Italian opera, and reappeared as 'verbal realism' in the Russia of the 1860s. The basic principle was always the search for truth and communication, and the rejection of abstract music which, in the meantime, had developed in its own way.

On the watershed between intellectualism and musical practice lay a minor theatrical genre which had some degree of contact with the subject of the analogy between music and language. The French called it *mélodrame*, the Germans *Melodrama*: it was a short 'lyrical scene' combining speech and orchestral commentary (the Italian equivalent, *melologo*, is a recent term coined by historians; the Italian word did not actually exist at that time, so foreign was the idea to the Italian sphere).

Its origins lie in Rousseau's *Pygmalion* (1770), and in what seems to be the result of his theory on the musical inferiority of the French language: 'convinced that the French language, lacking any clear accentuation, is not at all suited to music, least of all to recitative, I have imagined a type of drama in which words and music, rather than going together, are heard one after the other, and where the spoken phrase is in some way anticipated and prepared for by the musical phrase'.[25] The work was immediately successful throughout Europe, but the *mélodrame* did not flourish in France; it survived for a while in Spain at the hands of the poet and composer Tomás de Iriarte (1750–91), and caught on in the German countries, particularly on account of the *Konzertmeister* at Gotha, Jiři Antonín Benda. The transfer of a company of actors from Weimar to Gotha, the great actress Charlotte Brandes, and the example of *Pygmalion* encouraged Benda to adopt the new style with *Ariadne auf Naxos* and *Medea*, both dating from 1775. But Benda had his own cultural antecedents: he grew up with the Jesuits, cultivators of rhetoric and of the clear style of acting typified by the great monologues of the classical theatre, and he had taken a part in opera at Berlin as harpsichordist, showing a great deal of interest in the accompanied recitatives of Hasse and Jommelli. So, taking his cue from *Pygmalion*, he stepped into the field that Rousseau had studiously avoided: music's interference with the recitation, used at the emotional climaxes in the action, making sure that the rhythmic variety of the prose (Cicero's 'numerus'), the stresses of the recitation and the curves of the vocal intonation were balanced by corresponding moves in the music. Thus there opened a prospect extending beyond the horizon of literary men and playing upon the possibilities of instrumental music to 'speak'.

Mozart, who heard Benda's works at Mannheim in 1778, told his father: 'there is no singing in it, only recitation, to which the music is like a sort of obbligato accompaniment to a recitative. Now and then words are spoken while the music goes on, and this produces the finest effect ... Most operatic recitatives should be treated in this way – and only sung occasionally, when the words can be perfectly expressed by the music.'[26] General problems with recitative and the relationship between words and music in opera were always in the background. Benda's example was followed by Neefe, Reichardt, the group of composers at Mannheim (where Holzbauer wrote *La morte di Didone* in 1779) and J. C. F. Bach when he was working with Herder (*Philoktetes*, 1774); even Goethe wrote a *Proserpina* in 1776 to be treated in the form of a melodrama. The genre's popularity lasted about twenty years but then found its place in the *Singspiel* (see Chapter 20) and in incidental music, where it achieved its peak with Cherubini (*Les deux journées*), Beethoven (*Fidelio* and

Egmont) and Weber (*Der Freischütz* and *Preciosa*). Instrumental music, introduced to underline the voice and fill in the pauses in the dialogue, upset the relationship and put forward its own language of concise ideas, independent fragments of one or two bars that were to be very important for the component of realism in romantic opera, which went beyond the stylized conventions of *opera seria*. Yet the emotional nucleus, that 'finest effect' which Mozart spoke about when instrumental music was played under ordinary speech, was nevertheless a result of the linking of two means of expression, of the analogy which had been predicted for a long time by theorists, but which musicians had found more and more problematic.

15 *Opera seria* in the second half of the eighteenth century

Moving from the work of literary figures to that of musicians, one can gauge the old style's resistance towards modifications in the technical sphere. It was a case of continuous, slow changes rather than reform, and these changes did not really concern the relationship of the music with the text, the reality of expression and the question of perfect illusion, but were restricted to more musical matters: the connection between harmonic function and phrase length, the careful shaping of lines even in vocal coloratura, and symmetrical structures of various kinds. The contrast of major and minor tonal areas accentuated by the *empfindsam* style found its natural place in the dramatic field. The importance of the orchestra, the main medium of the rising symphonic style, could not but make itself felt; one should not, however, believe that an up-to-date orchestra, the use of harmonies for expression, the symmetrical construction of themes and, eventually, the inclusion of choruses and dances of French origin were symptoms of reformist visions, and that all the composers of the second half of the eighteenth century were reformers.

The well-known historical picture of Italian composers ready to appear as reformers on foreign stages (e.g. in Paris, at the French court at Parma, and in Stuttgart, Mannheim or Vienna), only later to return to their natural tendencies when they were working in Italy, should be viewed with caution and checked case by case.

Certainly in the north up-to-date writing about operatic reform was more widespread and informed, and a more cultured and influential bourgeoisie asserted the rights of a more rational style, but Naples, around the middle of the 1770s, was a centre of cultural reform equal to many north of the Alps. The cradle of opera 'in the Italian style' was international: Noverre's *ballet d'action* (1773), Gluck's *Orfeo* (in an altered version in 1774), the activity of the Nobile Accademia di Musica, inaugurated in 1777 with Gluck's *Paride ed Elena*, Traetta's *Ifigenia* presented in 1778 as a product of the vogue for Gluck, and various prefaces to librettos by intellectuals and poets such as Saverio Mattei, Luigi Serio and the Marchese di Corleto were all various indications that the ideals of reform opera also had firm roots in Naples. Yet it is equally true that Jommelli, in his later years at Naples, did not gain approval and wrote his late works for Lisbon. Nevertheless, the enrichment which Italians provided abroad may be attributed not only to their awareness of reform but also to the fact that instrumental music had achieved greater importance in those centres than in Italy (even an *opera buffa* like Paisiello's *Il re Teodoro in Venezia*, in which instrumental ideas often run away with the voice, failed in Naples after its success in Vienna). The real innovations were in fact in the instrumental sphere, while the formal shape of Metastasian *opera seria* remained, taking what pleasure it could in its capacity for absorption.

The figures who best represent this phase of 'internal reform' in Italian *opera seria* are Niccolò Jommelli (1714–74) and Tommaso Traetta (1727–79), both products of the Neapolitan conservatoires but connected with foreign centres for the most significant parts of their careers. It is indicative that Jommelli, after his début on the comic stage at Naples in 1737, took twenty years to reach the San Carlo theatre with an *opera seria*, *Temistocle*. From Rome, where he was *maestro* at St Peter's, Carl Eugen of Württemberg, a spiritual disciple of Frederick the Great, gave him the opportunity of returning to the theatre, attracting him to Stuttgart and his summer residence at Ludwigsburg. Except for a few journeys to Italy, Jommelli remained until 1769 at the Württemberg court, where he found the ground prepared in several directions. Tragic French art and *ballet d'action* were flourishing in the hands of Gaetano Vestris and Noverre (the latter produced his most important works here – *Médée et Jason* and *Psyché et l'Amour*); and the court maintained a high instrumental standard with Italian violinists secured by the duke (including Pasquale Bini, Antonio Lolli and Pietro Nardini), and kept up close links with neighbouring Mannheim (Holzbauer was at Stuttgart shortly before Jommelli's arrival). In short, there was a concurrence of various elements favourable to the Italian musician, who was able to choose his singers and instrumentalists. This was a golden age which later vanished as a result of the financial restrictions imposed by the Seven Years' War.

At Stuttgart Jommelli composed about thirty stage works, including seventeen *opere serie*, mostly on texts by Metastasio or Mattia Verazi, the court poet at Mannheim. The repertoire of subjects includes some of the commonest in *opera seria*: *Fetonte*, *Attilio Regolo*, *La clemenza di Tito*, *Lucio Vero*, *Andromaca* and *Enea nel Lazio*. The theme that stimulated Jommelli most was fatal passion, and he had the quality of a first-rate tragic musician. His conception of opera was stately and impassive, as the prevalence of major keys even in the most melancholy situations shows. The vocal display in his operas, for the most part sequences of detached thirds, has an instrumental precision and is still 'serious' and imposing, almost contradicting its function. Accompanied recitatives acquire greater and greater importance and are, like the arias into which they resolve, strict character studies, in which variations of tempo (e.g. Allegretto–Allegro con spirito–Andantino–Andante in the space of a few bars) occur whenever the text calls for it.

The magnificent spectacle – the settings are described in detail – is in line with the tradition of Lully and Rameau, but the need for dramatic continuity was not even noticed at Stuttgart, and Jommelli set Verazi's librettos as they stood, without worrying that the course of the action was interrupted every so often by seventeenth-century ethics (against women or concerning the fickleness of fortune); and if a character declares that he is angry like a river in flood, there is inevitably a 'simile aria' describing the rushing waters. The internal dramatization of the closed piece was the frontier that came closest to reform: breaking of the 'affects' and changes of rhythm, tonality and thematic figures (in the orchestra, patterns associated with the Mannheim symphonists recur) are all factors which go beyond the traditional aria; but although internally advanced in this way, they remain limited moments of tragedy, and the ever-present risk of their being isolated from the following aria is ignored. Certainly some passages seem to be linked together on a larger scale in a single dramatic sweep, as in Act III, scenes 6–7 of *Fetonte*, in which the chorus, 'motionless through fear', describes with terrible solemnity the death of Fetonte and Climene: 'Che spiagge! che lidi funesti!' ('What sad beaches and shores!'); but this happens more to emphasize the crucial moment of the tragedy than as a deliberate attempt to unify scenic complexes beyond the fundamental rhythm of Metastasian opera.

For Traetta, too, Naples was only the starting point (with *Farnace* at the San Carlo in 1751) of a career orientated towards the recognized centres of the European movement of reform. His first destination in the 1750s was Parma, a bastion of French influence between Lombardy and Habsburg Tuscany. Duke Philip of Bourbon and his intendant du Tillot wanted to turn it into a 'little Athens' in the light of the *Encyclopédie*. They invited Condillac as the Infante's tutor and drew into their orbit Goldoni, Algarotti, the scholar Saverio Bettinelli (the man who said that Italy had no culture of its own because of the Greeks and the Romans), the Platonist Mazza, the mathematician Keralio, the architect Petitot, who laid out gardens in the French style in the plain of Parma, and permanent French theatrical companies. *Tragédies lyriques* were staged in the season 1757–8 and Rameau's *Castor et Pollux* made a strong impression with its splendid scenery, but the obstacle of language and a style that was by now considered out of date, even in its country of origin, spurred on the energetic du Tillot, whose musical tastes probably lay with Rameau, to a more ambitious project. Since the most recent and brilliant culture was devoted to the French classics in the tragic theatre whilst in music it was completely Italianate, it was thought that the best style could be formed by combining French drama and Italian music. From this combination the type of opera described in Algarotti's *Saggio* would come to life on the stage, and, in another direction, a French opera translated into Italian was also tried at Dresden during the same period.

The experiment was entrusted to the court poet Carlo Innocenzo Frugoni, who was created superintendant of theatrical productions in 1754, and, in fact, to the young Traetta, who had made a name for himself at Naples, Rome, Venice and nearby Reggio Emilia with Metastasian operas. The theatrical foundation adopted was that of the *tragédie lyrique*, and Traetta's early works were in this style: *Ippolito ed Aricia* (1759), *I Tindaridi* (1760), translated by Frugoni from French originals set by Rameau more than twenty years earlier, and *Enea e Lavinia* (1761), another translation from Fontenelle. Traetta wrote some beautiful passages, neither more nor less than he had done in Metastasian operas, and certainly Frugoni, writing in an ornate style and impervious to theatrical trends, cannot have been a lively partner. Indeed, he was really the weak link in the whole project, and the fact that this was not foreseen shows the cultural limitations of even a man as active and well-informed as du Tillot.

The short experience with operatic reform was more useful to Traetta than to the court at Parma. This can be seen when the composer, without the responsibility of immediately creating reform opera there, came into contact with librettists more suitable than Frugoni, such as Verazi and Coltellini. In 1761, a year before Gluck's *Orfeo ed Euridice*, he produced a setting of *Armida* for Vienna, and in the following year one of his most important works, *Sofonisba*, for Mannheim. Here Traetta's empirical solution to the problem of dramatic unity – to take great care over the arias of one or two principal characters and to neglect the rest – is already apparent. This represented what might be called an 'aesthetic' path to unity, continuity by virtue of sheer artistic merit. Thus, with a series of very carefully composed arias, internally dramatized as in Jommelli, the emphasis is constantly thrown onto the protagonist and her husband-to-be, Siface, whose aristocratic, detached grief is sketched with broad, Handelian gestures. More impressionable than Jommelli, the young Traetta conformed more faithfully to the models of *tragédie lyrique*, as in the imposing scene of Sofonisba's suicide by poison. Many passages reveal a vital succession of simple recitatives which become *accompagnato* and broaden out into arias; and when Sofonisba, in Act II, Scene 6, wants to prevent the duel between Massinissa and Siface, the music is no longer that of an aria but amounts to declamation, musical drama, in which all the responsibility rests with the orchestra, while the voice limits itself to syllabic linking phrases. After *Sofonisba* Traetta occasionally modified the principles of reform, especially in *Ifigenia in Tauride* (1763) for Vienna and *Antigona* (1772) for St Petersburg. In the former, besides the key figures of Iphigenia and Orestes, the chorus is also important, but the episode in which the furies persecute the hero has no trace of realism or terror. This is epitomized in Orestes's aria, a piece which clearly illustrates the stylistic resistance of the Italian *opera seria* tradition. *Antigona* goes even further and is built on a single dominant character (tailored to the voice of Caterina Gabrielli, one of the greatest singers of the time), suitably matched by the chorus (the highly celebrated chorus of the Imperial Chapel at St Petersburg). The religious emotion of Sophocles's original, even though diluted by Coltellini, and the impending sense of death culminate in the funeral lament of Act II. Together with the final scene of Jommelli's *Fetonte*, it is one of the greatest contributions of Italian *opera seria* to the heroic 'Sublime', rediscovered in the study of antiquity, which pervaded a high proportion of European art around 1770.

In Jommelli and Traetta, despite their differences, Italian opera maintained a courtly grandeur that continued the baroque tradition. The appeal of the *galant* style advanced with the writers who began their careers around the 1760s, the generation of 'neo-Neapolitans', so called because of the fundamental change that is apparent even in their external adherence to the form of *opera seria*.

Gian Francesco De Majo (1732–70) was a typical 'neo-Neapolitan' who inherited a short-breathed style, with simple, gentle themes and a restrained vocal style whose virtuoso writing is not too hazardous. His short career fell almost completely within the decade 1760–70, with librettos by Zeno, Metastasio and the 'moderate' reformers Coltellini and Verazi. In *Almeria* (1761) his refusal to set the numerous choruses provided by Coltellini and his slight interest in accompanied recitatives are significant indications that he was largely unconcerned with the themes of the new movement. From Naples a four-year journey took him to central Europe at an important moment for reform: at Vienna, in the wake of Gluck's *Orfeo* and Traetta's *Ifigenia*, he put on *Alcide negli orti esperidi* (1764) and at Mannheim *Ifigenia in Tauride* (1764) and *Alessandro nelle Indie* (1766). De Majo's historical importance lies in the kind of musical style which he introduced into the context of *opera seria*, the concise *galant* tunes, the tenderness of some of the leading female characters, and the slender links with comic opera contained in the central sections of his arias. For the boy Mozart, who admired him at Naples when he visited there in 1770, the types of themes for use in Italian opera were mainly those of De Majo.

Even more tied up with Metastasio and Italian forms generally were the Bohemian Josef Mysliveček, who was very popular in Parma, Bologna and Naples, and Johann Christian Bach, who learnt Italian opera from Hasse and the Graun brothers, experimented with it in Turin (*Artaserse*) and Naples (*Catone in Utica*), and exported it to London. A born instrumentalist, J. C. Bach was at Mannheim in the early 1770s, where he put on *Temistocle* (1772), and then took another difficult step, this time to Paris with *Amadis de Gaule* (1779). The youthful output of Giuseppe Sarti (1729–1802), left as *Kapellmeister* in Copenhagen by the travelling company of the Mingotti brothers, was also based on Metastasio, as well as on Zeno. After gaining fame throughout Europe with his comic opera *Fra i due litiganti, il terzo gode* (1782), he was invited to St Petersburg by Catherine II, where with Coltellini he produced *Armida e Rinaldo*. In 1790 he collaborated on *Nachal'noye upravleniye Olega* (The early reign of Oleg), to a Russian libretto by the Empress dealing with the foundation of Moscow; the preface explains that the opera has 'imitated Greek music' in order to rise to the historical subject. The occasional use of consecutive octaves (as in the chaconne on a Slavonic folk song in Traetta's *Antigona*) is a little curiosity that cuts into the polished surface of the common operatic language at the end of the century, indifferent to nationalism and eccentricities.

A true departure from the course of Italian *opera seria*, a decisive turn as the result of a conscious effort, was, however, only to be achieved with the activity of Piccinni and Sacchini in Paris (see Chapter 18). Paisiello and Cimarosa, the last great Neapolitans (see Chapter 19), showed in the sphere of serious opera a strong faith in the Italian tradition. Paisiello, who was in Russia between 1777 and 1780, chose librettos by Metastasio for his *opere serie* and wrote to Galiani about *Alcide al bivio* that he had worked very hard on the accompanied recitatives, restricting coloratura and ritornellos:[27] precisely what Algarotti was trying to do with opera. Cimarosa's most successful serious work, *Gli Orazi e i Curiazi* (Venice, 1796), still openly exploits Neapolitan methods at a time when the *ancien régime* was dissolving. The librettist, Antonio Simeone Sografi, was a reformer, influenced at a distance by Benedetto Marcello's *Il teatro alla moda* with his two farces *Le convenienze teatrali* and *Le inconvenienze teatrali* (1794 and 1800); he prepared a text that was quite novel for Cimarosa, looking towards Gluck and the French composers if only in the way it places soloists and chorus in conspicuous confrontation (its source was Corneille, and the subject had been made famous about ten years earlier in a painting by David). Cimarosa responded like an Italian well acquainted with the requirements of reform opera: the da capo aria, restricted to a single affect, is completely replaced by the internally dramatized aria, while march rhythms and the heroic timbre in the tenor part of Marco Orazio reveal the new feeling of the Napoleonic era. But the martial tone is cultivated no more than is necessary to emphasize by contrast the tenderness of emotional feelings (Cimarosa's most authentic vein), while in the general delicacy of style he makes an easy marriage with comic opera, following the example of Mozart which at this time was beginning to become widespread.

16 Gluck in Vienna

Christoph Willibald Gluck (1714–87), born at Erasbach the son of a forester, had humble origins and a hard childhood, not unlike his contemporaries Diderot, the son of a cutler, and D'Alembert, who was brought up by the wife of a poor glass-worker. Nothing is known of his early years, which were spent following his father in the small centres of the Upper Palatinate, between the Juras of Franconia and the forests of Bohemia. It is likely that he took his first steps in music in ordinary schools, where the subject was carefully taught. This typical musician of the age of Enlightenment was always to have something of the peasant and the self-taught person about him; this is reflected in his cautious moderate decisions (always made after careful consideration), a reluctance to get excited, a lucid style and a passion for ideas and culture felt with the ardour of an outsider reaching them late in life. Furthermore, he had a confidence in dealing with the nobility and in managing himself as a public figure which showed that he could overcome the pressures of modern publicity that conditioned a profession no longer dependent on the courts.

In 1730 he seems to have enrolled at the Faculty of Philosophy at Prague. By the time he was twenty he was in Vienna as *Kammermusikus* to the same Lobkowitz family that employed his father as a forester. Popular with Prince Antonio Melzi, he followed him to Milan in 1737, where he studied with Sammartini. He wrote instrumental and sacred music side by side, and set out on his theatrical career in the footsteps of Metastasio and Hasse, making his début with *Artaserse* (1741). For a decade he worked assiduously, producing more than an opera a year, and not only for Milan and Venice; he moved to London in 1746 and then followed the most dynamic Italian musical troupe of the eighteenth century, that of the Mingotti brothers, into north-east Europe. In 1748 he was commissioned from Vienna to write *La Semiramide riconosciuta*, and two years later he presented *Ezio* at Prague and, in 1752, *La clemenza di Tito* at Naples, all to librettos by Metastasio (he strongly preferred the libretto of *La clemenza* to another text offered to him by the San Carlo). After he had set the Neapolitan musical circle talking about him, especially on account of his emphasis on the orchestra, which was regarded as excessive by local composers, he settled in Vienna at the end of the same year, 1752, where marriage to a well-to-do widow had in the meantime freed him of economic worries. In the Austrian capital he worked more calmly, without the spur of competition, allowing time for discussions with intellectual circles and theatre-lovers. Thus, slowly, the environment for 'Gluck's reform' developed. It was no different in its theatrical motivations from Algarotti's, Metastasian with French graftings, but here it was nourished by a combination of favourable circumstances which were missing in the transplant attempted by du Tillot at Parma or in the *ancien régime* court at Stuttgart.

Vienna had a cosmopolitan taste with very different roots: opera was by definition Italian and, since the beginning of the century, French culture had been familiar to the group centred on Prince Eugene. Halfway through the 1760s enlightened cosmopolitanism found an important representative in Josef von Sonnenfels. As theatrical censor he had banned improvised comedies, revealing his strict nationalistic taste in the *Briefe über die wienerische Schaubühne* (1767). Gluck entered the court circle in 1754 and, besides Metastasian operas, began to produce *opéra-comique* from 1758, following the trend that had been in vogue in Vienna for some years and that was later encouraged by the Seven Years' War, which reduced the possibility of costly spectacles. In this orientation towards France, the advice of an influential friend, Count Giacomo Durazzo, was valuable. He had arrived in Vienna as ambassador of the republic of Genoa, and in 1752 moved into the service of the imperial court. A passionate devotee of the theatre since his youth, Durazzo had been appointed 'director of theatrical affairs' by the minister Kaunitz, and for about ten years had the opportunity to perform in three rather restricted fields: *opéra-comique* centred on Vienna, *ballet d'action* with Hilverding and Gasparo Angiolini, and reformed *opera seria* (he invited Traetta and supported Gluck and Calzabigi with great diplomacy against Metastasio).

Durazzo and Ranieri de Calzabigi had known each other in Paris in 1754, where the latter was secretary to the Marquis de l'Hospital. More sensitive than most to the lure of the ancient world and full of plans in the theatrical field, Calzabigi had behind him a youth spent mainly at Naples, whence he had fled because of legal action over his involvement in a poisoning. He was already the kind of intellectual (the type that appears in Diderot's novels) in whom the boundary between scholar and adventurer was becoming less and less distinct, a new breed, widespread since the time at which, with the decline of the cultured priest or noblemen, the possible paths for the intellectual had become those of tutor in a rich family or of free, broad-minded entrepreneur, unafraid of swapping the gambling-house for the library. He arrived in Vienna as Kaunitz's secretary with a reputation as a financier, just in time to collaborate on the first official work of Gluck's reform, the pantomime ballet *Don Juan ou Le festin de pierre* (17 October 1761). The choreographer was the Florentine Gasparo Angiolini, the other important name in this encounter between the cosmopolitan Italy of the Enlightenment and the French art of stage dancing in the Vienna of Maria Theresa. Angiolini, then thirty years old, also enjoyed the favours of the court at Vienna, and had to find, as he himself was to say, the way to 'translate into pantomime a Comedy [Molière's *Le festin de pierre* in fact], a Drama and slightly later an entire Tragedy'.[28] A composer and, with his *Lettere a Monsieur Noverre sopra i balli pantomimi* (Milan, 1773) and *Riflessioni di Gasparo Angiolini sopra l'uso dei programmi nei balli pantomimi* (London, 1775), a theoretician about dancing, his canon was that of the 'expressive truth', something also fundamentally championed by Gaetano Guadagni, who a year later (1762) was to be the first Orpheus in Gluck's opera and for whom declamation meant expanded song. Guadagni was an interpreter; he had studied in London with David Garrick, the actor whom Noverre considered the greatest of those actors who could identify with the role and disappear within the character.

The next step in the reform was in fact *Orfeo ed Euridice* in the following year (5 October 1762). After the ballet, which was in an avant-garde style just illustrated by Noverre's *Lettres sur la danse* (1760), Gluck and Calzabigi aimed at the specific objective of tying together works and music, not yet in musical tragedy, but in a more modest genre, the *azione teatrale*. This was a cautious reform carried out by two fifty-year-olds, with a prevalence of professionalism over programmatic radicalism, as can be seen from Gluck's works of the following years: *Il trionfo di Clelia* on a Metastasio libretto for the inauguration of the Teatro Comunale in Bologna in 1763; *La rencontre imprévue* in 1764, an *opéra-comique* on a Turkish subject; *azioni teatrali* on texts by Metastasio in 1765; and *Telemacco o sia L'isola di Circe* to a libretto by Coltellini in 1765. The musical tragedy was eventually reached with *Alceste* (26 December 1767), another progressive collaboration with Calzabigi, this time accompanied in the preface to its publication (Vienna, 1769) by a programmatic manifesto (see Reading no. 6), a clarification and summary of the ideals of reform that had been widespread in Europe for a decade.

This theoretical awareness of the confluence of so many favourable factors must not prevent one from seeing clearly at this point the importance of Gluck the musician; it should not be thought that anyone else, provided that they were competent, open to the reforms and from the same kind of cultural environment, would have done what Gluck did. In what way had Calzabigi ventured not only beyond Metastasio's tragic dignity but also further than the innovatory promise of Coltellini or Verazi? It was essentially in the simplification of the scenario, which was reduced to a few fundamental points with the consequent suppression of secondary characters, the second or third couples who, like a system of concentric circles, conditioned the series of events through misunderstandings and revelations. Calzabigi's action was radical: others gave *opera seria* new life by shaking it up, enlivening the free spaces within the old structure; he, instead of inflicting injuries on it, pinned it down to a few scenes. Jommelli's *Fetonte* could still have ten scenes per act; *Orfeo ed Euridice* and *Alceste* have no more than two per act, and some acts have only a single scene. The whole of the first act of *Orfeo* may be regarded under the heading 'death of Eurydice'; the first scene of *Alceste*, in the same way, represents 'Admetus's death', the second 'Alcestis's sacrifice', and the whole of the last act 'Alcestis's death'. One cannot get away from these central concepts, which at times join into complementary unions, as in the second act of *Orfeo*, where the first scene (hell and the furies) and the second (the Elysian fields) constitute the two contrasted faces of nocturnal terror and divine peace according to the Enlightenment paradigm of the passage from darkness to light. Calzabigi had clearly understood that the real problem of reforming opera was that of dramatic continuity, but unlike so many of his illustrious colleagues he did not try to solve it: he skilfully avoided it by expanding sketches into great scenic pictures, achieving continuity at the cost of immobility. The influence of ballet is certainly decisive in the broad scale of *Orfeo* and *Alceste*; without words, and unable to keep the action going on various levels or to allude to detailed facts with the ease of recitative, ballet, especially when inspired by the severity of Greek theatre, had of necessity to condense its action into its essential points, into a few scenes which were immediately understandable, prolonged internally in slow periphrases.

In spite of all this, which had already been understood and accepted for a long time, the scenario still needed a type of music that would fill it out adequately, and this is where Gluck came in, the only musician at this time whose spirit of imagination had the capacity to imbue this immobility with feeling. In an age in which the *galant* style had circulated a language of short phrases, Gluck painted whole scenes with a single formative stroke and with a density of action which seemed to develop, as though bringing it out of cold storage, the direct influence of his acquaintance with Handel in London almost twenty years earlier. Jommelli and Traetta, in their intention of restoring nobility to Metastasian opera, dramatized the aria internally so that it tended towards accompanied recitative. For Gluck the aria was less important; from the opening bars of *Orfeo ed Euridice* it is clear that there is little likelihood of its becoming important, and in Orpheus's 'Chiamo il mio ben così' the firm autonomy of the closed piece is compromised by continual outbreaks of unprepared free recitation. In *Alceste* the aria's opening phrase is often hidden; one of the most important arias, 'Ombre, larve, compagne di morte' in Act I, scene 2, opens without forming a proper theme or anything to signal its beginning, but grows imperceptibly from the territory of recitative. Gluck looks beyond the aria to the scene, to the vast, motionless theatrical period prepared for him by Calzabigi, and he bears the whole span in mind with an intensity and control of overall range that are unmatched in the contemporary field.

In the ample space at its disposal, the chorus could now flow freely: it is no longer the kind of chorus which intervenes when allowed to by the conventions (in finales or ceremonies), but a continual presence whose relationship with the protagonist can also symbolize the contrast between the individual and the community, between private and public virtue, a cardinal point of classical ethics. Concentration on the theme of death is particularly indicative; if the funeral scene, the *tombeau*, was a familiar topic to the *tragédie lyrique* (there was also one in Traetta's *Tindaridi*, performed at Vienna in 1760), Gluck amplified this moment with ritual solemnity. In the opening of *Orfeo* and the ending of *Alceste* the funeral lament is split between soloists ('pleurants') and chorus (subsequently divided, in *Alceste*, into an on-stage chorus and one far off 'in the city'). Nothing shows the great amazement demonstrated by the deeper consciousness of the mid-eighteenth century in the face of antiquity better than the homorhythmic choral layout and the fatal structuring into a syllabic progression of 'Piangi [two notes] o patria [three notes], o Tessaglia [four notes]'.[29] A few years after the funeral scenes of *Orfeo* and *Alceste*, Lessing published a pamphlet, *Wie die Alten den Tod gebildet* (How the ancients imagined death; 1769), in which the medieval Christian's conception of death, with his dances of death, his hook-beaked falcons and other terrifying manifestations, is compared with the peaceful naturalness of pagan death, reflected in serene, composed symbols, the urn and the cippus (a monumental pillar). Gluck also bordered on this austere world in non-theatrical works from his last years, in *De profundis* (1782) for chorus and orchestra (without violins and using three trombones) and in the *Ode an der Tod* by Klopstock (1783). In 1785 he published at Vienna *Oden und Lieder von Klopstock*, seven songs for voice and keyboard in a syllabic style, monodies accompanied at will by an instrumental part in unison, to be sung at the piano by a single performer – short pieces which, at least through their poetic texts (especially *Die frühen Gräber*: 'early graves'), form a link with Mozart's *Lied der Trennung* and *Abendempfindung* (1787) under a twilight sky, firmly intent on probing the peace of the grave.

We have certainly come a long way from the cheerful element of opera, but it is precisely because he was stimulated by this withdrawal that Gluck's music appears as such a fresh voice in the twenty years between 1760 and 1780. If it has in the past been possible to regard Gluck the dramatist as superior to Gluck the musician, the misunderstanding should be attributed to the anomaly of his musical position with regard to the main currents of development. Other composers took the reform of *opera seria*, which tended to replace the abstract climate of the 'concert' of arias by a greater dramatic reality, closer to its fusion with elements of Italian comic opera inspired by Goldoni. Gluck, however, forged a trail which involved the curious mixture of Handelian sublimity and the melodic and rhythmic simplicity of French *opéra-comique* and Austrian folk song. There was another, even greater anomaly: sonata form was foreign to Gluck, even though, with its dynamic syntax and internal movement, it was becoming the vehicle of a type of music of action – it was the pattern of the mature Italian *opera buffa*, taken to its limits by Mozart, and the course which led to the close connection between instrumental and vocal, symphonic and stage music. Gluck led the way to the formal stability of the *Lied*, and he preferred the vertical conception, homorhythm, rare but decisive modulations and artful vocal lines to thematic contrast and the interweaving of dialogue. Nor does he show any sign of the apprenticeship common to all professional composers: sacred vocal counterpoint.

In Gluck's music, with its basic impermeability to sonata form, the orchestra's expressive function, cut off from the principles of harmonic operation that motivate its progress on the symphonic level, acquired total and absolute prominence. Timbre assumed crucial importance for the first time and, rightly or wrongly, it is with Gluck that one begins to speak of an orchestrator separate from the composer. But this is the case because Gluck's choices of sounds were derived not from the field of sonata form but from theatrical considerations, and in this respect, too, his experimental variety had few models to follow. The prominence of Orpheus's harp and the use of rare instruments (cornetts in *Orfeo*, cors anglais in *Alceste*) were not the only important innovations; the trio of trombones as a sign of earthly authority or an extraterrestrial symbol, the colour of the flute in its low register, and the use of horns, trumpets and timpani in subdued effects rather than in self-indulgent *fortissimos* are all inventions of Gluck which are firmly linked to the history of the orchestra. It fell to him, completely outside the tradition of the concerto and the symphony, to do away once and for all with the supporting harpsichord and look instead for harmonic completeness in the string group, relying on the viola as the means of linking violins and bass instruments into a cohesive whole.

With all his past as a composer of Metastasian operas and with all the links which can be put forward to connect him with the general problems of reform, the Gluck of *Orfeo* and *Alceste* was an unusual and untraditional musician, and it was from this point that the head-on collision with the theatre took on its unmistakable tone. Everyone around him was talking about reform opera, but with Gluck the reform went beyond the technical and musical sphere, entering not only the hall but also the heads of the audience. The reform works of Jommelli and Traetta were recognizable from their scores only to the professional; with Gluck the seriousness of the theatrical event was imposed on everybody, as if the stage itself were consecrated to something higher. In this way his musical theatre could be tedious but never courtly; though originating in the court, his music was no longer 'courtly' in the previous sense of the term.

17 Gluck in Paris

After *Alceste* the success of the trio Durazzo, Calzabigi and Gluck declined. In fact Durazzo, who was unpopular with the Empress, had settled in Venice as ambassador as early as 1764. The third opera from Gluck and Calzabigi, *Paride ed Elena*, was drawn from Ovid's *Heroides*; it is devoid of tragic content and does not have the vital creative character that distinguishes *Orfeo ed Euridice* and

Alceste. It was staged in 1770 without attracting much attention and it is significant that Gluck's fortune in Vienna failed just at the beginning of the decade which saw Haydn and Mozart assert themselves in the field of the sonata. Calzabigi, too, who was apparently implicated in an amorous scandal, disappeared from the Viennese court after 1771.

At this point, Gluck turned to another city, Paris, the unique centre which could act, as it had for the Italian *bouffons* and the Mannheim symphonists, as an international springboard for his work. Gluck and France met each other halfway, and the composer prepared the way with his usual skill, setting in motion high-level musical diplomacy between Vienna and France which involved his old singing pupil Marie-Antoinette, now wife of the Dauphin of France. His intermediary was a contemporary of his, the noble man of letters François Le Blanc du Roullet. Du Roullet arranged Racine's *Iphigénie en Aulide*, which was regarded by Algarotti and Diderot as the best possible source for an opera, as a libretto, and wrote the first of the letters to the *Mercure de France* (1 August 1772) which prepared the ground in the only effective way in a modern city – via the platform of the newspapers. To excite interest, du Roullet and Gluck restated, twenty years later, the arguments of the *querelle* of 1752–3, in particular contesting Rousseau's assumption about the French language's unsuitability for singing. Gluck illustrated his conception of opera in a letter to the *Mercure de France* (1 February 1773), at the same time announcing his *Iphigénie en Aulide*, which was to be staged the following year. For five years he dominated the theatrical life of Paris, following the first *Iphigénie* with French adaptations of Viennese works, *Orphée et Euridice* (1774) and *Alceste* (1776), and then *Armide* (1777), *Iphigénie en Tauride* and *Echo et Narcisse* (both 1779).

In spite of the congenial environment, Gluck did not find a Calzabigi in Paris (he did meet another adventurous literary figure, Beaumarchais, who in 1774 devised the libretto of *Tarare* for him, but it was a fruitless encounter). The series of French operas shows the fusion of the innovatory results of his Viennese experience and the historical tradition of the *tragédie lyrique* cultivated in its natural environment. Apart from the chaconne in the last act of *Armide* and the storm at sea in the introduction of *Iphigénie en Tauride*, clear evidence of French taste, the influence and immediate presence of the great trio Corneille, Racine and Molière led Gluck to create more many-sided characters. For the composer this meant rehabilitating the aria, not as an isolated piece (although many arias from these reform operas are 'parodies' of arias written in the past for Metastasian operas) but, in its relationship with accompanied recitative, as a central shaft of light on the character. Thus the two Iphigenias, Clytemnestra, Agamemnon and Orestes, amid continuous uncertainties and tensions, have a psychological flexibility unknown to the statuesque nature of Orpheus and Alcestis. As he became more French, Gluck came closer to Jommelli and Traetta with the 'character studies' which they presented in ariosos and dramatized arias. The chorus also took on a more varied role. The cruelty of the Greeks who demand their victim in *Iphigénie en Aulide* recalls the clamour of the crowd in Bach's Passions. The furies who torment Orestes in *Iphigénie en Tauride* do not give him time, as they did Orpheus, to manage a song, but only allow him snatched interjections in a declamatory style. The Scythians who drive Orestes and Pylades forward to the sacrifice, with insistent rhythms, violent unisons and the use of side drum, cymbals and triangle, have a barbaric character unknown to the classical choruses of *Alceste* (this was noticed by a reviewer from the *Journal de Paris*, who, surely influenced by the tragic end of Captain Cook three months earlier at the hands of the inhabitants of Hawaii, felt himself 'transported into the midst of cannibals dancing round the victim tied to the stake').[30]

The heroines, however, are invested with a celestial character (hell and the Elysian fields continue to be Gluck's two fundamental colours). If the second Iphigenia shows traces of Rameau's tragic grandeur, the first is completely enveloped in domestic tenderness, entirely suiting her 'bourgeois' situation as a woman torn between love for her father (Agamemnon) and for her lover (Achilles). Accompanied mainly by the woodwind, she was to leave her mark in the Elsas and Elisabeths of Wagner, who studied *Iphigénie en Aulide* in depth, and around her, in the finale of the second act, there is an aloof, respectful seriousness in which one can sense the tone of another French tradition – just for once not that of the grandiose, but that of Jansen, the Port-Royalists and Racine.

18 Gluck's influence

The fuss aroused by the 'Gluck affair' at Paris in 1774 was to affect other composers and to leave an indelible mark on French musical theatre. Responding to the initial move by du Roullet and Gluck, who had referred to the Franco-Italian *querelle* of 1752, the super-intendent of the Opéra, Vismes de Valgaye, and a group of scholars led by Jean François Marmontel (a friend of Diderot and D'Alembert and a collaborator on the *Encyclopédie*) fixed on an Italian to oppose Gluck, and succeeded in organizing a new clash in theatrical and musical circles which has passed into the annals as the *querelle* between the Gluckists and the Piccinnists. The chosen rival was none other than Piccinni, whose accomplices were the Neapolitan ambassador to Paris and the abbé Galiani, who in 1774 had praised Piccinni's *Alessandro nell'Indie* from Naples above *Orfeo ed Euridice*.

This rivalry was as deliberate as the *querelle des bouffons* of 1752 had been accidental, a sign of a climate saturated with literature and tired, bookish rhetoric. The controversy, furthermore, was without any underlying general theme; it was no longer a matter of the naturalness of *opera buffa* on the one hand and the dramatic realism of the *tragédie lyrique* on the other, but of two composers, one cosmopolitan and the other completely Italian, converging on a single genre, the French *tragédie lyrique*. Moreover, to make the confrontation easier to assess and to raise the temperature of public curiosity, the touchstone was to be the same libretto (Quinault's *Roland* revised by Marmontel) – a practice common in Italy but new to France. At this point Gluck disdainfully refused to descend into the arena and composed *Armide* on Quinault's original libretto dating from 1686. Piccinni, a 'très-honnête homme' as Galiani described him, [31] wrestled as best he could with the French scansion and 'bergerettes' and presented his *Roland* in 1778, without renouncing the tripartite aria, and emphasizing as much Neapolitan melody as he could: this was precisely what his supporters thought could easily be grafted onto the *tragédie lyrique* as an antidote to the 'cri', the cry of anguish and distress which Gluck used too often.

Supporting Piccinni, as well as Marmontel, were Jean-François de Laharpe, Nicolas Framery and Pierre-Louis Ginguené, Piccinni's first biographer and a future historian of Italian literature. Marmontel liked the inner calm of Piccinni's piece, which, according to him, was comparable to Racine, while Gluck's wild character reminded him of Shakespeare. [32] On Gluck's side were François Arnaud and Jean Baptiste-Antoine Suard, with whom Rousseau, won over by the *Iphigénie* of 1774 and not very interested in a French Piccinni, also sided. The events of the controversy, besides those in the *Mémoires pour servir à l'histoire de la révolution opérée dans la musique par M. le Chevalier Gluck* published by Leblond in 1781, can be reconstructed by consulting newspapers such as the *Mercure de*

France, the *Journal de Paris*, the *Journal de politique et de littérature* and the *Journal de musique historique, théorique et pratique* for the two years 1777–8.

But the musical proselytism of the culture of the 1750s did not repeat itself. New men, brought up to be interested in practical affairs, like Benjamin Franklin, the United States commissioner in Paris, or the historian John Symonds, had nothing to do with the *querelle*; lucky people these French, they seemed to say, they must live in a well-organized kingdom to get worked up over such things. It was indeed only a decade before the storming of the Bastille, but the Paris of 1752, the Paris of *La serva padrona*, had not been a much calmer city than the Paris of 1778. All the same, this irony would not have been possible then, and yet the appearance of the *bouffons* had brought into focus profound changes which could no longer be deferred.

Although he lacked courage (as is shown by his confession in the dedication of *Roland* to the queen),[33] Piccinni remained firmly rooted in Paris while Gluck, after the triumph of *Iphigénie en Tauride* and the lukewarm success of *Echo et Narcisse*, returned to Vienna in 1779. As director of the singing school that formed the nucleus for the future Conservatoire, Piccinni had the satisfaction of gaining the upper hand with his own *Iphigénie en Tauride* (1781), in which the fullness of the orchestration and the choral writing are more Gluckian than Gluck himself, and above all with *Didon* (1783). Here aria and recitative seem to be mutually supportive along the more typical lines of reform opera, recovering, after his attempts at tragedy, the intimate expressive qualities that had made him famous. The voice is predominant while the orchestra remains in the background, and this is the point at which any instrumental emancipation prompted by Gluck stops for the time being. Dido, a heroic woman and mistress of her own destiny, such a different woman from the Cecchina of 1760, is nevertheless a remarkable figure, precisely because of her adherence to the old melodic formulas.

Piccinni is one of the earliest composers of the old Neapolitan school whose long career crossed the stormy waters of the French Revolution. Confused by the events of 1789, he was tossed between Jacobin and Bourbon administrations, and could no longer feel at home in any environment.

From Paris, as Gluck had anticipated, his musical theatre became a European affair. The feeling that Gluck's works were exceptional spread only with difficulty, and operatic productions were kept going only by remaining open to experiments. In London in 1771 it

did not seem strange to present *Orfeo ed Euridice* for the first time
with additions by J.C. Bach and Guglielmi like an ordinary
eighteenth-century pasticcio. In Naples the opera was staged in 1774
with even more serious violations, and at Munich, in January 1775,
an *Orfeo ed Euridice* by Antonio Tozzi was produced to the same
Calzabigi libretto as that used by Gluck. Gluck's significance,
however, lay elsewhere, confirming that his importance was to be
found not in a theatrical concept, but in his music, in melodies,
harmonies and timbres; the originalities of Gluck's music are what
passed into circulation after the Paris season of 1774. Some years
before, the mild Boccherini had already explicitly returned to the
scene of the furies from the ballet *Don Juan* (an episode later
transferred to the Paris *Orphée*) in a symphony in D minor called
'La casa del diavolo'. Dittersdorf's programmatic symphony 'Andromeda's rescue' was also a true study of Gluck, and Orpheus's
descent into the underworld is parodied by Paisiello in *Socrate
immaginario* (1775). Ferdinando Giuseppe Bertoni from Lombardy
also composed an *Orfeo ed Euridice* (1776) on the same Calzabigi
libretto, confessing that he had taken Gluck as his example, 'per
seguirne le tracce' ('following in his footsteps').[34] In the same years
Canova completed his early statues, *Eurydice* (1775) and *Orpheus*
(1776), still on baroque lines and with openly melodramatic movements. Echoes of *Orfeo* can also be found in Traetta's *Cavaliere
errante* (1778) and were still to be heard in Salieri's *Grotta di Trofonio*
(1785) and Candeille's *Castor et Pollux* (1791). Later in Paris, in the
wake of Gluck, there was a revival in *opéra-comique* of the appeal of
parody, something which had almost disappeared in the twenty
years 1754–74 after the success of Italian *opera buffa; Iphigénie en
Aulide*, *Orphée*, *Alceste* and *Armide* were parodied over and over
again, by Moline and Dovigny, Rouhier and Deschamps, and
Favart and Guérin de Frémicourt. Even current musical events
became material for *opéra-comique*, in Billardon de Sauvigny's *Gluck-
istes et Piccinnistes* and Chabanon's *Esprit du parti ou les Querelles à
la mode*.

In the *tragédie lyrique* itself, Gluck's line extended mainly through
two Italians who had come together in Paris on the wave of the
confrontation between Gluck and Piccinni, Antonio Sacchini
(1730–86) and Antonio Salieri (1750–1825). They both foreshadowed the type of Italian musician who became an international
figure, a type that was to be common in the revolutionary and
imperial age up to the advent of Rossini.

Antonio Sacchini was born in Tuscany, but educated in Naples, and left the Italian stage behind quite early on. In 1770 he succeeded Jommelli at Stuttgart for two years and subsequently worked for a decade in London, alternating new works with re-adaptations of works written in Italy. In Paris he attracted the sympathies of the Italian party (especially Framery), to whom he offered the innate quality of a melodist and a lively succession of scenes, in contrast to the solemn tempos of Gluck's action. He approached the *tragédie lyrique*, however, with great caution, making his début with adaptations of earlier works; and for his mature work *Oedipe à Colone* (1786) he approached Nicolas-François Guillard, the librettist of Gluck's *Iphigénie en Tauride* and the principal inheritor of Gluck's tradition. Avoiding amorous intrigues and concentrating on public virtue, the right of the state and the struggle for power, the subject of *Oedipe à Colone* clearly reflects the taste of the Parisian middle classes on the brink of the Revolution, nourished by rationalism and ancient history. Sacchini's last opera, *Arvire et Evelina*, performed posthumously in 1788, was set in Ancient Britain, with druids and bards, and was full of invectives against the imperial eagles of Rome and hymns to the pure Celtic society. Guillard had very promptly presented Sacchini with a libretto full of early romantic sensibility, embracing the ideas of nature and night ('J'aime la sombre horreur de ce séjour sauvage', the barbarian Arvire sings),[35] the attraction of terror, Ossian, and the Breton forests. But this romanticism did not affect the music, which remains orientated towards the heroic style, with four-square cadences and wide intervals. Only in the choruses of the bards are more interesting protractions noticeable, as in the 'Symphonie douce et majestueuse' in E flat major in Act II, which is tinged with the priestly and masonic solemnity that was to re-echo in Mozart's *Die Zauberflöte* two years later.

Antonio Salieri was twenty years younger and even more international than Sacchini, his only Italian feature being a melodic style descended from Piccinni. With *Les Danaïdes*, he introduced himself to Paris in 1784 as a perfect champion of Gluck: he came from Vienna, where Gluck had returned five years earlier, and the opera was actually put on as a result of a collaboration between pupil and teacher (after a few performances Gluck stated that Salieri was the sole composer), and in fact the scenes of general despair in *Les Danaïdes*, on a libretto that Calzabigi had written for Gluck, are a faithful copy of situations to be found in Gluck. But rivalry with Sacchini, or with any Italian party, was no longer important; the following opera for the French stage, *Les Horaces* (1786), was to a libretto by Guillard, drawn, like Cimarosa's *Gli Orazi e i Curiazi* ten years later, from Corneille. Its overture, more than that of *Les Danaïdes*, follows Gluck's ideal that it should 'apprise the spectators of the nature of the action that is to be represented',[36] and the first scene, set in a temple and containing three contrasting arias for Camille, outlines a broad theatrical structure. However, the opera was not very successful and seemed to Beaumarchais 'un peu sévère pour Paris'.[37] On the other hand the predominance of the aria brought it close to the contemporary *Oedipe à Colone* by Sacchini; it achieved the balance which had been advocated by Guillard between the principles of Gluck and Piccinni and created a general solemnity of musico-scenic structure amid the appearance of new interests and literary sources a long way from Gluck's classical roots. The great success between 1783 and 1785 of works by Grétry such as *La caravan du Caire* or *Richard Coeur-de-Lion* was already beginning to show the popularity of the picturesque exotic and the theme of adventure. Salieri was also successful with his last Parisian work, *Tarare* (1787), an 'opera in the tragi-comical style' on the libretto that Beaumarchais had devised for Gluck in 1774; but, with its mixture of the heroic and the ridiculous and its instructional and commonplace aspects, it was a very long way from Gluck's stylistic compactness.

The rest of Salieri's career was spent in Vienna, his most successful output being in the area of comic opera. Well regarded by the court, dominating the Italian theatre at Vienna and becoming vice-president of the Tonkünstler-Societät until 1818, Salieri was to fulfil an important educational role; he taught singing and Italian prosody to Beethoven, Schubert, Liszt, Meyerbeer and other less illustrious pupils. His classes on vocal music, at a time when it had been placed in a critical position by the independence of instruments and when national romantic opera was developing, clearly exemplified the movement in which Italian opera was no longer taught from the stage but from the school-bench. In Paris, however, Gluck's legacy was left in the hands of French composers of secondary importance, skilful manufacturers of airs in a folky, dance-like idiom, a long way from Gluck's musical characteristics, but all determined after *Iphigénie en Aulide* of 1774 to turn over a new leaf and move on a bit further. They came mainly from the French provinces, like Pierre-Joseph Candeille (1744–1827) or Jean-Baptiste Lemoyne (1751–96), or from abroad, like Johann Christoph Vogel (1756–88). Candeille, after ballets, pastorals and *divertissements* on classical subjects (e.g. *Les Saturnales ou Tibulle et Délie*, 1777), also tried grand opera in five acts with *Pizarre ou La conquête de Pérou* (1785), in which the only influence from Gluck is the exotic stimulus of the ballet of the Scythians from *Iphigénie en Tauride*. But Candeille's only success was the adaptation with new arias and Gluckian instrumentation of Rameau's *Castor et Pollux* in 1791, while in 1793 *La Patrie reconnaissante ou L'Apothéose de Beaureparie* (on the death of a revolutionary French general) was already tied up with the topical interest in a new dimension of public music and 'funeral and triumphal' ceremonies that was to continue up to Berlioz.

If Gluck's following was mainly French, the influence of his work also resulted in several movements in the German countries where Italian opera had been condemned by Gottsched in the 1730s with the same arguments as those of French rationalism (e.g. Saint-Évremond). Halfway through the century a current of reform, using arguments similar to those of the Italian school from Muratori to Algarotti, took heart at Gluck's appearance, thinking that it had found its musician. A letter from Gluck as an old man to Carl August in Weimar dating from 1780[38] is tinged with melancholy due to the energies that he had spent on behalf of France, neglecting 'the inward impulse to write something' for the German stage; but this desire of the intellectual, clearly sensitive to the strong movement in national culture going on around him, could not find an echo in the musician born in 1714 for whom musical theatre transcended national boundaries even though it was in the Italian or the French language. Gluck's connections with the German element are summed up in his meeting with Klopstock, but they did not go beyond the setting of a few odes (*Oden*) and a few bardic songs for the *Hermannsschlacht* (1773). In 1774, on the brink of his departure for Paris, Gluck refused to set Herder's *Brutus*, just as two years later he dropped the proposal of an opera suggested to him by Wieland, in whose fantastic world he was certainly unable to live. Nevertheless Wieland, for whom 'classical' and 'exotic' came together in a poetic remoteness, was one of Gluck's most convinced supporters: simplicity of action and an opening overture suited to the plot are principles fully underlined in his *Versuch über das deutsche Singspiel* (1775).

Wieland contributed to the birth of German opera with two librettos, *Alceste* and *Rosamund*, set in 1773 and 1780 by Anton Schweitzer (1735–87). These are carefully constructed works, but still lack dramatic range because the Gluckian elements of the libretto are contradicted by the triple regime of simple recitative, accompanied recitative and aria. As a plot, *Rosamund*, being set in medieval England, was a novelty, and in fact the work was written for Mannheim, where Carl Theodor made persistent efforts to rid opera of every kind of Italian dominance. In 1775 the indefatigable duke founded the Palatinate Society for the study of the German language and literature, and arranged for the construction of a national German theatre. On the work's completion two years later, the inaugural opera was Holzbauer's *Günther von Schwarzburg*; it was the first German opera to be printed in full score (1776), and around its birth one can sense the awareness of a solemn moment, the laying of the foundation stone that was going to support a new genre. But with all its lively orchestration and abundance of accompanied recitative, this history of German patriotism was written in the language of reformed Metastasian opera. The difficult delivery of national German opera was not to take place in the courts with works dealing with famous historical subjects, but in the bourgeois city, where it derived from the humble field of the *Singspiel*.

19 Italian comic opera in the second half of the eighteenth century

The composers of the second half of the century continued basically along the lines of Piccinni's *La buona figliola* (1760), welcoming all its ideas in the way of 'musical comedy'. The field of Italian comic opera was undisturbed, spreading out smoothly, across a European network, and its continuous progress (unlike that of *opera seria*) was not even discussed from the point of view of the need for reform. Italian *opera buffa*, in its homeland and beyond, was required above all else to remain faithful to itself. This pledge was not contradicted by Piccinni's steady output (almost an opera a year until his move to Paris, without ever repeating his stroke of luck with *La buona figliola*), nor by the composers Pietro Guglielmi (1728–1804) and Pasquale Anfossi (1727–97). The last achieved such European fame with *L'incognita perseguitata* (Rome, 1773) that he rivalled Piccinni, and the nineteen-year-old Mozart turned confidently to his *La finta giardiniera* (1774) when he had to set the same libretto by Petrosellini a year later. Giuseppe Gazzaniga (1743–1818), who was active throughout Europe during the twenty years 1770–90, was also indebted to Piccinni (and to Porpora); he wrote *Il finto cieco* (1786) on a libretto by Lorenzo Da Ponte for Vienna. Da Ponte's name ushers in the greatest period of eighteenth-century Italian comic opera: along with Giovanni Battista Lorenzi, Giuseppe Petrosellini, Giovanni Bertati and Giovanni Battista Casti, he formed a group of the greatest comic librettists since Goldoni, representing for the development of comic opera what Calzabigi had been for *opera seria*.

This remarkable development, which reached its height with Mozart in the decade 1780–90, was given a decisive impulse by Giovanni Paisiello and Domenico Cimarosa, whose output covers the whole of the last thirty years of the century.

Paisiello (1740–1816), born at Taranto but taught, like Piccinni, at Sant'Onofrio in Naples, was the most 'Neapolitan' of the Italian composers. In the flow of his compositions, in his personal character and in his artistic mould there was a kind of incarnation of a strong Mediterranean mythology, made up of creative facility, naturalistic dialects and alternations between irrepressible burlesque and pathetic languor, the whole being built on a general basic cheerfulness (or was it sceptical detachment?). Paisiello did not have a 'theory' about comic opera, except in so far as he aimed to develop all the characteristics of *La buona figliola*, but he was more of a 'musician' than Piccinni – he had more harmonic instinct and more curiosity for everything that was going on beyond the Alps in the symphonic field. In his early Neapolitan period (up to 1776), besides setting librettos by Goldoni, Paisiello turned to Lorenzi, whose comedies gave up crude comic effects to reflect middle-class life, and to Cerlone, who was a kind of Neapolitan Gozzi, poised between the exoticism of *The thousand and one nights* and the vogue for stock characters. In *L'osteria di Marechiaro* (1768), amidst elves and Pulcinellas, Paisiello's Neapolitan nature is shown in his use of instruments like the colascione (a two- or three-stringed Neapolitan lute), the bagpipes and the mandolin.

Lorenzi, an authority on the sentimental English and French novel, wrote the librettos of *Il duello* (1774) – including the role of Clarice, Cecchina's sentimental successor – and *Socrate immaginario*, which in the two years 1774–5 signalled the Neapolitan period's point of arrival. A famous figure of the Neapolitan enlightenment, Ferdinando Galiani, also collaborated on *Socrate*, and its material is typically intellectual, making fun of the philosophical fashions and imitations of antiquity (Charles Palissot de Montenoy's *Les philosophes*, a heavy satire on the encyclopaedists, put on in Paris in 1760, had gained extraordinary notoriety). In its protagonist Don Tammaro, whose mind is deranged by the lives of the Greek philosophers as Don Quixote's had been over stories of the ancient knights, there was a clear allusion to a Neapolitan intellectual of the time, Saverio Mattei, who was obsessed by classical literature and Greek ideas and, furthermore, harassed by his wife – an extreme example of comic opera's precision in aiming not at a social class but at an individual person known to everybody – with the result that a royal order suspended performances because the libretto was considered 'indiscreet'.[39] But the indiscretion of *Socrate* was above all in Paisiello's comic vitality, much superior to Piccinni's mild cheerfulness through the vivid power of its themes and unexpected modulations. The descent into the underworld is parodied from Gluck's *Orfeo ed Euridice*, with its chorus and dance of the furies and with Don Tammaro who, like Orpheus, sings a cavatina over a triplet accompaniment, here in pidgin Greek (Calimera, calispera./ Agatonion Demonion,/ Pederaticon Socraticon').[40] Humour also cuts into the traditional narrative structures, being applied to a 'contemporary age' of disconcerting immediacy. In the 'ideal age' of *opera seria* the action is always set in its context by an introduction, and even in *La buona figliola* the first aria sung by Cecchina, in the garden surrounded by baskets of flowers, serves to establish her appropriate setting among fruit and vegetables. By the time of *Socrate* this was no longer the case; when the curtain goes up the opera's action has already begun, with Don Tammaro being thrown down the stairs by his wife, and only later does the audience discover its significance and the situations of the story.

Halfway through the 1770s at Naples even the court, which until then had identified itself only with the prestigious *opera seria* at the San Carlo, began to show an official interest in comic opera. The minister Tanucci (with his down-to-earth nature and his Tuscan good sense, completely foreign to the theatres) had already enjoyed Paisiello and Lorenzi's *L'idolo cinese* in 1767, but it was only from 1776 that King Ferdinand IV got into the habit of going to the Teatro Nuovo for comic opera. By this period, however, Paisiello's fame had spread beyond the borders of Italy, and his European career was continued in Russia; a new satire by Paisiello and Bertati on *I filosofi immaginari* (1777) provoked unrestrained laughter from Catherine II, a friend and correspondent of the encyclopaedists, and the opera was soon translated into French and German, reaching the stages of Paris and Vienna in 1780 and 1781 respectively. In the meantime, however, Beaumarchais' comedy *Le barbier de Séville* had arrived from Paris and was performed at St Petersburg in 1776, the year of Paisiello's arrival there. The opera based on it, *Il barbiere di Siviglia* of 1782, to a libretto requested from Petrosellini in Rome, was the second great success of Paisiello's Russian period, spreading and, as the hostility towards the appearance of Rossini's *Barbiere* more than thirty years later shows, gaining tenacity throughout the whole of Europe.

If these works on texts by Bertati and Petrosellini had the benefit of a unified narrative structure and a skilful organization of situations and characters, the most important achievement on the musical level was perhaps *Il re Teodoro in Venezia*, written by Paisiello in 1784 for the Viennese court. The librettist was Giovanni Battista Casti, the new imperial poet; he succeeded Metastasio in 1782 but, with his Voltairean sarcasm against all the established values and every kind of ideological and moral myth, was very different from his predecessor. Based on a passage from Voltaire's *Candide*, coupled with numerous references to everyday matters (in particular money, in its various forms of notes, loans and interest), the libretto of *Il re Teodoro* is nevertheless an anomaly compared with the common trend of Goldoni's works, with an extemporary treatment of the action, full of sophisticated whims and sudden inspirations. Paisiello entered this fanciful world with the confidence of full compositional maturity, reacting carefully to the variety of tone exhibited within the libretto. On the more purely comic level he allows the notes to run around the many word-games of Casti's sparkling language (e.g. 'Qual Berlich, qual Asmodeo/ Mi dirà qual diavol è', or the repetition 'Taci, taci' in the first finale, which rebounds among all the characters in a large-scale musical piece). He emphasizes words which cannot fail to be understood by means of sudden gaps in the harmony or by doubling the vocal line in unison or at the octave in all parts. He allows much structural development in the finales, with triplet ostinatos that push the action forward, and he increases further the range of expression, with an orchestra that seems to take over the comic vitality in dialogues between the strings and woodwind, with good-natured parodies of *opera seria* (e.g. the allegorical representation of Debt) and with an expressive nobility of a more robust type than that granted to the many descendants of Piccinni's Cecchina. The fact that *Il re Teodoro a Venezia* did not really fit into the widest current of Italian comic opera is confirmed by its cold reception by the public of Naples in April 1785. It did, however, achieve great success (at least for the first few years) at the Burgtheater in Vienna, where the opera was heard by Mozart and Da Ponte on the eve of *Le nozze di Figaro*.

These years, between 1785 and 1787, were decisive for eighteenth-century comic opera, which aimed more and more towards the ambitious goal of replacing situation comedy by an integral representation of society. Da Ponte speaks in his preface to *Le nozze di Figaro* (1786) of 'as it were a new kind of spectacle',[41] and the theme of the 'dynamics of the social classes' (rapidly and vehemently circulated by Beaumarchais' *Le mariage de Figaro* and Schiller's *Kabale und Liebe* in the same year, 1784) widely penetrated comic librettos, joining up on the musical side with the experience of the sonata and the symphony at the most violent point in this development. The Vienna of Joseph II in the 1780s became a privileged home for the success of musical comedy: in 1783 it witnessed Paisiello's *Il barbiere di Siviglia*, and in 1784 a revival of Piccinni's *La buona figliola* in a German translation. In 1785 the Spaniard Vicente Martín y Soler (1754–1806), popular with the court, appeared and made a great success in the following year with *Una cosa rara*, to such an extent that it overshadowed, at least in Vienna, Mozart's *Figaro*. The most popular work by Francesco Bianchi (1752–1810), *La villanella rapita* on a libretto by Bertati, also reached the Viennese stage in 1785; Mozart wrote two ensembles for this production, and another significant coincidence occurred in February 1787, when Gazzaniga and Bertati's *Don Giovanni Tenorio o sia Il convitato di pietra* was put on in Venice a few months before Mozart's *Don Giovanni* at Prague.

Out of such a mass of events, one more must be mentioned: *La grotta di Trofonio* of 1785, another brilliant libretto by Casti set to music by Antonio Salieri who had just returned to Vienna from Paris after revealing his Gluckian style in *Les Danaïdes*. The references to *Orfeo* are clear but limited, and Casti's language is certainly as far as one can get from Gluck's musical style even with such a symmetrical libretto (with the usual pairs of lovers who change their characters and inclinations every time they enter the cave of the magician Trofonio). Many melodies are in languid minor keys, as in *La buona figliola*, but the orchestral texture is drawn from Haydn and Mozart to a greater extent than in Paisiello. The trio 'Ma perché in ordine il tutto vada' from the first finale, with its discussion about the paths to be taken in the wood, is a starting point for the 'action piece' that was to be developed by Mozart and Da Ponte in *Don Giovanni* (e.g. 'Metà di voi qua vadano' from Act II, scene 1), and the expansive C minor that is associated with the cave and the spirits has only a Gluckian veneer but, with its rapid divisions into sections, is really in the mould of the Italo-Viennese sonata. It is not important that Salieri, fresh from his experiences with Gluck, may not have grasped Casti's irony towards metaphysics; indeed, his seriousness helped the spread of greater harmonic and thematic density within the bounds of comic opera at just the right moment.

Compared with *Il re Teodoro in Venezia* at the centre of this intensive Viennese season, Paisiello's following operas in the third period of his career at Naples and Paris are less significant. Nevertheless *L'amore contrastato*, also known as *La Molinara* (1788), with a rich variety of themes that were used for variations by composers as late as Beethoven and Paganini, and above all *Nina, o sia La pazza per amore* (performed in 1789 at the royal palace of Caserta), the final product of the *larmoyant* vein, found a wide following. But the still down-to-earth model of Cecchina disappeared in the French source of Benoît-Joseph Marsollier (*Nina ou La folle par amour*) in a passionate thirst for emotions and tears that shows new expressive poles. The success of Paisiello's *Nina* was above all posthumous: Desdemona in Rossini's *Otello* is a direct descendant, and Bellini still regarded it with admiration as a model for his last opera, *I puritani* (1835).

The comic approach of Domenico Cimarosa (1749–1801) was also unaffected by Casti's liveliness and tended not to take the path of a risky mixture of vocal and instrumental styles. His *Il matrimonio segreto* (1792) has always been regarded as the point of arrival of eighteenth-century Italian comic opera, the culmination of a genre that had started from the Teatro dei Fiorentini in Naples at the beginning of the century, had been enriched in Venice by the sentimental and realistic aspects of Goldoni, had been made much of (almost to its own surprise) by the *philosophes* in the Paris of the *Encyclopédie*, had passed into the great enlightened courts at St Petersburg and Vienna, exposing itself to the beneficial influence of instrumental music in modern Europe, and was now returning to its Neapolitan cradle at exactly the time when storm clouds were gathering in the sky on the other side of the Alps.

Cimarosa's career was similar to Paisiello's, with his early years at Naples, the conservatoire instead of the fireside, and hard work to gain popularity in Rome, Naples and Venice. Around 1780, through the success of his comic operas *L'italiana in Londra*, *Il pittore parigino* and *Giannina e Bernardone*, he was an important figure in the main European theatres, although he maintained firm roots in southern Italy; and like Paisiello, he achieved maturity in musical comedy halfway through the 1780s, with *Le trame deluse* (Rome, 1786). Then came the inevitable invitation from Catherine II to go to Russia (1787–91), followed by his return to Italy via Vienna and by the composition of *Il matrimonio segreto* for Vienna at the request of the new Emperor Leopold II, formerly Grand Duke of Tuscany and completely pro-Italian.

Welcomed as a triumph and repeated in its entirety the same evening at its first performance (a unique case in the annals of music), *Il matrimonio* was to obliterate for posterity all of Cimarosa's other operas and almost all other eighteenth-century comic operas except for Mozart's, becoming in the eyes of the following century a summary of the whole course of eighteenth-century opera, with serious adverse consequences. As with Paisiello's *Nina*, the libretto's sources had various European origins, from a set of engravings by Hogarth to plays by the elder Colman and by Garrick, and from Madame Riccoboni's *Sophie ou Le mariage caché* to J.A. Pierre's *Le mariage clandestin* (1790). Nevertheless Giovanni Bertati united everything into an organic sequence, evenly distributing the different aspects of the brilliant, the tender and the partly predictable surprise, and offering the aristocratic public once again the entertaining spectacle of the bourgeois simpleton, so easily duped, and his aspirations to rise to the ranks of the nobility – in short, the opposite of a Casti libretto. And if *Teodoro* was not popular at Naples, *Il matrimonio segreto*, produced there in 1793, was the centre of attention for 110 consecutive evenings. Cimarosa's music fitted this very flexible libretto like a glove, revealing in a direct, convincing form the linguistic achievements of musical comedy with which Paisiello and others had experimented and which Mozart realized so completely in his three Da Ponte operas. Never had comic opera sounded so 'Neapolitan' as in the cosmopolitan perfection of *Il matrimonio*: the Alberti bass makes its final appearance here (e.g. in Paolino's aria 'Pria che spunti in ciel l'aurora' from Act II, scene 4), the harmony (almost always in three real parts) is consonant, full of thirds and sixths, melodic appoggiaturas plainly reflect inflections of dialect, and 6/8 rhythms flow freely and gently, almost with a flavour of the sweetness of Nativity scenes and rosy complexions.

Despite all its delightful colour, the music of *Il matrimonio* has a melancholy timbre, and this may be why it was immediately mythicized (by Stendhal, for example) as a symbol of a golden age of innocent creation; but beyond this suggestion lay the result of currents of taste that were losing their power, or rather were colliding with larger issues. The 'quiet life' of the second half of the eighteenth century in Italy ended even at Naples with the revolution of 1799. Paisiello and Cimarosa, like Piccinni and Boccherini, were men and artists of the *ancien régime* and suffered the changes of those years in a traumatic way. Cimarosa, imprisoned by the Bourbon reaction, was driven into exile in Venice when he had hardly reached the age of fifty. Paisiello was only temporarily out of favour; he recovered as Napoleon Bonaparte's protégé and in 1802 went to Paris as director of the Emperor's chapel. All the doors were open to him, but Paris was no longer the place for him, and, in spite of the honours he received, he applied for leave after a year and returned to Naples; he suffered humiliation and bitterness at the restoration of the Bourbons, however, which hastened his death at a time when his name was beginning to be obscured by that of Rossini.

20 Other national forms of comic opera

There is an objective linguistic fact which distinguishes Italian *opera buffa* from all other forms of comic musical theatre: in the other forms the libretto was not set entirely to music, but was in part simply recited. The 'completely sung' opera was an Italian prerogative, while in French *opéra-comique*, German *Singspiel*, English ballad opera and Spanish *tonadilla*, musical pieces alternate with spoken sections.

In spite of this external difference, the European success of Italian comic opera in the years 1752–60 was reflected in the other forms of comic musical theatre, strengthening structures and encouraging a generally more authoritative tone. Paris, the springboard of the Italian *bouffons*, was in the front line of this new phenomenon. The Théâtre de l'Opéra-comique, successor to the theatres of the fairs, was well acquainted with the comedy interspersed with musical pieces, for the most part popular hit songs (*vaudevilles*) disguised by new words, but Pergolesi's *La serva padrona* and Rousseau's *Le devin du village* must have encouraged the progressive replacement of street melodies by original ariettas and arias written expressly for the theatrical occasion. This was the path taken by Egidio Romualdo Duni (1709–75), a Neapolitan pupil of Durante who settled in Paris in 1756 who, after a regular output of *opere serie*, had become acquainted with the *opéra-comique* in the 'French' court at Parma. In Paris, abandoning Metastasio for Favart and other lesser authors like Anseaume, he made a name for himself with *Le peintre amoureux de son modèle* (1757), *La fille mal gardée* (1758) and *L'isle des foux* (1760), an adaptation of Goldoni's *Arcifanfano*, introducing a new consistency of melodic and orchestral writing into the fragile structure of *opéra-comique*.

While the genre reached Vienna with the works written by Gluck between 1755 and 1764, Duni's example was followed in Paris by François-André Danican Philidor (1726–95) and Pierre-Alexandre Monsigny (1729–1817), both of whom had the melodic gifts of a Piccinni, especially Monsigny, who with *Le déserteur* (1769) made a name for himself in all the European theatres. But the name most associated with *opéra-comique* (partly because of his prolific output) is that of André-Ernest-Modeste Grétry (1741–1813), born at Liège and educated in Rome, but from 1767 until the end of his long career working mainly in Paris. His most successful creative period was from 1769 (*Tableau parlant*) to 1784, when he produced his masterpiece, *Richard Coeur-de-Lion*, the pace-setter for early romantic opera on account of its setting and theatrical ideas, such as the trappings of the chivalrous Middle Ages, the providential rescue of a character at the end of the opera, and the recurring theme of an aria sung by the squire Blondel. Through his airs, which flowed easily from his pen, Grétry elegantly overtook the transformations of the new France; Blondel's aria 'O Richard, o mon Roi!' was to become a kind of royalist hymn, but in the Reign of Terror Grétry's music fitted revolutionary subjects and marches written by order of the new government just as well. Gradually *opéra-comique* absorbed the principal elements of musical comedy which had matured in the Italian field; only the concerted piece remained characteristic of *opera buffa*, while in the French field the *vaudeville* always remained the favourite finale, with all the characters in turn singing various verses of the same song.

Less developed but more prone to excursions into folklore was the Spanish *tonadilla*, which began as a short interlude in plays and *opere serie* and was given independence towards the middle of the century on the stages of Madrid by the works of the flautist Luis Misón (died 1766). The use of typical instruments and Andalusian dances like *seguidillas* and *tiranas* (a very rich store of rewarding and exotic music) maintained the immediate Spanish characteristics of the *tonadilla* even when Italian influence, around the 1770s, was becoming dominant. The greatest exponent of this period was Blas de Laserna (1751–1816), who was induced to extend the frontiers of the style by the examples of Paisiello and Cimarosa without, however, adding anything to the dancing charm of his first production (his 'Tirana del Tripili' included in *Los maestros de la Raboso* was to be known throughout Europe during the nineteenth century).

For English ballad opera, too, weakened after the exploit of *The*

Other national forms of comic opera

beggar's opera (1728) by Gay and Pepusch, the period of recovery
came halfway through the century in the wake of *opera buffa* and
opéra-comique. A pasticcio by Arne, *Love in a village* (1762), following Galuppi's success in the 1760–1 season, was welcomed as the
first English comic opera, remaining in the repertoire in England for
a century and soon being exported to the colonies of America and
India. In fact it launched a fashion that flourished with the works of
Charles Dibdin (1745–1814) and Stephen Storace (1762–96) and
which was also open to adventurous subjects with supernatural
elements.

In Austria and Germany the play with music (*Singspiel*) found a
companion in the song tradition (the *Lied*) with which it progressed
side by side. The collection *Singende Muse an der Pleisse* (the Pleisse
was the river in Leipzig), in which, besides many pieces for solo
keyboard, the poet J. S. Scholze (known as Sperontes) published
poetry by himself and others, adapting to it dance melodies and
rhythms mainly of French origin, had already been popular between
1736 and 1750. But the stimulus to its exploitation on stage was
increased with the success of a ballad opera by Coffey, *The devil to
pay*, especially when, translated into German by C. F. Weisse with
new musical items by Standfuss, it was put on at Leipzig in 1752,
the year of *La serva padrona* at Paris. Johann Adam Hiller
(1728–1804), the most important composer of early *Singspiel* at
Leipzig, which was almost always based on French subjects, was
later to join up with Weisse; he achieved a popular success,
unprecedented in German-language opera, with *Die Jagd* (1770),
containing many *Lieder* which acquire nobility in contrast with the
Italian aria style reserved for characters of higher social status.

To this branch of northern *Singspiel*, in the footsteps of the pair
Hiller and Weisse, belong J. A. Benda, Neefe and Reichardt, but
halfway through the century a southern branch of German *Singspiel*
also developed; it was centred on Vienna and was almost impervious
to the idyll of French origin, being inspired exclusively by Viennese
humour through the typical stock characters of Hanswurst (Jack
Sausage), Kasperl and Hasenhut. Here, too, the supernatural was
popular, drawing freely on Wieland's fairy-tales but remaining cautious for the most part in its elements of comic surprise. While at
Vienna the vernacular comedy of Philipp Hafner (a hard drinker and
poet who satirized the Enlightenment writers in *Der Furchtsame* of
1764) or C. G. Klemm became obstructed by the rationalist severity
of Sonnenfels, the *Singspiel* was to enjoy the patronage of the
Emperor Joseph II, who wanted to see a 'national *Singspiel*' and

fixed on this area rather than on *opera seria* (as at Mannheim) to encourage a national form of German opera.

This movement produced Mozart's *Die Entführung aus dem Serail* in 1782, a work that suddenly raised the genre to heights inconceivable even to its strongest supporters; but on a more modest level the most typical representative of the Viennese *Singspiel* was Karl Ditters von Dittersdorf (see Chapter 25), who very skilfully fused elements of Italian opera (concerted action pieces and passages of vocal bravura) with the easy melodiousness appreciated by the Viennese public. With his first *Singspiel*, *Doktor und Apotheker* of 1786, he gained a success which was never repeated with any of his later works. The opera, on the other hand, shows all his characteristics: a syllabic style like Pergolesi's (*La serva padrona* was a fundamental experience for Dittersdorf); a comic talent epitomized by the captain Sturmwald with his wooden leg, one of the most vivid portraits from the gallery of military parodies in comic opera, from Tagliaferro in *La buona figliola* to various figures in the works of Anfossi and the aria 'Non più andrai' in Mozart's *Le nozze di Figaro*; and music of action in the finales, in which he was now trying to follow the model of Mozart's *Die Entführung aus dem Serail*. Leonore's aria 'Zufriedenheit gilt mir mehr als Kronen' ('Contentment is worth more than crowns'), a hymn to *mediocritas*, the moderate course of life living peacefully day by day, sums up a dimension implicit in the opera and explains the composer's lasting success in Vienna, already predictable as the 'Falstaff' of the German cities with its inclination to jollity, superficiality and sensual gaiety. Indeed, Dittersdorf's *Singspiel* has been seen as a distant but congenial forerunner of nineteenth-century operetta.

21 Sacred music

Although the abundant output of sacred music continued in the second half of the eighteenth century, it was a field that was growing weaker in independence and originality; it lacked interest and was excluded from the rising phenomena stimulated by public curiosity in theatrical and court events. In a general way the whole of Enlightenment culture had been leading up to this decadence. The differences of opinion between J. S. Bach and the younger Ernesti over the importance that sacred music should have in the Thomasschule had been early symptoms of new trends;[42] as the secular Enlightenment and the reforms limiting the Church's power became more established, the liturgy was required to become less complicated; in consequence, attention to sacred music decreased. This is what happened in the Vienna of Joseph II (1780–90) when, with the dissolution of monasteries and the abolition of religious festivals, church music was required to be unelaborate and to use few instruments, and it was the same in the extreme case of republican Paris (1790–1800), with the suppression of the clergy and Catholic rites. But even beyond these limited phenomena, even where worship was not restricted, as in Italy, or where the budget for religious commissions was unlimited, as in Spain, sacred music faded into the background as an area of creative experimentation and confined itself more and more to reflecting stage music, separated only by the liturgical or religious nature of the sung text.

The problem of the relationship between the Church and the theatre, on the other hand, became a matter of conscience for composers of sacred music in the later eighteenth century. By now it was obvious that for some time two paths had been leading in different directions: on the one hand that of an operatic language suitable for *opera seria*, freely welcomed into liturgical styles as an up-to-date element, and on the other that of a polyphonic, imitative language in the 'strict' or 'Palestrina' style, regarded as the voice of tradition (its survival in the full *galant* style is reminiscent of the use of Latin in eighteenth-century scientific treatises). Nothing was more familiar to the church than these contrasts of ancient and modern, but now there was something new. The church hierarchy was not very deeply committed to safeguarding a 'true' religious style; on the contrary, pastoral requirements made the authorities take a conciliatory view of the operatic fashion, which at least involved a common linguistic style. Benedict XIV's encyclical *Occasione imminentis Anni Sancti* of 1749, however, confirmed the incompatibility 'inter cantum ecclesiasticum et scaenicas modulationes' ('between church singing and stage melody').[43] The real guardians of the old-fashioned style, those who wanted a kind of church music free from theatrical profanities, were above all the men of learning, the scholars and the musical historians, such as Giovanni Battista Martini, Fux, Giovenale Sacchi, Martin Gerbert and Burney. Pergolesi's *Stabat Mater* (a true reflection of eighteenth-century religiousness) had shown the path that the *galant* style could take within sacred walls, but it was regarded with suspicion by Padre Martini (who in his *Esemplare o sia Saggio fondamentale pratico di contrappunto* (1774–5) examined the old polyphonic style in order to draw suitable models from it) as an example of the mellifluous cantabile style of theatrical music. The defence of an 'authentic' type of sacred music went hand in hand with the defence of counterpoint; just as there was a type of opera by literary men, so there was a type of sacred music by scholars, also encouraging a current of reform, even though it was more tedious in its tone and its critical arguments than that of the theatre.

Heedless of these complaints, the practical musician found in the Mass (and in the smaller genres such as psalms, odes, cantatas and motets) an acceptable compromise between the two languages of fugue and opera. The Ordinary of the Mass sung according to the Roman rite provided the musician with six sections: Kyrie, Gloria, Credo, Sanctus, Benedictus and Agnus Dei. The longer sections such as the Gloria and Credo were subdivided into smaller sections which were treated as closed pieces, arias or duets; the repetition of the Kyrie, the final sections of the Gloria and Credo, and the concluding 'amen' were treated in fugal style. The chorus also sang passages in a homophonic style like that in the finales of *opera seria*; the organ and the orchestra (with wind and timpani on solemn occasions) could be restricted simply to doubling the voices, or could be given free parts, depending on the time available and on the composer's imagination (although in the Pope's private Sistine Chapel not even the organ was allowed). An aspect of continuity with the past was achieved by the use of madrigalisms: words such as 'resurrexit', 'altissimus' and 'sepultus est' were frequently set using suitable melodic directions or choices of register.

In Italy the musical bilingualism of the Mass was encouraged by the presence of operatic composers – Jommelli, Anfossi, Guglielmini and Galuppi – as musical directors of the important churches in Naples, Rome and Venice. North of the Alps the influence of the 'Neapolitan'-style Mass was felt above all in Catholic Austria, in Vienna, Salzburg and the numerous monasteries; furthermore Italians, engaged for the court theatre, supplied examples on the spot, and their liturgical music and oratorios influenced composers such as Reutter, Wagenseil and, in his very early works, Haydn, all of whom were active in Vienna. Salzburg also had the advantage of a strong choral tradition (which was in fact getting weaker in Italy, where the very survival of counterpoint was being undermined); Michael Haydn (1737–1806), Joseph's younger brother, took advantage of this more than anyone, being based in the archiepiscopal centre from 1763 until his death. He was one of the few composers of the second half of the eighteenth century whose sacred works represent his most important contribution, not only on account of his enormous output, but also because of the serious interest shown in his treatment of the liturgical text and his consideration of its function within a wide historical range, from Fux's *Gradus ad Parnassum* (which Michael copied out himself in full) to Gregorian chant and the modern symphonic style.

It was from this Austrian background, the land of the symphony after 1770, that the Mass was due to receive new ideas. If the 'Neapolitan' Mass adopted the language of *opera seria*, the influence of the symphony and of sonata form in the last decades of the century became inevitable. Naturally the importance of the orchestra increased, but the most substantial effect was the development of overall homogeneity: there was no longer a mere string of arias, but a unified scheme, even in the Gloria and Credo, making use of variation, skilful repetitions that accentuated the organic unity, and thematic elaboration that strengthened the imitative counterpoint. It is possible to recognize in the general structure of Joseph Haydn's late Masses (composed between 1796 and 1802) the internal layout of true 'vocal symphonies', and Mozart's sacred works are similarly permeated by symphonic thought.

While the Mass continued in this fashion to be cultivated in southern Catholic Europe, the most relevant factor in London was the lasting success of Handel. Arne, Boyce and Samuel Arnold (who in 1787 began the publication of *The Works of Handel* which continued into thirty-six volumes) all worked in his shadow. English culture, then, was particularly inclined towards preserving the past, and Boyce edited an important three-volume collection of sacred compositions covering two centuries of English musical history, *Cathedral music* (1760–73), which was also published in a revised edition by Arnold (1790). At the beginning of the 1780s Handel's oratorios were also known in Vienna through the private concerts of the Gesellschaft der Associierten directed by Gottfried van Swieten, Prefect of the Imperial Library and an important figure in Viennese musical life. The cult of Handel was, however, given new impetus when in the last decade of the century Haydn discovered the Handelian oratorio in London and, with *The Creation* and *The Seasons*, grafted it onto Viennese music, in which Italy had been the dominant influence for a long time.

With Johann Sebastian Bach, however, the line of development remained beneath the surface. The Passion found a successor in Hamburg with Heinrich Rolle, but he followed the example of

Telemann's 'theatrical' Passion more than the spirit of Bach. Fidelity to the Gospel text of John or Matthew (already anachronistic in Bach's day) was rejected as pedantic and lacking in subjectivity; one of the most successful oratorios of the period immediately following Bach's death, Carl Heinrich Graun's *Der Tod Jesu* (1755), is in fact on a libretto written in the first person and in the present tense, and with its quiet, simple character, close to folk song, occupies a similar position in the Protestant sphere to that occupied by Pergolesi's *Stabat Mater* in the Catholic. The tendency to make poetic paraphrases of the Gospel became particularly important with librettos written by Herder, two of which, *Die Kindheit Jesu* and *Die Auferweckung Lazarus*, were set in 1773 by J. C. F. Bach.

Herder's work in this context prompted the fusion between religious poetry and folk song. While in the Catholic world the tradition of the south Italian pastorale and the 'cradle song' was not encouraged and in any case remained localized, in northern Germany the *geistliches Lied* persisted even when the aria and imitations of theatrical forms were more prominent. The energy that someone like Hiller, the founder of the Leipzig *Singspiel*, put into cultivating the simplest song (e.g. *Lieder für Kinder*) in many didactic and religious collections found few counterparts outside the German lands. Beside the spiritual song, the chorale, of course, continued in its form as a simple melody or in four-part harmony, a unique channel of continuity with Bach's cantatas and Passions. From the fusion of the chorale with religious and folk melodies and with instrumental styles that had grown up in a middle-class environment of patriotic traditions, a third path of European sacred music, following those of the opera and the symphony, was to emerge, and around the turn of the century this seemed the most suitable vehicle to express a renewed religious feeling.

III

HAYDN AND MOZART

22 *Sturm und Drang* and music

One of the most radical forms of opposition to the taste for pleasantness, formal refinement and expressive simplicity from which Arcadia, the rococo and the *galant* style were born was the German literary movement known as *Sturm und Drang*, which developed between 1770 and 1780, at the same time (but without any similar theoretical element) as many sectors of the musical sphere came to an important turning point.

The movement's name alludes to a play by Friedrich Maximilian Klinger of 1776 entitled *Sturm und Drang* (Storm and stress). Besides Klinger and other less important figures, Goethe, Herder, Johann Heinrich Merck, Jakob Lenz and Heinrich L. Wagner were all involved in the movement, which also gained more or less lasting sympathy with other young intellectuals and poets like Bürger, the Swiss pastor Lavater, and Schiller. In 1770 none of the members of this group had yet reached the age of thirty; their origins were middle-class and their economic means (except for Goethe's) modest. They were almost all starting off a career as a tutor, entering the service of a prince, or beginning life as a pastor, and they made themselves known through periodicals such as the *Frankfurter gelehrte Anzeigen, Thalia* and *Musenalmanac* (the magazine of the Göttingen school of poets). Shakespeare was their guardian spirit, but they found encouragement in contemporary, especially English and French, literature: Rousseau, Richardson, Young's *Night thoughts*, Warton's *The Pleasures of melancholy*, Gray's *Odes* and the heroic and tragic ballads of ancient English poetry published in 1765 by Bishop Thomas Percy. Strasbourg, the French city where Goethe was a student in 1770, was the principal meeting place and a favourable centre for forging artistic links; its cathedral was the starting point for a re-evaluation of Gothic architecture.

In the theatrical field, where their main technical interests lay, the *Sturm und Drang* group proposed the following basic principles: the substitution of Shakespeare for Aristotle as master of dramatic rules (in 1774 Lenz's *Anmerkungen übers Theater* was explicit on the subject); the adoption of the central character of the hero, whose development was to be the real subject of the action (instead of subordinating the characters to a plot organized around stock patterns) in a view of freedom not permitted in classical tragedy by the pagan idea of Fate; a general dislike for Gottsched and for all that he stood for regarding the dullness of rationalism or formal restrictions on the use of imagination; and, on the contrary, a form of art that went right to the heart of the matter, making the spectator relive the author's immediate feelings. In order to achieve these results they did not object to using a direct syntax and vocabulary, devoid of any classical weaknesses, or to the uncompromising exploitation of evil, provided that it was taken to grand proportions. This resulted in the upsetting of nature, which became wild and hostile, and outstanding examples of virtue, as well as great examples of moral evil, like H. L. Wagner's *Die Kindermörderin* (The child-murderess) of 1776, or the Plutarchan criminals in Schiller's *Die Räuber* (The robbers) of 1782. Another aspect of their opposition to Gottsched and to the elegant literature modelled in a spirit of cosmopolitan unity on the classics was their rediscovery of folk song and the sagas of the Poetic Edda. Shakespeare went side by side with the myth of Ossian, the famous literary fraud perpetrated by Macpherson, who around 1760 circulated *chansons de geste* about Caledonian heroes, and Klopstock (who returned to settle in Germany in 1770) provided evidence of German legends and history, also being an expert on matters of political freedom; the theme of the corruption of the courts and the shameful acts of princes was in fact another fundamental theme in the ideology of the *Sturm und Drang*.

Halfway through the 1770s the principles of the movement were summed up in Goethe's epistolary novel *Die Leiden des jungen Werthers* (The sorrows of young Werther; 1774), which, with its extraordinary success and countless imitations, provided a model of behaviour for a whole generation. When the protagonist (a painter) exclaimed in his enthusiasm for the new-found spring, 'I could not draw at all now, not a line, and yet I have never been a greater painter than I am now',[1] all the age-old tradition of the craftsmanship of art was upset and in its place aestheticism was outlined – art was not just the work itself, but the whole of life. To Werther, Klopstock and Ossian were as necessary as air; the reversal of common sense, beauty and agreeableness ('For a week we have had the most dreadful weather, and for me that is a good thing')[2] came naturally to him. He is full of mocking attacks against the stifling limitations of conformity ('Shame on you sober men! Shame on you wise men!'),[3] while in the presence of nature, disrupted by terrible yet wonderful flooding, he is full of longing for annihilation ('Ah, with open arms I was standing in front of the abyss and gasped "Down! down!" and lost myself in the ecstasy of having my torments, my sorrows go sweeping down there; rushing along with the waves!').[4] The *Sturm und Drang* was firmly disillusioned with attempts to make reality beautiful by means of clichés; a few references in *Werther* to the background of the country are sufficient to condemn the rustic joys of Arcadia, sweeping aside cottages and fake shepherds, who are shown here in their exhausting series of battles for survival. Something similar happened to the 'bella vita militar' (the 'fine military life')[5] so popular in *opera buffa*. Verri, travelling in Europe during the Seven Years' War, had already talked of the 'hopeless job' and 'fierce sadness' of soldiers,[6] and the same war returned as the background of Bürger's ballad *Leonore* (1773), which depicts a night ride on horseback which Death takes with the fiancée of a soldier who had fallen in battle.

In a real sense the *Sturm und Drang* remained restricted to the decade 1770–80. For Goethe it was a short, violent creative period, subsequently replaced by other scientific and administrative interests. For Herder, with his *Volkslieder* of 1778–9, folk song was a calming influence. Schiller, after *Die Räuber*, moved on to classical tragedy with *Die Braut von Messina* (The bride of Messina). And after 1780 Klinger took up a military career in the Russian army, as did Lenz, who, like Werther, was unable to adapt to life, and who died in Moscow in 1792, mentally ill and in misery. But beyond its significance as a chapter in the history of German literature, the *Sturm und Drang*, in a broader and more general sense, had four consequences: the appearance on the scene of 'committed art', with its related danger of over-emphasis and empty rhetoric; the revival of a heroic conception of life that the eighteenth century had forgotten; the development of a terrible seriousness that made the tone of the Protestant north felt against the southern Catholic tradition; and finally the redemption of restlessness and contradiction as artistic and moral values, as dimensions not to be played down or even less suppressed, but to be probed and explored so that they could be exploited more easily.

Interpreted in such a broad way, the *Sturm und Drang* raised a

mortgage which, in the musical field, could be fully paid off only by
the full romanticism of the period 1820–40. The *Sturm und Drang*
music of the 1770s as it is commonly understood can, however, be
restricted to two main stylistic areas: that of Gluck, with his strong
unisons, syncopations, gloomy orchestration and minor keys treated
more broadly than in the tender style of Piccinni's *Cecchina*; and, of
secondary importance, that of the *empfindsam* vocabulary of C. P. E.
Bach (see Chapter 5), with his philosophy of 'being moved in order
to move others'[7] and his inclination towards fantasy, which was
exaggerated to the point of eccentricity in sonatas by Müthel. Even
though Bürger's *Leonore* was promptly set to music by the *Singspiel*
composer Johann André, it was in the field of instrumental music
that the relationship between *Sturm und Drang* and music was fully
established, as always without any statements or proclamations of
principle. The comparison between Gluck and Shakespeare which
Marmontel proposed in the years of the Gluck controversy in Paris
was a simplification that was reapplied with journalistic eagerness to
the contemporary infatuation with Shakespeare promoted by the
Sturm und Drang movement in Germany. Gluck's theatrical ideas
were really poles apart from the *Sturm und Drang*, but nevertheless
the ballet music of the furies in *Don Juan* in 1761 had already
established a type of *Sturm und Drang* music, preceding literary
evidence by a decade and already showing that the importance of the
new movement was instrumental rather than vocal.

Around 1770 a stricter tone of expression was becoming more
successful; this included the minor-key vein of some of the Mannheim composers (e.g. Beck's Symphony op. 3 no. 3 of 1762), the
serious tone and more rapid movement in some of Haydn's symphonies between 1768 and 1772 (e.g. the finale of no. 39 in G minor
and nos. 44 and 45 in E minor and F sharp minor), and the agitation
shown by Boccherini in his Symphony op. 12 no. 4, and in chamber
works published in Paris between 1768 and 1771. Haydn's quartets
in F minor and G minor from op. 20 (1772) have an impassioned
seriousness which was inherited by Mozart's Quartet in D minor K
173 (1773), where it is motivated by a tragic anger with touches of
grotesque invention. This aggressive aspect is apparent above all in
the Symphony K 183 (1774) by the seventeen-year-old Mozart, who
opposed the rigidly conventional symphony/divertimento/serenade
that was still fashionable with the same impatience that Werther
showed for the common sense of his friend Albert or the mundane
meticulousness of the ambassador. It was music full of movement, a
new and particular type of swiftness: 'the dead ride quickly', as the

refrain from Bürger's *Leonore* says. The tendency to speak with a louder and more threatening voice became particularly important in the field of piano music. The opening of Clementi's Sonata op. 2 no. 2 (1779), with its new sonorous resources, free from embellishments, with its clamour of octaves emulating trumpets in the high register and with its 'orchestral' tremolo in the bass, caused a considerable stir. In 1777 Mozart played his K 284 in Augsburg on a piano with a sustaining pedal and wrote about it enthusiastically to his father.[8] Johann Christian Bach also included in his op. 17 collection (1779) a Sonata in C minor which can be seen as being in the footsteps of Mozart's K 310 written in Paris the year before and which tries to achieve the agitation of the *Sturm und Drang* within the old style of harpsichord writing.

This brief survey of music affected in varying degrees by the new goddess Restlessness draws exclusively on the field of sonata-type works, whose attractions Gluck ignored. It is, however, precisely here that the movement's importance lies, since the attributes of deliberate originality and the outbursts of rebelliousness drawn from the outlines of Gluck's sonority reacted with a vigorous current of formal organization that ran through sonata form in the same years. The tendency of *Sturm und Drang* music was to coagulate into increasingly prominent themes, but this was only one of the elements involved in the general move towards a coherent musical language which showed great skill in its almost virtuoso use of form.

23 The peak of sonata form

At the beginning of the 1770s Gluck felt that Vienna's theatrical climate was too limited and left the city; and yet at exactly that time Vienna was about to become the musical centre of Europe, the favoured seat of an increasingly mature musical culture, the source of a language so perfect and self-contained in all its aspects that it was to be taken as a model and defined simply as 'classical' (in the context of 'Viennese classicism'). But the heart of the experience was to be chiefly instrumental, with a massive output of sonatas, quartets and symphonies; even if in Mozart there was a link with the theatre, the development of the constituent elements of the musical language occurred in the instrumental field and, more precisely, in the field of sonata form.

At the time of its appearance in Europe within the sphere of the *galant* style (see Chapter 3), sonata form showed the general plan described on page 15. This was enough to satisfy the demands of clarity and simplicity (and also of performance) and to clear the ground of the scholastic type of composition based on counterpoint, but in the forty years 1770–1810, in the hands of Haydn, Mozart and Beethoven, sonata form was taken as a frame of reference for completely different profound and unpredictable ideas. A desire for discovery that had no time for scholastic stiffness filled every part of sonata form, working within with untiring strength and open-mindedly exploring every possibility; and all this was on a broad basis of common understanding, almost a code, that nowadays allows a general discussion, temporarily forgetting the individual writers.

The first step in this adventure involved overcoming the poetics of the *galant* style. The sonata of the 1750s was the antithesis of fugue and polyphonic elaboration based on imitation. Now the poetics of simplicity and naturalness (in whose light J. S. Bach had been considered artificial) had had their day; there was an increasing return of concern for counterpoint, at first in a 'programmatic' way, with the inclusion of old-fashioned fugues as sonata or quartet movements and with the use of passages of canonic writing in the course of individual movements. Vienna, the leading centre for traditional contrapuntalists like Fux or Caldara, asserted its rights here, but by now intellectuals such as van Swieten were also working there; he had come from the Berlin of Marpurg and C. P. E. Bach and was a channel through which a different type of counterpoint from Fux's – that of J. S. Bach – became familiar. In the light of this rediscovery of Bach in Vienna at the end of the 1770s, fugal sections forcefully included in the course of the sonata tended to break up into the free autonomy of several simultaneous parts. A dialogue style grew up as a kind of secular heritage of religious counterpoint, while the *galant* poetics of pleasantness were not contradicted but continued on a higher intellectual plane, as a delight in thinking and building with sounds. It became common to refer to the act of talking together in company; for Goethe a quartet was like 'four intelligent people conversing',[9] and William Jones (in his *Treatise of Music* of 1784) went so far as to distinguish Haydn and Boccherini from Handel, comparing the first two with familiar conversation at a tea-table as opposed to the oratory of the court or the pulpit. These new discursive possibilities, which transformed the idea of sociability and the understanding of how to live, and thus completely removed the erudite aspect from the revaluation of counterpoint, worked their way particularly into the second section of the sonata's plan, the short period of digression between exposition and recapitulation. This part of sonata form was extended and intensified, limiting itself to the development of ideas from the exposition by means of variation technique and imitative interweaving that could be achieved as a result of the rediscovery of counterpoint. This section's growth in every way was to be the central thread running through the development of sonata form during the period. In its full capacity it can be called 'development', or better still 'Ausführung' or 'Durchführung' as the German theorists called it, thereby involving the idea of 'leading' or 'guiding' the thematic material towards its inherent possibilities. The string quartet, with its capacity for polyphony within a consistent timbre, was one of the favourite fields for this experimentation, and Vienna surpassed even the powerful publishing trade in Paris during the decade 1780–90 in the publication of quartets.

Another goal to be aimed at was greater thematic potential. The type of theme which grew out of the fusion of dance and the aria and could be easily localized was no longer sufficient; the theme began to grow in status, became more personal, and had more character. If Lavater was thinking of founding a science, physiognomy, by observing people's faces, the sonata's success now seemed to depend on the 'face' of the theme, with a clearly recognizable character and features; and a 'physiognomy of keys' (C minor, E flat major and F major), if not of themes, was suggested by Schubart at the end of his *Ideen zu einer Ästhetik der Tonkunst*, published posthumously in 1806. The abbé Vogler (*Mannheimer Tonschule*, 1778) assigned roles to the two main themes ('the first being the stronger, which supplies the material for the development ['Ausführung'], the second being the gentler, which relieves the heated commotion and bolsters the ear with a pleasing contrast').[10] First and second themes tended more and more, in fact, to take on their own physiognomies which were not always easily categorized, and in reality went beyond Vogler's classification. The new emotional temperature and the dynamism of the *Sturm und Drang* with its emphasis on contrasts could hold many surprises as far as expectations of overall structure were concerned.

A third and decisive step beyond the realm of the *galant* sonata was the concern for coherence, the welding together of individual parts of the form into a requisite unity. This did not contradict the idea of thematic growth; there was a compromise between the physiognomy of the theme and its use in the course of the composition. The staticism of the theme and the dynamism of development converged; the theme tended to dissolve into developmental ideas, and developmental ideas tended to solidify at a thematic level. In this tension the distinction between main and secondary parts, the essential and the ornamental, disappeared.

The characteristic aspect of the new formal framework was the importance assigned to the development. This was the heart of the new sonata form, and it tended to encroach on the exposition and recapitulation, since linking passages, codas or other elements drawn from the themes could be anticipations of or supplements to the development. On the other hand, codas or cadential sections could acquire a prominence which allowed them to be defined as a 'third theme'.

The whole piece was held together by the 'harmonic principle', its unified organization into a functional hierarchy of 'tonal areas'; the more the scale of the development extended the chequered tonal plan, the more harmonic links had to come into play to bring about the return to the original key. The points on this route (tonic, dominant and subdominant, with the whole spectrum of related keys) fixed the boundaries of a syntactical structure that kept the memory continually busy; the first theme in the recapitulation sounds different from the identical one (on paper, that is) in the exposition because it has passed through the development. In the succession of tonal areas it is as if everything is compared with preceding or following elements in the temporal chain. Time, gauged by the memory, becomes the true material of sonata form even to the detriment of the theme: 'these Allegros sometimes do not even have a theme and seem to begin in the middle,' Mayr wrote of Haydn,[11] for whom tonal planning was in fact so significant that it enabled the code of sonata form to function even when some elements were missing, such as when 'second themes' are built out of first themes simply transposed into a new key, or when infringements of the code are immediately contradicted from a harmonic standpoint, like the 'false recapitulations' where Haydn pretends to begin the recapitulation but uses the 'wrong' key.

Thus, while theorists and scholars went to fantastic lengths to uphold analogies between music and language, the real self-contained language of music – the very notion of a 'musical language', in fact – was born in the instrumental field of sonatas and quartets. This process, which had no theoretical manifestations (except for vague formulas like that of 'an entirely new and special way' used by Haydn about his op. 33 quartets of 1781),[12] was exclusively the result of 'abstract' musical thought – that is, it was not externally influenced by literary culture as was opera. Rousseau referred to Fontenelle's 'Sonate, que me veux-tu?' to confirm instrumental music's inferiority to vocal music, the only kind worthy of the status of 'arts d'imitation'.[13] In 1779 Goethe wrote to the composer Kayser that, in the context of *Lieder*, melodies could and should be 'eigne, bestimmte und runde' ('individual, precise and straightforward');[14] but in the field of the sonata the precise, compact melody could be of only limited use, while even unrefined elements and subsidiary details, so long as they were related to the whole, were fully acceptable. To understand a sonata enthusiasm was no longer enough; it took a degree of unquestionable skill. If the harpsichordist of the 1750s offered simple sonatas at the request of a new amateur public, the sonata form of thirty years later climbed the hard ladder of technique to the highest rung, while Haydn and Mozart aimed increasingly to raise the amateur to a more expert level of professionalism. By this time fugue had become out of date and sonata form seemed the most likely means of satisfying the recurrent temptation of the art of music: 'Flemingism' – the ivory tower, the fun of composition and the purely musical satisfaction to which above all Renaissance polyphony, especially that of the Flemish, had given free rein.

Free from all schemes and contexts except for those of an abstract musical language, with its own motivations and significance, mature sonata form was nevertheless rooted in its time and would have been unthinkable outside the final decades of the eighteenth century, the great European capitals, and the rationalism of a powerful and innovatory middle class. With all its independence of instrumental vocabulary, sonata form reflected the century's theatrical inclination, the dynamism of the comedy and the structure of the *Bildungsroman*. With the increased importance of their different natures, the two themes could now act like two characters, and the boldness of the developmental passages and the cohesion of the whole could outline a succession of events: the presentation of the figures (exposition), the plot (development) and the solution or 'agnitio' (recapitulation) with theme-characters that reappear with greater experience. Confirmation of this correspondence can be seen in the 'action music' which evolved in parallel in opera: Mozart's great operatic finales are really born from the spirit of elaboration and the imposing unity of conception of the sonata's development.

Another unmistakable sign of the times was the mark of rationalism. Sonata form of 1780–90 (the decade in which Kant's fame spread throughout Germany) was no longer satisfied with a general sympathy for systematization and 'clarté' (clarity), but sank its roots into a rationalism that governed all its moves with the logical behaviour of deduction, analogy, and conclusion. Basically the development became in fact a 'critique' of the themes, their limits and their combinatory possibilities, the deepest possible deciphering of the physiognomies presented in the exposition. The syntax of the sonata worked out by Viennese classicism, taking the themes out of their niches, transforming substance into function and individual detail into continuity, showed a tendency comparable to the revolution performed by Kant's critique of logic. While Kant mocked Swedenborg's theosophy and all metaphysical theory (he claimed that one cannot understand spiritual matters, one can only bear witness with moral behaviour), the expression 'thinker in music' could be legitimately used again thirty years after Bach's *Art of fugue*. The rococo, Arcadia and the *galant* disappeared, without even resorting to the programmatic passion of the *Sturm und Drang*, simply through a wider exercise of reason.

Finally, sonata form was an intensely 'civic' form of expression. The discovery of the modern city as a great adventure, translated into internal dynamism of movement, is apparent in symphonies by Haydn and above all by Mozart written halfway through the 1780s, in the feverish haste of their finales and their nervous vitality on a detailed level (the overture to *Le nozze di Figaro* is a supreme example of the new dynamism that could enter music). These are the years in which people began to forsake nature and the pleasures of the countryside, preferring the contemplation of luxury and the ease of travelling, of trading and of changing one's condition and life-style that the big city offered. And it was permissible even to be suspicious of nature; nature included the mushrooms that had poisoned Schobert, as well as the inhabitants of Hawaii who, completely unaware of the noble savage that was widespread in literary fiction, had killed Captain Cook.

The organic unity that grew up in the sonata form of the first movement of symphonies, sonatas and quartets also naturally affected the whole works within these genres, producing an increasingly unified conception of their various movements. No movement could claim complete isolation from the others any longer; sometimes the developmental impetuosity of the first Allegro was strong enough to discourage the use of an Adagio as the second movement, preferring instead a minuet or scherzo because of its more vigorous rhythmic character. The minuet as a finale for the whole composition was bound to die out; it was jeopardized by the weight of the first movement and was obliged to give up its position to a closing Allegro which strengthened a structure that would otherwise have leaned towards the opening. The later extension of the sonata principle to all the movements was a sure sign of commitment towards unity; it penetrated the Andante or Adagio, which was usually in the simple mould of a song, sometimes even reached the minuet, and became common in the finale in place of the familiar rondo when the essentially hybrid sonata-rondo form common in Haydn and Mozart (where one of the recurring elements of the rondo is given the status of a second theme) was not used.

The message of unification and the optimism of an emphasis on reason left in the end a clear mark in the use of an old structural element, the slow introduction to the first movement. This Adagio–Allegro structure, well known to the baroque era especially in France, sometimes lost its ceremonial character in the sphere of Viennese classicism so that it could be used to symbolize the passage from darkness to light, from chaos to rational order. Haydn illustrates this process at the opening of his oratorio *The Creation*, but the contrast is stronger in the field of sonata form; by using frequent dissonances in the few bars of the introduction, like horrors born from the sleep of reason, and making them disappear when the first theme, with its promise of industriousness, looms on the horizon, sonata form simply repeated in its own new terms the parable of the victory of light over darkness predicted by the Enlightenment in all the areas of civilized life.

24 Franz Joseph Haydn

In the course of his long life, Haydn (1732–1809) embraced almost all the musical changes of the period considered in the present volume. He was born when Bach was working at Leipzig on the Mass in B minor and he died nearly twenty years after Mozart, at a time when Beethoven had already written his Fifth and Sixth Symphonies. He was a direct protagonist in or witness to every event contained within these limits, on the levels of language, taste, and the social organization of music.

The identification of Haydn ('the father of the symphony') with sonata form began while he was still alive, and if he was not literally its father, he was certainly its greatest teacher, from its first steps up to adulthood. The cliché of a simple, good-natured Haydn should, however, be accepted much more cautiously, even though this view is long-standing, dating at least from the times of E. T. A. Hoffmann and the first consideration of the trio Haydn, Mozart and Beethoven as a true unity. Since then it has been difficult to look at Haydn without an implied comparison with Mozart and Beethoven; 'Papa Haydn' is a simplification which grew up in the shadow of *Don Giovanni* and the 'Eroica'.

His whole output still presents, in its characteristics and dimensions, many aspects of the baroque era. At least until 1790 Haydn's work can be regarded as the last great product of patronage in the musical field. His prolific production is worthy of preceding generations: more than a hundred symphonies, over eighty quartets and as many divertimentos, and more than twenty stage works; and around 175 chamber works involving the baryton (a kind of viola da gamba provided with extra strings which vibrate in sympathy) – just because it was the instrument that Haydn's master happened to play. His dealings with all the musical genres, with every kind of instrumental and vocal work, whether sacred or secular (*opera seria, opera buffa*, cantatas, Masses, oratorios and *Lieder*), also give the impression of another age. And yet there are a few small cracks in this great building and a few hidden inner qualities: theatrical music was set aside once Mozart's greatness in this field became apparent; concertos and divertimentos almost disappeared after 1780 in favour of symphonies and quartets; while the late collections of Scottish, Irish and Welsh folk songs, along with passages in *The Seasons* representing the common Austrian people, reveal a curiosity and an interest in the new romantic taste.

A model life

Haydn's life is surrounded by an aura reminiscent of that around certain episodes from the life of St Francis. Few biographies are so rich in anecdotes, trivial episodes and remarks that are unforgettable for their wit and candour (the only note of discord is his bad-tempered denigration of Sammartini). And few biographies have a chapter like the one concerning his friendship with Mozart, especially in the history of music, which does not usually involve men like Pylades or Pirithous. But his exemplary behaviour was also facilitated by the succession of events, which, whether through the chance of circumstances or through his intuition or his soundness of character, were always in harmony with the changes of the times and always coincided with favourable opportunities. Haydn always took the right steps in his life; as a court employee he worked calmly, without quarrelling with the people who provided his commissions, and as a free agent he successfully made his own name in the risky and chaotic world of business.

This supreme instrumental composer was not a virtuoso on any instrument and entered music through the vocal door as a result of the beauty of his voice as a child. From Rohrau (in southern Austria), where he was born into a farmworker's family, he was entrusted at the tender age of five to the rector of a school in Hainburg, and from here, thanks to one of the many people who scoured the Austrian province looking for treble voices, he was taken in by the choir school of St Stephen's in Vienna. He received his musical education at this centre, in a regime which involved a large amount of self-tuition in many fields, including the harpsichord and violin, as well as polyphony in the church style and the open-air serenades of the dance bands. His serious application to Fux's *Gradus* and to Italian oratorio (which combined in Vienna with the genre known as *sepolcro*) did not obliterate the cheerful peasant background which was to remain indelible and to become combined with erudition in an individual manner. On his dismissal from the choir when his voice broke, he was turned out on the street at the age of eighteen and probably worked persistently during the decade 1750–61 to make himself a name, writing Masses, chamber music and even a *Singspiel* on a French subject. He was supported by famous Italians in Vienna like Porpora and Metastasio, but the Austrian aristocracy also began to notice him, and his first divertimentos for string quartet and his earliest symphonies originated between 1757 and 1759 in the summer residences of the Counts Fürnberg and Morzin.

In 1761 Haydn's life settled down for about thirty years: he entered the service of one of Europe's richest and most distinguished families, as assistant *Kapellmeister* to the Esterházy of Galántha, Hungarian Catholics who supported the Habsburg throne in the old struggle against the Turks. The musician was engaged by Paul Anton but, when the latter died in 1762, his brother Nicolaus, known as 'the Magnificent', became his real protector and patron. Nicolaus had been a general in the Austrian army in the Seven Years' War and was now about fifty, a passionate music lover who played the baryton (an instrument that was by then out of fashion but was worthy of the prince's aspiration on account of its complex difficulties). The chapel (an orchestra, a church choir and various singers) followed the court as it moved around: it was at Vienna during the winter, at Eisenstadt (south of Vienna) for the greater part of the year, and occasionally visited other seats. But that was not all; the legend of Versailles led Nicolaus to transform a hunting-lodge just to the south of Neusiedlersee, a deserted place infested with malaria, into a splendid residence that astonished travellers and guests from all over the world. The new court, the result of enormous expense, was christened Esterháza and inaugurated in 1766 just as Haydn succeeded Gregor Werner as principal *Kapellmeister*.

At Esterháza there was an opera house seating five hundred and a little marionette theatre, decorated with shells and coloured stones, to whose scale *opere serie* were reduced. Travelling companies stayed at the castle for months, performing Shakespeare, Lessing and Schiller. The *sala terrena* of the main palace was used for formal concerts and there were frequent musical events, with two operas and two concerts a week besides the daily chamber performances in the various apartments and occasional entertainments in honour of distinguished guests (for the visit of the Empress Maria Theresa in 1773, Haydn wrote his Symphony no. 50 and the opera *L'infedeltà delusa*). Haydn lived and worked in this golden retreat, supplying all the music that he was asked for in an isolation that was broken only by brief trips to Vienna. Disagreements over commissions were slight, or wisely restrained, and they would seem to have been offset by having at his disposal an orchestra which he could use for all kinds of experiments. 'Cut off from the world', he was to say one day, 'I had to become original'[15] – one of the many shrewd remarks that give his biography its flavour and reveal a contented disposition, prepared to go to any reasonable length to remain happy.

From the secluded southern shore of the Neusiedlersee, Haydn's fame slowly began to spread. In the decade 1760–70 manuscript copies of his compositions circulated in the main Austrian monasteries and the houses of Italian and French noblemen; in France, Holland and England the first pirated publications appeared around 1764 (no system of copyright existed at the time). A decade later Haydn personally edited his first legitimate publications and from 1780 he had a publisher, Artaria of Vienna, at his disposal.

The first foreign recognition came from Spain. In 1781 a letter arrived at Esterháza through Artaria from another retreat, Las Arenas in Old Castile, from the Italian Boccherini, who was full of ardent admiration for 'Sigr. Giuseppe Haidn' and gave evidence that his music was well known in Spain.[16] The commission for music to go with sermons on the *Seven last words of the Saviour on the cross* (seven Adagios for orchestra lasting about ten minutes each) arrived from Cádiz Cathedral in 1785, while the previous year the Paris society of 'Concert de la Loge Olympique' had already asked Haydn for six suitable symphonies – all commissions which were gladly authorized by Nicolaus since Haydn, after all, appeared to the world as Prince Esterházy of Galántha's *Kapellmeister*. Halfway through the 1780s his works were the most widely printed of any in France and England: in London the publisher Forster had published eighty-two of his symphonies by 1787, and in 1784 the *European Magazine* had already come out with a biography of the composer. Italy, the mother of instrumental music, regarded him as a great composer, and in 1780 the Philharmonic Society of Modena elected him to its membership. The musical aristocracy of Europe knocked on Haydn's door and he received requests from King Friedrich Wilhelm II of Prussia, a great lover of the cello, and even from the coarse Ferdinand IV of Naples, who commissioned five concertos from him in 1786 for his favourite instrument, the 'lira organizzata' as Haydn called it, really a popular kind of hurdy-gurdy which was easy to master. The Corellian phenomenon of an instrumental musician who gained a reputation superior to any that could be achieved in the theatrical field repeated itself, on a larger scale due to greater efficiency in methods of circulation; and, as with Corelli a century before, there was a similar flood of forgeries, since publishers and copyists did not have any scruples about writing the name Joseph Haydn on works by his brother Michael, Vanhal, Ordonez, Leopold Hofmann or Dittersdorf to increase the value of their product.

In September 1790, a year after the outbreak of the French Revolution, the internationally known composer found himself suddenly a free man due to the death of his patron, Nicolaus the Magnificent. The new Esterházy, Prince Anton, only kept him nominally in his service, granting him an annual pension of two thousand florins but in practice leaving him to go where he liked. Thus Haydn broke away from the *ancien régime* like a falling ripe fruit, and from patronage entered the new world of the free profession. Looking at it from outside, everything was all right; life was fine and offered the right opportunities. Within his own mind, the extent to which livery had by now lost its attraction for the *Kapellmeister* is suggested by what almost amounts to his flight from Esterháza, abandoning property and valuables, to Vienna, which attracted Haydn more and more because of the fond ties and friendships that he had formed and cultivated at a distance for some time, and because of its society life, its domestic music and its connections with publishers.

He certainly received plenty of new offers to enter the service of powerful men, above all from Ferdinand IV of Naples, but events were forestalled just at the right moment by the dynamic and effective German violinist Johann Peter Salomon, a London concert impresario who quickly persuaded Haydn to tour England. This choice too was a propitious one, and the London adventure was preferred to safe employment in Italy, where he also had a strong desire to live and whose language he had known since his youth. Haydn chose freedom, but he also chose instrumental music rather than opera, the symphony orchestra instead of the lira organizzata, and the real music of the impresarios instead of the mythical music of Arcadian shepherds.

There were two London visits, in 1791–2 and 1794–5. He was invested with a doctoral degree *honoris causa* at Oxford University and gained triumphs in the public concert halls; he met musicians from all over the world who were based in London (some of whom were already well known in Vienna) such as Gyrowetz, Dussek, Clementi, Cramer and the Storaces; and he was involved with three rival concert societies and performances of oratorios during Lent at Covent Garden and Drury Lane. The vigorous sixty-year-old composer was filled with new life, inspiring him with numerous ideas that were to be brought to fruition in the final period of his career.

His notebooks from this London period are full of candid exclamations about the scale and vitality of the modern metropolis. There are astonished notes of details – figures on the number of buildings, the death-rate and the amount of coal consumed – and to the man used to the silence of Esterháza or to orderly Viennese etiquette, the excitement and din of the streets, with their famous cries from the hoards of pedlars, seemed 'unbearable' (though this was noted with a hint of pleasure).[17]

Tired of the modern life, Haydn returned to his native land in 1795 at the invitation of the new prince, Nicolaus II, who wanted to rebuild the choir and orchestra. The fourth Esterházy, as the composer was well aware, was mainly interested in sacred music, and Haydn's six late Masses date from this time; the works by Handel which he had heard in London had already orientated him towards his own form of grand symphonic choral composition. Haydn found an even more suitable area for this renewed sympathy with the dimensions of oratorio in the circle presided over by van Swieten, the Viennese disciple of Bach and Handel. The *Seven last words* were transformed into an oratorio (1796) with one of van Swieten's texts, and he was also the author of the librettos, based on English originals, of *The Creation* (1798) and *The Seasons* (1801), whose public performances in Vienna (especially the revival of *The Creation* in March 1808 at the University's Hall in the presence of Beethoven) were to be the consecration of Haydn's glory in his native Austria.

The point that Haydn had reached at the dawn of the new century can be judged by the final anecdote of his life, perhaps the loveliest little story in the whole history of music. In May 1809 the composer was dying in Vienna, which was being besieged by French troops and abandoned by the aristocracy. On one of his last days a French soldier, an officer of the hussars, turned up at the composer's house, causing apprehension in the household which was already imagining Haydn ending up like Archimedes, run through by a Roman soldier while drawing figures in the sand. The officer, however, with a fine tenor voice, sang the aria about Man's creation ('Mit Würd' und Hoheit'), moving the gentle old man to tears. Napoleon Bonaparte, too, detailed a guard of honour in front of his door; it was the homage of the 'quidams', as Julie's father had called them, of citizens loyal no longer to the King but to the State and to republican virtues, who were by now on the march throughout the world, patrons of a culture born of the aristocracy and inherited from them on the basis of individual reputations and merits.

Half a century of music

Haydn's career encompassed about fifty working years (1750–1801), in which it is possible to distinguish three main periods: twenty years, 1750–70, of progressive maturity based on the baroque and *galant* styles; the period 1770–95, which was spent exploring sonata form and which ended in London with his last word on the symphony; and the final Viennese years, 1795–1809, in which the great oratorios stand out. Knowledge of his work, which during the nineteenth century was limited to *The Creation* and a few of his last symphonies, has only quite recently become comprehensive – a vital condition for appreciating the vast range which he covered.

The early influences on Haydn were Italian and Viennese: Vivaldi, the Italian opera overture and Sammartini for instrumental music; Wagenseil and Rutini for the keyboard; and Fux and the polyphonic tradition of St Stephen's for vocal music.

Many Vivaldi concertos, including *Le quattro stagioni*, were in

Paul Anton Esterházy's library at Eisenstadt, and it was the prince who suggested in 1761 that Haydn should set the 'times of day' to music in the three symphonies with titles in the French style, 'Le matin', 'Le midi' and 'Le soir'. Dividing up the day or year, involving the lesson that while everything is changing virtue or reason is constant, was a common theme, and Gregor Werner, the Esterházys' principal *Kapellmeister*, had published in 1748 a *Curious musical calendar* in twelve parts representing the months of the year. *Die Tageszeiten* was also the topic of a successful little poem by Zachariae, but Haydn stopped at 'Le soir' and omitted 'La nuit', where the Leipzig poet had raised a hymn to Young and the poetry of night in accordance with a sensibility that for the moment did not find any response in music. Haydn's three symphonies were, in fact, a modern version of Vivaldi's *Stagioni* in terms of a primitive sonata form, and the model of Vivaldi is apparent in the use of solo instruments, instrumental recitatives, and the abundance (also typical of Sammartini's early symphonies) of sequential passages.

The move away from the form of the concerto and towards that of the symphony took a long time. The Symphonies nos. 13 and 40 (1763) end with fugues on Fuxian themes; the Symphony no. 34 is not far removed from the *sonata da chiesa*, and the Adagio of no. 36 for 'violino principale' and 'violoncello solo' is like a movement of a baroque double concerto. Haydn was generally very interested in the concerto between 1763 and 1766 and wrote several of them for his colleague Luigi Tomasini, violinist at the Esterházy court. Unexpected solo passages in the symphonies are tied up with instrumentalists at the chapel, such as the solo oboe part in no. 38 for Vittorino Colombazzo, who had just been engaged in 1768. Sequences, themes with striking rhythms (in the style of Vivaldi), echo effects and minor keys without any feeling of tragedy, taken from the sentimentalism of Piccinni's *La Cecchina*, are all characteristic of his works up to around 1766. More personal features became established in the finales (with folk ideas of 'Hungarian' origin) and in the minuets, which were orientated towards a French rococo ceremoniousness or a heavier, rustic rhythmic style of an Austrian kind.

Between 1766 and 1770 there was a perceptible change in his music influenced by various factors, including restrictions imposed by his duties and traumatic experiences in his life, such as his succession, following Werner's death, to the post of principal *Kapellmeister*, with the consequent task of writing sacred music, or the danger to his life caused by a serious illness (several Masses and the *Stabat Mater* in G minor seem to have been written as a votive offering to the Virgin Mary for his recovery). Furthermore, around 1769–70 Haydn was rather badly treated by some northern news-papers (in Hamburg and Leipzig), with the usual charges against Austria and the south: they lacked nobility, they had no idealiz-ation but an excess of humour and Hungarian rusticality, they smelt of the stable, and they were full of exotic eccentricities (the trio of the minuet from the Symphony no. 28 seemed 'Balkan' to Leipzig critics).[18] The sudden strengthening of symphonic language, the more aggressive minor key modelled on Gluck's furies, dynamic syncopation, and the *Sturm und Drang* tensions of the Symphonies nos. 39, 44, 45 and 49, along with the polyphonic mastery exhibited in the fugues of the op. 20 quartets: all these slight but definite manifestations of unrest seemed like a reply to those puristic, intel-lectual critics on two fronts – that of dramatic expression and that of musical doctrine.

The fact is that at the beginning of the 1770s Haydn was almost a new musician. Instrumental solos were rarely used in the symphonic field after 1766; a sonata like no. 19 of 1767, although called 'Diver-timento', was already a true 'piano sonata' with no more traces of the *galant* harpsichord style. The regular metrical structure of four-bar phrases became dominant, concertante-style improvisations were abandoned, and irregularity and imagination were directed rather into the harmonic channel, realizing the great discursive possibilities of modulation. The discovery, for example, that an E may be used as the tonic of the key of E, the third of C, the fifth of A or the leading note of F, and that one can draw together the threads of all these relationships, made up fully for the loss of the varied colours and improvisation of the baroque. Then there was greater emphasis on themes, which was sometimes almost palpably obvious: the theme which opens the Symphony no. 39, with its rests that are more important than the notes, even though it is marked *piano*, contains a power that is far superior to the rambling energetic enthusiasm of the Mannheim composers. From this point the nicknames given to Haydn's symphonies (e.g. 'Mercury', 'La Passione', 'The School-master' and 'Il distratto') become more frequent, and this was another external symptom of his objective pictorial faculties.

This highly nervous side of Haydn, who was committed to extricating himself from the pleasure-loving rococo of serenades and divertimentos, is one of the most interesting of his long career. It has recently been established that Haydn directed Gluck's *Orfeo ed Euridice* at Eisenstadt, and in fact Gluck's influence (in extended static harmonies and string tremolos) is present in several thematic ideas. The other pole of the musical *Sturm und Drang*, that of C. P. E. Bach, is also present: the Piano Sonata no. 20 in C minor of 1771 really represents, in its typical groping around, with rounded-off points at every significant cadence, an adoption of that model, placed in a broader and more expert formal frame. In Berlin and Hamburg people certainly recognized in it a portrait of Emanuel Bach in full relief.

In the second half of the 1770s, at least in the symphonic field, the creative tension of the period 1768–74 levelled off into a certain indulgence. Nevertheless, the decade 1774–84 showed Haydn's greatest commitment to the operatic field. Haydn's stage works, all written for the court at Esterháza, involved not only the charming world of Goldoni (*Lo speziale*, 1768, *Le pescatrici*, 1769, and *Il mondo della luna*, 1777) but also *opera seria*: Metastasio's *L'isola disabitata* (1779) is a *tour de force* of accompanied recitatives in pure reform tradition. Successions of pieces that are masterly in their vocal suitability and instrumental integration, Haydn's operas nevertheless lack theatrical strategy. He did not have the taste for mystification that denotes the theatrical genius. This can be seen clearly in an opera like *La fedeltà premiata* (1780), precisely in its high quality of invention and writing, with tender Piccinnian accents, skilful instrumentation, very lively arias and grand finales, but with no malice and no irony (the character of Perrucchetto shows what Mozart's Cherubino would be like without his erotic streak), and especially with its libretto by Lorenzi, which brushes up an Arcadia from *Aminta* or *Il pastor fido*, direct predecessors of *La buona figliola*, and that only four years before *Le mariage de Figaro*. Haydn was conscious with admirable clarity of his relationship with the theatre after Mozart's great Italian works. Although in a letter of 1781 to his publisher he had praised *L'isola disabitata* and *La fedeltà premiata*, attributing their lack of success to his hermit's life, in December 1787 he replied to the Prague theatre which had asked him for an opera to put on after *Don Giovanni* that all his operas had been conceived for the private circle of Esterháza, beyond which they would have no effect.[19] It would have been quite another matter to write a new opera, but the risk was too great, 'for scarcely any man can brook comparison with the great Mozart'.

The open-mindedness that was lacking in stage works written for the small clique of Esterháza produced new results in instrumental music, which easily reached the public in every corner of the world through the publishing houses. The six Quartets op. 33 (published in 1782) were the first obvious product of the fervour for quartets that pervaded Viennese circles in the decade 1780–90. The possibilities of the language of sonata form from strict economy of means (the second theme is often suppressed in favour of a more thorough exploitation of the first) to prodigious inventive freedom established themselves and grew in these works. Haydn's music became full of jokes and traps for the listener, and comedy of a theatrical kind became unrestrained when the situations were purely musical (the surprise ending of the second quartet leaves the listener with the feeling that he has been taken in, that all his expectations have been frustrated). The flexibility of language exhibited by the four instruments is more than worthy of the phrase 'an entirely new and special way' that Haydn used in presenting the collection. The Largo cantabile of the fifth quartet is an open reference to Gluck, not to the furies but to the opposite pole, the contemplative peace of 'Che puro ciel'. The themes of the scherzos have the catchy precision of the *Singspiel*, and those of the second movements generally adopt the spacious language of the vocal aria. In other words, these quartets present a collection of characteristics which would have been unthinkable ten years earlier and which are entirely conditioned by the rules of a language with punctuation, nominative and oblique cases, question marks and sentence construction that cuts out the dead wood of the baroque sequence.

Similar effects permeated the symphonic field, especially when in 1785 the Esterházys' *Kapellmeister* was commissioned to write not for the palace's *sala terrena* but for Paris, and not for the small court band but for the most important orchestra of the time. The six 'Paris' symphonies (nos. 82–7), composed between 1785 and 1786, and presented at the Concert de la Loge Olympique, and immediately afterwards at the Concert Spirituel (to which may be added the next five, nos. 88–92, also conceived for performances in Paris), reveal an extremely extrovert Haydn, determined to exploit as far as possible the most brilliant orchestral colours, as well as the fondness for jokes that was already apparent in the quartets. The finale of the Symphony no. 82 (nicknamed 'The Bear') is an exciting peasant (or bear) dance in which the composer was not afraid to mix refined thinking with the heavy stomping of peasants. Sometimes (as in the independent vitality of the acciaccaturas in the first movement of the Symphony no. 83 or the finale of no. 86) the eighteenth century and the *galant* style are mirrored, yet mimicry and ironic detachment are stressed. Instead of a fusion of the *galant* and the scholarly there is often a fusion of the *galant* and the popular or, rather, a surpassing of the *précieuse* origin of the *galant* style in favour of the popular gesture. It fell to an Austrian subject to reveal music's coquettish possibilities to the Parisians and to produce for the first time a type of music that made one feel like moving and fidgeting, far from the haughtiness of the baroque suite and the insipidity of the *galant* pastorale.

The spirit of individualization and the capacity for representation are most prominent in small-scale sections, like the trios of minuets. Sometimes the strings have phrases of open and almost uncontrolled melancholy over robust, rustic fifths in the basses; other trios (e.g. those in the minuets of the Symphonies nos. 85 and 86) have the limited but perfect quality of a toy, with the bassoon developing its ideas over the waltz rhythm of pizzicato strings. The slow movements are sometimes little nocturnes marked 'allegretto', suitable for dancing on tiptoe; in no. 85 this movement is called 'Romance' and the theme is taken from a popular French song, 'La gentille et jeune Lisette'; and in no. 86 the Callotian term 'Capriccio' is confirmed in ghostly or at least theatrical accents.[20] As with the Quartets op. 33, all these non-structural details gain their significance from the energy of the underlying sonata form; the principle of thematic elaboration and the adventurous play of modulation become established with clear evidence that can be unequivocally understood. Nevertheless, credit is due to the reviewer from the *Mercure de France* who recognized this at first hearing when he praised Haydn for knowing how to 'derive such rich and varied developments ("développemens") from a single subject'.[21] This economy of themes, an antidote against the theatrical temptations of sonata form, is evident above all in the six Quartets op. 50 (1787), where second themes are normally avoided. It is an indication of a desire for unity, rivalling fugue, as well as of Haydn's frugality of invention, which was in this respect a long way from the intellectual voracity displayed by Mozart during the same period.

After Paris, Haydn travelled to London, the other capital of European symphonic trade. Here he made his appearance with a few symphonies that were new even to the very well-informed British public, such as no. 92, which was written in Vienna in 1789 and later christened the 'Oxford' because it was performed in the famous city as a gesture of thanks for his doctorate. The furious finale, which filled the audience of the Sheldonian Theatre with enthusiasm, emphasizes the importance of the last movement, continuing a trend that was already apparent in the 'Paris' symphonies and their contemporaries (e.g. no. 88), and almost rivalling the expressive agapes of the Adagios in sonatas by C. P. E. Bach and his followers.

Franz Joseph Haydn

In his two London trips during the first half of the 1790s, Haydn crowned his symphonic achievement with the last twelve symphonies (nos. 93–104), written for the Salomon concerts. This series summed up the qualities of his own symphonies and those of others, and became an obligatory model not only for musicians close to Haydn in London and Vienna but also for Beethoven, Schubert, Rossini and Weber. Without rhetorical coldness, there is in the 'London' symphonies an amplification of elements which had been familiar in Haydn for about twenty years. Compared with the 'Paris' works there is a greater formal composure in these symphonies, especially in the second set (nos. 99–104). The orchestra already includes clarinets, trumpets and timpani as standard instruments, though they had previously been used only in 'solemn' symphonies which had their own festive colours; and the whole texture, even in the transparency of its counterpoint, reveals a coarser grain, the use of an artist's brush instead of an engraver's tool – it is reasonable to suppose that Mozart's three great symphonies of 1788 (the 'Jupiter' was published in 1793, between the first and second London visits) may have influenced him in this severe, monumental direction.

Compared with previous quartets and symphonies, and with a few specific exceptions such as no. 102, there is yet another, less radical feature of the sonata principle in the 'London' symphonies. There are clear divisions between tune and accompaniment (many themes are in two real parts) and even a return of the Alberti bass; this predilection, along with ever-increasing thematic characterization, means that for listeners of later generations many themes approach the simple warmth of Rossini. There was also room in this tolerant broadness of outlook for a return to the use of concertante soloists: the cello solo in the trio of the minuet of the Symphony no. 95, the coda to the Andante of no. 96 (involving concertino and ripieno) and the finale of no. 98, with violin solos and an almost ghostly reappearance of the harpsichord obbligato in the final bars, are all allusions to the baroque concerto, clearly encouraged in London by the concerts of the 'Academy of Ancient Music', which kept in circulation works by Handel, Corelli and Geminiani. But these and other cheerful departures from sonata organization were formulated on the other side of the fence from the 'baroquisms' of the early symphonies. The code of sonata form was present here more than ever, confirmed by the denials themselves, and never before had Haydn showed such faith in the comprehensibility of musical language as he did now; from this point of view the 'London' symphonies are one of the clearest proofs of the whole civilization of the Enlightenment.

In the wake of symphonies like nos. 88 and 92, the 'London' symphonies also emphasize the importance of the last movement. If there is any tiny blemish it must be looked for in the slow movements, especially when the form of theme and variations recurs with the narrow strophic regularity that Mozart had already removed from his three symphonies of 1788. These Andantes are certainly masterly and beautiful (that of no. 101, 'The Clock', transforms the regular ticking into a gem of musical jewellery), but one waits impatiently for the minuet and above all the finale. In Symphonies nos. 94, 96, 97 and 98 a type of finale that breaks into a run with whispered *pianissimo* ideas reaches perfection; the music crackles and laughs beneath the surface. In the finales of nos. 99 and 103, contrapuntal episodes that are perhaps modelled on Mozart's 'Jupiter' are emphasized, while in the last symphony (no. 104) the closing Presto, a type of bear dance set in motion by an imagination of overflowing vitality, confirms its loyalty to rustic values; it is a full stop in every sense, and even Beethoven was to find it a serious problem to do something different within the confines of the playful finale.

The post-London work of Haydn's last seven years is summed up mainly in the symphonic choral works: the late Masses and the oratorios *The Creation* and *The Seasons*. When he returned to Vienna in 1795, Haydn had closed many accounts, not only in the genre of the symphony: his last sonata, no. 52 in E flat, was written in London in 1794, in the circle of one of the most advanced pianistic schools in Europe, and is a great concert sonata, comparable on account of its broad conception with the 'London' symphonies and, in its final renunciation of the harpsichord, with Beethoven's contemporary op. 2 sonatas. The fifteen or so trios for piano, violin and cello written in 1794 and 1795 are also no longer piano sonatas 'doubled' by the other instruments, but real chamber music in the sense already indicated by Mozart. Only in the quartets was the last word yet to arrive, with opp. 76 and 77 in 1797–9.

The six late Masses, at the calm confluence of sonata form, symphonic style and imitative polyphony, were written, one a year from 1796 to 1802, at the request of Nicolaus II Esterházy as name-day presents for his wife Maria Josepha Hermenegild. This circumstance, while religious iconoclasm was spreading in revolutionary France and after what was really a mockery of the liturgical Mass, Léonard Bourdon's *Le tombeau des imposteurs et l'inauguration du temple de la vérité* (1793), had appeared on the stage, gave these works the sense of an Austrian fidelity to the fine Catholic tradition. But on the level of their musical content, despite the influence they exerted on Cherubini and Schubert and even Bruckner, they are works of tedious dignity with a senatorial tone that makes one think nostalgically of the more unrestrained 'Short Masses' (where the instruments are restricted to two violins and organ) of Haydn's earlier years.

The two oratorios present a very different case. *The Creation* (1798) is bound up with the first steps of a 'historical' awareness of music. The retrospection mischievously present in the 'London' symphonies was made more solemn and profound in the oratorios by the use of choral forces and recourse to the model of Handel (*Messiah*, performed in German in Hamburg in 1772, had been revived in Vienna in 1788–90 in Mozart's arrangement, while Haydn had heard it in 1791 in Westminster Abbey). The chorus 'Vollendet ist das grosse Werk' ('Achieved is the glorious work'), no. 26 of *The Creation*, is a perfect carbon copy of Handel; it is music written with the past in view, but there is more participation and warmth in this Handelian style than in the 'original' Masses with their forced polyphony. Furthermore, on the contemporary front, all the symbolism tied up with the oratorio's subject provokes Haydn's innate realistic inclination towards the story and the sketch; the formulas used for the natural elements (water and air) and for wild and domestic animals make *The Creation* and *The Seasons* into a kind of encyclopaedia of the natural and musical sciences that remained fashionable for a good part of the nineteenth century.

The Mozartian accent that was noticeable in the best 'London' symphonies became more apparent in the works written during the early years of Mozart's posthumous fame. Many arias, especially in *The Seasons*, begin in a manner fit for Papageno, while the picture of winter's desolation, almost a mirror of the human condition, presents a seriousness that is Masonic in tone. This seriousness also runs through the Adagios of the Quartets opp. 76 and 77, which can be fruitfully explored for signs of Haydn's concern with Mozart; the obvious recollection of the Quartet K 421 in the opening of the second quartet of op. 76 provides evidence of the continuity of a posthumous dialogue with Mozart in that special area of the Viennese sonata style. The expressive use of instruments in the more spacious style already foreseen in the 'London' symphonies and with hindsight described as Rossinian also returns in the two oratorios. Indeed, the aria about the creation of man (no. 24), the one the French officer sang at Haydn's bedside, has the superficial fluency and symmetry of a Rossini aria. In *The Seasons* the light staccato that heralds the downpour is a model for the storm in *Il barbiere di Siviglia*, while the chorus no. 2 ('Komm holder Lenz') of peasants greeting the spring, with its familiar 6/8 time, paves the way for countless rosy dawns in early-nineteenth-century Italian opera.

Outside the framework of sonata form, the purely instrumental sections of *The Seasons* also contain new nuances. Each season has a short symphonic prelude, and these four intense pictures are richer than the famous 'Representation of Chaos' that opens *The Creation*. The introduction to 'Summer' is particularly significant, with its gloomy orchestration in unison, representing the anxious wait for the early morning light. It was the time that Goethe stressed, the 'Tag vor dem Tage', the morning before the dawn which heralds work and all 'valuable manly industry';[22] and in the well-ordered universe of *The Creation* and *The Seasons*, where everything is in its proper place and everything has its use, there is a note of the kind of bourgeois morality that occurs in Goethe's contemporary elegy *Hermann und Dorothea* (1797). Hermann's mother could easily live in the countryside of *The Seasons*, so neat and tidy, as, worried about her son, she crosses the garden in a hurry, but not enough of a hurry to prevent her from tidying up a stake or removing a caterpillar from a cabbage, 'since an industrious woman never takes a step without purpose'.[23] As well as bourgeois virtue there is also a little of that Austrian *mediocritas* that appears in Sonnenfels' *Reflections of a German patriot* (1793), a violent invective against the tumultuous innovations brought about by the French Revolution.

From other clear signs it is apparent that the almost seventy-year-old Haydn had been aware of some branches of the romantic growth that was flourishing around him. In the third part of *The Creation*, Uriel's statement 'pure harmony descends on ravish'd earth' is entrusted not to four-part strings, traditional in similar appearances, but to the mysterious timbre of the horn. In the aria 'Hier steht der Wandrer nun' from *The Seasons*, words like 'Wandrer', 'Frost', 'Schnee', 'Schritt' and 'Pfad' (wanderer, frost, snow, step and track) appear, all specific ideas present in Schubert's *Winterreise*. In the hunting episode the horns play not distinct melodies, but pure sound-signals, while the chorus throws around exotic cries of 'Tajo! Tajo! Halali! Halali!' with a positive, newly coined realism that contrasts with the sporting display of earlier musical hunts (e.g. in Symphony no. 73 and a scene from *La fedeltà premiata*); and the choruses of games and domestic tasks that appear in 'Winter' have the earthy aspect of 'Volkston'; they are choruses of 'Burschen', a crowd of strong young men of the kind later to be found in *Der Freischütz*.

25 Other paths of the sonata style; Dittersdorf and Boccherini

The historical development that is apparent in Haydn, the gradual replacement of the late baroque and *galant* styles by the logic of sonata form, was followed sporadically and with varying degrees of success throughout Europe by the generation born between 1730 and 1740. These composers were aware of Haydn's importance and took him as their model, but they were all less disposed than he was to cast the skin of the *galant* musician, and they tended to be more restricted by the fact that they lived in isolated country residences; a few were also naively interested in a more immediate exploitation of Gluck within the boundaries of instrumental music. Turning to them after the Haydn and Mozart of the 1780s, one has the impression that the rococo was not in fact dead, but only dozing within more straightforward forms, and that sacred polyphony was similarly preserved as a cold exercise. Polyphonic doctrine and the *galant*–rococo style were still phenomena which did not overlap but existed simultaneously yet independently of each other. This independence might have been a good thing; the trouble was that the first lacked passion in its conception and the second lacked the courage to follow the path of enjoyment as far as it could go.

This division was evident, especially in Austria, in the large number of little musical artisans who created a web of musical industriousness in the shadow of Haydn and Mozart. The erudite tradition of Fux had J. G. Albrechtsberger (1736–1809) as its main follower, a product of the musical culture of the monasteries near Vienna (Klosterneuburg and Melk Abbey) who after 1772 settled in the capital, where he was to become famous as a teacher. In the instrumental field he treated the keyboard (organ and harpsichord) like a professional, but his idea of a cantabile style was (as with Werner, Haydn's predecessor with the Esterházy family) still that of Corelli and Tartini. The symphonic output that ran parallel with Haydn's was partly the work of his brother Michael and of the Spanish violinist Carlos d'Ordonez (1734–86), who remained faithful to the three-movement form, as did the Bohemian Johann Baptist Vanhal (1739–1813), the composer of minor-key symphonies in a distinct *Sturm und Drang* vein, which were welcomed in northern Europe with a success similar to Haydn's. Also active in the field of piano music, Vanhal managed, with his military sonata dealing with the battle of Aboukir (1798), to put into practice the fashion at the end of the century for programmatic pieces.

But the most versatile member of this Viennese circle was Karl Ditters von Dittersdorf (1739–99), a typical representative of late-eighteenth-century Austria in his style and cultural approach. He was trained as a violinist and made a name for himself as a virtuoso in Viennese churches and in the orchestras of the aristocracy. He had the opportunity to gain a literary knowledge that left its mark in his articles and theoretical writings, in his posthumously published autobiography, and in the intellectualism of his six surviving symphonies inspired by Ovid's *Metamorphoses* (1785), which contain picturesque references to the fall of Phaeton, Actaeon's hunt and his dogs, the murmuring of streams and the croaking of frogs. In 1763 he travelled to Italy with Gluck, and later got to know Haydn and Mozart: a late source describes a Viennese quartet with Haydn as the first violin, Dittersdorf as the second, Mozart on the viola and Vanhal on the cello,[24] and Dittersdorf often appeared in Vienna and Berlin, even though the greater part of his activity was in country courts, at Oradea in Hungary and Johannisberg near Jauernig, and in the castle of Rothlotta in Bohemia, where he died.

Dittersdorf carried on from Wagenseil, *La serva padrona* and the *galant* style, with which he combined folk inflections and the French taste for rondeau and minuet themes drawing on the *opéra-comique*, from which grew his greatest success, the *Singspiel Der Apotheker und der Doktor* (see Chapter 20). His internationalism is apparent in the *Sinfonia nel gusto di cinque nazioni* (1767), which has a 'German' (that is a Mannheim) Allegro, an 'Italian' Andante, an 'English' Allegretto, a 'French' minuet with a 'Turkish' trio, and an international, that is, a Viennese finale. In his programmatic symphonies the model of Gluck is inevitably prominent: movements like the dance of the furies and minuets portraying the Elysian fields, for example, are evident in 'Andromeda's rescue', in whose central Larghetto a concertante oboe develops a lament that revives the solemnity of Handel. The six quartets of 1788 are inspired by the strict example of the quartets of Haydn and Mozart; the use of counterpoint is nevertheless avoided, and while the first violin dominates for the most part, the four instruments are often linked in pairs, and there are many cadential passages that reveal the ever-present influence of Italian violin writing from Vivaldi to Tartini. On the other hand, ideas which are simply juxtaposed with no transition reveal Dittersdorf's slight sensitivity to more radical experiments in sonata structure.

With its intense musical life and the attraction that it exerted on smaller centres and residences, the Vienna of the 1770s was by now the musical capital of the German-speaking countries. It had taken the place of Mannheim; Mozart still benefited from the latter city's instrumental vitality and concert life in 1778, but in that very year the elector Carl Theodor moved to Munich and the centre rapidly degenerated, the members of the school moving increasingly to France or, in the elector's retinue, to Munich. The tendency towards experimentation typical of the first generation of Mannheim composers can still be found in symphonies by Franz Beck, but Christian Cannabich (1731–99) and Carl Joseph Toeschi (1731–88) wrote in a fossilized language, and even the refined Carl Stamitz, Johann's elder son, a virtuoso on the violin and the viola, ran aground on the French symphonie concertante, which was foreign to the views of modern symphonic thought. The outlet for academic ideas was created later in the form of an institution, the Mannheim Tonschule, founded by Georg Joseph Vogler (1749–1814) in 1776 under the elector's patronage. A very gifted teacher, Vogler mixed instrumental technique, acoustical science and old-fashioned learning with free experimental interests that Mozart was to find disgusting because of their amateurism, but which were nevertheless to influence pupils such as Weber and Meyerbeer in his last years at Darmstadt.

In Paris, on the death of La Pouplinière (1763), who had made his orchestra a copy of the one at Mannheim, the legacy of private music was inherited by Prince Conti and the Baron de Bagge; however, public initiatives were more energetic (see Chapter 27), while the publishing trade became more organized and efficient. Haydn's circulation originated in 1764 from Paris, where Boccherini's works also were published from 1767 up to the late 1790s. A current, comparable with that between Paris and Mannheim, was set up between Italy and Paris that contrasted with the Viennese pole epitomized by Haydn's success in Paris (1786–7) and the later activity of his disciple Pleyel.

Faithful to its vocation, Paris was more important as an international stage than for the symphonies of its composers, such as Jean Baptiste Davaux (1742–1822), Simon Le Duc (1745–77) and Henri

Joseph Riegel (1741–99) which parallel the continuous output of the inexorable Gossec. The favourite genre of the French was the symphonie concertante, whose formal characteristics were shared by their trios and quartets. In 1780, while interest in the sonata-type quartet was reaching its peak in Vienna, Davaux published six concertante quartets on popular tunes, thus anticipating a future fashion. They are loose in structure and contain no hint of conceptual development, though they are attentive to the realism of the popular theme; even in the middle of the Revolution, Davaux's *Symphonie concertante mêlée d'airs patriotiques* (1794) demonstrated the success of the old form in the Parisian environment. The connection with Gluck, much more noticeable in Paris after *Iphigénie en Aulide* (1774), was also foreign to the more typical musical scene of Vienna; the sonatas 'for harpsichord' (meaning, by this time, the piano) and violin by the Alsatian Johann Friedrich Edelmann (1749–94), with their directions 'avec tristesse' and 'très lentement, d'un ton lugubre', place themselves midway between C. P. E. Bach and Gluck.

Italian instrumental music of the 1770s was, for the greater part, a European phenomenon, and was not practised primarily in Italy itself, except in Lombardy and Piedmont, which were islands of professional stability, and in Tuscany, which was to some extent linked with Vienna by the Lorraine dynasty. In 1770, after almost twenty years of European concerts, the violinist Gaetano Pugnani (1731–98), a leading member of the violin school founded by Somis, returned to Turin. After 1770 he published (mainly in London, Paris and Amsterdam) works with old-fashioned titles, 'Overtures in eight parts' and 'Trio sonatas', as well as concertos, symphonies and sonatas for violin and keyboard in which an inner refinement of the *galant* taste, dull and rather sterile, emerges beyond the paths frequented in Vienna. It is an aspect, a different level of stylistic assurance, that is exploited in Boccherini, a reluctance to follow the more radical models of modern sonata style, avoiding their schemes and remaining faithful to the roots of the Italian violinistic tradition in the concerto. In his last years, nevertheless, Pugnani contended with the leading *Sturm und Drang* text, Goethe's *Werther*, in a kind of musical translation of the novel into twenty-two instrumental pieces that, probably through Masonic links, was successfully performed at Vienna's Burgtheater itself in 1796. Even though it is loyal to French customs in its concertante traits, the work shows an influence of Gluck, Haydn and Mozart that would have been unthinkable in the writer of Corellian sonatas; the symphonic breadth in some of the scenes of nature and the intensity of many minor-key passages are without comparison in the whole of Italian music from the second half of the century.

The other Italian training ground for violinists was Tuscany, in particular the cities of Leghorn and Lucca. Pietro Nardini (1722–93), who returned home to Leghorn in 1766 from the Stuttgart of Carl Eugen and Jommelli, came directly from the school of Tartini. As a result of his arrival, a quartet in the modern concert sense of the term was soon formed in Milan on the basis of Sammartini's instrumental culture. This information was provided many years later by one of the members, Giuseppe Cambini, in an article about quartet music which appeared in the *Allgemeine musikalische Zeitung* of 1804,[25] and for a few months this quartet of Tuscans – Nardini and his pupil Filippo Manfredi as violinists, Cambini on the viola and Boccherini on the cello – must have been an important landmark in Italian instrumental music between Lombardy and Tuscany. By the beginning of 1768, however, Boccherini, Manfredi and Cambini were already in Paris; Cambini (1746?–1825?) settled there permanently, becoming just as French as his operatic colleagues and writing more than eighty symphonies concertantes and 174 quartets, all of which were published between 1773 and 1809. Composing and teaching (and publishing tutors on singing, the violin and the flute), Cambini passed through the years of the Revolution, for which he wrote various hymns 'à la Victoire', 'à l'Égalité' and 'à l'Être suprême'. By shortly after 1770 the small Tuscan group had disbanded; Nardini settled in Florence, still publishing in London and Amsterdam, and Manfredi returned to Lucca in 1772, giving up his association with Boccherini, who had in the meantime moved from Paris to Madrid.

The early years of Luigi Boccherini (1743–1805) show the difficulties that a musician seriously dedicated to instrumental music found in continuing to work in Italy. The son of a double bass player in the Palatine chapel of Lucca, trained in playing the cello and in composition, he was hardly fifteen when he went to Vienna with his family (his father, and his brother and sister, who were dancers) and was engaged as a member of the court theatre's orchestra. Without any regular arrangement he alternated between staying in Lucca and in Vienna during Gluck's most significant years: the same years in which Haydn entered the service of the Esterházy family. The six String Trios op. 1, which were praised by Gluck, and the six Quartets op. 2 appeared between 1760 and 1761, and both collections were published a few years later in Paris. In 1764 he entered the service of the Palatine chapel at Lucca, and in the following two years he and his father played at Pavia and Cremona as cellists in the orchestra of Sammartini, whose acquaintance, after that of Gluck, proved a fundamental experience for Boccherini. His activity with the Tuscan quartet, for which at the moment the only known written evidence is Cambini's late article, but which is difficult to ignore when one considers the scale of the op. 2 quartets (to which the enlarged scoring for string orchestra, customary at that time, cannot be applied) dates from the same years (1766–7).

In 1767 and 1768 Boccherini busied himself in Paris. He played with Manfredi at the Concert Spirituel and in 1767 (three years after Haydn's first quartets) published the Trios op. 1 and the Quartets op. 2; the six Sonatas for harpsichord and violin op. 5 published in 1769 bear witness to his European fame with their countless manuscript copies and various English, German and Dutch reprints. But in 1768 he felt that the offer of an old-style secure post at the court of Madrid was preferable to his position as a free musician, one among the many who were having to make their way in Europe's most crowded musical centre. Thus began his long period in Spain (1768–1805), almost forty years in a country rich in music but socially rigid, a land of lonely careers (such as those of Domenico Scarlatti and Antonio Soler) from which one had to get away, as Martín y Soler did, if one wanted to gain an international reputation.

For more than fifteen years Boccherini was chamber composer to the Infante Don Luis (King Charles III's brother) in Madrid and at the Las Arenas palace in the province of Avila, where he had at his disposal a quartet formed from a family of musicians, the Font family. This was a fruitful period, comparable with those of Domenico Scarlatti in Spain and of Haydn at Esterháza in so far as these composers all produced music in isolation for a small audience, always the same type of pieces for the same type of people. On the Infante's death in 1785 Boccherini passed into the service of the Benavente-Osuna family, and his income also included a pension from Friedrich Wilhelm II of Prussia, the great lover of the cello who appointed him chamber composer with the duty of sending all his new works to Berlin. But the end of the *ancien régime* seriously affected the composer: the King of Prussia's pension was revoked and his patrons left Spain. Still, the French 'quidams' liked Boccherini and for a short time he was supported by Lucien Bonaparte, the French ambassador to Madrid (1800–01). On the latter's departure, however, Boccherini remained trapped in Madrid with a royal pension and the small profits from his works, managed by the publisher Pleyel in Paris, who was ungenerous towards the composer. Family deaths and illnesses also embittered the last years before the composer's death in May 1805.

Boccherini's isolation in Spain, nevertheless, was not quite like Domenico Scarlatti's, and as a result of fairly favourable opportunities his music always remained on the musical markets of central Europe. In a letter of 1780 to the Viennese publisher Artaria he recalled sending thirty works to the press on Paris, Venice, Madrid, England and Holland;[26] in the years 1767–76, which probably contained the best of his prolific output, Paris was above all the springboard that launched his international reputation. At the beginning of the 1770s Boccherini still stood on equal terms with Haydn and Mozart on account of his melodic gift, his technical maturity in his treatment of the quartet, his variety of language, and his enthusiastic openness to contemporary values. The Adagio in D minor of the first quartet of op. 6 (1769) and the corresponding movement in the contemporary fifth trio of op. 9 adhere with singular directness to the tone of a confession, the accent of speech and the grim gloominess of the *Sturm und Drang*. Like Dittersdorf and others, Boccherini incorporated elements of Gluck's style into sonata-form works, with sforzato unisons, leaps and chromaticisms (e.g. in the finale of the second quartet of op. 6 in C minor); this is also clear in the fourth symphony of op. 12 with its 'chaconne qui représente l'Enfer et qui a été faite à l'imitation de celle de Mr. Gluck dans le Festin de pierre'. Yet at the same time the distant and almost opposite voice of Vivaldi was also present, unmistakable in the minor-key openings of the op. 2 and op. 27 quartets. Some of the Grave movements in these works even go so far as to repeat and expand the courtly and rather frigid lament of Corelli. Rome had been the birthplace of the Italian violin style at the end of the seventeenth century, and it was this style that still influenced Europe in the 1770s, although it was by then centred on Paris, and had been adapted to suit the modern sonata form.

The six Symphonies op. 12 (1771), whose vigorous tone reveals a decisive change from the model of Sammartini, played their part in the European panorama; the masterpiece is not perhaps the famous no. 4, with its Gluckian approach, but the gentle no. 3 in C major, whose first movement throbs with a Piccinnian sensibility that is one of the most telling statements of Italian symphonic writing. The most convincing lesson is found in the slow movements – the Andantino of the first symphony, the Andante amoroso of the third, the Adagio non tanto of the fifth (with its understanding of the lyrical possibilities of the horn, which were almost unknown at that time in Vienna) and the Larghetto in A minor of the sixth – all movements in which the melodic brush-stroke has a persuasive power and a skill at moving from one phrase to another which was able to influence even Haydn and Mozart. Only the finales, held back by festive long-windedness, are weak; they detract from the prominence of the minuets, whose trios tend to suggest elements of the concerto. The Symphonies op. 35 of about ten years later (1782) are also notable, but compared with Haydn, whose influence is by now perceptible, the position is reversed: op. 35 remained in manuscript – the appearance of the 'Paris' symphonies (1787) must have made them a lost cause.

That the style of the Viennese sonata was completely foreign to Boccherini is clear at first sight in the most typical section of his output, the string quintet, a field in which the Tuscan composer worked alone without any real precedents. Indeed, the fact that he persisted in composing quintets until the end of the century (he wrote a total of 184, of which 113 are for two violins, viola and two cellos), while after 1780 the symphony and the quartet were the up-and-coming genres, is an indication of an unusual linguistic temperament; but even within these early quintet collections, opp. 10, 11 and 13 (1771–2), unsurpassed in their originality and abundance of ideas, the discourse extends along paths unrelated to the most radical developments of sonata composition. Boccherini worked on the basis not of individual themes but of a tangle of lyrical ideas, a radiant melodiousness that runs equally through both first and second themes and both major and minor keys: a much more artful and sophisticated 'singende Allegro' than that of the harpsichordists twenty years earlier. It is not really necessary to point out the workmanship of the themes, although it is certainly there, or the contrast between first and second themes that appears from time to time; the fact is that the cardinal problem of sonata form, the contradiction between the static (the prominence of the theme) and the dynamic (the concept of development), did not concern him – it is avoided by the use of three, four, or even more themes, each one more winning than the last, in a fundamental friendship of ideas. And then, Boccherini seems to say in the early quintets, why attack the amateur or the connoisseur with Allegros which are crammed full of ideas from the outset (to say nothing of the inane sparkling openings in the Mannheim style)? Better to begin with these Andantinos, Amorosos, gently flowing Andantes, Allegrettos or pastoral Larghettos – conciliatory introductions which do not rule out later ideas or even important statements in the course of the gradual unfolding of the discourse in sections less well qualified to display them.

Even a distant look at Boccherini shows signs of a calm and conservative outlook. With an artisan's way of looking at things he divided his chamber output into 'opere grandi' (works in four movements) and 'opere piccole' (works in two movements), selling the latter for half the price of the former. He was prepared to make transcriptions and to alter a part from one instrument to another. He remained loyal to the minuet, showing no hurry to replace it with the scherzo and, far from restricting himself to the chirpy rococo of the famous minuet from the Quintet op. 11 no. 5 (which became exceptionally successful only at the end of the nineteenth century), he found in this eighteenth-century stereotype an area that was open to every possibility. He never felt irritated by Arcadia; this is clearly shown by the rustic tone of his Pastorales, a kind of country music that was also shared by Paisiello and in general was typical of the whole of the second half of the eighteenth century in Italy. The only openly up-to-date element was his recourse to Spanish folk music: Boccherini was too modest in considering his Andalusian dances (*fandangos* and *tiranas*) and descriptive ideas (e.g. in 'Musica notturna delle strade di Madrid') as being of limited scope and not saleable beyond the Spanish borders. His interest in the guitar around 1798–9 (the same time as Fernando Ferrandiere's *The art of playing the guitar* appeared) also reflects the musical customs of Boccherini's new home; he arranged the piano part of a few late quintets for the guitar for the Marquis de Benavente, and above all, a sure sign that he was held in high regard, he transformed one of his happiest youthful quintets, op. 10 no. 4, into a symphony for orchestra with concertante guitar.

Certainly, thinking back from the depths of the last years to the Boccherini of 1768–70, one may wonder what would have happened to him if he had lived in Paris, London, Vienna or Berlin rather than in Spain (one may also wonder what would have happened to Haydn if he had remained walled up at Esterháza). Boccherini's historical misfortune, however, was not so much that he did not meet a Salomon as that he relied on assumptions orientated more to the past than to the future, rather like Cimarosa in his last difficult years in Italy. A late piece like the melancholy Larghetto of the second quartet op. 58 (1799), in the middle of three dull movements, still provides a surprise with its depth of calculated exploration which has no real precedent except, to some extent, the Adagios of

Haydn's *Seven last words*. Even in Boccherini there is, nevertheless, an air of grandeur that goes beyond the *galant* world, but it seems to originate more from a religious attitude of withdrawing into seclusion than from the affirmation of the more decisive and open-minded worldly values of Vienna, Paris or London. Boccherini had really made his greatest contribution to European instrumental culture with his impermeability to any of the basic problems of modern sonata form, with his relaxed manner and with his enjoyment in the beauty of invention, which interested Mozart, a great lover of irregularity and of the unusual hidden under a regular guise, much more than Haydn.

26 Mozart

In view of Mozart's ability to grasp what was essential in every genre almost without the knowledge of any model, it will be useful to sum up in a rapid introductory sketch the stylistic opportunities of the musical world around 1770.

A variety of styles

In general terms, the various elements which had led up to this point and which now overlapped with the works of Mozart can be presented as follows:

(a) The extrovert side of the *galant* style; the cantabile melody ('singende Allegro') and the Alberti bass were obvious manifestations of it, and regular phrase structure was its most consistent characteristic. The chief models were J. C. Bach, who was well known in London, Wagenseil and others of his circle in Vienna, and the Italians Galuppi, Paradisi and Rutini, who were known through English and German editions.

(b) The serious side of the *galant* style, the *empfindsam* style of C. P. E. Bach and the depressive aspects of Schobert and Eckhardt associated with Paris: minor keys, harmonic experimentation and fanciful preludes that suspend strophic regularity and continuously delay the point of arrival.

(c) The 'stile osservato', i.e. counterpoint treated as an academic exercise in the context of sacred music, a popular style which imitated Palestrina in its tonal harmony, and which was liked by academics and was well known in Salzburg.

(d) Extemporary, 'secular' counterpoint, an imitative style within a regime of free conversation, which was developed in unforeseen ways following the discovery of Johann Sebastian Bach by van Swieten's Viennese circle.

(e) The principle of thematic clarity, of searching for themes that were easily identifiable by their fusion of dance rhythms and the melodic articulation of the aria or popular song.

(f) The principle of thematic elaboration: not only ornamental variations but also the 'critical' use of themes and the exploration of their possibilities. Here Haydn showed the way more than anyone else, but Boccherini also developed ideas originated by Johann Stamitz, Sammartini and other lesser composers.

(g) The heroic style, i.e. Italian *opera seria* and Gluck: declamation, the dramatic tension of accompanied recitative, the use of the chorus, and themes with a courtly air.

(h) The Italian, comic style, in particular the continuity of the concerted act finale, at first along the lines of Goldoni and Piccinni and then along the more elaborate lines of Casti and Paisiello.

(i) The comic vernacular style: the German and Viennese *Singspiel*, the more light-hearted aspects of Italian *opera buffa* and later musical jokes of popular origin.

A few selected 'negatives' are also important, rejections of institutions or stylistic attitudes that Mozart had nevertheless observed:

(a) Instrumental recitative. Compared with Haydn, who sometimes borrowed this style from Emanuel Bach, and others who associated it with Gluck, this hybrid was foreign to Mozart, to whom it must have smacked of experiments and halfway measures. The fact that he must, nevertheless, have been aware of it is shown by the recitative-like cadences in the Adagios of the piano concertos (above all K 271).

(b) Melodrama. After Mannheim's infatuation with Benda's works (see Chapter 14), Mozart's use of this style was a modest extension. Here too, as with instrumental recitative, the message of experimentation was not made for Mozart's ears.

(c) The sentimental, pathetic style, the style of the various Cecchinas of the time, with 6/8 time, morbid minor keys and gentle appoggiaturas. Mozart, after paying tribute to it with *La finta giardiniera*, was impervious to its more affected forms, but it is quite certain that he knew about them. Barbarina, looking for the pin in the last act of *Le nozze di Figaro*, is the synthesis of all the 'buone figliole', orphans or foundlings, who inhabit the musical eighteenth century.

Some of the genres in this outline (*opera seria*, comic opera and sacred polyphony), already had a long tradition before Mozart, others (the symphony, the quartet and the *Singspiel*) had taken shape more recently, and others (the piano employed in chamber music and with the orchestra) really only began with him; but all were drawn into his creative sphere, producing in the brief space of some twenty years (1770-91) an extraordinary achievement which could be surpassed only by composers who questioned the most basic formal principles. Mozart's power as an assimilator also went beyond general points of reference, finding material in lesser works, in ideas of even the poorest composers, and in characteristics and performing abilities of singers and instrumentalists. Everything was put to good use in the most varied and coherent stylistic universe that the history of music had known since Bach's time.

There was, however, a further innovatory element. Mozart was not only the greatest in everything that was already in circulation, but was also able to operate at a second level, establishing a network of nuances and complex relationships between pre-existing musical ideas and the composer's own selection and use of them. If he drew freely on what had already been said, he also made connections on a previously unknown scale and set up reciprocal interactions between different styles, handling stock characters and clichés without ever getting into a muddle with them and forming for himself a musical language that was capable of anything.

Mozart's journeys

Wolfgang Amadeus Mozart was born in Salzburg on 27 January 1756. His musical training was the educational masterpiece of his father Leopold, a cultured man who was educated at the Jesuit Gymnasium in Augsburg and was violinist and *Kapellmeister* in the prince–archbishop's court. Wolfgang's musical education is shown in the *Notenbücher*, collections of short pieces in the *galant* style assembled by Leopold which include, like photographs from real life, the first little minuets which Wolfgang spelled out at the age of five or six, lovingly retouched by his father. If his father's house was a unique musical establishment (reminiscent of that of the Bachs), other composers were also able to influence the young boy in his native city, a small centre but with a traditionally rich musical life encouraged by the prince–archbishops, sometimes in competition with Vienna. J. E. Eberlin, A. C. Adlgasser and Michael Haydn were other sound models for Wolfgang, serious professionals who were largely busy among the choirs and organs of Salzburg's many churches.

But Salzburg was not able to provide a suitable setting in Leopold's eyes for his son's prodigious musical qualities, and so travel, with a rather rash precociousness, became one of the fundamental experiences of Wolfgang's early years. They were very different journeys from those in fashion at the time, the tours of connoisseurs looking for monuments and works of art (and also, in the case of Burney, for music). These were working holidays, tiring and marked by illnesses; education was quite accidental and what mattered was making known to the world a phenomenon in the form of a six-year-old child who played, improvised and composed, and, in the meantime, looking for suitable centres of work.

The first trips were in 1762: to Munich, one of the German gateways of Italian opera, and in the autumn to Vienna, where Wolfgang discovered Wagenseil and, along with his sister Maria Anna (Nannerl), created a short-lived stir at court. Following this first visit (which occurred while Gluck's *Orfeo ed Euridice* was being put on at the Burgtheater, a fact which is completely ignored in Leopold's letters), Vienna was to be the frequent destination of journeys until the decisive move there in 1781, though hopes of a court post, which had seemed only natural and appropriate, were always frustrated. A whistle-stop tour of north-east Europe which lasted three years was commenced in 1763: Munich, Augsburg, Trier, Mainz, Frankfurt (where the fourteen-year-old Goethe attended Mozart's concert), Bonn, Brussels, Paris, London, Amsterdam, The Hague and Paris again, returning home via Switzerland at the end of 1766. His acquaintance with J. C. Bach, Schobert and the Mannheim orchestra were all salient experiences. In Paris the encyclopaedist Grimm predicted Wolfgang's genius for the stage,[27] while at this time the composer was writing his first sonatas for violin and keyboard, his first symphonies and his first arias on texts by Metastasio. In short, even in the view of the prudent Leopold, Wolfgang seemed destined for the most glorious career.

After three years spent at Salzburg devoted mainly to occasional stage performances, Leopold reckoned that Wolfgang was mature enough to confront Italian opera in its natural home, and the two made three trips to Italy. The first (December 1769 – March 1771) was a complete triumph marked by honours and generous tokens of recognition from the old Italian academies; it took in Verona, Mantua, Milan, Bologna, Florence, Rome and Naples, and from there the return journey north also called at Turin and Venice. The fourteen-year-old Mozart met Piccinni and Noverre at Milan, Giovanni Battista Martini at Bologna and Nardini at Florence, and encountered *opera seria* and *opera buffa* at Naples, Roman polyphony, and the still-productive instrumental vein of the regions along the Po valley (it was in an inn at Lodi, one day in March, that for no obvious practical reasons he wrote his first quartet). After the success of *Mitridate*, which was produced at Milan in 1770, Archduke Ferdinand, the Governor of Lombardy, wanted to employ Mozart, but the step was discouraged by the archduke's mother, the great Maria Theresa, who advised him from Vienna 'to prevent your burdening yourself with useless people' who would degrade his service by going 'about the world like beggars'.[28]

The second and third journeys both involved shorter stays centered on Milan (August – December 1771 and September 1772 to June 1773) to put on the serenata *Ascanio in Alba* (on a text by Parini for Archduke Ferdinand's wedding) and the *opera seria Lucio Silla*. The limited interest which the latter aroused, not being followed by other commissions and so concluding rather than opening an Italian career, shows that the fame of the boy prodigy was declining. He was sixteen, was no longer a phenomenon, and had to make his way among numerous rivals armed with something more than an adolescent smile; deep down, even his father had neither the flair nor the persistent determination to gain pre-eminent positions for his son that were in any way worthy of his talent. There now began a period in which the awareness of his immense capabilities and the desire to compete on a European scale conflicted more and more with the dependent musician's obedience to his old social status. In this case the contrast was sharpened by the personality of the new bishop, Hieronymus, Count of Colloredo (who succeeded the kind Siegmund von Schrattenbach in 1772), a modern man, a follower of the Enlightenment with rigid requirements concerning his own duties and those of others – and therefore a very awkward patron. There was by now a dangerous conflict between the twenty-year-old Mozart who wrote the Symphony K 183 and the Concerto K 271 between 1773 and 1777 and his position as *Konzertmeister* in the rather baroque Salzburg, and it did not take much to turn it into open warfare.

The two poles towards which Mozart inclined after his Italian travels were Vienna and Munich. He spent the summer of 1773 in Vienna, still with his father, with the declared aim of gaining a court post, but the only important outcome was his acquaintance with

Haydn's early masterpieces. At the end of 1774 Mozart was in Munich, but here too the success of *La finta giardiniera* did not produce any lasting results. In 1776 he was champing at the bit; he wrote a dejected letter to Padre Martini ('I live in a country where music leads a struggling existence')[29] and got ready to leave for Italy. The permission that Colloredo had previously granted, however, was revoked, and for the first time Mozart abandoned life as a servant and set out on his most important journey, not with his father but with his mother, a companion to advise rather than to instruct. The two left in September 1777 via Munich, where people were beginning to talk about a German national theatre, and Mannheim. Here Mozart allowed himself a long break, making contact with the second generation of the Mannheim school (Cannabich, the flautist Wendling, the oboist Ramm and the great singer Raaff) at a time when even the elector Carl Theodor himself was concerned with German opera (see Chapter 18). Mozart attended rehearsals of Schweitzer's *Rosamund* and was enthusiastic about Holzbauer's *Günther* and especially Benda's melodramas. He fell in love with Aloysia Weber, the excellent singer with whom he dreamt of a voyage to Italy, intending to make his fortune in the theatres like Wilhelm Meister with Marianne. This was the first appearance of the romantic side of Mozart's character that worried his father so much; in fact Leopold complained bitterly from Salzburg that he should not lose himself in the rank and file of provincial music, and urged him to move on to Paris.[30]

Mother and son arrived in the French capital in March 1778. The symphony for the Concert Spirituel (K 297) was favourably received, but the phenomenal reception of Stamitz was not repeated. Paris was no longer the same for the twenty-two-year-old Mozart as it had been in 1763, nor had the anonymous public of the concert hall much in common with the audience at the house of Prince Conti which had acclaimed him as a child. Grimm had no way of turning him into the success that he had predicted fifteen years earlier, and theatres, impresarios and journalists were too busy with a controversy between Gluck and Piccinni to show any interest in a young Austrian. In this instance Mozart acted on his own initiative, giving private lessons in high society and publishing six violin sonatas with Sieber's firm, but this was hardly sufficient to establish himself or to pay off the debt which the family had incurred during the journey. With Noverre, too, there was nothing concrete, and he was not even able to find support from his old teacher, J. C. Bach, whom he ran into again in Paris and who was already in difficulties on his own account. Then on top of everything came his mother's sudden death, followed immediately by evidence of his Aloysia's indifference towards him. It was in these crucial experiences, in spite of a lack of practical success, that the value of the trip to Paris lay: the direct encounter with life's less pleasant surprises and the sense of confusion in a foreign country that was becoming increasingly disturbed by social tensions and divisions. The fact that Mozart does not mention this aspect in his letters does not matter; absorbing everything, without any trace of selectivity, was indeed the achievement of maturity.

In the twelve years after his return home from Paris there were only occasional short periods when Mozart was away from Vienna, where he settled in 1781, and he did not venture beyond the German-speaking countries again. He made several visits to Prague and to Munich, Mannheim and Mainz, and he even went as far as Berlin and Frankfurt; the journey to the free imperial city of Frankfurt (1790) a year before his death was the most moving of all, as it was just the opposite of the carefree experience of his childhood travels. Mozart went there for the coronation celebrations of Leopold II and to encourage his career by drawing attention to himself, but the concerts given at his expense passed unnoticed; the city was completely taken up with the celebrations and ceremonies, and (as Metternich shows in his memoirs) scarcely paid any attention to the appearance of French exiles, the unintentional but eloquent heralds of a profound disturbance which was about to spill over into Europe.

An independent profession

The fundamental event of Mozart's life was his decision to leave the musical service of a court and to maintain himself as a free professional, selling his music directly to the public of a big city. It does not matter that he may have been forced into it by circumstances; certainly his deliberateness did not have the romantic aura of Schiller, who ran away from the Duke of Württemberg's castle in 1782, but the step is no less significant because it was the result of eight years of conflict. Other musicians before him, including J. C. Bach and many more obscure musicians, had left a secure chapel post for the uncertain profession within a city, especially when the Seven Years' War made terrible inroads on the coffers of the central monarchies and the number of dependants had to be reduced somewhat. But in Mozart's case it was to become symbolic, not only because he is a figure of such great stature, but also because of the violent friction of the time at which it happened, a few years before the French Revolution. Bach's imprisonment by Duke Wilhelm Ernst of Weimar half a century earlier did not cause a sensation in the social history of music, but the rebellion of Mozart, who was alien to any pretence, was to assume the significance of a declaration of war between the new bourgeois world and the old regime of artistic production. Even the material failure of the action ultimately gave its instigator the further legendary aspect of being the victim.

On returning to Salzburg after his Paris adventures at the beginning of 1779, Mozart was again included on the rolls of the archbishop's court as cathedral organist; but the monotony of service was soon broken by an important theatrical commission, *Idomeneo* for Munich, and it was really the opera's favourable outcome that increased Mozart's faith in himself and persuaded him to oppose Colloredo in a determined fashion when the latter, about to depart for Vienna following the death of Maria Theresa, required him to go to the city as part of his retinue. At first the composer obeyed and in March 1781 he was given rooms in the headquarters of the Teutonic Order, where the musicians sat at table with the cooks and valets – a fine come-down after the respect that Carl Theodor had just shown him. The most intolerable insult was not this, however, but the veto imposed on the free, direct running of his musical finances. A benefit evening at the Kärntnertor theatre with one of his symphonies and a piano concerto (and people shouting 'bravo!' during the performance) caused him to write an excited letter to his father: 'Well, how much do you suppose I should make if I were to give a concert of my own, now that the public has got to know me? Only this arch-booby [*erzlimmel*] of ours will not allow it.'[31] A little later, quite the opposite occurred; the arch-booby (meaning the archbishop) made him play for his guests without giving him a ducat more than the ordinary salary that he had received in Salzburg, while that very evening Mozart had been invited by the Countess Thun, whose guests included the Emperor! In short, when in May the Salzburg troupe was asked to follow its master back to the little green, rainy city on the Salzach, hemmed in by the Mönchsberg and the Kapuzinerberg, Mozart felt that his feet had become firmly planted on Viennese soil and could not even consider packing up. There were arguments and noisy scenes with the archbishop; he was called a scoundrel, and finally (in June) Count Arco, the chief steward, threw him out, giving him, moreover, a sacrilegious kick, suddenly propelling Mozart and with him the 'modern musician' into the state of an independent professional artist.

This condition as an independent musician lasted ten years, the final years of his life. His introduction to the new regime of private initiative and competition succeeded for a few years, with open success on the basis of which Mozart, had he had a tenth of the ability of a Gluck or a Grétry at getting on with people, could have set himself up for the rest of his life. On Christmas Eve 1781 he played before the Emperor and the Grand Duke of Russia in a musical competition with an Italian who was becoming increasingly well known, Muzio Clementi. In 1782 he aroused the Burgtheater's enthusiasm with *Die Entführung aus dem Serail* (The abduction from the harem), and on the wave of its success reckoned that he would be able to put on one of his operas each year for the 'national' theatre patronized by Joseph II. Between 1782 and 1783 he met in succession Haydn, van Swieten and Lorenzo Da Ponte – something which would have been unthinkable in Salzburg. But his trump card seemed to be the public concert, a territory which he entered with the series of concertos for piano and orchestra of 1782–6 written for his performances in public concert-halls (the Augarten-Saal and the Mehlgrube) or private rooms in van Swieten's home; the list of subscribers to a concert of 1784 which contains the finest names in Joseph's Vienna shows how widely he was respected. Other channels through which the independent musician could earn a living were also put to use, including private lessons and a good relationship with a publisher: Artaria published six sonatas for violin and piano in 1781, two piano sonatas for four hands in 1783 and another three ordinary piano sonatas the following year. 1785, however, was the golden year, with the publication of, among other works, the six quartets dedicated to Haydn, three piano concertos and two symphonies. The great step seemed to have been taken; the musician had made a place for himself in the city and in 1782 he married Constanza Weber, Aloysia's sister, with whose family he had taken refuge after his break with the archbishop. The feeling of being part of the establishment must have been an important factor in his entry to Masonic lodges. His father visited him at Vienna and saw his son's success for himself, being moved by the praise which he heard from the lips of Haydn, who described Mozart as 'the greatest composer known to me'.[32]

Yet from this peak Mozart's fortune began a rapid decline which coincided exactly with the height of his creative powers. In the spring of 1786, a little while before *Le nozze di Figaro*, one of his

series of concerts attracted the remarkable number of 120 subscribers, but with Vienna, after *Figaro*, there was no longer the basis
of an *entente cordiale*. At first the opera did well, so well that after its
third performance Joseph II had to forbid encores of the ensembles,
but then the opera moved on to German cities in the German
translation by Knigge and Vulpius; in Vienna the court and the
aristocracy (except for van Swieten) preferred to turn to Paisiello,
Sarti and Martín y Soler. Mozart would have liked to try Paris again,
but his father refused to finance him. He was, however, presented
with new prospects in Prague, a city which was enlivened by a spirit
of rivalry with Vienna. Here, where he had friends and admirers,
Mozart achieved the great successes of his final years: *Le nozze di
Figaro* was received enthusiastically in the season 1786–7, and in
1787 *Don Giovanni* was a triumph. Even Vienna took notice and
Mozart was appointed 'court composer' in place of Gluck who died
in that year, but the appointment was little more than honorary and
the only commissions were society dances, minuets, contredanses
and German dances. Mozart wrote about a hundred of them
between 1788 and 1791, and in his catalogue they seem to be signs of
a setback, tributes to a patron less tangible but no less stringent than
the archbishop – the market for functional music.

In 1789 he left for Berlin, hoping for a post at the court of
Friedrich Wilhelm II; he returned with no more than an order for
six quartets (of which he was to write only three) and six piano
sonatas (of which he wrote only one). That summer of 1789, spent in
Vienna, was the unhappiest of Mozart's life; demands for money
became more and more frequent and he turned increasingly to loyal
Masonic friends even for small sums. *Così fan tutte*, commissioned
by the court, was put on in January 1790, but the state mourning for
the death of Joseph II interrupted its initially quite good reception.
Even with the reorganizations and changes connected with the
accession of Leopold II, in a period of economic restrictions and
little interest in music, Mozart did not succeed in getting the post of
second *Kapellmeister* for which he was hoping by this time, rowing
against the tide towards the old status of the dependent musician. In
his final year (1791), an individual who wished to remain anonymous
commissioned him to write a Requiem and a mysterious envoy
appeared every so often to arrange for its collection. Mozart's
emotional psyche was disturbed and the work remained unfinished;
this was the most 'romantic' episode of his life.

In the summer of 1791 the inhabitants of Prague were still
greeting their Mozart enthusiastically after *La clemenza di Tito*,

written for the coronation of Leopold II as King of Bohemia, and at the end of September *Die Zauberflöte*, given in Vienna in front of the bourgeois public of the Theater auf der Wieden, achieved an immediate success which took him back to the popularity of his early Viennese years. But it was too late to repay debts to a man who had become worn out by illness and fatigue, and he died on 5 December 1791.

Why did Mozart pay such a high price for independence? Beyond the biographical evidence of a man who was not really cut out for organizing his own career, what historical basis was missing from his introduction into the independent profession which Haydn managed with a single step, confirming a position that he had in fact already reached? The Austria of the 1770s, strongly influenced by the three figures of Maria Theresa, Metastasio and Hasse, certainly turned out to be more hostile than indifferent to the young musician from Salzburg, but his lack of success in Joseph's Vienna, after the good position he had reached in 1785, has still not been explained satisfactorily. Reasons for his split with the Viennese aristocracy offered in 'social' terms usually set great store by the revolutionary energy of *Le nozze di Figaro*. Yet this judgement is the result of a view conditioned by the French Revolution, which nobody was thinking about in Vienna in 1786, and in any case does not take into account the extent to which the subversive element present in Beaumarchais' comedy was watered down in Da Ponte's libretto for Mozart.

The reason for the opera's limited success was perhaps more prosaic, and should be looked for in the complexity of its musical texture. The only full account of the work (in the *Wiener Realzeitung* of 11 July 1786) talks of serious difficulties of performance;[33] Count Zinzendorf, a typical member of the Viennese nobility, considered the opera merely 'boring',[34] and Joseph II, complaining to Dittersdorf that in Mozart the singers were deafened by the orchestra, was probably referring to *Figaro*.[35] For Dittersdorf, Mozart's works, like Klopstock's, had to be read more than once to be understood in all their beauty,[36] and the *Chronik von Berlin* wrote as late as 1790 that *Le nozze di Figaro* was a piece for experts. If these were opinions that were current in the north, in the homeland of C. P. E. Bach, Marpurg and Forkel, then the richness of Mozart's language must have made even less of an impression on the Viennese court, which already favoured the distinctive cantabile style of Martín y Soler's *Una cosa rara* and the cheerful vein of Dittersdorf's *Doktor und Apotheker*, and later found its ideal opera in Cimarosa's *Il matrimonio segreto*. Furthermore, Mozart provided all that richness and novelty of musical thinking without any plans or manifestos and without the help of publicity in an age full of intellectualism and theoretical statements; the intellectual Gluck was successful, but not the non-intellectual Mozart, who was set apart by the fact that he went directly to the heart of problems only through his music.

Mozart's lack of a secure basis of success in the instrumental field appears even more surprising. It can be taken for granted that the praise Mozart received in Vienna as a *performer* may have concealed the *composer* of the piano concertos, whose symphonic conception he had originated in the years 1781–5; but even as a concert pianist Mozart was to find himself at a disadvantage. The prototype of the new concert artist was Muzio Clementi, with whom Mozart had played in front of the Emperor in 1781. Clementi left England backed up by a network of European connections with publishers and instrument makers, and above all with an international vision of concert activity, while Mozart's level was that of the city. The composer who had travelled so much in his childhood stopped exactly when the time of the travelling virtuoso arrived.

Finally, without digressing too far into conjecture, his lack of recognition can also be ascribed to the brevity of his life. It was a question of time: Mozart was about to become successful with the more progressive European bourgeoisie. In the autumn of 1790 he had received several invitations from London, from Salomon, naturally, who was thinking of putting him alongside Haydn in his concerts, and from the director of the opera, Robert May O'Reilly, who wanted him to write for the London stage. He received similar offers from Amsterdam, and prominent Hungarian noblemen also declared that they were prepared to keep Mozart with an annual subsidy of a thousand florins. Here aspects of growing nationalism after decades of Italian dominance certainly came into play, and a 'German' interest in Mozart was apparent in cities like Mainz, Mannheim and Munich which, like Prague, rated him much more highly than Vienna. But it was too early for these seeds of nationalism to come together to help Mozart to the same extent that they were to support Beethoven. The intervening period was not long, but in it occurred the rise of Napoleon and the invasion of Vienna through which Joseph II's vague aspiration developed into the patriotism of the Napoleonic era, the feeling for the fatherland reawakened by Napoleon and then turned against him in the form of German patriotism. The Austrian aristocracy and bourgeoisie were to come together in support of Beethoven, protecting him from material problems, tolerating all his tantrums and avoiding any possibility that he might wish to leave the country: this was a new union between patronage and an independent profession that did not yet exist for Mozart in the decade 1781–91.

The music up to the departure from Salzburg

Mozart died when he was only thirty-five – halfway through life according to Dante's calculation; but it is always claimed that the course of his life developed twice as quickly as normal, and from this reasonable assumption there follow two consequences. First, Mozart's output (in itself enormous, comparable in quantity to that of healthy and long-lived champions of the baroque age like Draghi, Telemann and Hasse) was not suddenly cut short by death, but is a complete, finite universe which embraces all the musical genres of the time. And secondly, when one considers his famous precociousness, his perfect works came relatively late. For someone who had begun to write minuets at the age of six, symphonies at eight and Masses and operas at twelve, he reached maturity late, at the age of seventeen, after a rather long apprenticeship.

The chronological picture of Mozart's work is based on certain dates which more or less correspond with the last three decades of his life: 1763–73, the decade of his development; 1773–81, the period of his maturity up to the break with Salzburg; and 1781–91, the final decade in Vienna.

The works from his childhood may be categorized as explorations of musical styles; they display a keen respect for the individual characteristics of the different styles, which he had acquired as the result of the dynamic alternation between his examination of examples during his travels and his reworking of them in the periods at Salzburg. The symphonies from his London voyage (1765), K 16, 19 and 22, are in three movements and represent a type of Italian opera overture modelled on J. C. Bach and Abel; they contain a succession of ideas in the *galant* spirit and exploit the 'singende Allegro'. On the other hand, in the Andantes, at least the one in C minor in K 16, there is serious emotion in the manner of Schobert. On his return home he immediately adopted, in the symphonies written in Vienna from 1767 to 1768 (K 43, 45 and 48), the four-movement pattern with the minuet as the third movement; these works include elements of the *galant* style (which was well known also to Monn, Wagenseil and Starzer) and add the serious note that is typical of the Viennese baroque.

The opposing styles of the *galant* and the erudite intermingle in the twenty-seven symphonies written during the years of his Italian journeys, and it is the same with the series of quartets. Here, too, the early works are 'Italian', written spontaneously ('to while away the time' according to Leopold)[37] not long after they had crossed the Alps, in the inns of Lodi or Bozen. The quartets K 156–60 were composed in Milan at the same time as *Lucio Silla* and are in the style of Sammartini and Boccherini; they show a more uniform level of writing than the symphonies, but are more advanced and more passionate. They focus on the slow movement (which, in four cases out of five, is in the minor key, with plentiful expression marks), and extend, as it were, the tragic pathos of *Lucio Silla*, with its scene at night by Mario's tomb. But a new direction suddenly appeared with the six Viennese quartets (K 168–73) completed in the summer of 1773 under the influence of Haydn. The Italian ideal of the cantabile style, proclaimed by Boccherini with his quintets published in Paris in 1771, was temporarily abandoned in favour of a more rigorous formal definition in the footsteps of Haydn's op. 20 quartets and Gassmann's six quartets dating from the same year, 1773; whole movements are replaced by fugues, imitative writing is widespread, themes are intensively developed, and the four-movement structure is firmly established.

Mozart's early development, then, took place entirely within the instrumental field, but in the close examination that he was continually making of contemporary musical events, opera could not be postponed for long. The first exercises in stage music, between 1766 and 1768, occurred at Salzburg: a sacred *Singspiel* (*Die Schuldigkeit des ersten Gebots*, written in collaboration with Michael Haydn and Adlgasser) and a comedy in Latin (*Apollo et Hyacinthus*) written for the university. But with two works of 1768 written for Vienna, the *opera buffa La finta semplice*, to a libretto by Coltellini after Goldoni, and the *Singspiel Bastien und Bastienne*, using Rousseau and Favart as sources, the twelve-year-old Mozart already found himself in the mainstream of European taste, while the operas for Milan, the result of the Italian journeys, were inevitably to be overshadowed by the dense vegetation of *opera seria* from Metastasio, Hasse, Jommelli and J. C. Bach.

The 'historical destiny' of genres is a view that emerges firmly when one looks at the swift passage from the stereotype of Metastasian opera (*Lucio Silla*) to the symphonies of the end of 1773 and the first few months of 1774 (K 183, 200 and 201), for which it is useless to look for models among his contemporaries. While Sieber was publishing Haydn's *Sturm und Drang* symphonies in Paris

(1773), Mozart at Salzburg, too, shook off the weak or vainly rhetorical background of the *galant* symphonic output. K 183 in G minor is the symphony which owes most to the *Sturm und Drang* style; the heroic profile of its themes, fashioned with broad strokes, has a fatal character unknown even to Haydn, mixed with a severity drawn from roots buried in sacred music or *opera seria*, but everything is governed by an inflexibility of thematic outline and an emotional *Streben* ('striving') that makes the work's first and last movements worthy contemporaries of Goethe's *Prometheus*. Exactly the same rejection of approximations, but on the horizon of the most cheerful optimism, appears in K 201. Here, too, the *galant* style is superseded, but from within, homeopathically almost, and is pushed to previously unknown extremes of melodic delicacy, thematic sophistication and enchanting sensuousness. The achievements of this fundamental year (1774) are immediately noticeable in other sectors, in the comic opera *La finta giardiniera*, written for Munich, in which the sentimental affinities with Piccinni and Anfossi are swamped by instrumental richness, and in the six early piano sonatas, which appear unusually late considering that the instrument had been available for more than ten years. Here the most striking work is the Sonata in D major K 284, which, along with Clementi's op. 2 (1779), made the harpsichord redundant with its variety of touch (from virtuoso articulation to cantabile) and with a liking for a symphonic-style weight of sound. But unusual aspects are also to be found in smaller details, especially, for example, in the opening of K 282 (a sonata which has two minuets in the style of the string trio probably descended from Boccherini), three bars that somehow recall the ancient, inexpressible calm of some of the slow preludes of the *Well-tempered Clavier*, an unmistakable sign of his separation from the common herd, a breath of air from other planets completely unknown to Bach's sons, to Galuppi and to Haydn.

It appears from a letter to Padre Martini that opera dominated Mozart's thoughts in 1776: 'As for the theatre,' he wrote, 'we are in a bad way for lack of singers. We have no castrati . . . '[38] He made up for the scarcity 'by writing chamber music and music for the church' to keep himself amused. The period 1775–7 represents an adjustment to his position as *Konzertmeister* at Salzburg; he wrote many locally-commissioned works, from *Il rè pastore*, to celebrate the visit of the Archduke Maximilian to Salzburg in 1775, to entertainment genres (with gems such as the Divertimento K 247 or the Serenade K 250) and, on the other side of the coin, the Masses (K 257–9, 262 and 275), where the conciseness typical of the Enlightenment and required by the archbishop did not rule out references to the style of opera and the concerto, made possible by the close relationships between genres in the Austrian baroque. There was another sudden leap forward in this period with the concerto for instrumental soloist and orchestra. The five violin concertos, a synthesis of the Italian knowledge of the violin filtered through his father Leopold, date from 1775, and the three early piano concertos from 1776; they are all, however, overshadowed by the Concerto in E flat major K 271 of January 1777. The presence in Salzburg of a Parisian pianist, Mlle Jeunehomme, who does not otherwise appear in contemporary reports, seems to have been the immediate stimulus for this bold masterpiece, which was written on the eve of Mozart's journey to Paris and which explored an entirely different world from the concerto for strings and keyboard of Galuppi, Serini, Wagenseil, and Johann Christoph Friedrich and Johann Christian Bach. After four bars for the piano, which butts in straight away, the E flat major tonality takes on the calculated sumptuousness which it was to retain alone until *Die Zauberflöte* and Beethoven's 'Eroica' Symphony. The moody depression of the *Sturm und Drang* comes to a halt in the C minor Adagio, in which the piano comes unusually close to the style of instrumental recitative, while the finale re-establishes architectonic solemnity, completing a unified conception of the three movements which had never before been so thoroughly realized.

Other explorations in the instrumental field occurred during the visits to Mannheim and Paris in 1777–8, even though he was composing at a relaxed pace. The Mannheim composers' academicism, which had no future, was overtaken on their home territory by some sonatas for violin and piano (K 296 and 301–3) which returned to a genre that had ceased with Schobert, developing it into an equal dialogue between the two instruments. In Paris the Sonatas in A minor K 310 for piano and in E minor K 304 for violin and piano represented a revival, at times even an agitated one, of *Sturm und Drang* elements, but in the more flexible moulds of chamber music; the style of Gluck, with its minute details of a type not permitted by the elevated heroic rhetoric of the Symphony K 183, was entirely avoided.

Beside these examples of solo music (which also include sonatas like K 331 with the 'alla turca' finale and K 332 in a spacious F major), his symphonic output, which was still the area on which it was necessary to concentrate in Paris, has less intrinsic value. The Symphony K 297 is in three movements in the French manner with the addition of the clarinets that were missing at Salzburg, but, with its general tone of militaristic stiffness, it is like a modernized Stamitz symphony. (The Sinfonia concertante in E flat for wind written by Mozart for his friends at Mannheim was, however, very different: it represents the epitome of a type of composition based on encounters and conversations, as it were, between the instruments, but was nevertheless turned down by the director of the Concert Spirituel.) But the great symphonic harvest of his experience in Mannheim and Paris matured almost as soon as he returned to Salzburg, in the two years 1779–80, and culminated in the Sinfonia concertante K 364 for violin and viola and the Symphony in C major K 338. Especially with the latter, the composer who had left for Paris as a hopeful youth from the country and was returning disillusioned and with an empty purse seemed to be giving his fellow-citizens an arrogant reminder of his mastery. The opening shakes the listener from head to foot with its geometrical fusion of fanciful thematic models in the Mannheim style and the rapid pulse of its underlying rhythm, while in the second movement the Lombard rhythms which Sammartini and J. C. Bach loved, solid and bottom-heavy ornamental figures, improvise a comedy of irresistible mimic power.

After Mozart had put his livery back on, the same robust conception can be found again in sacred works like the Mass K 337, the *Vesperae solennes de confessore* K 339, and in particular the majestic Kyrie K 341. But after Paris, Mozart, scarcely satisfied with the arias he had written at Mannheim for Aloysia, Dorothea Wendling and Raaff, longed to return to writing for the theatre. To supplement the enthusiasm for the theatre that he had experienced at Munich and Mannheim, the cradles of national opera, he now encountered companies passing through Salzburg: Johannes Böhm's company in 1779, followed in the autumn of 1780 by the troupe of Emanuel Schikaneder, a true prototype of those captains of theatrical fortune whose feats were celebrated in Goethe's *Wilhelm Meister*. In productions by Schikaneder Mozart saw in succession Lessing's *Emilia Gallotti*, Gozzi's *Le due notti affannose*, Beaumarchais' *Le barbier de Séville* and Shakespeare's *Hamlet*, while for Böhm's company he wrote incidental music for Gebler's play *Thamos, König in Aegypten* which takes into account Benda's melodramas and, in the choruses, Gluck and the *tragédie lyrique*, both of which he had scrupulously avoided the year before in Paris.

But the time for confronting and getting rid of this complex of values, from Jommelli to Gluck, finally came in 1781 with *Idomeneo*, commissioned from Munich by Carl Theodor, who had thought of Mozart for the main opera of the carnival season. Although the

poetic language of its libretto (by Giambattista Varesco) is Metastasian, Mozart's great *opera seria* is, from the point of view of its
dramatic structure, closer to a *tragédie lyrique* (the importance of the
chorus, and scenes like the shipwreck inspiring descriptive music
which is, moreover, treated with great care, are enough to separate it
from even the most reformed Italian operas). Gluck is present in
specific external references, the most obvious of which is the subterranean voice that pronounces the divine sentence, which, like the
oracle in *Alceste*, is accompanied by trombones. For the first time,
at the age of twenty-five, Mozart was able to devote all his energies
to the most ambitious genre of the time. But he was still a lover of
melody and still thirsty for the different possibilities of music, and
he entered the highly artificial sea of *opera seria* with unfurled sails.
The result was that the profusion of themes and wide-ranging
flexible harmonies end up placing him poles apart from the static
quality of Gluck, while an open cantabile vein of Italian origin runs
within the limits of the French framework. In the specific area of
opera seria, however, *Idomeneo* presents an unprecedented intensity
of ideas, from the plasticity of accompanied recitative to the weighty
archaism from which the broad themes of arias and choruses
originate, and which culminates in the imposing heights of the
chorus 'O voto tremendo, spettacolo orrendo'. This passage in C
minor, over a solemn triplet rhythm (which comes again in *Don
Giovanni* for the Commendatore's death, presented in a constantly
changing light by means of modulations), returns to the tragic scale
of 'Che spiagge! Che lidi funesti!' in Jommelli's *Fetonte*, creating at
the same time a type of funereal heroism on which Beethoven was to
draw extensively in the funeral march of the 'Eroica' Symphony.
The last twenty years of the century began with the severe tone of
classicism; the *galant* style was finished, thanks not only to Gluck
but also to the man who had provided its most skilful monument in
serenades and divertimentos. In the cries of 'O!' which set the tone
of Mozart's mighty chorus, one can sense once more the sublime
awe of the three shouts of 'Herr!' which open Bach's St John
Passion, strains that music had not known for about half a century.

The Viennese decade

Compared with the preceding picture, the whole of Mozart's work at
Vienna under the new conditions of professional independence
reveals the clear minimization of the two genres most closely linked
with the life of the Salzburg court, music for the church and music

for entertainment. The effect of his freedom stops at this external observation; there were no other abrupt changes of direction except for the sudden run of piano concertos. The maturity of Mozart's language was well established by 1780, however, and was certainly something out of the ordinary. At Vienna his genius fermented and reacted from its heights to encounters that would have been difficult to envisage in the provincial isolation of Salzburg: encounters with Bach's counterpoint (the assimilation of which was his final acquisition on the purely musical level), with the phenomenon of the public piano concert, with the new kind of musical comedy of Casti and Paisiello, the plays of Beaumarchais and the librettos of Da Ponte, with the ideals of the human brotherhood of Freemasonry, and, once again, with national German opera.

With *Die Entführung aus dem Serail*, performed at the Burgtheater in the summer of 1782, the *Singspiel* reached unsuspected heights, which, with their comic Turkish style, remained unsurpassed; as Goethe was to say to Dittersdorf, the work 'marked a new era'.[39] At the same time as he was composing *Die Entführung*, Mozart put his embryonic philosophy of the theatre on paper in two letters to his father (see Reading no. 8) which declare, in opposition to Gluck and the 'literary opera', the supremacy of music over poetry (which must be 'the obedient daughter of the former').[40] He had already written home from Mannheim (1777) that his 'dearest wish' was to compose a *Singspiel*;[41] in fact the whole of *Die Entführung* is pervaded by great joy, a realm of perfect happiness and a sublimation of fun. This can be seen everywhere: in exhilarating arias, real outbursts of joy like 'Welche Wonne, welche Lust' or 'Vivat Bacchus'; in janissary choruses that resemble those in Holzbauer's *Günther* but move along more quickly and are covered, as it were, in Turkish spices; in serenades and romances full of yearning for the south; in the comedy of Osmin with the hyperbole of his low notes, like those of a baroque Cyclops; and also in the feverish vitality of the instruments, especially the woodwind, never before unleashed with such effervescence in an operatic score (which dates from the same period as the wind serenades K 361 and 388, which were written for Salzburg but are fit to rank among Mozart's greatest masterpieces). The importance Mozart attributed to the humble German genre, besides its symphonic scale and commitment, emerges from the accompanied recitatives, in one of which (no. 20) two young men, having made an unsuccessful attempt at escape and being convinced that they are living their last moments, seem like two noble souls discussing the hereafter, something which is also suggested by the libretto's use of Pietist vocabulary (which includes the words 'Seele', 'Pein', 'Todesschmerz' and 'Seligkeit'). This is, perhaps, a lapse in the opera's joyful mood and a break in its incredible momentum, but it is also a preparation for the sublimity of the final moral expressed by the pascha Selim, a worthy heir of Boccaccio's Saladin in the penultimate story of his *Decameron*, a shrewd, generous and tolerant man.

Mozart's great experience in 1782, around the time of *Die Entführung* and slightly after, was his discovery in van Swieten's library of J. S. Bach's *Well-tempered Clavier* and *Art of fugue* (and perhaps other works) and of Handel's oratorios, as well as new pieces by W. F. and C. P. E. Bach. Mozart's study of the Bachs is documented by his transcriptions of six fugues (one by W. F. and five by J. S. Bach) for string trio and of five fugues from the *Well-tempered Clavier* for string quartet, by the Fugue for two pianos K 426 and by various fugal fragments for piano (two or four hands), all of which testify to an insatiable passion for musical ideas. Although the works in which this neo-contrapuntal style appears in an explicit and almost programmatic way are not very numerous (the famous examples include the finale of the Quartet K 387, the finale of the 'Jupiter' Symphony, sections of the unfinished Mass K 427 and of the Requiem, the outer movements of the Sonata K 576 and the overture to *Die Zauberflöte*), the whole of Mozart's writing became to some extent impregnated with it. The string quartet, however, must naturally have seemed the best area in which to test this new grafting of counterpoint onto sonata form, that most austere of musical genres which Mozart had left alone for nine years and which he now reconsidered (in the Viennese environment, which was keenly interested in the quartet) with his six quartets dedicated to Haydn (K 387, 421, 428, 458, 464 and 465). In fact the signal for directing this energy came once again from Haydn, from his op. 33 quartets of 1781, with which Mozart's set displays clear affinities; but his apprenticeship with Bach, largely displayed on the canvas of the string quartet, also left obvious signs, not only in thematic ideas which were already conceived in four parts, but in a broader rhythmic style and a wider compositional range encouraged by the unpredictable dimensions of Bach's harmonic vocabulary.

The quartets dedicated to Haydn enthusiastically accept the challenge thrown down by the view of the sonata principle as a link between *static* emphasis on themes and the *dynamic* current of development and variation, and the balance that is established between richness of ideas and conceptual elaboration is the result of an impressive effort. No less than three years, a long time in terms of Mozart's creative periods, elapsed between the composition of the first quartet (1782) and the publication of the whole set (1785), and the autographs show a quantity of corrections that is very unusual in the manuscripts of Mozart's works that have come down to us (a legacy which, with its very meagre proportion of sketches, second thoughts, deletions and inserted leaves, can bring to mind the biblical temple of Solomon, built without the noise of hammers and pickaxes because it was made up of stones which had been fully finished off in the quarry). It was also natural that the vigorous ideas must have seemed tiresome to the Viennese, even though they were more favourably disposed towards the quartet than ever before. For the *Wiener Zeitung* of 1787 it was a pity that Mozart 'in his truly splendid artistic principle of becoming an innovator, [had] gone too far in a direction that would certainly achieve less in the way of feeling and the heart'.[42] This was half a century after Scheibe's criticisms of Bach, but the ideology of the *galant* style was still alive halfway through the 1780s.

If the quartets are the works most permeated by the sonata principle, the piano concertos represent its free paraphrase. The three concertos written in 1782 (K 413–15) are inferior to K 271 in their boldness of conception, but the standard of this Salzburg work was reached again with the series of six concertos written in 1784 (K 449–51, 453, 456 and 459) and was surpassed by the three concertos of 1786 (K 488, 491 and 503), and again in Mozart's final years by K 537 and 595. The discovery, made entirely by Mozart, of the sound of the piano juxtaposed with or enveloped by the orchestra and, within this scheme, of the piano combined with individual families of instruments (in particular the woodwind) makes this genre, in Goethe's terms, a kind of realm of Mothers for Mozart's creativity.[43] In the piano concerto, more than in the severe timbre of the string quartet and the concise ideal of the symphony, sonata form found itself continually exposed to new ideas even within the traditional three-movement structure: the piano enters or finishes with completely new themes, never used elsewhere; second themes or suggestions of development are introduced outside their normal environment; codas and transitional passages are full of ideas that take on a thematic dignity, fooling the analyst in his attempt to classify them as third, fourth or umpteenth themes; and there is a fondness for variations and whimsical passages that are only restrained by the imposing rhythmic unity.

The type of virtuosity employed in these concertos (and virtuosity had to be present in works with which Mozart attempted to please Vienna) turned out to be an essentially intellectual one. The performing difficulties are little more than those of the solo sonatas for piano; but there is greater employment of leaps, broken octaves and unexpected rapid chord progressions, and there is above all greater emphasis on the left hand, which is freed from its sustaining function in the symphonic structure and is often required to double the right. These are the signs of composition on a larger scale, suitable for the concert-hall, but there is no search for new pianistic techniques such as those developed by Clementi in London. More typical of Mozart's piano concertos is the broad range between their extremes of expression; in this respect the concertos are more direct than Mozart's other works which often exploit his genius for understatement. The Concertos in D minor K 466 and C minor K 491 are shaken by stormy outbursts, true precedents for the darker moments of *Don Giovanni*, while an Olympian optimism, combining a Handelian inheritance with hints of revolutionary marches, shines from the majestic heart of the Concerto K 503. The Andantes almost all tend towards the cantabile style of the romance, but their mood varies from the blissful cantilena to the sorrowful lament in which the strings' sighing syncopations and the woodwind's countermelodies against the piano seem like sad fellow-travellers. The rondo finales are based mainly on popular themes suitable for the *Singspiel* and release streams of provocative gaiety, with an outrageous liking for fun which nevertheless does not rule out the sweet flavour of affection. These characteristics are reflected in the contemporary use of the piano in chamber music, which includes the marvellous Quintet for piano and wind K 452 (1784), the two Quartets for piano and strings K 478 and 493 (1785–6) and the various trios written between 1786 and 1788, all of which are highly original works. The piano sonata, too, above all K 457 in C minor (1784), was open to a vast symphonic expression not found in any of the many examples in C minor produced by J. C. Bach and Haydn.

After four years Mozart returned with these riches to the theatre, entering the realm of musical comedy with *Le nozze di Figaro* and *Don Giovanni* (1787). The 'dearest wish', his desire to write opera, was apparent in his return to unfinished works like *L'oca del Cairo* (1783) and *Lo sposo deluso*, and also in *Der Schauspieldirektor* (The impresario, 1786), and was encouraged by his perception of the common root between dramatic dynamism and instrumental forms; he drew in his leaning towards the stage on the vocabulary of the sonata and the concerto, on exposition, development and recapitulation, and on variations, modulations and interrupted cadences. The correspondence of these formulas with human affairs, whether the most commonplace or the most exceptional, their identification with the marvellous intricacy of life, was the thread that Mozart had to unravel, whatever the tangle he must have felt confronting him when he decided on Beaumarchais' *Le mariage de Figaro* as a libretto. The choice was entirely Mozart's, not the librettist's, and however much it may have been due to the success of Paisiello's *Il barbiere di Siviglia*, it suggests a greater need for caution before passing judgement upon Mozart's 'lack of culture' simply because he did not spout quotations and theories (and no doubt there are still some who would reproach him for having passed unwittingly and indifferently through the Roman forums when no longer a child). The ability to link up the reciprocal tensions of the language of the sonata on the one hand and psychological stage action on the other must have seemed to him a much more ambitious goal than the study of classical Greece and archaeological reconstructions for the benefit of contemporary culture, or even than the resolution of the conflicts between public and private with their predetermined prejudices. In this light, his unique instrumental apprenticeship put him in a much more favourable position than Paisiello and Cimarosa, who were also shrewd men of the theatre, but for whom the instrumental side had only to smooth the way for the vocal, not to penetrate and influence it with the complete freedom shown by Mozart.

Even though his material was in effect still the same as that of traditional *opera buffa*, Mozart, with his skill in the field of instrumental music, turned a page in the chapter of musical comedy. He disposed once and for all of Arcadia and the dull remnants of pastoral life which still survived to a small degree in Paisiello and the Italians. The 'urban' element of sonata form asserted its rights; the countryside was left to the clumsy company of *Ein musikalischer Spass* K 522, and *Le nozze di Figaro* immersed itself from the opening notes of the overture (with which the very concept of 'nervousness' entered the history of music) in the swift, bustling rhythm of city life. It was this new inner swiftness that nourished Mozart's 'action music', penetrating even into solo arias and flowing naturally through the act finales, those 'types of short plays or little self-contained dramas' as Da Ponte called them.[44] The finales of Act II of *Figaro* and Act I of *Don Giovanni* are movements of musical thought that seem to reveal in their play of vertical and horizontal combinations the practices of Bach, particularly some of the great structures in the cantatas and

Passions. There are many musical aspects which push the two operas beyond the theatrical genres from which they originate. In *Figaro*, the nocturnal feeling of the last act rediscovers the uneasy ambiguity of Shakespeare's *A Midsummer Night's Dream*; it is full of staccatos, pizzicatos, string passages to be played at the point of the bow and interrupted serenades, all of which are put forward in the 'Puck-style' of early romanticism. In *Don Giovanni* the surmounting of comic barriers was due not only to the presence of entire scenes which are objectively tragic (the death on stage right at the beginning contradicted Metastasian and French taste, which made its actors die behind the scenes) but also, on a strictly musical level, to unexpected polyphonic structures (e.g. 'Tutto, tutto già si sa' in the finale to Act I), to changes of tempo for a few bars, and to sudden unisons which expand towards cosmic solemnity and are completely eccentric as far as the theatrical situation in its narrow sense is concerned.

Le nozze di Figaro and *Don Giovanni* were, however, the result neither of the simple grafting of abstract instrumental values onto two librettos, artful though they were, nor of a truly original union of Bach and French or Italian eighteenth-century comedy, but of the interaction between the two, which demanded a corresponding maturation of uniquely theatrical features. The clear division between good and evil characters, still present in *Idomeneo* and *Die Entführung aus dem Serail*, was destined to fall away as artificial; to achieve this it was necessary to be interested in man as he is, not, as Gluck and Beethoven were, in man as he ought to be. The characters of the two operas are real men and women, frustrated by conflicting forces. They do not refer to anything outside themselves, and they are not symbols; the mystery of their personalities (into which people will always continue to probe) is simply that of *being*. We do not know them once and for all, but, as in real life, through their external and internal movement, their situations and their states of mind, and here lies the crux of the connection with sonata form, which is essentially movement, development and temporality in action.

Besides transforming the stock types of comedy into real characters (e.g. the servant–mistress into Susanna and the jealous man into the Count), Mozart also confronted new ideas and created characters with complex motivations, something familiar to the subtle analysis of literary practice, but foreign to the summary typecasting of musical theatre: Cherubino, for example, is upset by the erotic disturbance of adolescence which, like Goethe's Ganymed, always seems to be saying 'I am coming, I am coming! but where? ah, where?';[45] and the Countess senses the continuous work of time and already sees herself descending the slope of old age. And then there is Don Giovanni, who is newer and more complex than all the others. There is, certainly, a symbolic element in him: his sin, well known to the western Christian tradition, is lack of restraint ('quale eccesso!' and 'gravi eccessi' are frequent comments on his activities), and when in the last act he faces divine judgement and, less repentant than ever, refuses to see in the Commendatore anything other than a 'vecchio infatuato' (crazy old man), he qualifies as a worthy follower of a whole secular, enlightened tradition. But never has a symbol had more fluency of movement and a greater capacity for driving forward theatrical action and for arousing complicity or direct sympathy. There is in Don Giovanni something of the dominant personality of the *Sturm und Drang* type, like Götz and Prometheus, who stand firmly between light and shade; but there is also a Renaissance grandeur and harmony, and the decision at the end of the first act ('Ma non manca in me coraggio, non mi perdo o mi confondo' – 'But I've got plenty of courage, I'm not going to lose heart or be disconcerted') suggests a relationship with certain characters in the *Decameron*, who, in the direst straits, only manage to get out of trouble by their wits and sporting ingenuity.

Finally, these newly minted characters often find themselves dropped into situations which are also objectively new: Susanna and the Countess, for example, dress up Cherubino and are astonished, with a trace of envy, at his pale skin; and Don Giovanni tries to make Don Ottavio and Donna Anna believe that Donna Elivra is mad, while at the same time whispering to her to be prudent and not to attract attention. Had music ever before been thought capable of realizing such delicate and complex situations? Is there anything more unstable or more fickle than the sexuality which runs through *Le nozze di Figaro*? And yet Mozart's theatrical instinct preferred this probing into man's biological nature to the exploration of the dynamics of the social classes as propounded by Beaumarchais; no licentiousness, however risqué, of contemporary libertine literature goes so deeply into psychosomatic eroticism as, for example, 'mi pizzica, mi stuzzica', 'come la man mi pizzica' and 'come il polmon mi s'altera',[46] and no swooning reaches the ecstasy of Susanna's aria 'Deh vieni, non tardar, o gioia bella'. From this point of view *Le nozze di Figaro* and *Don Giovanni* are among the very few examples of non-moralizing theatre; the happy ending of the former is paralleled by the honest ending of the latter, but how long the Count's faithfulness will last and how much Don Giovanni's punishment placates Donna Anna and Zerlina is not made clear, and things are left in an ambiguity which is the only certainty as far as the human heart is concerned.

A consciousness of summing up, comparable to the seal which *Le nozze di Figaro* and *Don Giovanni* set on the whole of Italian musical comedy, also appeared in the symphonic field, which Mozart cultivated in the Viennese decade with an unusual economy (he wrote only six symphonies) but with a previously unmatched commitment. The first symphony of the group, K 385, dates from 1782; it was linked with *Die Entführung aus dem Serail* and with the Haffner family from Salzburg, who had commissioned it from Mozart. The symphony begins with an idea that recalls the opening of the first symphony of op. 18 by J. C. Bach (1781), but this is only a localized hint – almost as if it were a grateful salute to an old teacher – whose outlines are disturbed by an anti-Arcadian fury and a feverish nervousness of movement. A seriousness of elaboration close to that of the string quartets dedicated to Haydn, but set in the rich frame of the symphony orchestra, is present in the Symphonies K 425 (1783) and 504 (1786). Finally, after the two great Italian stage works, the three symphonies K 543, 550 and 551, which have always been in the repertoire and on which the knowledge of Mozart as a symphonist was to be based in the nineteenth century, were written as a group in the summer of 1788. In K 543, the E flat major tonality confirms the spaciousness anticipated by the Piano Concerto K 271. Something of Handel's stately splendour (rare in Mozart) stirs in the slow introduction, while a sense of greatness, heralding heroic deeds close at hand, is derived from the generous provision of ideas and from the movement's rhythmic energy; together with the first movement of the Piano Concerto K 503, it was an important work for Beethoven. The Symphony K 550, too, is a summary of all the dramatic fervour connected with the key of G minor; but the tragic rhetoric is overtaken by the disturbing individuality of its themes and the tension of its harmonic ellipses, and the finale again recalls the *Sturm und Drang* through the desperate force with which it attacks the darkest regions of sensibility. After Mozart had exhausted the gloomier side of his inspiration, K 551 in C major finds in its title 'Jupiter' an accurate indication of its radiant nature; the architecture in movement that makes up the finale is a perfect union of fugue and sonata form, tossed off with divine cheerfulness by a composer who felt that he was putting a full stop to the form that he had taken up, like a little plant in bud, twenty years earlier, between London, Vienna and the Po valley.

In the first part of the Viennese decade, from *Die Entführung aus dem Serail* to the 'Jupiter' Symphony, Mozart's output flowed like a raging torrent, tending to conclude almost systematically chapters which he had opened earlier. In the course of the last three years his setback on the professional level made it less homogeneous, and he was compelled to mix works undertaken reluctantly with others accepted enthusiastically, following his own inner judgement. There was also a flowering, reminiscent of an earlier aversion to large-scale forms, of humble occasional pieces from a composer who had always written for everyone, but who now distinguished between pieces for the public and pieces for himself or for the innocent enjoyment of small circles of admirers. The works written out of necessity are never far from a statuesque frigidity, precisely because they are magisterial; their complete detachment was later to make them susceptible to both condemnation and uneasy misgivings.

This characteristic is occasionally apparent in works written for the court at Berlin – the late quartets, the quintets composed between 1789 and 1791, and the last piano sonata (K 576), whose first theme, truly fit for a Prussian soldier, is subjected to polyphonic elaborations which restore to the keyboard the counterpoint of the *Well-tempered Clavier* and the *Goldberg Variations*. But detachment from his material is evident above all in *Così fan tutte* and *La clemenza di Tito*; Mozart, who in *Don Giovanni* had united the parallel paths of *opera buffa* and *opera seria*, leaving an important legacy to the following century, had, because of the circumstances of his life, to part them again and to return to Metastasio's separation of comic and serious with two quintessential operas in these respective genres.

In *Così fan tutte* Mozart and Da Ponte returned to all the functions and customs of comic opera with a lucidity fostered by the most pitiless tone of the sceptical and rationalist eighteenth century. The Rousseau–Goldonian sentimentalist remains completely silent; there are no grand finales, as in *Figaro* and *Don Giovanni*, but rather an economy of movement and a transparency of outline achieved by pure musical invention. The very success of the trick, with its game of symmetries, relies upon a reduction in the human quality of the characters. The nocturnal scene of *Le nozze di Figaro* also involves dressing up, but here the deception fails in the end because the voice, the only stable element in a foolish game of attractions, gives itself away: Susanna forgets to alter her voice and Figaro immediately recognizes 'la voce che adoro' ('the voice that I adore'), while, in her turn, Susanna notices the Count's arrival in the same way ('Questi è il conte, alla voce il conosco' – 'That's the Count, I recognize his voice'). Donna Anna, too, recognizes her seducer's voice from its timbre, the most sensual of aural phenomena ('gli ultimi accenti,/ che l'empio proferì, tutta la voce/ richiamar nel cor mio di quell'indegno/ che nel mio appartamento . . . '),[47] – and the same was to apply, in *Die Zauberflöte*, to Tamino and Pamina. This is a race of people with very keen ears, worthy offspring of the musician who wrote some parts only after hearing the voices of the singers who were to perform them; whereas the couples who are cynically changed and then restored to each other by Don Alfonso do not recognize voices, and do not have the emotional experience which would enable them to do so. In this way the ambiguous fun of *Così fan tutte* remains attached to the characters who proclaim it ('io crepo se non rido' – 'I'll burst if I don't laugh') and does not create involvement beyond the footlights. It certainly did not involve the actor Friedrich Ludwig Schröder, who performed Wieland's translations of Shakespeare, Lessing and Goethe, tending more and more to the grandiloquence of Iffland and Kotzebue, and who in 1791 judged the opera to be a 'miserable thing which lowers all women'[48] – evidence of a new spirituality compared with which *Così fan tutte* smacked of the *ancien régime*, although the opera does not seem to have stimulated many other comments in the troubled historical times. Mozart's contact with Metastasio's *La clemenza di Tito*, which the librettist Caterino Mazzolà tried to modernize by introducing ensembles, can seem even colder. In effect it was the swansong of eighteenth-century *opera seria*, sung by Mozart in an elaborate and irrefutably masterly fashion despite his hurry (it was written in about four weeks), with a more aristocratic manner than ever, without a nod to the fashion of the times and without the slightest doubt concerning its anachronistic character.

If *La clemenza di Tito* was set in a timeless light, *Die Zauberflöte*, on the contrary, was the opera by Mozart that was most influenced by the 'spirit of the times', a manifestation that sums up the whole Austrian Enlightenment and at the same time early German nationalism: Goethe, Herder, Hegel, all were to some extent affected by it, and Beethoven regarded it with veneration. It was to be an inexhaustible source for the 'romantic opera' of Weber, Marschner, Lortzing and Spohr, branching out beyond the German countries in the work of the Slavs Smetana and Dvořák and, even at the end of the nineteenth century, in that of Rimsky-Korsakov.

The rapid pursuit of happiness, which is seen in the return to a lost but rightful lover and is reflected in various passages such as Figaro and Susanna's 'Ah corriamo, mio bene,/ E le pene compensi il piacer'[49] and Don Giovanni and Zerlina's 'Andiam andiam mio bene/ a ristorar le pene,'[50] becomes explicit in *Die Zauberflöte*, where it is controlled by a moral message: the pursuit is encouraged not merely by impulse, but by a community of wise men who extend a friendly hand to anyone wanting to leave darkness for light and to achieve happiness in the only way permitted to man, through wisdom. The point at which the two armed men, having laid aside the armour of the Lutheran chorale, fit in with Tamino's dance rhythm when he has recognized Pamina's voice, clearly shows Mozart's moral philosophy: beneath the hard surface are two kindly guides who support the man in his difficult journey ('Ja, ja, das ist Paminens Stimme! Wohl dir! nun kann sie mit dir geh'n, nun trennet euch kein Schicksal mehr').[51] The current of solidarity gives a new meaning to the re-established division between good and evil that was abandoned by the Italian operas of fifty years earlier. Now the division was restored according to the morphological laws of the fairy-tale, but it was not simply a step back towards the *commedia dell'arte* and marionette theatre; if the characters were marionettes at all, they were those discovered in the loft by Wilhelm Meister, or those idealized by Kleist in *Über das Marionettentheater* (1810) – that is, they were symbols of a state of innocence, of freedom from worldly cares and from the contradictions of reason.

Even more than *Die Entführung aus dem Serail*, *Die Zauberflöte* transcended the limits within which the *Singspiel* had remained until then, not so much through the complexity of its musical language (*Die Entführung* is possibly superior from this point of view because of its elaborate concertante approach) as through its exceptional range of different expressive styles. These vary from the humorous pathos of the *Lieder* of Papageno, the famous incarnation of the golden state of nature (he is not concerned with *Streben*), to the dazzling, brittle virtuosity of the Queen of Night; from the heavenly singing of Tamino and Pamina, who place their trust in the magic power of sound to overcome the test of fire, to the sublimity of Sarastro and the priests, and the burnished gold of their choruses to Isis and Osiris: priestly solemnity, but also secular severity, the result of a union between the *Lied* and the chorale that was still to echo in Weber's choruses of huntsmen – priests of the temple of the forest. This air of mystery and apprehensive melancholy that occurs in many passages of late Mozart – the motet *Ave verum* written for a boys' chorus from a school in Baden, the little works for mechanical organ, the veiled tones of the Clarinet Concerto, and the Masonic nobility already present in many of the Andantes in the piano concertos – is fully present in *Die Zauberflöte*; the opera places a final seal on Mozart's creative work, apart from the Requiem which was left incomplete. It can also be seen as a happy conclusion: the exotic sound of the glockenspiel played by Papageno and the pure polyphony of the three boys are just the most obvious musical signs of the recovery of an original purity, of the lost paradise in search of which Kleist was to commit suicide at the age of thirty-four, the same age as Mozart when he wrote, in *Die Zauberflöte*, his last will and testament.

Thus Mozart, who never consciously thought of reforming anything and whose character was the furthest imaginable from the statement of principles, had systematically developed all the musical genres of his time. His attitude was not far from that of the comedian in the prologue, 'Vorspiel auf dem Theater', of *Faust*: 'Suppose I talked about posterity, who'd give us any fun today?'[52] and yet *opera seria*, *opera buffa*, *Singspiel*, sacred music, symphony, concerto and chamber music had all been adapted by Mozart. Moreover, some of the early stirrings of romanticism had come to touch many of his works and to give them the transcendental glow that is missing in Haydn and that makes Mozart, even when he is rooted in the commonplace, unique. Goethe must have meant this when he considered (probably wrongly) that Mozart would have been the only person capable of setting *Faust* to music, and Mörike was to seize on this in his short story *Mozart auf der Reise nach Prag*, intermingling with the carefree journey through the crags of the Moravian mountain range and the long pleasant evening heat the continuous presentiment of death. Hoffmann was to declare in no uncertain terms that Mozart was romantic, meaning that in his music one sensed the man with all the various shades of his state of mind: not just one affection, a single nerve, but a simultaneous and changing group of them; and for this generation the knowledge of Mozart was reduced to a summary: *Figaro*, *Don Giovanni*, *Die Zauberflöte* and the symphonies of 1788.

Considered as a whole, the extraordinarily diverse span of Mozart's creativity, from the international rococo of the early years to the *Ave verum* and *Die Zauberflöte* is valued for what it is, a true internal revolution which extended the possibilities of communication through music to unknown limits. Mozart left behind a musical language that was incomparably enriched, not so much in neologisms as in syntax, in the violation of the destructive eighteenth-century sediment of strophic regularity. Mozart's oscillation between *Gemütlichkeit* (cordiality) and *Sehnsucht* (nostalgic yearning), typically Austrian and marvellously portrayed by Mörike, was only the most metaphysical of the ambivalences brought about by his language: there were also those between tragedy and comedy; between learned and *galant* styles; between demonic *Streben* and unconditional abandonment to events and the beauty of the present; and between aristocratic coldness or weary isolation and popular extroversion taken as far as the most outrageous hedonism, an everlasting source for the cheerful vein of composers like Lortzing, Nicolai and Johann Strauss the Younger. Everything that had been separate and classifiable became mutually connected, and from this fusion comes the feeling of joy and the lump in one's throat that is the fingerprint of late Mozart. From here some ideas advanced until they were superimposed on Schubert in a union whose basis was Viennese culture and compared with which Beethoven was to seem, at first sight, like an outsider from Germany who was more open to French winds of change.

IV

BEETHOVEN

27 The transformation in musical life at the end of the eighteenth century

In few other periods has the social world of music suddenly undergone such vast and radical changes as it did in the years 1770–1820. The life of a musician in 1810 was more like that of one of his present-day colleagues than the life of a *maestro di cappella* in 1760. The present circle for the production and diffusion of music is still largely that bequeathed by the final decades of the eighteenth century, when the industrial revolution and the bourgeoisie under the leadership of the state changed the face of the greater part of the countries of Europe.

The period's great social changes mainly involved, in the musical field, the replacement of the *maestro di cappella* with the independent professional musician. The old *maestro di cappella*, like other salaried persons in the service of a gentleman or a council, was a servant of greater or lesser rank depending on his patron's inclination or on the fame that he himself enjoyed. In any case he had a series of stipulated duties: to compose or direct performances of every type of music required by the public or private life of the chapel or municipality; to enforce discipline and see to the good behaviour of the musical personnel; and to buy instruments, to check that they were working properly, and to supervise the musical library. A composition belonged not to the composer but to his master, and it could not be published without the latter's consent. Around 1769 there was an important argument on this point involving Jommelli and Carl Eugen of Württemberg (who even contested the musician's right to have a copy of his scores), and later works written for private orchestras, such as those of the Princes Esterházy or Lobkowitz, also belonged to the families; even Beethoven at first had to observe an exclusive right that lasted from six months to a year, and was only later able to publish freely. The dependent musician could not usually accept outside commissions without authorization (as was the case with Haydn when he wrote for Cádiz or Paris, and with Boccherini when he sent quintets from Madrid to the King of Prussia). Resignation was at his master's discretion; in 1717 Bach was placed under arrest for insistently asking to leave the service of Wilhelm Ernst, Duke of Weimar, and in 1721 Graupner was unable to gain permission from Ernst Ludwig, Landgrave of Hessen-Darmstadt, and had to turn down the post which he had been offered as Cantor at Leipzig. It was written into Haydn's contract of 1761 with the Esterházy family that leave had to be requested six months in advance, but the prince nevertheless had the authority to refuse it.

The figure of the independent musician very gradually made headway in the second half of the eighteenth century, while the system of absolute patronage fell into decline. In some cases it collapsed through internal breakdown, as happened with Carl Eugen, who could not meet the expenses for the theatres of Stuttgart and Ludwigsburg, but the first jolt to the old regime came with the Seven Years' War (1756–63). A stream of German and Bohemian musicians, mainly from the most affected cities (like Dresden, where the orchestra which had been formed by Hasse was scattered to the four winds), headed for the centres of Paris, London and Vienna. At Paris in 1776 the minister Turgot suppressed the guilds of arts and crafts (among them the musicians' guild, the Confrérie de Menestriers de St Julien), and a rudimentary recognition of the composer's rights was affirmed in an order which gave him part of the takings from performances of his works. Some eminent or fortunate composers freed themselves from the old status, as Haydn did in Austria in 1790. Finally, the decisive blow which removed this status was provided by the wars and upheavals of the Napoleonic era; after 1815 the situation had changed almost everywhere, the musician had become an independent professional, whether he wanted it or not, with various possibilities before him from which to choose.

Maestri di cappella and employees in various capacities left without patronage and a fixed salary now had three main ways of earning their living through music: the sale of their own work to a publisher (and that meant taking instrumental music more seriously than anything else, since the publication of a stage work was still very unusual); public concerts supported by subscription; and private music lessons. The nations in which the institution of the public concert, music printing, and a substantial class of people directly interested in making music flourished thus came to the fore. The musical decline of Italy, where these three aspects were lifeless or on the way to extinction, and where the old academies had neither the dynamism nor the turnover of the modern societies run by citizens in England, France and many German cities, must be seen in this light.

Public concerts were already being given in London at the end of the seventeenth century and in the Collegia Musica in Frankfurt and Hamburg shortly afterwards; but the most famous institution was the Concert Spirituel founded in 1725 in Paris, in the Tuileries Palace, by Anne Danican Philidor. Called 'Spirituel' because its concerts took place in the two weeks of Easter and in the religious festivals during which the theatres were closed, and administered at one time by the Académie Royale de Musique and run as an independent enterprise, the Concert became the chief centre of attraction in Parisian concert life from the middle of the 1770s. It was much more lively than the private institutions, although the latter were also active, following as they did in the footsteps of the orchestras of Prince Conti, the Baron de Bagge and La Pouplinière. The repertoire, as was normal at that time, consisted of alternate instrumental pieces and vocal arias from operas, and the names of Piccinni and Paisiello were joined more and more frequently after 1777 by that of Haydn. In 1784 the Concert Spirituel moved from the Salle des Suisses to the larger Salle des Machines, while other societies, such as the Concert des Amateurs (which became the Concert de la Loge Olympique in 1780, the organization that commissioned the 'Paris' symphonies from Haydn), also entered the field. In his rural seclusion, accustomed to a fixed salary (sometimes, it is true, accompanied by extra payments), Haydn was astonished by the money he was offered – twenty-five louis d'or for each symphony and five more to publish the six symphonies in France. A piece of music could, then, be valued for its intrinsic quality, besides its generic occasional function for public events.

In London there was competition between the Bach–Abel Concerts (1764–82), the Concerts of Ancient Music (1776), which were supported by the court and were largely devoted to Handel, and the Professional Concerts (1783–93) founded by Clementi, Cramer and Salomon, the last of whom turned independent with the Salomon Concerts (1791–5). In Leipzig, the Grosses Concert was founded in 1743 by sixteen businessmen; after the Seven Years' War, Johann Adam Hiller renamed the institution the Liebhaber Konzert

(Amateurs' Concert), then the name changed again to the French-style Concert Spirituel (1766), and in 1781 it finally became the still-existing Gewandhaus Concert. A Concert Spirituel was also formed at Berlin in 1785 by Reichardt, and the years around the turn of the century saw the birth of musical societies, especially for choral singing, in several German cities: the Singakademie in Berlin (1791), the Singverein in Leipzig (1802), the Gesangverein in Lübeck (1805), and the Caecilienverein in Frankfurt (1818).

At Vienna the aristocracy was involved with the bourgeoisie and the instrumental players to such an extent that the necessity to form concert societies of the London and Paris type was felt relatively late – no earlier, in fact, than 1782, when concerts were organized by an Englishman, Philipp Martin, in the Augarten pavilion where Mozart appeared as a pianist. Concerts in aristocratic houses were open to all music lovers; those in Prince Lichnowsky's house were a regular Friday morning rendezvous, in which even the professionals who played in the evening at the Burgtheater would take part. Musicians could hire the auditorium of a theatre directly as impresarios themselves, playing for their own profit, while the organization and diffusion of musical culture spread to societies of professionals or amateurs like the Gesellschaft der Musikfreunde (1813).

The other incentive to free activity came from the diffusion and progress of music printing. Although there was no copyright law, there were more opportunities for a composer, even if he had only a mediocre reputation, to get his own instrumental works published than there had been in the past. The system of reservation by subscription also became common for publications, which were announced at the appropriate time by public notices in the newspapers. By the mid-1760s, publishers in Paris and London, encouraged by the success of the Mannheim school, had already set up a new technique of retailing, the 'Symphonie périodique' (or 'Periodical Overture'); rather than putting onto the market volumes containing groups of six symphonies or quartets by one composer, it seemed more convenient, 'pour faciliter le choix de Mrss. les Amateurs de la Musique',[1] to put out works one at a time, alternating various composers in weekly or monthly instalments by subscription. But it was new printing techniques that enlarged the market in a decisive way; although the copperplate method of printing had already offered the possibility of using plates that were cheaper than those of copper, it was above all lithography (i.e. changing from the plate to a special type of limestone that was tried out by Senefelder around 1796) which provided advantages in the cost and the number of copies that could be printed and which promptly became widespread.

In the second half of the eighteenth century the chief centre of music printing was Paris, where there was a host of publishers, including Sieber, Bérault, Venier, Imbault and Richault, almost all with branches in the main European cities. Rivalry with London (Walsh, Bremner and Corri) was very strong; J. Julius Hummel was working in Amsterdam and Berlin; the oldest German publisher was Breitkopf of Leipzig, who later worked in association with Härtel; Schlesinger was working in Berlin, and Schott in Mainz; and in Vienna Artaria, the publisher of Haydn and of many works by Mozart and Beethoven, stood out above Torricella, the Bureau des Arts et d'Industrie, Mollo and Hoffmeister. Italy, the world leader in the art of music printing, now took lessons abroad: in 1807 the twenty-two-year-old Milanese copyist Giovanni Ricordi was working in Leipzig at the firm of Breitkopf and Härtel, and a year later he began his own business in Milan.

Music lovers who joined together in concert or cultural societies nevertheless wanted to get to know the music at first hand or at least to make it known to their families, as a sign of their affluence; thus there was a far greater number of pupils than that offered by some princely families to provide work for the modern musician of the big cities. It was a phenomenon that was particularly connected with the popularity of the piano, whose makers, like the Érards (Paris and London), the Heynes (Vienna), the Steins (Augsburg and Vienna), Johannes Zumpe and Broadwood (London), and Schiedmayer (Erlangen, near Nuremberg), achieved around the mid-1770s great technical breakthroughs in the area of strength and intensity of tone. Around 1780 Hofrat Bauer of Berlin experimented with a colossal piano christened the 'Crescendo', a pyramid three metres high and one metre wide, with metal strings, three pedals and a mechanical device for key transposition; but the real path of development lay rather with the small-scale instrument, the upright piano that Matthias Müller began to build in the early nineteenth century, opening up to the instrument the inexhaustible market of domestic music on a vast scale. Playing in concerts, publishing, giving private lessons and selling instruments could of course be practised at the same time: Clementi in London and Ignaz Pleyel in Paris were publishers and piano makers besides being composers and concert performers; and Le Duc and Gossec organized concerts in Paris. For others the profession extended beyond musical frontiers: Viotti in London, after failing as a theatrical impresario, ventured into the

French wine business instead of exploiting his talent as a violinist, and for some time Reichardt managed salt mines at Halle. The impression that some people were incapable of regarding music as a free profession provides evidence of a state of uncertainty and a readiness to try anything; a thorough survey of this aspect would probably take some of the glory away from Grétry's words when he remembered having assisted in a 'revolution among musicians that slightly preceded the great political revolution. Yes, I remember it well, the musicians, whom public opinion scorned, suddenly got up and rejected the humiliation that was being heaped upon them.'[2]

It is scarcely necessary to observe that this freedom did not in itself give any guarantee of artistic quality to the musician of modern history, who, free from immediate detailed instructions from his master or protector, could be subject in a similar way to the kind of demand imposed by the musical market. It is important to draw attention to a few general aspects revealed by the new course: above all to the competitive spirit, a symptom of the sense of energy and movement that the Seven Years' War had already imprinted on the weak life of Europe. In Paris in 1774 Gluck and Piccinni were to have rivalled each other over the same libretto, and in 1781 the director of the Concert Spirituel, Legros, increased interest in Haydn's *Stabat Mater* by comparing it with two other settings, Pergolesi's everlasting work and another by a certain 'père Vito'. The stimulus of rivalry appeared in composition competitions and above all in the concert field, where a technical maturity and a growing skill in the use of instruments that had up to now been of limited soloistic capabilities became established. On looking through the records of the Paris Concert Spirituel alone, it is clear that the violin and the human voice, which had been dominant up to 1760, were no longer unrivalled: in 1764 a horn player from Strasbourg, Jean Joseph Rodolphe, after working at Parma and Stuttgart at the time of Traetta and Jommelli, demonstrated the virtuoso possibilities of the hunting horn; and soloists on the oboe and flute, and slightly later on the clarinet and bassoon, appeared regularly from the 1770s onwards. The harpsichord was not popular owing to its limited volume of sound, but with the fortepiano the position changed; Mme Lechantre used it in 1768, one of the first times that it had been used in a public concert, and from 1780 pianists became more and more numerous. The organ, however, disappeared, while soloists on the harp, the guitar and the mandolin put in occasional appearances.

A subsequent widening of the historical horizon of the music that was performed corresponded to the expansion of instrumental frontiers. The composers of 1770–80, however prolific and industrious, could not fulfil the requirements of concert societies, and so people looked to earlier music. Not only in London, with the Concerts of Ancient Music (where 'ancient' meant music of twenty or thirty years earlier, i.e. Handel), and in Vienna, with the Konzerte alter Musik (1816), but also elsewhere, music began to be considered as being no longer an exclusively contemporary art, and works by practically unknown composers who were no longer alive were drawn from the past, sometimes in order to provide comparisons with living composers. The idea became established that the repertory piece might have just as much novelty value as a new work, and the whole situation was reflected in reviews, articles and discussions at the dawn of a new historical awareness.

The theatrical *querelles*, especially the one between Gluck and Piccinni, had already helped to widen the historical horizon because people dug into the past in order to strengthen their own ideas. So, too, in the theory of teaching, respect for one's predecessors gave a stronger foundation for teaching methods; Clementi, for example, published works by Scarlatti and Bach. But the expansion of documentation by this time allowed the birth of music historiography as an independent activity: Padre Martini's *Storia della musica* (1757–81) and *Esemplare: Saggio di contrappunto* (1774), the Jesuit Antonio Eximeno's *Dell' origine e delle regole della musica colla istoria del suo progresso, decadenza e rinnovazione* (1774) and the Benedictine Martin Gerbert's *Scriptores ecclesiastici de musica sacra* (1784) are some of the final impressive contributions of religious culture to the field of music; but new voices appeared with the 1770s. The music historian and organist Charles Burney did not have much faith in the educational value of music, considering it a diversion and a luxury, but it was to his credit that he did not try to prove theories or confirm positions of dominance, and instead of being interested in the origins, progress and decay of every type of music, he was interested in the musicians of his day. He became a musical traveller, and in publishing *The present state of music in France and Italy* (1771) and *The present state of music in Germany, the Netherlands, and United Provinces* (1773) he presented the reader with a real kind of music instead of a literary one reconstructed on classical Greek and Latin models. In 1776 the *General history of music* by another Englishman, the lawyer John Hawkins, appeared at the same time as the first volume of a similar *General history* by Burney. A complete

awareness of historical writing as a profession was shown by
Nikolaus Forkel, a product of the great academy of learning in
Göttingen, who already tended to consider music in the context of
general philosophical and artistic history. Forkel held courses at the
Georg August University which were attended by A. W. Schlegel,
Tieck, Wackenroder and Humboldt; in 1788 he published the
Allgemeine Geschichte der Musik, in 1792 the *Allgemeine Literatur der
Musik* (an early scientific musical biography), and in 1802 the mono-
graph *Über Johann Sebastian Bachs Leben, Kunst und Kunstwerke*,
one of the first steps towards the rediscovery of Bach, comple-
menting the activity of van Swieten in Vienna and that of Carl
Friedrich Zelter, Goethe's musical adviser, in the Berlin choral
societies.

In effect, especially in the German cities, lasting links were forged
between music and culture based on general problems of critical
methodology, historiography and aesthetics, the science of art and
beauty which, following Kant's *Critique of judgement* (1790), already
had its own distinct, independent life in relation to other spheres of
learning. If one wanted to illustrate the typical musical intellect of
the late eighteenth century, one would no longer think of Padre
Martini, who remained rooted in Bologna, but rather of someone
like Reichardt, who registered at the University of Königsberg,
passed through the German cities on concert tours as a pianist and
violinist, and was associated with C. P. E. Bach, Haydn and Beethoven just as he was with Klopstock, Goethe, Herder and Lavater.
He rediscovered Bach, linking him with the feeling for the Gothic
that Strasbourg Cathedral aroused in Goethe; in Italy he experienced
the revelation of Palestrina, and he got to know Handel's music in
London and Gluck's in Paris. Points of reference increased and
adapted to one another, and increasingly numerous and binding
ideas for current music came from the background of history. The
assumption in Hegel's *Aesthetics* that 'the conditions of our present
time are not favourable to art' in fact meant that in the early years of
the nineteenth century the modern artist was not only more and
more influenced 'by the loud voice of reflection all around him', but
also stood within a similar world of reflections, nourished by knowledge and the history of art. Furthermore, he 'could not by any act
of will and decision abstract himself from it; not could he by special
education or removal from the relations of life contrive and organize
a special solitude to replace what he has lost' (i.e. Greek art or the
golden age of the late medieval period).[3] In the musical field, then,
this extremely fertile process began in the last decades of the eight-

eenth century with the new society's first steps beyond the immediate utility of music and beyond its nature as an art of the present, without a past and without a history.

28 Music and the French Revolution

The period of roughly a quarter of a century (1789–1813) which included the French Revolution and the Napoleonic Empire was, as far as political, social and civil upheavals are concerned, the greatest turning point in the historical period dealt with in the present work. France returned to the height of European esteem in every sense, and became the object of analysis and discussion, praise and condemnation; the Revolution immediately became a European talking point through eye-witnesses, accounts of travellers or emigrants, and letters or reports from Paris that were published in journals, especially in England and in German cities, which were very rich in periodicals. And it became all the more so in autumn 1792 when, on 20 September at Valmy, the revolutionary and republican army of Dumouriez and Kellermann forced the Austro-Russian troops led by the Duke of Brunswick, a veteran of the Seven Years' War, into retreat. This victory of a makeshift army of citizens against the mercenary armies of old dynastic Europe was hailed enthusiastically even outside France: Kant, Herder, Klopstock, Lavater, Alfieri and Goethe (who was present on the battlefield) all regarded that day as the beginning of a new period of history. 'Heliopolis, in the last year of the old obscurantism' was the verdict offered by Fichte in his *Zurückforderung der Denkfreiheit von den Fürsten Europens* (1793).[4]

This broad agreement in European intellectual life up to 1793 is explained by the immediately contemporary interpretation of the Revolution: it seemed to be the necessary extension of a revolution that had already been undertaken in philosophy, literature and the arts. Ideas about the rights and the value of man, the argument against tyranny and the praise of virtue and feeling were all themes of Enlightenment culture which ran through fiction and through the theatre inspired by the middle classes of the second half of the eighteenth century: this is what happened as a result, people said, with a predictable time-lag between literature and reality. This interpretation certainly did not help an understanding of the real revolution, the Terror of 1793–4, and in fact many people who had previously hailed the Revolution enthusiastically now condemned it, while others were faced with the problem of justifying it. For everyone, at any rate, it was a powerful and lasting reason to examine one's own position and to rethink traditions and customs, a violent shock that upset consciences, a confrontation with real social problems that were unknown to the rather vague outburst of the *Sturm und Drang*; and so it was an inexhaustible source of suggestions and ideas for investigation for the following era, a legacy of experiences for the whole of European history, whatever one might consider the initial cause to have been.

In considering the effects of the French Revolution in the musical field it is usual to attach great importance, with hindsight, to certain episodes in operas written around the time of the Revolution, thus emphasizing the literary content of the libretto. In this way advance notice of the Revolution has been heard in 'Se vuol ballare signor contino' from *Le nozze di Figaro* (1786), the quintet 'Viva la libertà' from *Don Giovanni* (1787) and the finale of Salieri's *Tarare* (1787; 'Homme ta grandeur, sur la terre,/ N'appartient point à ton état:/ Elle est toute á ton caractère'),[5] while, in musical terms, unisons, sforzatos and minor keys in a *Sturm und Drang* mould have been given revolutionary significance. But this approach, which hinges on the fact that these works were composed only shortly before 1789 or were connected with Paris, derives from the classic interpretation already mentioned of the Revolution as a consequence of previous innovations on a cultural level, and does not take into account artistic works written in a totally different environment and which have nothing in common with 'revolutionary' music. Also from the point of view of non-musical content, the almost total lack of interest shown in the four performances of *Le nozze di Figaro* in Paris in 1793 should be pointed out; Méhul's *Hymne pour la fête des époux* (1798), which appeals to God in a soft C major *andante* to make 'par le chaste hymen nos moeurs incorruptibles', is an example of the sort of music, far removed from nocturnal intrigues or Cherubino's agitation, that could be born of the experience of the Revolution.

The musical repercussions of the Revolution should be noticed first of all from the point of view of the organization and development of certain genres; the new phenomenon, which had never before existed on such a vast scale, was state intervention in artistic production and circulation. Instrumental music had no immediate relevance, and was therefore neglected; the concert life of Paris, the richest in Europe along with that of London, almost ceased, while attention turned to the theatre. From April 1790 the former

Académie Royale de Musique, the Opéra, became the responsibility of the city of Paris, which ran it through a committee. The National Assembly declared that theatrical activities were free from any form of official control, and improvised companies and entrepreneurs and cheap forms of theatrical performances grew up. The traditional ban on theatrical activity during Holy Week, the time of the Concert Spirituel, was abolished; in August 1793 a motion of the Convention proposed that three times a week (once at the expense of the state) the theatres should put on *tragédies républicaines* like those of *Brutus*, *William Tell* and *Caïus Gracchus*',[6] and similarly that performances contrary to 'l'esprit de la révolution' should be banned and their directors arrested and punished. When France was besieged (in June 1793), the Opéra put on Louis Jardin's *Le siège de Thionville*, the preface of whose libretto praised the use of the memorable subject as the choice of citizens who loved to see on stage 'those virile republican virtues which victoriously oppose the timid and *fantastique* virtues of monarchies'.[7] In spite of all this, the Opéra's theatre, exceeding mere stagnation in classical subjects (e.g. *Fabius* and *Horatius Coclès*), showed a glaring rigidity in its repertoire: Piccinni's *Didon* was performed 250 times up to 1826, Salieri's *Les Danaïdes* 127 times up to 1828, and Sacchini's *Oedipe à Colone* 583 times up to 1844. It was a completely different case with *opéra-comique* at the Favart and Feydeau theatres, two of the places most sensitive to the new musical life of Paris. In the early years of the Revolution *opéra-comique* was distinguished not so much by its republican topics, with characters like Brutus and Gracchus, as by its immediate reflection of contemporary events and its suitability as a medium for current news as a result of its more flexible structure and its division of sung and spoken parts. In 1794 the Favart and the Feydeau competed over the staging of the death of Barra and finished together on 5 June with Grétry's *Joseph Barra* and Jadin and Léger's *L'apothéose du jeune Barra*. The tone of the genre of *opéra-comique* rose, as witness its new names: *comédie héroïque*, *fait historique* and *trait civique*. The Jacobin theatre's commitment was also felt in Italy, and in Milan F. S. Salfi, in the preface to *La congiura Pisoniana* (1797), proposed a type of work that aimed at 'education' and the 'heart' rather than the ear; these proposals did not, however, take root in the formal structure of fully sung opera, which remained the only type able to suit Italian taste.

Furthermore, beyond the theatres and concert-halls, the Revolution caused a flood of music written for open-air performance in streets and squares. An impressive number of songs (over two thousand are known from between 1789 and 1794) were written by professionals or by occasional poets and musicians, original compositions or parodies of well-known tunes with new words. On a more general level, the new state, having got rid of the Catholic church, aimed at creating a new religion, with its sacred texts (the constitution), its symbolism, its new cults (Reason and the Supreme Being) and its liturgical songs: odes, marches, military music and hymns to liberty, to nature, for wedding feasts, for agricultural festivals, and for the departure and return of the army became the most typical kinds of music for revolutionary use. In festivals on the square of the Bastille or the Champ de Mars to celebrate historical days (such as 14 July and 10 August) or in praise of those who had fallen in the Revolution, a new liturgy *en plein air* materialized which had as ministers ranks of players and singers and the Opéra's corps de ballet; the décor and movements were supervised by Jacques-Louis David, who acted as artistic director and who was trusted by the revolutionary (and later imperial) government in all artistic matters. The Requiem Mass found its open-air equivalent in the funeral march, following a grandiose musical view of death that was to have such a hold on Berlioz. The attention that was paid to music as a medium for propaganda gave a new stimulus to the profession of teaching; in 1789 an officer of the *Garde Nationale*, Bernard Sarrette, founded the band of the guards with forty-five musicians; it was promoted in 1793 to the Institut National de Musique and in 1795 to the Paris Conservatoire, and was directed by Sarrette himself until 1814, with many professors from the original military nucleus. A movement also started up to safeguard and catalogue the libraries and instruments abandoned by aristocratic exiles or prisoners which went to make up the first stocks of the Bibliothèque Nationale.

With so much material the problem of a typology of revolutionary music passes into the background; especially in the early years, people seized hold of what music there was, the genres that were readily available. At the beginning of 1790 a document entitled *Suppression de toutes les académies* appeared in circulation in Paris (it was even introduced into German universities and rejected there by indignant critics) which proposed, after the suppression of the clergy decreed by the National Assembly, the abolition of the academies, which were 'the clergy of sciences, literature and the arts'. But there was no movement of that kind in music; Gluck and Sacchini were very popular, and it was enough to adapt republican words (in some cases written by Marie-Joseph Chénier) to their choruses, such as 'Poursuivons jusqu'au trépas' from the former's *Armide*, or 'Grand Dieu! de mille maux' from the latter's *Dardanus*, which was thought to be much more suitable than a generalized Te Deum to celebrate the first anniversary of the 14 July. August Vestris continued to be the great star of ballet at the Opéra. The overture to *Démophon* by Vogel, a follower of Gluck, was performed in 1791 by a band of twelve hundred instruments, including a dozen tam-tams, in the Champ de Mars in honour of the victims of Nancy; and the triumph of Rameau's *Castor et Pollux*, modernized by Candeille and given at the Opéra over a hundred times between 1791 and 1800, is significant. And if the *tragédie lyrique* was still popular, more flexible and attractive genres like the *opéra-comique* were even more successful; when the Opéra reopened its doors after a seven-day closure on 21 July 1789, it revived Rousseau's *Le devin du village* 'in aid of poor workers'. Old composers who had made their careers under the *ancien régime*, like Grétry and Gossec, were happily accepted, and Gossec became almost the official musician of the early years of the Revolution. The legacy of the aristocratic, courtly suite was still drawn on through the *pas de manoeuvre* and *marches*: *Ça ira*, the prototype of revolutionary songs and, along with the *Marseillaise* by the soldier–poet Rouget de Lisle, the only song that later retained its fame, was taken from a fashionable work well known to everybody, Bécourt's contredanse *Le Carillon National*.

The symbolic weight with which these texts were charged eventually gave their musical themes an unfamiliar importance as the unwitting bearers of contents that were foreign to them in origin. Between 1790 and 1793 newspapers like the *Chronique de Paris* or the *Orateur du peuple* were full of references to the success and circulation of songs of a revolutionary tone – a group of people, for example, managed to get *Ça ira* played on the organ, a sacred instrument for the divine office, and there was another performance of the song which replaced a Te Deum – references to what amount to no more than elementary debates dealing with music which enlarged its emotional sphere and its relationship with real life.

Nevertheless it would be too much of a limitation to reduce the French Revolution's influence on music to the purely functional level; it had an effect, too, on musical language itself. The first obvious phenomenon to be displayed was the extraordinary advance made by wind instruments through their technical progress and varied usage. Sarrette founded the *Magazin national de musique*, a monthly periodical of patriotic hymns with a circulation of twelve thousand which spread wind music into every city in France and added to the rapid publication of 'methods' for playing the clarinet, horn, bassoon and trumpet. Percussion instruments, though less susceptible to immediate developments, received the same stimulus, making use of a variety of sounds that were already familiar from the janissary military bands: there are tam-tam and bass-drum rolls in Gossec's *Marche lugubre (pour orchestre militaire)* and a cannon is actually required in the same composer's *Triomphe de la République*, along with a gigantic orchestra of woodwind and brass. Descriptive, programmatic music made increasing use of new ideas; the 'battle' genre revived its laurels which had been left to wither since the *galant* era, often making use of detailed captions. A Bohemian living in London, Franz Koczwara, became famous for *The Battle of Prague* (1788), a sonata inspired by an episode in the Seven Years' War, but the genre became especially popular with the Napoleonic wars, producing pieces such as *La bataille d'Austerlitz* (1805) for piano and violin and *La bataille d'Iéna* (1807) by Jacques-Marie Beauvarlet-Charpentier. The programmatic character of such works, in fact, took on the aspect of numerous quotations, in the form of a *pot-pourri*, of national hymns with their unfailing and effective significance, almost like a coat-of-arms in sound (this is also the case with Beethoven's 'Battle Symphony', which is part of this line of development). The strategic importance of these themes, on the other hand, led to a rich output of variations and fantasias on arias or patriotic hymns, which proved an early spoke in the wheels of the stricter sonata style.

Another effect of the revolutionary decade was to increase the circulation of spacious, solemn and excessive musical styles. Many of Gossec's works were really still on a small scale, and gay dances (like the *carmagnole*) had the easy gait of the *opéra-comique* or the Italian-style 6/8 (Cherubini's *Hymne pour la fête de la jeunesse*, 10 Germinal 1799,[8] could be viewed as a simplified version of 'Giovinetti che fate all'amore' from *Don Giovanni*). But a slow and massive tone, with a simple form, became common in the revolutionary hymn, especially when it was in E flat major; Gossec's *Hymne à Voltaire* for three male voices (1791) and *Hymne à la Liberté* 'at sunrise on the square of the Bastille' (1793) already recalled the tender Masonic and Habsburg E flat major of Mozart's *Die Zauberflöte*. Méhul liked an even more open spaciousness, and Cherubini's *Ode sur le 18 Fructidor* (1798)[9] had a width of range and a breadth of manner that almost suggests a Handel with French citizenship. The expanded conception of harmonic rhythm (long stretches of tonic or dominant for several bars and long pedal notes) became increasingly established, something which was totally opposed to the logic of sonata form, where no single bar is without purpose. The simple unison chorus which replaced intricate polyphony, apart from helping performance by non-professional singers, was given noble connotations through its historical reference to Greek music which had apparently produced so many memorable effects in listeners' minds, even without using harmony and vertical combinations of sounds.

Basically, this liking for the grand and the static meant a strengthening of Gluck's values and their development *en plein air*, in the march and in harmony, as the wind band had shown. Of the two branches of development of the *Sturm und Drang* in music, Gluck and the sensibility of C. P. E. Bach, it was the first that continued in the early nineteenth century; the other one, the branch of fantasy and conversation in short phrases, rapidly became exhausted, and by the beginning of the new century it was already difficult to find any real trace of it.

29 The origins of romanticism

Around the last decade of the eighteenth century, in the years of the French Revolution and the European wars, all the currents which since about 1760 had been moving in the most varied fashion away from the old artistic ideal based on sentiment disciplined by reason and involving the imitation of models of excellence, a careful choice of fine material, and a formal balance established themselves with the first manifestations of the 'romantic' movement in its historical sense.

The category of 'popular' culture now appeared with indisputable clarity; the anthologies of folk poetry already popular with the *Sturm und Drang* movement and the followers of Ossian, such as Thomas Percy's *Reliques of ancient English poetry* (1765), which was translated and imitated in Germany by Goethe, Schiller and Bürger, and later in France by Hugo and in Italy by Berchet and Prati, and which was followed up by Walter Scott in his *Border minstrelsy* (1802–3), were in fact among the cradles of romanticism. Folk songs reflected even better than the work of an individual poet the hearts of peoples in their primitive phase, each one different from the rest and recognizable by the roots it had sunk in particular customs, stories and legends; this was the fundamental idea of the *Volkslieder*, 'songs of every people and country' (1778–9) published by Herder. It seemed impossible at that time to guarantee noble and sincere feelings without a definite country of origin, and in Herder's footsteps the scope widened, from Pratsch's *Russian folksongs* (1790), from which Beethoven took his 'Russian themes' in the op. 59 quartets, to Thomas Moore's *Irish melodies* (1807).

The emphasis on the popular brought with it a new consideration of nature as a single entity with man. In 1796–7 Schiller published *Über naive und sentimentalische Dichtung*, defining poetry in which unity with nature is unconscious as 'naive', and that which consciously searches for that unity as 'sentimental'. But even within current taste the tone and situation of the natural setting and surroundings were changing: it was no longer the time for pleasant general scenes like sea-shores and country areas without strict geographical locations, but for Switzerland, Scotland, the Tyrol and Savoy, which stripped away privileges reserved for Arcadia and Partenope's gardens. The discovery of Alpine nature was the order of the day as a result of the early climbs made between 1780 and 1790 and the *Voyages dans les Alpes* (1779–96) published by the Genevan geologist Horace-Bénédict de Saussure. The *air savoyard* achieved a success that was to last for a long time, from Dalayrac's *Les deux petits savoyards* (1789), which remained in the repertoire for forty years, to Cherubini's *Les deux journées* (1800), and its echo can still be heard in Donizetti's *Linda di Chamounix* (1842). Dances like the schottische (the 'German polka') and the Ländler threatened the minuet's supremacy and paved the way for the success of the waltz. From Switzerland came the *ranz des vaches*, an Alpine melody sung or played on the alphorn to bring in the scattered herds and later stylized in 6/8 in works on Swiss subjects.

Just as important as the position of nature defined in geographical terms is that of the history of individuals and of the fatherland. In 1790, at the imperial celebrations at Frankfurt, Iffland's *Friedrich von Austria*, not Mozart's piano concertos, was the main production. Karoline Pichler and Joseph von Collin wrote plays and poems dedicated to Rudolf, the founder of the Habsburg dynasty. The 'Habsburg legend' grew up: in 1804 Francis II, Emperor of the Germanic Holy Roman Empire, had himself crowned Francis I, Emperor of Austria, with an act of chancery that created a legendary form of the Austrian supremacy in Europe that had actually been lost by then to Prussia and to Napoleon.

Many seeds thrown out by the *Sturm und Drang* were consciously matured and developed: Heidelberg's 'romantic circle' (Arnim and Brentano), Novalis, Tieck and others, disagreeing with Voss and Goethe, turned their attention to the north, to German myths and the Niebelung legend. A chorus of Valkyries had already put in an appearance in a 'heroic' *Singspiel* by the Dane J. E. Hartmann, *Balders død* (The death of Balder; 1779), but in 1808 La Motte-Fouqué revived Sigurd (the old name for Siegfried) in a play which later became part of the trilogy *Der Held des Nordens* (The hero of the north; 1810), and in 1811 he provided a compendium of all the romantic themes in his short story *Undine*. Ossian, with his retinue of heroes and poets, appeared on the Parisian stage with Lesueur's *Ossian ou Les bards* (1804) and Méhul's *Uthal* (1806); but the romanticism of the scenes and situations did not affect the music, apart from a few superficial choices of instrumental timbres (e.g. the harp). In any case there was none of the poetic fermentation provoked by the Ossianic theme in contemporary French painting, in the luminous white figures of Gérard's *Ossian évoque les fantômes au son de la harpe sur les bords du Lora* or in the moonlit collection of plaster casts in Ingres' *Le songe d'Ossian*. The passion for the Ancient and the discovery of the Orient which had ruffled the smooth surface of the middle of the eighteenth century tended to unite in romantic taste; Georg Friedrich Creuzer's *Symbolik und Mythologie der alten Völker, besonders der Griechen* (1810–12), a work in which the classical tradition was orientalized and romanticized, came from the Heidelberg circle, providing evidence of a single sensibility resulting from causes which had been cross-fertilizing since the 1760s.

But there was not only the north; Italy, too, which had lost its European supremacy under the impulse of national cultures, returned to the foreground, no longer as the mistress of the arts and philosophy, but as the 'Italie pittoresque'. An English aristocrat, Horace Walpole, had begun a horror story, *The Castle of Otranto* (1764), set, with deliberately calculated effects, in a fictitious southern Italy, and people were to become increasingly attracted to Italy with its castles and confessionals, especially writers who did not know it directly but who were nevertheless inspired by a profound yearning for the south. The glories of literary Italy, too, were the object of new attention. Dante, the least read of the Italian poets during the eighteenth century, was studied passionately at Berlin and Jena by the romantic circle of the 'Athenäum'; he was considered 'the holy founder and father of modern poetry' by Friedrich Schlegel,[10] the Italian teacher of Schelling, who, in his turn, recognized in *La Divina Commedia* a style that was 'always unique, a world on its own'.[11] Dante was also at the centre of the interests of Ginguené, the man who in 1811 published the first volume of the *Histoire littéraire d'Italie*. This rediscovery of the most famous voices of medieval Italy is matched by a widespread re-emergence of religious sensibility. For Chateaubriand (*Génie du Christianisme*, 1802) the modern world owed everything to Christianity, 'the most poetic [religion], the most human, the most favourable to liberty, to the arts and to literature'.[12] Carlo Dolci's *St Cecilia* in the Dresden art gallery thrilled the early generations of romantics with its holiness. In 1810 a group of painters, the Nazarenes, moved from Vienna to Rome, drawing on Christian tradition rather than the classical past; they had read in Wackenroder's *Herzensergiessungen eines kunstliebenden Klosterbruders* (Outbursts from the heart of an art-loving monk; 1797) of artists (such as Fra Angelico) who worked and prayed like ancient knights. The revaluation of the aesthetic quality of the Christian religion was accompanied by the re-establishment of a moral interpretation of love, a familiar link between the sacred and the secular. The eighteenth century, even at its most restrained, had never pretended to make the life of feelings and love coincide with that of marriage, whose purpose was above all the raising of children. In the turbulent climate of the revolutionary years, the distinction between the two spheres became less tolerable, and people sought the benefits of a firm union, emphasizing the value of fidelity and conjugal love and regarding their violation as a cause for concern; nineteenth-century fiction and opera were largely monogamous and often involved the related themes of jealousy and betrayal, which was regarded as a sin.

It is generally recognized that the French Revolution was foreign to the romantic movement; it was a new vision of an old conflict between the rational, mathematical tendency of France and the sentimental current which had been spreading to Europe from England, Switzerland and the German states since the early eighteenth century, with an increasingly firm faith in the personal, in love and sorrow. The Revolution made things level and uniform; it worshipped Reason and rejected fantasies. Chateaubriand discovered in exile the charm of the Breton forests and the English poets Milton, Gray and Young, while Jacobite Paris seemed a closed world to him, like Lycurgus's Sparta.

But there is no foreignness to romanticism in the style of the music. The love of newsworthy events and the contemporary element that was popular in *opéra-comique* favoured an aspect of realism, an accurate location and a conciseness without circumlocution that was to give romantic opera many ideas. The contribution made by the enriched scoring for wind instruments became evident later on; one only has to think of the number of romantic emotions that were to pass through the horn's winding, hazardous tubing. The spacious metre of the hymn and the expanded melodic phrase were also to provide useful ideas, as were folk-like themes, especially those of dances more rhythmic and more vigorous than the minuet. And then there were not only romantic subjects (the Middle Ages, Scotland and Nordic legends) but a romantic tone, the tone of enthusiastic personal discovery of new areas of thought and feeling; and the Revolution gave the world a display of gigantic energy and positive enthusiasm with few parallels in modern history. The success which Cherubini enjoyed in the years 1790–1800, in the eyes not only of Beethoven but also of Weber, and the interest in Méhul's *Joseph* shown by Weber and also by the young Wagner were early indications of a new continuity and a conscious influence that passed neatly over the differences in national roots. One could say that true musical romanticism arrived later than the literary romanticism of Hölderlin, Novalis and Tieck, but the twenty years of the Revolution and of Napoleon served more to clarify it than to distort it, providing the outburst of the *Sturm und Drang* with a worthy rival, new musical subjects and new material with which to contend and react.

30 Musical theatre in Europe up to Rossini. French opera; Cherubini, Spontini and Mayr

The operatic scene in the decades around the turn of the century shows some changes in the traditional geography of music. The most significant voices were no longer to be heard in Italy; after Cimarosa Italian opera was to some extent provincial and remote. The Neapolitan conservatoires still boasted good teachers – Nicola Sala, Giacomo Tritto and Fedele Fenaroli – but what more could they say to the musical Europe of Haydn, Mozart and the young Beethoven? The most talented Italians, furthermore, had gone abroad, settled the other side of the Alps and adopted foreign languages and customs.

In Naples, Nicola Antonio ·Zingarelli (1752–1837) followed a typical career for an eighteenth-century operatic composer, with a prolific output largely dealing with classical subjects. In 1790 he visited Paris, where he wrote a setting of Marmontel's libretto *Antigone*, but he avoided the Revolution and moved to Milan, where he achieved his greatest success with *Giulietta e Romeo* (1796). He was still writing operas up to 1811 which again, in their Neapolitan outlook, showed only a few thematic traces of Mozart. Later his activity centred on church music, written in the style of Palestrina, and on teaching; he taught, among others, Bellini and Mercadante. Also producing numerous works, this time in the comic field, Valentino Fioraventi (1764–1837), who is well known for *Le cantatrici villane* (1799), and Pietro Generali (1772–1832) were to have similar musical fortunes; they were both employed by Neapolitan theatres and Roman churches, and in both cases this activity was broken by periods of employment as artistic directors in theatres in Lisbon and Barcelona respectively.

Even Austria and Germany, which after producing Haydn and Mozart seemed the most likely candidates to succeed Italy, were not really right for the operatic genre. Mozart had died in 1791, Haydn did not write any further operas after his first London visit, and Beethoven encountered serious difficulties in getting one to work; Vienna remained chiefly a centre of instrumental culture. What did continue to flourish, after Dittersdorf and *Die Zauberflöte*, was the genre of *Singspiel* in the hands of Johann Schenk and Wenzel Müller, who provided a link with Viennese operetta. The work of Joseph Weigl (1766–1846), one of the best-known personalities of Beethoven's generation and the object of numerous sets of variations on account of his talent for writing themes, was largely for the stage. *Die Schweizerfamilie* (The Swiss family; 1809) is one of his most typical works, an idyllic hymn to the *Heimat* (homeland) dressed throughout in mountain mythology (with shepherds, rustic huts, peaks and valleys); 6/8 time is predominant and *andantino* is the most common pace of movement, with neat themes (such as the opening one) like the newly whitewashed fronts of Alpine chalets. Were it not for Jacob's *Lied*, in a penetrating and tortuous G minor, anticipating Schubert's 'Wo ein treues Herze' in *Die schöne Müllerin*, and were it not for the melancholy tone of the final *Lied* (in A minor with D sharps) shared by the flute and the voice of Emmeline, 'Only in the country where we are born does peace smile and happiness flourish' – a successful theme which gave rise within and outside Vienna to numerous *variations pastorales* and was even taken up again by Liszt in the Swiss piece *Le mal du pays* from his *Années de pèlerinage* – it would seem to be a kind of Arcadia lifted up into the mountains.

Stronger chords were heard in Paris, where *opéra-comique*, from such an independent outward appearance, demonstrated a surprising capacity for change. The French city, which was something between a republic and an empire, was the true capital of European musical theatre: a success in Paris meant a world success – this was a rule already proved by Gluck which was to hold true until Verdi and Wagner.

One type of opera which grew out of *opéra-comique*, and is definable on the basis of its plot, was very successful and is a good reflection of the taste of the revolutionary period; this was the so-called *pièce à sauvetage* or 'rescue opera', i.e. an opera which ends with a rescue of the protagonist, hero or heroine, who has been kept hidden throughout by brave friends or locked up by a cruel tyrant. In Italy the genre achieved limited popularity: the pretence of the *deus ex machina* was calmly accepted, but the fact that the saviour was a man, indeed a ruler, a powerful person arriving with his followers in the nick of time, was not very credible in Italy at the end of the eighteenth century. This may have been due to the realism of the Italian character typified by Boccaccio, Machiavelli and the Neapolitan followers of the Enlightenment, but there was certainly also a general lack of the type of enthusiasm that was widespread in revolutionary France. The situation of imprisonment and eventual release, an early romantic enrichment of *opéra-comique*, was already present in works like Monsigny's *Le déserteur* (1769), Grétry's *Richard Coeur-de-lion* (1784) and Dalayrac's *Raoul, Sire de Créqui* (1789); but in the 1790s the theme became widespread, especially after the Terror: the law of September 1793 concerning suspects, the number – around 200,000 – of French exiles, and the abundant news reports of tip-offs and arrests gave much greater importance to fear, heroism, imprisonment, liberation, and to domestic peace and the quiet life, fostering a religious sense of the precariousness of existence – it was not so much the kind of intuition and intelligence found in Beaumarchais' comedy as faith in Providence that helped one to find one's way. A famous book by de Maistre, the *Considérations sur la France* (1796), had clearly brought France to the attention of Europe as the main instrument of a Providence that warns and guides humanity along the right path by means of revolutions. The success of these romantic events with happy resolutions is seen in the convergence of several composers on the same plots. *Lodoïska* was set (in different versions) around the turn of the century by

Cherubini, Kreutzer, Mayr and Paër; but few plots met with the popularity of *Léonore ou l'amour conjugal*, a libretto 'from real life' by the magistrate Jean Nicolas Bouilly, taken from one of his direct experiences as administrator of a French department during the Terror. A woman from Touraine, dressed as a working boy in male clothing, gets into a prison where she knows her husband is unjustly held, and has the courage to aim a revolver at the prison governor at the decisive moment, while in the distance a trumpet call signals the minister's arrival which resolves everything. The subject was immediately staged at the Feydeau with music by Pierre Gaveaux (1798), a pupil of Beck (a member of the Mannheim school) at Bordeaux, but then passed into the hands of Paër (1804), Mayr (1805) and finally Beethoven (1805), who found in it the only theatrical material to his liking.

Musically, this operatic genre had its roots in the symphonic field. The castrato, the symbol of the immorality of an age which violated nature for aesthetic satisfaction, disappeared. The orchestral scoring, with many wind solos, took on a weight and impetus unknown to the old *opéra-comique*. The chorus played an active part, and soloistic vocal writing is often found even in static ensembles. Folk songs and picturesque arias, whose nationalities or more precise settings were realistically indicated, were common, but curiously enough this was a type of opera without grand melodies: a new dramatic language was mysteriously formed with a vocabulary of diminished sevenths, chromatic scales and menacing tremolos. A notion of 'dramatic music' almost completely separate from that of abstract music grew up. Colours were heightened, and the dynamics *ff* and even *fff* were no longer uncommon. There was a current, which can often seem exaggerated to the modern listener, that almost raised characters and situations to a higher plane than usual. The female role typically adopted a heroic character; while business and the activity of life distracted the man from his passions, the woman 'brooded' on hers. This was an idea, also taken up by Diderot (*Sur les femmes*), that was very widespread in the eighteenth century; but now the intensity of feeling even affected the busy woman, and in his own memoirs Bouilly gives evidence of having found in the heroic renunciation of women of every age and class, and in their determination to assist in misfortune, 'the strength to bear the cruelty and humiliation of men', like sheep threatened by hungry wolves.[13]

Dressing up in male clothing with the aim of following husbands or fiancés into battle was already common, but this was the result not merely of curiosity on the part of 'la dama soldato' (as the title of Gazzaniga's opera describes her), but of her faithfulness to her partner and her spirit of sacrifice, which was modelled on that of famous women of republican Rome: the heroic aspect ran through everything. The woman tied to the home or devoted to women's work went through a less successful period. Even Goethe acknowledged that he wanted to raise Dorothea from mediocrity, and represented her as a warrior maiden in one episode (in which she drives back the straying Frenchmen with the slashes of her sabre).[14] Noble, strong women, who sacrifice their ringlets and when necessary take up arms to save their companion's or husband's life, became common in novels and operas.

Luigi Cherubini (1760–1842) settled in Paris in the most significant period for the heroic revaluation of *opéra-comique*, and was the musician who embodied perhaps more than anyone else the historical crisis in Italian music at the end of the eighteenth century. Born in Florence the son of a musician, he approached Italian opera through Giuseppe Sarti, with whom he worked in Bologna and Milan between the ages of eighteen and twenty. For a long time he was involved in the business of writing 'additional pieces' for operas by other Italian and foreign composers. But there was also a Tuscan element in Cherubini, based on the Florentine counterpoint and organ writing of Giovanni Maria Casini, and later of Bartolomeo and Alessandro Felici, with whom he studied counterpoint in the manner of Padre Martini; he wrote Masses and cantatas for churches and religious colleges – a latent basis that Cherubini would never forget.

In 1784 he left Italy, first for London and then for Paris, where he met Viotti and wrote several Masonic cantatas. In 1787 he was one of the violinists who played in Haydn's 'Paris' symphonies and in 1788 he made his debut at the Opéra with *Démophoon*. The energy and the strong four-square rhythms associated with the key of C minor (in the overture and the opening of Act II) speak plainly: this is the C minor of Gluck encouraged by the experience of the Viennese symphony. Cherubini, unlike composers such as Piccinni, Sacchini and Paisiello, did not have a Neapolitan heritage which could be exchanged with the tradition of the *tragédie lyrique*; it cost him nothing to give equal importance to the orchestra and the voices, drawing the latter in fact into the symphonic orbit of the former. And if his angular, jerky melodic writing did not meet with the popularity of *Didon* or *Oedipe à Colone*, this provided all the more reason to turn without hesitation to *opéra-comique* and rescue operas.

The decade 1790–1800 was the happiest in the composer's long career; a newcomer in the most dangerous and changeable city in the world's artistic scene, the thirty-year-old Cherubini played the triangle in Sarrette's republican band, composed hymns and marches, received official appointments and put on four works at the Feydeau – *Lodoïska* (1791), *Eliza* (1794), *Médée* (1797) and *Les deux journées* (1800) – which made him Paris's leading musician.

In *Lodoïska*, set in a chivalrous Poland with providential raids by the Tartars, there was no longer room for graceful and catchy ideas, traditional ingredients of *opéra-comique*; even his melodic writing has an instrumental character, in the line of Mozart and Haydn rather than Paisiello and Cimarosa. A rapid style proved particularly effective in the act finales which explain the rescue opera's success as something contrived to make an impression on a public which is never lost from view. In *Les deux journées*, though far from the age of Mazarin, the emotion of the immediate crisis (derived from another real-life subject by Bouilly) and the value of the worthy action are more than ever present. Cherubini's tendency towards fragmentation, especially in the *mélodrames*, shows itself in pregnant and wholly original harmonies and in carefully calculated depths of tenderness. The contrast between good and evil is fully worked out in musical terms and is developed on a scale that is more than just personal. Thus, set against the clearly articulated rhythms of cruel soldiers, there are flowing choruses of country folk (akin to those in Haydn's *The Seasons*) and the Savoyard aria of the water-carrier Mickeli which, like a friendly word of reassurance, reappears at several points in the opera. In *Eliza ou Le voyage aux glaciers du Mont Saint-Bernard*, the threatening danger which in other works comes from some wicked person is assigned to the hostile nature of the Alps. Choruses of monks in the hospice, with lanterns, pickaxes, blankets and sacks of provisions, appeal to heaven for mercy towards the unfortunate people who risk their lives amid the ice and precipices. This scenario is typical of paintings by Caspar D. Friedrich, but is not reflected in the music, which remains impermeable to nature's terribleness and is more influenced by the popular choruses of the inhabitants of the Aosta valley going to work in France, and by the *ranz des vaches* of the alpine guides.

Médée achieved results of unequalled immediacy and vigour. The appropriate setting for classical material should have been the Opéra, but by good fortune the customary scanty structure of the *opéra-comique* – the use of both singing and speaking, the extended gestures, the slow, stately gait of the dance and the intellectualism of *déclamation* – took the work to the Feydeau. The force that emanates from the title role makes no concessions to the traditional aura of the sorceress, full of longing for revenge and annihilation, and is a landmark in musical theatre that sets itself up in opposition to the contemporary worship of the extreme products of Italian delicacy, Paisiello's *Nina* and Cimarosa's *Gli Orazi e i Curiazi*. Furthermore, there are no prominent themes in *Médée*; its melodies cannot be easily remembered, and the field is held by a mysterious force of energy that surrounds the protagonist. The orchestra surrounds and supports the voice, and the harmonic exploration suggests the resulting melodies. The D minor of *Don Giovanni* and the Concerto K 466 is clearly present, and so too is Gluck's method of progression by means of repeated cells, but these cells are merged with the broad harmonic rhythm of the ode or the revolutionary hymn (in Act III, Médée's descent from the mountain covers twelve bars of unvaried D minor), or converge in unison choruses, with bare orchestral harmonies, often in octaves, as the ancient Greeks are said to have performed them; sometimes, however, the Mozartian turn of phrase is broken up by details, by sforzatos which have an analytical function, or by augmented or diminished chords which reveal the distortion of Médée's mind.

The importance of Cherubini's first decade in Paris really lies not in his general dramatic influence, but in the quality of his musical ideas – it is these that make up his theatricality. After 1800 a difficult period began. His relationship with Napoleon, the ruler of France and all its cultural policies, involved a lack of sympathy on both sides; and even to the eyes of the public in Paris Cherubini now seemed to lack the one thing that could be expected from an Italian – a melodic gift. Furthermore, the Feydeau theatre had ceased to exist and the Opéra was becoming the real temple of imperial glory; thus, while Napoleon invited Paisiello to Paris and was later to look favourably on Paër and Spontini, Cherubini was left with his teaching at the Conservatoire and with two spells abroad, following the success of his 'revolutionary' operas in German lands. In Berlin, *Lodoïska* was put on in 1797, *Médée* (in German) in 1800 and *Les deux journées* in 1802. In the same year all three operas were given in Vienna during a memorable theatrical season in which, in the presence of Beethoven who was soon to produce *Fidelio*, they rather played the part of Paisiello's *Teodoro* opposite Mozart's *Le nozze di Figaro*.

Meanwhile in Paris Cherubini put on a performance of Mozart's Requiem at the Conservatoire, and in 1803 he returned to the Opéra with *Anacréon ou L'amour fugitif*; the opera was completely unsuccessful, not only because the plot contained no element of any type of heroism or noble patriotic feelings, but also because of the contradictions and problems that it revealed. In the overture one senses the mark of a mature symphonic imagination, with ethereal string phrases that were not without their influence on the *idée fixe* of Berlioz's *Symphonie fantastique*. Mozart, even more than Haydn, became a point of continual reference in the relation between voice and orchestra and in the admirable instrumental introductions to the arias; but the recitatives are ponderous, the musical pieces are all alike, and there is no longer the fluent agility of *opéra-comique*, nor even the entirely Italian shrewdness in not juxtaposing pieces in the same mood. This was pure music, certainly, not dramatic; but it was of second-rate quality, with predictable structures, beautiful – one could even call them original – ideas, but nothing that forms a solid conversation beyond the four-bar phrases. In 1805 Cherubini visited Vienna, where he met the elderly Haydn and Beethoven, who acclaimed him as the greatest living dramatic composer. With *Faniska* (1806), a *Singspiel* put on at the Kärntnertor theatre shortly after *Fidelio*, Cherubini returned to the 'rescue' plot and found once more the incisiveness of his earlier operas with clear traces of early Beethoven (Faniska's aria in Act II, 'Allzu tief sind des Herzens Wunden', is one of the greatest points of contact by a contemporary with the sphere of Beethoven). But Cherubini returned from Vienna empty-handed, and in fact found himself even more isolated in Paris after the triumph of Spontini's *La Vestale*.

In an artistic life that was gradually becoming more and more shadowy, his interest in sacred music revived. Here, even more than in the theatre, the contradictions of Cherubini's rich personality came to the surface in the equal use, side by side, of the vocal style of Palestrina and of imitative textures and musical ideas in a new harmonic and symphonic mould which was close to the compact nature of the chorale and in which the orchestra is once again the unit of inventive measurement. But the first style, the vocal counterpoint which Cherubini had learnt in Italy and displayed in the depressing academicism of the Credo for double choir, had lost all its bite after the 'Jupiter' finale, and only Cherubini's indecisive nature, loyal to positions that had previously been superseded, could keep it alive rather than discarding it. Thus the most impressive part of the huge *Messe solennelle* of 1811, which was written for no particular external reason, is the Crucifixus section, in which the voice is reduced to a simple repeated note over changing string and woodwind harmonies; and even in the Benedictus, the sublime atmosphere of the instrumental introduction is only spoilt by the entry of the voices.

In 1813, as if competing with Spontini, Cherubini again appeared at the Opéra with *Les Abencérages* (a subject by de Jouy, the librettist of *La Vestale*), a love story set against the background of war between Christians and Saracens for possession of Granada. Cherubini kept up with the times on the grandiose scale that linked the final phase of the *tragédie lyrique* with nineteenth-century grand opera. But the seriousness of *Les Abencérages* was contrary to all the magnificence and lack of restraint that it involved, and the most genuine moments of the vast work lie in the persuasive use of instrumental ideas and the priestly choruses that give the finales a real and profound spaciousness (in the line of *Die Zauberflöte*); they are successors to the grand funeral scenes of *opera seria* with, in addition, a new religious air.

After the fall of Napoleon, nothing was further from Cherubini's nature than to try to regain the leading position in the musical life of Paris that his by now European fame would easily have given him. The excitement that followed Napoleon's fall, with its illusion of wiping out twenty years of history and returning to the old regime, was not for him. A disenchanted Tuscan, Cherubini knew only too well that the world had changed and that the Italian Rossini and the young romantics from the other side of the Rhine were new voices, voices from which he felt equally distant, although he had provided them with decisive stimuli. He continued along his path: his stature as a teacher became consolidated, and he took over the direction of the Conservatoire in 1822, while his *Cours de contrepoint et fugue* (put together by his pupils) was to acquire such authority that it seemed in the eyes of the twenty-five-year-old Berlioz to symbolize academic composition. The Cherubini of the Restoration showed little interest in the theatre, where he was overtaken by his students (Auber and Halévy), and he reserved his intermittent bursts of energy for sacred music and a few instrumental works. The latter are essentially epitomized in the Symphony in D major (1815, composed for London at Clementi's invitation) and in six string quartets, the first from 1814 and the others written much later (see Chapter 31). But Cherubini's late work focused above all on sacred music, the two Masses for the coronation of Louis XVIII (1819) and Charles X (1825) and in particular the two Requiems for chorus and orchestra without vocal soloists. The first (1816, in C minor), composed in memory of the King beheaded by the Revolution, is a work of

continual emotional tension; the chorus, when it is treated homo-
phonically or in only two parts, quite softly, with short, faint woodwind phrases, introduces sonorities that continue in Mendelssohn
and even in the Brahms of the *German Requiem*. The other Requiem
appeared twenty years later (1836), at the centre of a golden decade
of European romanticism, after Rossini and Bellini, and after the
revival by Mendelssohn of Bach's St Matthew Passion. In D minor,
like Mozart's Requiem, it no longer has any trace of Palestrina's
style and the chorus itself is reduced to male voices alone. This
enigmatic and controversial work was conceived by the composer for
his own funeral, so that, like Canova, he had built his own funeral
monument with his own hands – an eloquent sign of the spiritual
condition of an Italy that beyond the Alps was called 'the land of the
dead'[15] and which had fallen back on the poetry of the graveyard that
had its true heart in the city of Cherubini's birth, in the tombs of
Santa Croce.

The numerous paths of Cherubini's career have taken us away from
the decade 1790–1800 which left behind so much in the field of
musical theatre. Around Cherubini, in those years, there was in fact
a whole generation of thirty-year-olds who passed through the early
years of the Revolution, contributed to the birth of the Conservatoire in Paris, and devoted themselves to the thematic enlarge-
ment of *opéra-comique*. They were more limited figures and followed
a straighter path than Cherubini, mainly on account of their more
restricted human and artistic motives; for some the new climate of
the Revolution remained the limit and the justification of their
musical activity.

While the prolific output of Nicolas–Marie Dalayrac (1753–1809)
continued with *opéra-comique* based on the model of Grétry, Jean-
François Lesueur (1760–1837) and Étienne-Nicolas Méhul
(1763–1817), following in Cherubini's footsteps, attempted a bold
enrichment of its contents, turning to adventurous, Ossianic or
biblical subjects. Lesueur, after being a provincial choirmaster,
established himself in 1793 at the Feydeau theatre with *La caverne*, a
story of bandits ending with a rescue: in Act II Alphonse, disguised
as a blind minstrel, gets into the robbers' cave where his fiancée is
being held prisoner, and his song arouses strange feelings within the
girl, a situation which makes a great impression through the swift,
straightforward music which accompanies it. The following year,
with *Paul et Virginie*, Lesueur exploited the extraordinary success of
a romance by Bernardin de Saint-Pierre set in the fabulous tropical

Ile de France. A few arias from *Ossian ou Les bardes* (1804) were called 'romantiques' but, as in Cherubini's *Eliza*, not much of the new material arouses any musical interest, except for the prominent sound of the harp, which was to leave noticeable traces in the young Berlioz. In 1809, following the example of Méhul's *Joseph*, Lesueur put on *La Mort d'Adam*, a 'tragédie lyrique réligieuse' permeated by Klopstockian grandeur.

Méhul, brought up as an organist and with strong instrumental interests, reached the stage in the wake of Gluck; of all the revolutionary group, he was the one who as an intellectual adopted the new course most firmly and who became the typical musician of the early French republic. After publishing six keyboard sonatas which are more orchestral than pianistic in style, he attracted attention at the Favart theatre with *Euphrosine* (1790), a singular mixture of Gluck and Haydn. Méhul had in effect the instinctive nature of a symphonist (see Chapter 31), as is apparent in the aggressive overture to *Stratonice* (1792) and in the opening of *Le jeune Henry* (1797); the opera was a failure but the overture, christened *Jagd Sinfonie*, became a favourite piece for German concert seasons and was well known to everyone from Beethoven to Mendelssohn. Much romantic material was collected together in *Mélidore et Phrosine* (1794), a story about adventures at sea very similar to Lesueur's contemporary *Paul et Virginie*; here, too, naive rushing scales depict frequent storms, but most important of all is Mélidore's 'prayer scene', where he anxiously awaits his beloved, who has to swim across the water to reach him: his Christian prayer is one of the earliest in operatic history, and is another symptom of *opéra-comique*'s fondness for realism and everyday affairs in its most dynamic period. But Méhul found his most suitable plot in the story of Joseph and his brothers, summed up in *Joseph* (1807), an oratorio-like opera with no female roles, devoted to the theme of paternal and filial love. The hollow spaciousness of the harmonies (with many octave doublings), the Gregorian 'incipits', the unison choruses harmonized only at the cadences, and the antiphonal structure with blocks of vocal and orchestral sound betray a deliberate reconstruction of the old style (for example in the opening of the second act with the chorus 'Dieu d'Israel') which could be called 'neoclassical' but for Méhul's lack of the delicate and intellectual skill required by this style.

More in keeping with the mould of Monsigny, Grétry and Dalayrac, however, was Adrien Boïeldieu (1775–1834), a member along with Méhul and Cherubini of the republic's musical triumvirate and a piano teacher at the Conservatoire. His adherence to the humorous vein was based on the liking for melody which Boïeldieu cultivated much more than loud noises and stark harmonies; there is, nevertheless, a ready sentimentality in *La famille suisse* (1797), and *Béniowski* (1800) is a fully fledged rescue opera. In the early years of the Empire Boïeldieu returned to cheerful subjects, rich in dance melodies, and this was the style introduced into Russia when he moved there as *maestro di cappella* to Alexander I between 1804 and 1810, leaving influences that were still to be felt in the melodic writing of Glinka. On his return home, in the years of the Restoration, he was to write his masterpiece, *La dame blanche* (1825, with a libretto by Eugène Scribe), a mixture of legend and realism, drama and comedy, with all the characteristics of the following historical period.

The Paris which crowned Napoleon as the French Emperor in 1804 was considerably different from the Paris of ten years before. A new, very rich class of bankers, businessmen and industrialists had taken possession of the city's civic and cultural life, but imperial pomp was not going to be accepted completely in music by the generation of 1760 – not by Cherubini, who was becoming more and more withdrawn and was at that time more interested in his Viennese successes; not by Boïeldieu in Russia; and not even by Méhul, who remained loyal to a republican naivety. Lesueur had displayed the bombastic style in *Ossian*, which was liked by the Emperor despite its lack of ideas, but this work had the excessive haziness of the northern mists; somehow a return to Rome was needed, and not so much to republican Rome, of which the Revolution was so fond, but to imperial Rome, with its fasces, eagles and thrones. With the early years of the nineteenth century, the excitement produced by reality and by true reports of current events had been exhausted; the necessity for celebration led back to the tendency towards idealization and to the dignity of traditional French opera. The tropics and Alpine regions were left in favour of a descent into a confused imperial city. The person who perceived this new trend and expressed it at just the right time was another Italian working abroad, Gaspare Spontini (1774–1851), who settled in Paris in 1803 at the height of Napoleon's fortune.

Educated in Naples, Spontini gave up even less in Italy than Cherubini had, but he understood the position that a musician could hold in society with a solid confidence which was the complete opposite of Cherubini. Like Gluck, he made sure of a firm circle of important friends: the Érards, piano and harp makers; intellectuals such as Lacépède, the naturalist and supporter of Gluck who became president of the senate under Napoleon; music historians like François-Joseph Fétis; and above all the Empress Josephine and the great bourgeois families with their salons presided over by famous women such as Madame de Staël or Juliette Récamier, the extremely beautiful woman who dressed like an ancient Roman, always in white, with a red fichu in her hair like a Creole as the only decoration.

Spontini appeared at the Feydeau theatre in 1804 with *Milton* (dedicated to the Empress), a 'true story' about the poet who after the fall of Cromwell took refuge in a friend's house. There is, then, something of the rescue opera in it, but more important than the incorporation of unpredictable events is a general sensitivity to the style of the *Lied* and the already assimilated presence of Mozart, Haydn and early Beethoven. Spontini's success was nevertheless founded on his inclination to grandiloquence and his instinct for the solemn liturgy of the stage, adopted with a dedication and shrewdness which was lacking in Cherubini and even in Méhul, whose ideas of grandiosity remained that of the army's *Chants du départ*. The libretto of *La Vestale*, moreover, which Étienne de Jouy had taken from Winckelmann, had been offered to Boïeldieu and Méhul and turned down by both before it came into Spontini's hands. Spontini, however, found it to his taste and achieved a return to Winckelmann, the greatest authority in the ancient field, but without the intellectual vigour of Gluck, the holy awe in the face of the gods. Antiquity, however, was treated calmly, being restricted to illustrative details, and it was no longer the sole nucleus of the inspiration of the plot. Spontini and de Jouy's skill lay in their setting in an extravagant classical frame of a moving middle-class situation, a conflict between love and loyalty to the vows of a priestess, vows that were taken in a moment of error and, in the absence of the unshakeable virtue of Gluckian figures, were subsequently regretted.

The musical key to the whole opera lies in the 'Evening hymn' which opens Act II; it is in a terse C major, more stately and measured than a revolutionary hymn, in a relaxed twilight mixture of chorus and horns, more memorable than the priests' choruses in *Die Zauberflöte* and containing the popular element that led directly to *Der Freischütz*. Spontini returned to the theme of the Evening hymn after the happy dénouement, thus marking it out as the most important in the opera: it is a strategic move that aims openly at popularity and reveals a man of the theatre who is more determined than Cherubini to achieve his desired result, and *La Vestale* was, in fact, a great European success, even on the Italian stages, a model for effects and attitudes up to Rossini and Meyerbeer. Despite numerous second thoughts, it presents a simpler language than Cherubini's; the dotted rhythm and the rising interval of the fourth are constantly present, and on these Spontini builds numerous small thematic cells (of three or five notes at the most) which are continually repeated to increase tension at all the key moments. This is a technique already established in *Médée*, but here it is adapted and used without restriction, in a way that would be unthinkable in a symphony. In fact, although keeping the orchestra at the centre of affairs, Spontini's language is not that of the sonata, but originates once again from Gluck, whose path had been broadened by twenty years of experience, by way of Salieri, Piccinni, Sacchini, Cherubini and Méhul; and in *La Vestale* in Paris the public thought that they saw before them the *tragédie lyrique* brought once again to life, with its rational, universal characters, uncontaminated by the distinctive and specific details of peoples and nations.

Things became more complicated with Spontini's second great work, *Fernando Cortez ou La conquête du Mexique* (1809); the subject has an exotic, barbaric element, but Spontini did not feel the attraction of other lands, and the exoticism is reduced to old 'Turkish' formulas and the use of castanets for Mexican dances. The celebration at the end (Napoleon attended its première) reaches levels difficult to surpass: everyone is benevolent, especially the rulers (Cortez and Montezuma), with the sole exception of the Mexican priests who, beside Montezuma's generosity, could well symbolize the intrigues of ministers and politicians. The burning of ships and the use of cavalry assured its colossal and grand scenic effect; the rhythm of the march dominates the work (in Act II Spontini does not hesitate to introduce it into a love duet between Cortez and Amazily), and examples such as this open the path to the Italian 'risorgimento' style of pieces like 'Suoni la tromba' from Bellini's *I puritani*. Nevertheless, the opera's memorable moments are in the choruses, not only those of triumph but also those of sorrow; in the first scene, with the chorus of Spanish prisoners thinking of their distant homeland, and in the opening of Act II there are simple melodies, almost dirges, with an internal harmonic poetry made up of full triads and diatonic sequences in which something of the imminent revival of Palestrina can be felt.

Spontini did not suffer immediate repercussions at the fall of Napoleon; he was appointed court dramatic composer by Louis XVIII, but the Opéra (which took back its former name as Académie Royale de Musique) lost importance and was not regarded by the

Restoration as a suitable place for its celebrations. This can be seen in Spontini's third important opera, *Olympie*, begun in 1815 but not staged until 1819. Taken from a tragedy by Voltaire, the opera returns to the classical subjects of *La Vestale*, and shows by means of a new use of musical elaboration how important the orchestra can be in musical theatre. But it got a lukewarm reception from the Parisian public before the Duc de Berry's assassination led to the suspension of its performances.

In May 1820 Spontini left Paris for Berlin, where Friedrich Wilhelm III valued him sufficiently to appoint him *Kapellmeister* and *Generalmusikdirektor*. His difficult position in the Prussian capital during the years 1820–42 was bound up with the history of German musical romanticism. Certainly Spontini, like Reichardt, worked to renew an operatic taste that was still the Italianate one of Frederick the Great's court; but in fact they made Berlin a centre for Gluck (Hoffmann's story 'Ritter Gluck' was set in Berlin). Spontini immediately put on *Olympie* in a German translation by Hoffmann (1821), after having revised the third act; but the distinctive features of his early Berlin years are really his approaches to romantic sources, like the collection of oriental romances *Lalla Rookh* by Thomas Moore (which Schumann and Berlioz loved), for which he wrote incidental music (1821): 'occasional works', as Spontini called them – such as *Nurmahal* (1822) and *Alcidor* (1825) taken from *The thousand and one nights* – all works written in the wake of *Der Freischütz* (1821) and to some degree bordering on romanticism while showing at the same time the limits of their foreign style.

In spite of his choice of suitable material (German history), these impassable limits were confirmed by Spontini's last important work, *Agnes von Hohenstaufen*, which was produced in 1829 and revised in 1837, but was not revived again and was left unpublished even at the composer's death in 1851. The *Lied* style which pervades the 'occasional works' is overwhelmed here by a kind of top-speed 'sound-engineering'; full of erudition in every bar, the opera shows signs of formal deterioration in its dramatic stature, with passages of deliberate, hard-earned excitement in its desperate search for a final chord. The 'popular' is represented by passages of stereotyped cantabile writing, like trips into the country, which contrast with the purely superficial strictness of the recitatives, with muddy orchestral chords similar to those provided more lightly by the harpsichord in eighteenth-century opera. Certainly the pearl, the great finale of Act II, stands out all the more strongly against this grey background; with its state of ecstatic excitement and its sacred conception of harmony, it is full of life, revealing a grand musical nature within a theatrical conception that was by now worn out. The necessary continuity generally missing in the opera is present in this finale, from the storm to the nuns' chorale (with a wind band imitating the organ) and Agnes's appeals, which are full of deep lyricism, clouded by disappointment and resignation. With all his good ideas and insights, Spontini was really a long way from early German romanticism in this twilight mood that was bringing to an end the period of musical cosmopolitanism with Paris as its capital. Spontini could only accompany it solemnly to the grave; he could not break free of it, let alone replace it with new romantic values.

Working on the international scene in this crucial period in European history (1790–1813) were other Italians who were much more reluctant than Cherubini and Spontini to give up the Neapolitan formulas, and were all destined to give way in the face of Rossini and the romantic opera of Weber and Marschner.

Francesco Morlacchi (1784–1841), a pupil of Zingarelli in Naples and Stanislao Mattei in Bologna, was the least affected by new ideas. From 1810 he was *Kapellmeister* at Dresden and in 1811 he gained a reputation in Italian theatre with the popularity of his *Raoul de Créqui*, a subject already used by Dalayrac for a rescue *opéra-comique*. Italian opera in the city that had belonged to Hasse ended with Morlacchi; it was, in fact, in Dresden from 1817 that the standard-bearer of the new trends, Weber, was seriously to oppose him with opera in German, and his court position was to be inherited by Wagner. Ferdinando Paër (1771–1839) came from Parma and was a more flexible and capable figure who made a name for himself in Italian theatres with works following on from Paisiello and Cimarosa. In 1797 he went to Vienna where he produced a few rescue works, the most significant of which is *Camilla ossia Il sotterraneo* on a libretto by Carpani taken from the French. Although melodic dominance is fundamental in Paër, this work is one of the closest Italian approaches to the naturalism of revolutionary *opéra-comique*: a waltz appears; comic parts, or ones which are neutral in character, are mixed in at decisive moments; and, when required, the music is adapted, as in *mélodrame*, to fill in gaps for action, which are indicated in the stage directions (e.g. 'The duke orders his writing desk to be brought. He begins to write. He tears up what he has written. He takes the portrait out of the desk and gazes at it. He kisses it. He holds it to his heart. He sighs. He slams shut the writing desk and rushes off.')[16] – humble actions without words that are completely new to the courtly and literary tradition of Italian opera. In the same style as *Camilla* are *Lodoïska, Leonora ossia L'amor coniugale* and *Agnese*, the last produced at Parma in 1809 and for a long time proclaimed as a model by those who were to find Rossini noisy.[17] But the prolific Paër combined elements of all the genres, even the heroic genre derived from Metastasio, as in *Achille* (1801), about which Napoleon was enthusiastic when he heard it at Warsaw a few years after its Viennese première. Patroclus's funeral, which is in C minor and contains syncopated sforzatos and side-drum rolls, continues the succession of revolutionary and Napoleonic funeral marches that was by this time on the verge of receiving the definitive seal which Beethoven's 'Eroica' Symphony set on this genre. Paër was summoned by Napoleon to direct the court chapel and arrived in Paris in 1807, but as a composer he was not very important. As the director of the Théâtre des Italiens he acted in an underhand manner against Spontini in the latter's final years at Paris, and tried to block Rossini's path; when he was no longer successful, he followed Boïeldieu into *opéra-comique* and wrote *Le maître de chapelle* (1821), which remained, along with *Agnese*, his most successful work.

In Italy, nevertheless, between Cimarosa and Rossini, it was not the operas of itinerant composers like Spontini and Paër that were the centre of attention; the dominant figure was a foreigner, Johannes Simon Mayr (1763–1845), a Bavarian educated by the Jesuits in Ingolstadt, a contemporary of Cherubini and Méhul who avoided Paris and settled in the provincial calm of Bergamo. His religious, literary and musical education was not that of an Italian opera composer; furthermore, his chief interest lay in sacred music, and it was to devote himself to this that he had come down to Bergamo and the ancient centre of S. Maria Maggiore. His interest in opera began in Venice, where he settled in 1790 to study with Bertoni and where he made his début with *Saffo* (1794), which was later followed by about seventy operas, all in Italian, as well as by oratorios in Latin and Italian. But once he became *maestro di cappella* he remained at Bergamo and turned down offers from every city in Europe and even an invitation from Napoleon, who wanted him to go to Paris.

As an intellectual Mayr was a German, and many historical, critical and autobiographical passages give evidence of his range of interests, his understanding of the language of Haydn, Mozart and Beethoven, and his admiration for Clementi and, around 1837, for Chopin. At Bergamo he conducted Haydn's *The Creation* in 1809, formed the Lezioni Caritatevoli di Musica in 1805 (where he had

Donizetti as a pupil) and founded the Unione Filarmonica in 1822 to promote the works of Vienna's holy fathers. But as an operatic composer he was an Italian whose reference points were Piccinni and the French vein stemming from Gluck. Hence, although he possessed a roundness of vocal line unknown to Cherubini, the heart of the matter for him, too, was the orchestra – an orchestra whose way of thinking was not that of the sonata, but that of Gluck, which does not contain the symphonic–vocal synthesis of Mozart's action music (although Mayr knew it well), but which exploits the late symphonies of Mozart and Haydn to theatrical ends. For this reason he was successful in Italy, especially with the Cherubinian *Lodoïska* (1796), *Ginevra di Scozia* (1801) and *Medea in Corinto* (1813). This last work, which was performed in Naples and is based on a text by Felice Romani (the future librettist of Bellini and Donizetti), is, in spite of its rapid shifts between maternal love and the thirst for revenge, possibly his most musically accomplished opera. Its agitation and the protagonist's tragic manner are based on a simplification of the Mozart of the G minor Symphony K 550; Creusa is often portrayed by the 'angelic' sound of the harp. Nevertheless, as was traditional in Gluck's operas, the great passages are for the chorus; they include the scene in a subterranean cell in the second act, in which trombones are used for the chorus of furies, and the opera's finale, which is an example of the sublime tragic style, with pulsating bass notes and blocks of sound which build up in a terraced manner, and with ideas formed through familiarity with Mozart's great minor-key passages – it is a model for the scene of the plague of darkness in Rossini's *Mosè*, but with individual figures which stand out like statues in high relief.

Medea in Corinto was staged in 1813, the year of the revolution of Rossini, who shortly afterwards became the talk of the town in Naples with *Elisabetta*. For Mayr, as for Fenaroli, Valentino Fioraventi and Pietro Generali, it was time to move on to sacred music; but for Mayr this was a pleasure, since it perfectly suited his nature as a musician and as a musical intellectual.

31 The new instrumental schools

Instrumental music around the end of the eighteenth century took on an importance unknown to earlier periods. Basically, it was an outlet towards which the whole of the second half of the eighteenth century had been orientated, particularly from the 1770s. Opera had always been the genre which was most talked about; Gluck in Paris caused rivers of ink to be spilt, and Rousseau was able to write that instrumental music on its own 'est peu de chose'.[18] But in the meantime instrumental music had formed its own path; with sonata form it had acquired a perfect autonomous language, and along with the institution of the public concert and the technical advancement of instruments, the publishing industry had spread Haydn and Mozart throughout Europe. Now instrumental music took the lead and was the area from which the most substantial and precious new ideas came. This can be seen in the 'operatic symphonism' of *opéra-comique* in the years of the Revolution, and is borne out in the dramatic works of Cherubini, Mayr and Spontini; and there was a surge from the theatre back into the concert hall, for from the overtures to Cherubini's *Médée*, *Les deux journées* and *Anacréon*, from Méhul's overtures, and from many of Spontini's purely orchestral passages came ideas and models for symphonies and sonatas (the quartet remained more sheltered) which ran parallel with the strict instrumental examples of Haydn and Mozart.

But the end of the eighteenth century and the early years of the nineteenth saw the appearance of a new generation of instrumentalists who wrote in a stereotyped way for the theatres, or indeed ignored them altogether, and who rooted themselves in the profession, either teaching or performing, with a partial but profound vision that prepared the ground for the great instrumental adventures of the decade 1830–40. The most dynamic field was that of the piano, the instrument which continued to change and prosper in the fifty years 1770–1820; and the most typical musician of this professional phenomenon was, like Cherubini and Spontini, an Italian by birth who became a European, Muzio Clementi (1752–1832), the composer of about eighty sonatas, various other piano pieces (capriccios, variations, toccatas and dances) and an impressive didactic output which remains the basis of modern piano technique. Concert artist, teacher, piano maker and publisher: the epithet 'father of the pianoforte' which is usually applied to him is justified in many ways.

Clementi was born in Rome and received early training as an organist, but he was scarcely fourteen when Peter Beckford, a British gentleman and a Member of Parliament, took him to England, promising to take care of his education and his introduction into London's musical life. The boy studied for seven years, apparently self-taught, in his protector's home in Dorset; at the age of twenty-one he moved to London as harpsichordist at the King's Theatre, gave his first concerts, and published his first sonatas. The second sonata of op. 2, printed by Welcker in 1779, was still marked for 'harpsichord or pianoforte' – but then the piano was not claimed as the only possible medium in any other contemporary works. It is in C major and has only two movements, a Presto and a rondo ('spiritoso') – there is no Adagio or Andante. The opening contains little inventiveness, originality or dialogue; these are replaced by a rough, clipped thematic style with shrill octaves in the right hand, a coarse octave tremolo in the left, biting successions of scales and arpeggios, and contrasts of register and touch. There is something of the energy that Mozart affirmed in his Symphony in G minor K 183, but here it is transformed into the major key, with a delight in efficiency and a fullness of sound that breaks through the walls of the salon of the 'connoisseurs and amateurs', the walls which were essential to the sensitive Emanuel Bach. Sensibility is the ingredient furthest from Clementi's Sonata op. 2 no. 2.

After seven years of working in London, the moment for his first concert arrived in the two years 1780–1, during a tour to Paris and Vienna, where Clementi met Haydn and Mozart and played before the Emperor (see Chapter 27). In 1782 the three Sonatas op. 7 were printed in Vienna, representing Clementi's greatest effort to approach the models of the Viennese sonata in its most brilliant decade. The clearest evidence in this direction is the third sonata's first movement, whose development is longer than its exposition and twice the length of its recapitulation, and whose first theme is extensively developed, including an appearance in longer note values. All blatant exploitations of technique are restrained, and they appear only in the octaves in the finale and in the use of full chords employing all the fingers – a particular characteristic of Clementi's. And how Vienna must have liked the first theme, written in straight-forward harmony in four real parts, the second theme, which as often in Haydn is derived from the first, and the connection between the last bars of the first and second movements!

The Sonatas op. 12, which appeared in London in 1784, presented once again on an even more triumphant scale the full pianistic sonority of op. 2, with octaves, double trills and wide hand-crossings. Nevertheless, this solid model was by now evolving in two directions: on the one hand, it tended towards a concentration of feeling, a carefully finished work which reflected the knowledge of Mozart – there is eloquent evidence of this in the Adagios and Larghettos; and on the other there was a move towards simplification which re-emphasized the Alberti bass (judiciously absent from op. 7 no. 3) and in every case a clear separation of tune and accompaniment, as in a faster and more direct *galant* style. In effect Clementi's exploration of the sonata, which occurred mainly in the twenty years 1782–1802, shows a clear independence from Viennese models. These were sometimes present in isolated features or individual phrases, but never in the overall formal structure, as is shown at a glance by the reduction of development sections (after the exploit of the third sonata of op. 7), which were rapidly replaced by variations, unpredictable digressions of an improvisatory kind, or sequences of pure pianistic formulas.

But for Clementi the canvas of sonata form was sufficient; indeed, he actually required certain formal resources when ordering all the ideas suggested to him by the keyboard. The final variations of the third sonata of op. 23 (1790), on a theme later introduced by Beethoven into his Septet, completely liberate the ornamental variation in the light of new pianistic sonorities. The fourth sonata of op. 25 (1790) opens with a Maestoso e cantabile which has simple but extraordinarily thick, massive harmonies, so that the thumb has to bend round clumsily to depress two white keys at the same time. In the fifth sonata of the same collection, in F sharp minor, the first movement, although it has almost no development, is a work of a complete strictness that comes from the assimilation of Domenico Scarlatti's *Trenta Essercizi* (in particular no. 25, in the same key), a model of the severity avoided by the *galant* style but always clearly present in London. The impetus and functional use of ornamentation are taken from the great Neapolitan and rearranged within the piano's symphonic possibilities, culminating in a coda that has a majesty unknown (at least on the piano) even to Mozart and that must have appealed greatly to the twenty-year-old Beethoven, who was a great admirer of this piece. The three Sonatas op. 37 of 1798 were also important, especially the second, which shows its proximity to the birth of Haydn's 'London' symphonies in its thematic typology (in the finale) and its broad sweep of modulation. But the best of Clementi's sonatas are perhaps those of the op. 40 collection, which appeared in London in 1802. The opening of the second sonata, in B minor, shows the extent of Clementi's greatness as well as his limits: it is a slow introduction in the style of an open confession, the complete opposite of all the self-restraint of the British, in which the musical fragments and the new harmonic language that emerges (the perceptive use of added-sixth harmony and the cutting effect of chromatic passing notes) are so pregnant that the first movement proper (Allegro), although very sturdy, represents a step backwards when compared with the introduction. In the third sonata, too, nothing equals the first theme, with its false modulation to G major – a device which Beethoven took up exactly in his Sonata op. 28.

With his op. 40, Clementi must have felt that he had gone as far as he could, and he temporarily stopped writing sonatas. He returned to the genre in later years, in 1821, with his op. 50, dedicated to Luigi Cherubini, in which the third sonata in G minor entitled *Didone abbandonata – Scena tragica* stands out. This is a large-scale work, among Clementi's most polished, but it is pervaded by his open sentimentality and a certain frigid superfluity which is a long way from the essential nature of his early works. Dedicated to a man of the theatre and theoretically aiming at a new scenic effect, *Didone* was one of the last of Clementi's instrumental works to be published; in the twenty years that separate it from op. 40 Beethoven had written all his piano sonatas between op. 31 and op. 109.

The study of piano technique in its historical and physiological foundations, along with a scholarly inclination, was already apparent in the abundance of canons in the first and third sonatas of op. 40, but it came openly to the surface with his series of didactic works. For Clementi, who from 1800 no longer appeared in public as a pianist, technical difficulties – problems of articulation, fingering and touch – were neither obstacles nor opportunities for showing off, but a real method of education, a method which matured in England, which is still today at the forefront of the teaching world. In 1790 he published in London the mainly canonic *Préludes ou Exercices* 'in the major and minor keys', followed by the *Introduction to the art of playing on the piano-forte*, which appeared in London in 1801 and was immediately reprinted in Vienna, Leipzig, Paris and Italy. But the great encyclopaedia of piano technique was contained in the hundred pieces of *Gradus ad Parnassum, or The art of playing on the piano-forte*, in three volumes (1817–26), which was printed almost simultaneously in London, Paris and Leipzig. Even with so much emphasis on climbing the Parnassus of the professional concert pianist, Clementi had not overlooked the interest in little hands and the groundwork for performance; he had already provided elementary models of style and phrasing with his *Sonatine* op. 36 (1798), which followed a middle course between didactic and free composition, and along with the teaching collections of Daniel G. Türk, prepared the ground for Schumann's pieces for the young.

But sonatas, methods and studies still did not exhaust Clementi's multifarious interests. This intellectual of the piano wrote pieces and cadenzas 'in the style of' Haydn, Mozart, Koželuh, Sterkel and Vanhal, and dug into the instrument's past, publishing in 1791 twelve sonatas under the title *Scarlatti's chefs-d'oeuvre, for the harpsichord or piano-forte* (two of which are spurious) and, between 1803 and 1815, the anthology *Selection of practical harmony, for the organ or pianoforte*. This work opens with a compendium of contrapuntal technique which contains examples by himself and Fux of simple, double and florid counterpoint, followed by fugatos, canons and fugues by Kirnberger, Padre Martini, Perti, C. P. E. Bach, Porpora, Albrechtsberger, Telemann, Eberlin and Marpurg. One fugue transcribed by Clementi comes from Mozart's Requiem; J. S. Bach's French Suite in G major (BWV 816) also appears (with the order of the movements rearranged) as a difficult exercise in finger technique – a different world from the fugue, the chorale and the Lutheran parishes. Clementi's fame grew with his withdrawal from concerts and his business trips; as publisher and owner (along with Collard) of a piano factory, he paid several visits to Paris, St Petersburg, Berlin, Leipzig, Rome, Milan and Vienna. In Vienna in 1807, he met Beethoven and taught Czerny and Moscheles, the final links of a chain that was to join up with Chopin. Meanwhile (1804–19) Breitkopf in Leipzig published his 'complete works' in thirteen instalments, a satisfaction granted to few of his contemporaries.

Thus for about forty years (1780–1820) Clementi was a leading European figure. Over him hangs Mozart's negative judgement that he was a mere 'mechanicus', without an ounce of feeling or taste, only good for churning out notes, scales and double thirds.[19] A variety of evidence can be cited in his defence: numerous Adagios and Andantes with a flexible, expressive tenderness, and numerous flashes of direct folk elements in waltzes, Swiss songs, schottisches, monferrinas (Piedmontese country dances), accompaniments in the style of the hurdy-gurdy or bagpipes over held fifths, and fragments of folky scales (e.g. D major with a G sharp). But Mozart's objection, from his own point of view, was legitimate and clear: Clementi was a 'mechanicus' not because of the dominant technical aspect, with its percussive scales in both hands, note-doublings and basses which are left bare to cadence between tonic and dominant, but because of his use of these elements in relation to the sonata. Clementi did not feel that the sonata was sacred, and did not have the sense of commitment towards its organic unity which Mozart felt even more than Haydn. In the middle of an exposition or a development he could come out with a passage of double sixths and concentrate on it to the extent of forgetting the continuity of the sonata; and

Mozart must also have disliked Clementi's spotlight on the piano, a piano of English construction with stronger strings and heavier hammers than those in Vienna. It was the Mozart of the piano combined with other instruments in chamber music or with the orchestra in concertos, where the sharp sonorities were rounded off amid woodwind and strings, that was opposed to Clementi; but Mozart's ideal sound was no longer shared by the taste of the period, which was increasingly interested in volume and mechanicalness. For Beethoven, Clementi was a fundamental acquisition – not the Clementi who adapted himself to Vienna, the one of op. 7 which Haydn liked and which was to influence even Schubert, but rather the 'mechanical' Clementi of the abundant arpeggios and the weighty technique of octaves, double thirds and double trills. The technical requirements of Beethoven's piano music were those of Clementi's, not those of Mozart's.

A prevailing interest in the piano, an involvement in concerts, in teaching and in business, the publication of tutors and occasional failure and escapes from debt are all common elements in the biographies of the generation that followed the old-fashioned *maestro di cappella*. Clementi's fame in the years 1790–1810 was seriously rivalled by the Bohemian Leopold Antonin Koželuh (1747–1818), who settled in Vienna, where he published piano sonatas and cultivated every type of composition. It was music that poured out free from care, with a discursive fluency that was to become common in post-Mozartian Vienna and was to some extent even dangerous when it did not involve a thorough investigation of ideas or technical interests. Koželuh produced some music in a popular style: between 1793 and 1797 he published in London a collection of Scottish songs and a number of smaller groups of *Lieder*, Italian 'Arietts' and French airs, and even introduced Scottish tunes into his piano sonatas (see, for example, his op. 52). This liking for character pieces, for programmatic works with references to these subjects or to Swiss and Alpine scenery, which were popular in contemporary stage settings, was very widespread after 1790 and tempered the rigour of the sonata style put forward by Haydn and Mozart in the 1780s. Publishers like Preston in London and folklorists like Thompson in Edinburgh tried to satisfy the interest in England that was spreading throughout post-Napoleonic Europe by publishing collections of folk songs for voices and small chamber groups (often with short introductions and postludes), which were commissioned from all the leading composers of the time, including Haydn and

Beethoven; their picturesque titles contrast with those of the professional methods and studies which continued just as vigorously in Clementi's footsteps.

The biography of another Bohemian, Jan Ladislav Dussek (1760–1812), is very similar to that of Clementi. He studied in Paris as an organist, but he too accepted the protection of a nobleman (from Holland), whom he followed as a teacher and pianist. In 1783 he met C. P. E. Bach in Hamburg and abandoned teaching to become a concert performer on the piano and the glass harmonica, making a reputation for himself in the leading countries of Europe. In the decade 1790–1800 he worked in London, where he met Haydn and Clementi (who appreciated his 'cantabile touch' and the full sonority which he achieved by the clever use of the pedal), played at the Salomon concerts, entered into a partnership with his father-in-law Corri in a publishing firm that subsequently failed, and escaped the fetters of Newgate prison by fleeing to Hamburg; he was to end his career in Paris as music master to Prince Talleyrand and as a concert organizer. His *Instructions on the art of playing the pianoforte* (London, 1796) provide evidence of his interest in piano teaching, but in his sonatas he is less strict than Clementi; nevertheless, his collections opp. 9, 31 and 39, and in particular op. 35 (dedicated to Clementi), contain thematic ideas that were immediately taken up by Beethoven in his early piano sonatas. From the general relaxation of form, lyrical oases emerge in the Adagios (perhaps under the influence of C. P. E. Bach), while Czech folk melodies and dances abound in the Allegros. Programmatic titles, too, such as *Le combat naval* for violin, cello and piano with timpani ad libitum, *La mort de Marie Antoinette* and *The Farewell*, reflect a new expressive direction, to some extent an equivalent in the instrumental field of the appeal to emotions and the affective quality that the revolutionary period had provoked in the theatre with the rescue opera.

A few composers moved a considerable distance away from the conventional instrumental tradition. Daniel Gottlieb Steibelt (1765–1823) from Berlin was regarded by Clementi as 'a charlatan';[20] the composer of more than 130 sonatas for piano alone or with other instruments, he oscillated between Paris and London and later, to get away from creditors, moved to St Petersburg to direct French opera. The title of one of his concertos for piano and orchestra, *Voyage sur le Mont Bernard*, recalls Cherubini's *Eliza*, but the pieces which became all the rage in London between 1796 and 1798 were the bacchanals for piano and tambourine which were performed by the pianist partnered by his attractive wife. (Even Clementi, and one can imagine with what disgust, bowed to the fashion for the picturesque and adapted his waltzes for piano to be accompanied by tambourine and triangle.) Some of Clementi's immediate pupils in London were more severe, such as Johann Baptist Cramer (1771–1858), with his collection of strict studies op. 100, or the Irishman John Field (1782–1837), who followed his teacher to St Petersburg and stayed there as a teacher who was much sought after. Yet even for them the sonata was no longer the heart of their output, being replaced by studies and, in Field's case, by nocturnes and romances, a sphere of action that was close to more elevated romantic culture.

If London in the period 1790–1810 seemed to be the European capital of the piano, Paris still belonged to the violin, the concerto and the quartet in the Franco-Italian sense. In the final years of the Concert Spirituel the last champions of the Piedmontese violin school, Antonio Bartolomeo Bruni from Cuneo and Giovanni Battista Viotti from Vercelli, came to Paris. Bruni (1757–1821) was solo violinist at the Théâtre de Monsieur (later the Feydeau) run by Viotti; he also wrote for the stage and achieved a memorable result with *Claudine* (1794), an *opéra-comique* based on an affectionate short story by Florian. He became involved in the new political movement, being the member of the Commission Temporaire des Arts in charge of making an inventory of musical instruments and collections belonging to political exiles and convicts. He published ten books of 'quatuors concertants', more than twenty sets of duets for two violins (a very fashionable genre in Paris), and a few didactic works.

Viotti's biography (1755–1824) is much more tortuous. He arrived in Paris in 1781, played at the Concert Spirituel, made friends with Cherubini and the French violinists Baillot, Kreutzer and Rode, and ventured into the theatrical business. The Revolution severed his career, and under the charge of having links with the royal family he was forced to leave Paris during the Reign of Terror. In London, Viotti played for the Salomon concerts and had another go at a theatrical career, but sympathetic republican opinions persuaded him to take refuge in the country near Hamburg. On his return to London in 1810, patronized by an upper-middle-class family who loved him like a brother, he was nevertheless unable to manage as a purely musical professional, and he embarked on a wine business. After the fall of Napoleon he made a final bid for Paris with an attempt at running the Opéra during Spontini's period, finding it, however, a very different climate from that of his youth.

Viotti did not have Cherubini's temperament, nor Bruni's capacity for adaptation; he was rather like Paisiello and Cimarosa in that wherever he went he suffered repercussions from the Revolution. He was a peaceful character, and, so far as one can tell from letters and other evidence, frank and open, something which is also suggested by the canzonettas of 1804 'Vo triste e placido' and 'O cara semplicità', written for his amiable patrons and signed 'Viottino'. A great violinist, Viotti was a long way from the new conception of virtuosity elaborated by Paganini in his *Caprices* around 1817; he was an artist of the eighteenth century whose education was based on Piedmontese order and on the England of George III. The rhythm of the march, with ascending fourths or fifths, is a characteristic of his Allegros, especially in his early period; but at the opposite extreme there are the limpid melodic curves of the 'pastorales' which appear in the serenades for two violins from the London years, the pale colour of minor-key themes, and the sorrowful references to Mozartian ideas. In the twenty-nine concertos for violin and orchestra, the soloistic peaks of the first Parisian group are followed by a more clearly articulated symphonic organization in the nine written in London. The best examples, however, were really written during the daily confusion between his flight from Paris and his first steps in London: they include the Concerto no. 22 in A minor published by Corri in 1793 and dedicated to Cherubini, whose dramatic style is truly evoked by the *agitato* finale. In this stormy manner, and even more in the broad cantabile dimensions of the Adagio in E major, Viotti, like Cherubini and Clementi, became European, but without breaking away so clearly from his mother country; he was anchored to an instrument that could no longer be improved and to the Italian violin technique that had been handed down continuously and patiently for a century.

As a quartet composer, Viotti became a leading figure in the Parisian tradition in the mould of Cambini's 'quatuor brillant'. He often begins like Boccherini with an Andante or an Aria, once even with an *Andante romantico*, while his brilliancy is evident in the finales, which are sometimes in the style of a polonaise. Close links were in fact established between Viotti and French violin-playing: J. Pierre Joseph Rode (1774–1830), Viotti's pupil, was violinist to the Emperor in 1800 and for a decade was at the top of the tree, writing concertos, 'quatuors brillants', duets for two violins, and the *Caprices en forme d'études dans les 24 tons de la gamme*, published in

Berlin in 1815 just before Paganini's *Caprices*. Rode, in collaboration with Pierre Baillot (1771–1842) and Rodolphe Kreutzer (1776–1831) also published a violin method 'adoptée par le Conservatoire'; Baillot had studied in Italy, had become Cherubini's pupil in Paris, was introduced to the Feydeau by Viotti, and distinguished himself through his effective gifts as a moving spirit in the instrumental field. Kreutzer, too, who had made his début as a boy at the Concert Spirituel, overcame the stagnation of concert life during the revolutionary years, making a name for himself in the theatre with successful subjects such as *Paul et Virginie* and *Lodoïska* (1791), and later teaching the violin at the Conservatoire from the institution's foundation. His fame as a teacher and a concert performer, increased by successful tours throughout Europe, remains linked to the forty studies (*Études* or *Caprices*) printed around 1807; in Vienna in 1798 he met Beethoven, who later dedicated to him the Sonata op. 47, which has passed into history, abetted by Tolstoy's novel, as the 'Kreutzer' Sonata.

The growing interest in the string quartet promoted by Baillot also led to the six quartets by Cherubini, who was meanwhile receiving compliments and dedications from accomplished musicians like Viotti and Clementi. His point of departure was the 'quatuor concertant' or 'brillant' from Boccherini to Cambini, from Viotti to Kreutzer, as is suggested by his juxtaposition of various motives instead of the thematic continuity of Haydn and Mozart and by the superiority of the first violin. Here Cherubini was able to exploit the symphonic experience he had gained in his great operatic overtures, his indestructible seriousness and his method of harmonic elaboration, and to achieve a rare synthesis with the only obvious model, the Parisian string quartet. The first three quartets were not published until 1836, and they did not escape the attention of Schumann, who reviewed them in the *Neue Zeitschrift für Musik* and was struck by their brilliance but was uneasy because he could not find, in a composer who was considered everywhere to be 'German', 'the familiar mother tongue', the language of Haydn, Mozart and Beethoven;[21] this was a legitimate puzzle, because the field of the Italo-Parisian quartet in which Cherubini worked was summoned to a new problematic existence. This was also the case to some extent with Méhul's four symphonies written between 1809 and 1810, which made people in Paris talk of the birth of a 'French symphonist' to succeed Haydn and Mozart. The first of these works, in G minor, opens with a theme of solemn, tragic rhetoric just like the opening of Cherubini's *Médée* (an overture which also left its mark on the first of Boïeldieu's piano sonatas op. 2). Mendelssohn conducted Méhul's symphony in Leipzig in the 1837–8 season, and Schumann was amazed by its similarity to the first movement, scherzo and finale of Beethoven's Fifth Symphony; but as in Cherubini's quartets, here, too, Schumann did not hear the 'mother tongue', though he was impressed by its outbursts of originality. There was, then, a clear symphonic path of operatic composers, apparent on first hearing, from Gluck through Cherubini to Méhul, which ran alongside the orthodox path of Sammartini, Stamitz, Boccherini, Haydn and Mozart.

Ignaz Joseph Pleyel (1757–1831) was not an instrumental virtuoso, but was important for his varied activities. An Austrian by birth, he was a pupil of Vanhal and Haydn and a friend of Paisiello and Cimarosa, both of whom he had met in Italy. When the Revolution broke out he was at Strasbourg, where he organized the Pleyel–Schönfeld concerts, later moving to London to direct the Professional Concerts in competition with the Salomon concerts. He was arrested in Strasbourg in 1793 because he had property there, but saved himself by swiftly composing revolutionary hymns, and by 1795 he had settled in Paris, where he published a *Nouvelle méthode de pianoforte* in collaboration with Dussek and where he founded a publishing house and a piano factory which was to become increasingly important in the new century. At this point he abandoned his superficial but prolific composition of quartets, symphonies, and trios and duets for various instruments, a catalogue of which it would be difficult to compile because of the number of transcriptions, arrangements and false attributions. An itinerary from Vienna to Paris was also followed by the Bohemian Antonin Reicha (1770–1836), a friend of Salieri and Beethoven and a pupil of Albrechtsberger, who instilled in him at Paris a contrapuntal strictness and a vocation for teaching. His treatises on melody and harmony helped his succession of Méhul as teacher of counterpoint and fugue at the Conservatoire, but his name remains linked mainly with the *Traité de haute composition musicale* published between 1824 and 1826, around the time that Berlioz became his pupil. Almost all the examples in the treatise are for wind quartet (woodwind and horn), following Reicha's main interest in refining and professionalizing the passion for wind music which became widespread through the music of the Revolution.

If London and Paris were the richest centres of innovation, no one in Vienna was any longer in a position, after Haydn's death in 1809, to match Beethoven, who was the sole, absolute ruler. Nevertheless, two Czech composers enjoyed a certain degree of fame: Joseph Gelínek (1758–1825), well known above all for his light piano variations on operatic themes, and Adalbert Gyrowetz (1763–1850), a prolific writer of symphonies and chamber music published between 1790 and 1814. Gyrowetz's slow movements are often variations on hit tunes, 'narrow-gauge' music without formal problems, in which Haydn, Mozart, Clementi and Beethoven are watered down into simple and immediately appreciable forms. Johann F. X. Sterkel (1750–1817), the priest and organist whom Mozart disliked on account of his habit of playing too fast,[22] worked in Mainz and Würzburg. Entirely dedicated to instrumental music, he published around eighty sonatas between 1774 and 1807, displaying an elegant cantabile style on top of a persistent texture of learned counterpoint. Johann Friedrich Reichardt was poised between the old and the new, and, as we have seen (in Chapter 27), was more important as a critic and musical historian than as a composer; he wrote, among countless works in every genre, about sixty sonatas for harpsichord, clavichord, and (later) piano. The early ones are firmly in the Berlin mould with the stamp of C. P. E. Bach in the limitation of each movement to a single 'affect'; but he dabbled in the 'declamatory style' and even after 1793, when Haydn's influence made his music more substantial, he always had something of the dilettante composer about him. In Vienna in 1808 he heard Beethoven's pupil, Dorothea von Ertmann, play some of the master's works, op. 13 (the 'Pathétique'), op. 26, op. 27 no. 2 and op. 57 in F minor; and in fact one of his sonatas in the key of F minor makes no secret of being written in the shadow of Beethoven's great work.

Italy too, especially in northern and central areas, benefited from a European instrumental culture supplied mainly by Austria. Milan, where the Conservatory of music was set up in 1808, was the main centre. Alessandro Rolla (1757–1841), a teacher at the Conservatory, the director of the orchestra at the new La Scala theatre, and the writer of didactic works and of concertos and trios mostly published in Paris, and the pianist Francesco Giuseppe Pollini (1762–1846), an Austrian born at Ljubljana who settled in Milan in 1790, stood out in the early years of the century. Pollini also published a *Metodo per clavicembalo* (1811 – it was actually concerned with the piano, not the harpsichord), along with variations and fantasias on operatic themes (even some by Rossini), often preceded by introductions with surprising harmonic experimentation which are much more important than the variations that follow them. But the piano sonatas, which remained in manuscript, are also rich in their musical content; they are modelled on Clementi as well as Haydn and Mozart, and have lively themes which are rather held back by the excessive regularity typical of Italians following the Viennese example. Pollini also wrote stage works such as *L'orfanella svizzera* and *La casetta nei boschi* (produced in Milan at the end of the eighteenth century) and romances like Goethe's 'Sai qual è l'amena sponda?' and Ossian's 'Canto di Selma': pieces which, like the Turinese Pugnani's orchestral suite based on *Werther*, show the entrance of European literary culture scarcely after it had crossed the Alps, a little vanguard of romanticism in the land of classicism.

Italy's isolation from the European instrumental movement is evident above all in the symphony, which in Italy could still be interpreted as a musical piece in a single movement, often linked with the liturgical service. This type of work was written in Bologna by Stanislao Mattei (1750–1825), a pupil of Padre Martini and his successor at the church of San Francesco (after the Napoleonic occupation some of his symphonies were, however, rearranged in a richer form for public concerts), and especially, for Naples Cathedral, by Nicola Zingarelli. So the only Italian voice of European importance was to be Paganini, who came from northern Italy, where the roots of instrumental music were stronger. His *24 Caprices* (published by Ricordi in 1820) were written around 1817, when the first volume of Clementi's *Gradus* appeared in London, and were high points of the new instrumental professionalism. But within the twenty-year-old Paganini there was not only the controlled mastery of Clementi, but also a demonic restlessness that opened up new horizons of virtuosity, so that the great romantic family of Chopin, Schumann, Berlioz, Liszt and Brahms was to use him as a springboard towards new goals, while Clementi was left in peace, and it was only much later that Debussy was to sketch an affectionate portrait of him. Paganini became an international reference point during his great concert tour of 1828–34, and so was a long way from Italy, which contented itself in the meantime with instrumentalists (mainly violinists) who had returned home in the period following Napoleon after long periods abroad. Nevertheless, it was thanks to them – Radicati in Bologna, Giorgetti in Florence and Polledro in Turin – that the taste for chamber music was to survive the high operatic tide in Italy.

Apart from the piano and violin, with their vast range of exploration, other less illustrious instruments also achieved a more solid technical awareness at the beginning of the new century, benefiting from the piano's progress and the general success of the language of the sonata. This was the case with the guitar, in the hands of the Spaniard Fernando Sor (1778–1839), who worked in Paris and London in the years 1813–15, and the Italian Mauro Giuliani (1781–1829), who lived in Vienna between 1807 and 1819; it was also true of the double bass, which was promoted to the rank of a solo instrument by Domenico Dragonetti (1763–1846), a concert artist well known everywhere, in whom Haydn showed an interest in London in 1794, as did Beethoven in Vienna in 1799. Later on the harp became entitled to independent status, especially in Paris with the makers Naderman and then Érard (who in 1811 constructed the new harp 'à double mouvement', i.e. with a double action involving pedals which could be depressed in two positions). Soloists and composers like Jacques-Georges Cousineau, François-Joseph Naderman and Robert-Nicolas-Charles Bochsa published tutors, taught at the Conservatoire and printed sonatas for solo harp or duets for harp and piano or violin, or for two harps, making familiar an instrument which had already earned itself considerable status in stage works by Lesueur and Boïeldieu. The harp entered important households as a gem of imperial-style furniture, and enjoyed a prestige that overcame its practical limitations because of its suggestions of antiquity and because of literary references to the Aeolian harp, the instrument of oriental origin whose strings were set in vibration by the wind. Ossianic poetry was full of Aeolian harps, which were also the object of a text by Mörike (*An eine Aeolsharfe*) and were elevated to mystical levels in an ode by Schiller, where the whole of creation is interpreted as an Aeolian harp which quivers and resounds. In 1789 a maker by the name of Schnel tried to adapt the principle of the Aeolian harp to the keyboard, and designed an 'aero-clavichord' which used artificial jets of air, but greater success was achieved by the gradual tendency to adopt characteristics of the harp in piano writing, so that Schumann could later compare Chopin's first study op. 25 with the sound of an Aeolian harp.

The glass harmonica invented by Benjamin Franklin (a set of glass bowls made to vibrate by means of friction from moistened finger-tips) belongs to the same 'ethereal' class; it was a contraption that was much in vogue in Austria and Germany, was not disdained by Mozart and Beethoven, and was used in concerts by Dussek. In the field of cratfsmanship, the passion for inventing instruments had already been reflected in the vogue for 'mechanical' instruments which did not require a player: such machines were usually equipped with a wooden cylinder with little metal spikes fixed into it which press down resonant metal levers, like the barrel organ which

Mozart used in some of his late pieces and which was so common in English churches from around 1795 onwards, replacing the organist and jeopardizing the profession, or like the *Flötenuhr* devised by one of Prince Nicolaus II Esterházy's librarians, combining an ordinary clock with a collection of little pipes and bells. But some instruments were constructed at the beginning of the nineteenth century which mechanically reproduced the entire orchestra: like Flight and Robson's Apollonicon or the Panharmonicon built by Johann Nepomuk Maelzel, mechanician to the Viennese court, who arranged works by Cherubini, Haydn and Handel for his instruments, besides obtaining from Beethoven his 'Battle Symphony' (*Wellington's Victory in the Battle of Vittoria*). Out of this whole confused museum of sound machines only the metronome, perfected by Winkel and Maelzel (1816) and then produced on a large scale by a Parisian industry, has remained alive. Greeted optimistically at its appearance as a messenger of the composer's precise wishes concerning movement, the metronome was an early form of opposition to the classical conception of artistic freedom, which found itself confronted by a machine that could control its progress; the early theorists of the 'death of art', of the decadence of innocent art as a result of the betrayal of the sentimental by the rational, were already making gloomy predictions based on the impassive precision of the boorish pendulum.

32 Beethoven

After following the changes in musical theatre during the French Revolution and the Napoleonic Empire, the reflections of nationalistic and patriotic feelings in characteristic pieces, and the rapid progress of a new type of technical professionalism, our attention is brought back by the appearance of Beethoven's name to the organic unity of the linguistic achievements established by the sonata principle which matured in Vienna in the decade 1780–90: that is, to be precise, in the quartets, symphonies, sonatas and concertos of Haydn and Mozart, which in pure musical terms were the richest legacy available to a young beginner.

Yet the rigorous application of the sonata principle was, by the 1790s, only one of several possibilities. Italian opera, with *Il matrimonio segreto* (1792), was still extraordinarily successful, an indication of its apparently everlasting good health, and in Paris, with

Cherubini's *Lodoïska* in 1791, a new type of French opera, full of youthful energy, was also advanced. In the instrumental field, the virtuoso piano school in London was a strong attraction, and the Parisian 'concertant' or 'brillant' style also presented independent and distinctive features, which were also apparent in Vienna in the young generations that scorned the fluency of Haydn and Mozart. Count Waldstein told the young Beethoven, when the latter was about to go to Vienna in 1792, that he was to 'receive Mozart's spirit from Haydn's hands':[23] more than just a general viaticum, this was an invitation to maintain one course in preference to others which were also legitimately available. But Beethoven was to interpret the exhortation in his own way: he was to inherit the legacy of Haydn and Mozart without renouncing anything that was going on outside this magic circle in a musical Europe which had not waited long before trying out other paths. The vexed and pointless question of whether Beethoven may be defined as a 'classical' or a 'romantic' composer stems from the fact that he absorbed all the new ideas which had emerged in a disorderly and riotous fashion in the years 1790–1810, but measured them with the yardstick of the most rigorous approach to the sonata principle, onto which he grafted himself directly. His position is not one of a focal point at which everything naturally converges, but one of a testing ground for a collection of elements which were not made to go together, and which were already following hundreds of independent paths beyond his sphere of operation. Beethoven achieved this union on his own, with a strength of mind and will comparable to the marriage of counterpoint and harmony undertaken a century before by the great Bach.

Beethoven's character

Ludwig van Beethoven was born in Bonn on 16 December 1770 into a family of Flemish origin which had emigrated to the Electorate of Cologne. After Bonn, the geographical setting of his biography is confined to Vienna: he moved there in 1792, at the age of just over twenty, with the idea of returning home sooner or later, but instead stayed for the rest of his life. His few small journeys are of negligible importance – a concert tour in 1796 (to Nuremberg, Prague, Dresden and Berlin) when he was still thinking of becoming a concert pianist, short spells in Hungary or Bohemia with the family of some nobleman or other, and summer visits all spent in the country close to Vienna. Longer journeys, in particular to London, remained purely hypothetical; his was on the whole a life of poor external circumstances, even though in some respects, especially in the emotional sphere, little is yet known about him.

The early years spent at Bonn were a poor version of Mozart's childhood. Beethoven also had a musician for a father, but he was only a tenor in the choir of the Elector Maximilian Franz, more inclined to drink than to teach his son. Ludwig's successes as a child prodigy – a few concerts and some early publications – did not yield anything apart from the appointment as organist in the court chapel in 1784. His early studies were instrumental – he learnt the piano, the organ and the violin from his father and other members of the chapel; his mother's poor health and eventual death when Ludwig was scarcely seventeen made these early years even more miserable. Bonn's importance to Beethoven lay beyond domestic walls, in his period of study with a real master, Neefe, a great admirer of C. P. E. Bach, a staunch Protestant, and a convinced champion of missionary art, and in his acquaintance through Neefe with Count Waldstein and the family of the Court Councillor, Stephan von Breuning. Here Beethoven was welcomed as a son and experienced all the openness and intellectual intimacy of domestic tranquillity that fate had denied him. In Breuning's house he shared in the charitable light which emanated from his wife Helene; they read Klopstock, Schiller and Goethe and discussed (in the first decade of Kant's popularity) the value of education as a spiritual adventure. It is not therefore surprising to find Beethoven in 1789 enrolled on the philosophy course at Bonn University, which had just been founded by Maximilian Franz and was full of Enlightenment ideas, and in which works by Rousseau and the Encyclopaedists had a wide circulation. *Opéra-comique* and *Singspiel* translated from French librettos were common at the court theatre in Bonn, but musically this little city on the left bank of the Rhine was provincial, and the Elector wisely let himself be persuaded by Waldstein, the Breuning family and Neefe to allow the young organist to spend some time in Vienna; especially as Haydn in person, passing through Bonn on his return from London, had spoken very highly of a cantata by the promising local twenty-year-old on the death of the Emperor Joseph II.

Beethoven settled in Vienna in November 1792. He studied for a little while with Haydn (who was not very interested in his pupil and who, in any case, returned to London in 1794) and, more profitably, under Johann Schenk and Albrechtsberger during a year of intense activity. For about a decade he went (though only sporadically) to

Antonio Salieri, in deference to the consistently high esteem reserved for the Italian language and vocal style. Within a few years (1792–5) Beethoven made a name for himself as an independent artist, his own impresario according to the new social role of the musician. The passage from the court to the free profession came about without any hesitation; the French republican troops had effectively done this for him by overthrowing the Electorate of Cologne with its associated musical chapel at Bonn. After losing his post, Beethoven worked on his own; stage work, which had been indispensable to a composer's career ten years earlier, was not even considered. In 1795 he appeared for the first time in public as a pianist, and in the same year Artaria published his Trios op. 1, which were followed every year by new works divided among the major Viennese publishers. In the early years of the nineteenth century, although Haydn's patriarchal star was still shining, Beethoven was the favourite of the city's musical life, and around 1810 he was regarded everywhere as the leading musician in Europe. He was considered as such by Bettina Brentano, who did her utmost to bring about the historic meeting with Goethe at Teplitz, and he was also seen in this light in the days of the Congress of Vienna (1814–15). Even when Rossini's star rose slightly later, Beethoven's supremacy remained undamaged, especially within German culture.

In Beethoven's career, despite its independent course, the institution of patronage still occupied a decisive position; among those who made considerable contributions to his economic independence were Prince Carl von Lichnowsky, at one time Mozart's pupil and a very loyal friend with whom Beethoven lived for a long time, the Counts Zmeskáll, Gleichenstein and Razumovsky, Archduke Rudolph, Emperor Leopold II's brother, and the Princes Franz Joseph Lobkowitz and Ferdinand Kinsky. The last three, at the beginning of 1809, guaranteed the composer an annual income of four thousand florins, on the sole condition that he stayed in Vienna, to write the kind of music he most wanted to. Indeed the composer was presented in 1808 with the opportunity of moving to Kassel as Jerome Bonaparte's *Kapellmeister*, an almost paradoxical situation: a French refugee from the Revolution offered Beethoven an old-style post as *Kapellmeister*, while the Austrian aristocracy sought to maintain him as an independent professional. This gesture by the three noblemen shows how important the musician was considered to be at this period; half a century earlier Klopstock had been taken in and financed in Copenhagen by Frederik V of

Denmark so that he could devote himself in peace to *Der Messias*, but this sort of recognition was unprecedented in music.

The great affliction in Beethoven's life was deafness, the first symptoms of which appeared as early as 1795. It gradually forced him to abandon his career as a pianist, which at that time he was pursuing not just as a soloist but in conjunction with orchestras and with other players. In 1802, at the age of thirty-two, the composer, after passing through violent conflicts, accepted his infirmity as irrefutable and was on the verge of despair, something which is echoed in a couple of letters and in the 'Heiligenstadt Testament' (6 October 1802) addressed to his brothers. His deafness became total around 1818, and from this date begin the 'conversation books' through which Beethoven still communicated with the world by getting the people he was talking with to write down their questions; 137 of these books have survived. His deafness was tied up with his solitary existence and the setbacks of his love affairs and prospective marriages; almost all of these (at least, of those we know anything about) involved noblewomen like Therese and Josephine Brunswick or Therese Malfatti, and were as a result doomed to failure from the start. Beethoven's family role in his final years was that of an uncle. In 1815, on the death of his brother Caspar Carl, he took under his turbulent protection his seven-year-old nephew Karl, fighting for him with a mother whose honesty was far from exemplary, and finally obtaining guardianship of him in 1820. He had, however, very modest results as far as the boy's education was concerned, in spite of the best of intentions (he wanted to make a classical philologist of him), something which proved a source of anxiety and bitterness in the final period of his life.

At first sight Beethoven's character has many *Sturm und Drang* features, with deep fits of depression, a lack of emotional self-control, many eccentricities and frequent changes of mood: 'You are frightening when you are so cheerful,' Lotte said to Werther,[24] and many thought the same about Beethoven (among them Goethe, who wrote: 'Unfortunately he is an utterly untamed personality').[25] Over and over again he showed numerous characteristics of his generation: the attraction/repulsion for Napoleon Bonaparte (shared by Kleist, Grillparzer and Hegel); the craving for legal equality with the aristocracy; the intellectual love of England, which was (compared with Metternich's Austria) the home of democracy and freedom; the passion for the classical world; and the belief in the betterment of humanity. For a long time he was not on very good terms with

Vienna; Haydn and Mozart's favourite city was regarded by Beethoven with superiority and intolerance. In 1794, when people everywhere were afraid of revolutions, he mocked the 'Austrian mediocritas' in a letter to the publisher Simrock in Bonn: 'so long as an Austrian can get his brown ale and his little sausages,' he wrote, 'he is not likely to revolt'.[26] His native country, the Rhineland, represented a fundamental ideal of his early years: a 'beautiful country' to which he longed to return (as he still wrote in 1801) to exercise his art 'only for the benefit of the poor'.[27] The uninformed reply to someone asking him for advice was that there were too many musicians in Vienna,[28] and that it would be better to live in Paris(!): 'I have already become accustomed to the basest and vilest treatment in Vienna', he wrote with obvious exaggeration to the poet Collin.[29] For a long time he complained about the worsening musical conditions and the bad orchestras, and he looked with admiration at the north; when he wrote to Breitkopf at Leipzig or to Bettina Brentano at Berlin, he talked about those cities as beacons of musical culture, and every so often he spoke of wanting to move, without ever getting round to it. Only after 1808, following the proof of his princely friends' generosity, and even more after the gunshots and the French occupation, did his sympathy for the old imperial city increase slightly. In 1812, in a letter to the German firm of Breitkopf, he actually managed to declare himself a 'poor Austrian musical drudge'.[30] But even then the pleasure-loving, pagan Vienna, sceptical and disenchanted, was not for him; Beethoven propounded a new ideal of strictness that developed in his isolation. After so much sociability, something which is at the root of the most perfect sonata style, he affirmed the value of *redire in se ipsum*, of the isolated creator that the eighteenth century had ended up by putting to one side.

Tied up with Beethoven's character is his thirst for culture. Few other musicians, and very few before him, talked so much about books and literature. There are in the 'note books' countless more or less explicit quotations from Schiller, Goethe, Kant, Rousseau and Plutarch, and references to Greek and Roman history and Indian philosophy. He was familiar with Schiller's *Don Carlos* and Goethe's *Faust*, and quotations sprang from his pen with the ironic detachment of an intellectual (for example when, referring to a change of rooms, he quotes: 'my world is the universe').[31] He received copies of Bahrdt's version of Tacitus and of Bothe's translation of Euripides's tragedies. The publisher Breitkopf was bombarded with requests about the complete edition of Wieland that was late in coming out, and about works by Goethe and Schiller which Beethoven ordered, claiming that they were his favourite poets, along with 'Ossian and Homer, though unfortunately I can read the latter only in translation' (a real annoyance, in all probability).[32] 'Have you read Goethe's *Wilhelm Meister* and Shakespeare in Schlegel's translation?' he asked Therese Malfatti in 1810: 'One has so much leisure in the country'.[33] He also had a literary style all his own: an exceptional liking for verbal *jonglerie* and double meanings (a trait that shows itself particularly in his correspondence with Zmeskáll), a taste for stylistic imitation, with borrowings from military and authoritarian jargon, and a whole gradation of tone ranging from a materialism drawn from Shakespeare or Rabelais to the biblical aspect of Klopstock.

Despite all this, Beethoven was not a composer who knew Sophocles better than harmony, as Ambros was to point out with concern halfway through the nineteenth century.[34] He was still above all a technician; he considered his ear (albeit an afflicted one) the 'most noble part' of himself, and no instrument held any secrets for him. He was on friendly terms with many performers (especially singers and violinists), whom he called 'brothers in art' (the entire span of his quartets was bound up with the Viennese concert activity of the violinist Ignaz Schuppanzigh). He did not talk much about his music, and then only in technical terms; but precisely because of this, because he operated on the basis of the greatest possible professionalism, his enthusiasm for contemporary culture acquired an unprecedented symbolic value which could not be claimed even by the varied interests of men like Reichardt and Rochlitz, who, like so many others (especially in German lands) had already made a useful combination of music and culture. On this culture, which he had regarded as a conquered land since his early years in Bonn, Beethoven laid the foundations for the position to be assigned to music at the summit of human activity. Mozart's 'Jupiter' Symphony also reveals a very elevated conception of music, but Beethoven, inspired by a romantic Neoplatonism that saw beauty and goodness spreading their reflections on man through art, was more specific. While the erudite Villoteau proposed in 1807 that the original root of the word 'music' came from the Hebrew 'mou-isès' meaning wisdom,[35] Beethoven with his stature whole-heartedly encouraged music's need to play a leading role in the education of man.

Even within the musical sphere, then, there was a 'literary' Beethoven with a new vitality. In 1801 he became enthusiastic with the publisher Hoffmeister over the project of publishing the works of

Johann Sebastian Bach, and in 1809 he asked Breitkopf for as many as possible of the scores in his possession – everything that he had in stock by Haydn, Mozart, and J. S. and C. P. E. Bach, since, he reminded him, 'my greatest pleasure is to play at the homes of some true friends of music works that I have never or seldom seen'.[36] Beethoven, then, made music even when he was not working, for his 'greatest pleasure', which was the pleasure of increasing his range of knowledge and of discovering new reflections of beauty and goodness; and the novelty of his attitude lies above all in the partiality of his choices and in satisfying his encyclopaedic curiosity. Mozart's adherence to music was more universal; Beethoven, however, introduces himself with one of his 'visions of the world', that is to say, an interpretation of the world starting from only a few elements; that is why he objected, for example, to *Don Giovanni* because of its immoral content, which was, in his view, unworthy of Mozart's genius.

Beethoven's artistic ideology was that of progress through an unattainable aim assigned by Nature. Schiller's proposal in *Über den Gebrauch des Chors in der Tragödie* (On the use of the chorus in tragedy, the introduction to *Die Braut von Messina*) could have been made by him: 'What art does not yet have it should acquire; the chance lack of resources should not limit the creative imagination of the poet. He sets as his aim the highest, he strives towards an ideal; the practical arts can accommodate themselves to what is available.'[37] Now, from this point of view, Mozart's art is a practical one, especially when he writes a solo part *after* having heard the voice that will be singing it. The leap from the real to the possible is, however, the new approach that Beethoven suggests to the nineteenth-century musician, persuading him, furthermore, that this is the only way in which music becomes worthy of composition.

Difficulties and obstacles on this road became opportunities and encouragements to make great progress, and in this is revealed the salient trait of Beethoven's character, at least up to 1810–15 – his enthusiasm for dissent and conflict as conditions for improvement. It was, fundamentally, a motive of a distantly religious kind (the infamous duality of the world, body and soul, God and the world) to which Luther had attached much importance, preaching (in his commentary to the Lord's Prayer) a warning for anyone who finds in himself 'only one desire rather than two contrasting ones'.[38] But the healthy condition of conflict had by this time been secularized within the culture of the Enlightenment as an irreplaceable means of education. Rousseau taught Émile that the noble savage is not really noble, because his nobility does not cost him anything; born in the depths of a forest, 'not having to fight anything in order to follow his own inclinations',[39] his nobility is worthless. For Julie, too, was not virtue perhaps 'un état de guerre'? Beethoven is pervaded by this concept of the value of difficulty; only in this way, playing on the educational significance of the test and on the missionary character attributed to art, can one try to reclimb the slope of one's own personal limitations. The only true evil would be to have no desire for action. Wilhelm Meister regards the director Melina, whose misery was caused by his own character, not by his profession, in the same way: 'There is nothing on earth which is not attended by difficulty. Only an inner drive, a desire and love help us to overcome obstacles, to blaze trails and to lift us above the narrow horizons by which others are miserably constrained by their timidity.'[40]

Beethoven's art worked towards these ideas, and was totally orientated towards a state of happiness situated at infinity; everything had still to be achieved, but the goal was no less certain for that reason. Mozart's happiness was that of the golden age, for it lay behind the artist, who was anxious to return to it. Beethoven's happiness lay in front of him; it was a region to be discovered, and through this his art has a positive basis and an optimistic tone apparent even in the profound spheres of a Largo e mesto, an Arioso dolente or a funeral march in C minor. For Beethoven, progress was a duty. In Haydn and Mozart, great leaps forward were instigated by external events (orders from Paris or London, commissions from important theatres), and that did not detract in any way from the sheer beauty of the results; but the fact that in Beethoven the impulse to make progress came solely from within, from the heart of his artistic desire, is an aspect which introduces a new light into the history of music.

Beethoven's language

As a whole, Beethoven's work appears to be generally less ramified than Mozart's. Three great blocks of works stand out: the thirty-two piano sonatas, the nine symphonies and the sixteen string quartets (the overtures and concertos can be classed along with the symphonies, and the remaining chamber music with the sonatas and quartets). One stage work, *Fidelio*, and the *Missa solemnis* stand like isolated rocks above a sea of related compositions.

While subdivision into *genres* is fashionable with Mozart, with Beethoven subdivision into chronological *styles* is more successful, something which was proposed in a famous book by Lenz (*Beethoven et ses trois styles*, 1852) and supported by his method of working on groups of compositions from different genres (e.g. on two symphonies, a concerto and two sonatas) at the same time. Compared with Haydn and Mozart, Beethoven wrote relatively few works in each genre; freed from the requirements of immediate occasions, each work had to have an inner justification, and so it was natural that there was an increase in breadth and variety, excluding the traditional collections of sonatas published in groups of six or symphonies in groups of ten. The time taken by the creative process increased beyond measure; except in a very few cases Beethoven no longer wrote under commission and had no deadlines to be honoured – even when he did have them he did not keep to them – and his work had to pass through the sieve of his inexorable personal requirements. The openly confessed joy of composition was mixed up with the torment of critical obstinacy, documented in a vast amount of preparatory work, sketches, changes of mind and last-minute corrections which contradict the romantic fetish for spontaneity.

Beethoven's sources also form a clear enough constellation: first of all Mozart and Haydn, but above all Mozart. Beethoven really saturated himself in some of Mozart's works, the late symphonies, the last ten piano concertos, *Le nozze di Figaro*, *Don Giovanni* and *Die Zauberflöte*, deriving from them the same discursive principles. Haydn, especially in the early years, influenced him more in individual well-defined ideas, in the sudden, precise thematic statement and the surprise modulation. In Mozart, moreover, Beethoven found that the character of many keys was clearly established: C minor and E flat major are tactical choices made in the wake of Mozart's examples; Sarastro's E major is also the key of many of Beethoven's Adagios which are pervaded by an air of calm; the use of F major as a pastoral key was derived more from Haydn's *The Seasons* than from Mozart, who had little interest in the bucolic – but among the instances of this key that are difficult to ignore there is the affectionate vein of 'Batti, batti, o bel Masetto' from *Don Giovanni*, whose subject could be disparaged without compromising the great value of the musical score.

A second important store of ideas was found on the Gluck–Cherubini front. Beethoven grasped absolutely clearly the common root of the 'democratic' aspect of revolutionary music in the *Garde Nationale* style and the majestic, heroic vein of *opera seria*, and achieved an incredible synthesis. His D minor (e.g. the Largo e mesto from his Sonata op. 10 no. 3 and the first movement of the Sonata op. 31 no. 2) is derived equally from Mozart's Concerto K 466, the oath scene in Act I of *Don Giovanni*, the High Priest's incantation in Gluck's *Alceste*, and the numerous instances of D minor in Cherubini's *Médée*. The triplets in the funeral march of the 'Eroica' Symphony are an exaggeration of the pulsations in the chorus 'O voto tremendo' in Mozart's *Idomeneo*. The trombones introduced in the Fifth Symphony have their ancestors in Gluck, not in the symphonic field. Cherubini had a direct influence on *Fidelio*, as did Clementi (especially his mechanical aspect) and Dussek in the field of piano technique. Mozart, Haydn, Gluck, Cherubini and Clementi constitute the major sources; the influence of a composer like C. P. E. Bach was weaker, and the rococo sharpness of someone like Dittersdorf is hardly noticeable. The real Italians, composers like Cimarosa and Paisiello, were of negligible importance since they were filtered through Mozart. Beethoven did not dwell much on the past; Handel was more important to him than Bach, by whom he knew above all the *Well-tempered Clavier*, but as a whole Beethoven's art was entirely sustained by contemporary values.

The pre-eminence of instrumental over vocal music reached a conscious affirmation with Beethoven. All the instruments (except the harp that was so popular with the Ossianics) were objects of continual experimentation, and among Beethoven's autographs there are numerous annotations concerning various kinds of instrumental problems. Some preparatory sketches for the 'Eroica' coincide with examples and notes about the characteristics of the natural horn covered in January 1801 by an article in the *Allgemeine musikalische Zeitung*. This kind of problem did not easily escape him, but no instrument was explored so deeply as the pianoforte: 'so far as the manner of playing it is concerned,' he wrote to the composer and teacher Streicher in 1796, 'the pianoforte is still the least studied and developed of all instruments; often one thinks that one is merely listening to a harp', while 'provided one can feel the music, one can also make the pianoforte sing'.[41] But beyond the ideal of singing, his investigations concentrated on exploring its qualities as an instrument: parallel lines two or three octaves apart are new inventions of timbre even for Clementi, and notes which are restruck without being detached or legatos which defy the instrument's incisive nature create a new manner of playing which requires a firm hand and profound articulation.

The principal unifying factor throughout Beethoven's work nevertheless lies in the formal field, that is, in sonata form, which, whether it is present in full profile or is foreshortened, paraphrased, contradicted or superficially absent, always operates as a fundamental frame of reference. Beethoven found himself faced with a perfect form in works by Haydn and Mozart which have all the nobility of the satisfaction of perfection. To go any further he had to upset the complicated equilibrium which supported it, and the first effective lever was one of thematic contrast, the differentiation between first and second themes. An ideal of inner coherence which suggested concealing contrasts and differences was close to Emanuel Bach's heart and was also favoured by Boccherini and Dittersdorf in their more refined works. Haydn also shared this approach, even though he did play on ambiguities and disguises; and so did Clementi, who had known how the presentation of the same theme in different tonal areas might be something appropriate for skilled listeners. For Beethoven, however, the difference in character between the two themes was an article of faith, and even when the two individuals were derived from a single root (as in the Sonata in F minor op. 57) the common material is transformed to such an extent that it undermines a balance which for Beethoven was no longer possible.

Beethoven's second lever was to deepen the contradiction from which sonata form derived its energy: the contradiction between staticism in its emphasis on themes and dynamism in the way in which they return and are developed and varied. At this time few people had Beethoven's genius for themes, and no one succeeded more than he did in extracting from their incumbent presence all the possibilities of movement. And this process of creating momentum, however adventurous it became, had no place for gratuitous combinations of themes; Beethoven kept clearly in mind the weak point of sonata form – the transition from the development to the recapitulation – and built up to that point throughout the development, whose function was to prepare for it. A panoramic view also embraced the reciprocal relationship of all the movements; there are, for example, sonatas which open with preliminary Adagios, slow introductions that return in a very unusual fashion within the Allegro (as in the *Sonate pathétique* op. 13), conditioning its structure, and final movements that exhibit a magnetic attraction over the preceding Adagio or scherzo without allowing it to finish. In short, the whole picture of the sonata was in turmoil during a process that lasted until about 1810, the boundary of a new problematical settlement.

Beethoven's harmony, in the general sense of tonal functions, was that of Haydn and Mozart in the period 1780–90. Real innovations in this field were made only in Beethoven's late works with his moderate recourse to modal traits (the 'ancient modes', as a note of 1808 puts it) or, in the opposite direction, to extreme chromaticism created by a radical conception of polyphony. Small-scale innovations of detail could include greater freedom of modulation, unprepared dissonances and the frequent use of added-ninth chords; more consistent innovations lay in the pianistic field, in dense sonorities in the low register or rapid successions of adjacent notes that form a cluster bordering on noise; here Beethoven was a very long way from Mozart (who said that 'music . . . must never cease to be music')[42] and was more receptive to the English piano school. But his real difference from Haydn and Mozart was his slowing down of harmonic rhythm and his projection of tonal functions onto a broader rhythmic foundation. Especially in the symphonies, but also in the quartets and sonatas with a more symphonic approach, spans of dominant harmony which put off their resolution for 18–20 bars are common, as are equally long affirmations of the tonic, a clear legacy from revolutionary odes and hymns.

The great change in melodic writing involved breaking off the identification of vocal and instrumental music which was the basis of the Viennese classical style. For Beethoven, melody was no longer an unambiguous notion, but a spectrum of infinite shades, from the unvocal and inarticulate motto to the cantilena based on the triad, with sensitive pauses on the main degrees of the scale, as in any music. Beethoven's melody always has an instrumental root, even in passages of the most fluid cantabile style; his contemporaries became aware of this when (like Giuseppe Carpani) they recognized in him not singing but a 'desire interrupted by singing'.[43] The working hypothesis of a modern scholar such as Schering, who linked Beethoven's themes with the poetry read by the composer (the details of which are, of course, impossible to discover), is valid only in so far as it is impossible to confirm, and amounts to an unattainable extreme of the instrumental stylization of singing.[44] This attitude towards melody explains Beethoven's sympathy for instrumental recitative, which is used to an extent that is not sufficiently explained by its precedents in C. P. E. Bach or Haydn. He uses it in various circumstances, from the consignment of declamatory passages in the style of *opera seria* to the piano, the string quartet or the double basses of the Ninth Symphony, to accents, articulations and recitative-like fits and starts that break up the metric regularity achieved by the eighteenth-century sonata. The greatest instrumental composer of his time was totally in favour of using unpronounceable words, as it were, thus resurrecting the old belief in a dormant spirit within the strings of the instrument which the artist awakened and engaged in a mysterious conversation.

In short, harmony and melody converge in the field of rhythm, in which the innovations are better known. Here the most important elements are syncopations emphasized by sforzatos and off-beat accents assigned to full chords on the piano, sharp pizzicatos on the strings and weighty sonorities of brass and timpani, a sign of unease which in the Viennese environment of composers like Dittersdorf, Weigl and Gelínek, Beethoven could use as a singular call to energy and action. More regular than Mozart in his use of two-bar phrases, which also dominate many works by other composers, Beethoven made up for this with constant changes of tempo in fits of accelerations and relaxations that give his language a distinctly anthropomorphic character. A few anthropological metaphors inserted above the stave are in themselves significant: 'exhausted, plaintive', 'reviving by degrees' (op. 110), 'oppressed' (op. 130) and 'feeling new strength' (op. 132); but more indicative than anything else is the question of tempo in general. Bach, almost without using markings concerning movement, does not leave the performer in any real doubt concerning his contrasts of tempo, and even for Mozart, *allegro*, *adagio* and *presto* were sufficient opening instructions, since they fell within the performing tradition without any substantial variation. But for Beethoven, even when he uses detailed indications in his own language or trusts in the mathematical time of the metronome, tempo is a problem that is always a matter of question, and generations of conductors and pianists will imagine afresh each time, watch in hand, the tempo of the 'Eroica', the Fifth Symphony, or op. 106 with different results, giving the concert-going public a great deal to think about.

Finally, from the language's anthropomorphic character is derived the symbolic density of Beethoven's music, the object of countless interpretations from his time to today and of constant discussions about what might lie behind the notes. A varied and sensational literature that cannot be ignored as circumstantial evidence bears witness to this anxiety to cross the Rubicon of abstract music which Beethoven has provoked far more than any other musician of the past. There is, in fact, nothing beyond the notes of Beethoven's music, yet one cannot conceive of the question's not being asked; and within this tantalizing situation lies the reason for the rhetoric devoted to Beethoven, and at the same time for his immense and consistent popularity.

The music up to the French invasion of Vienna (1809)

There is almost nothing by the Beethoven of the Bonn years that is completely spontaneous, though this period covered a considerable period of time (1770–92). His first exercises were in harmony, and contain traces of the theoretical works of Kirnberger, Vogel and Mattheson; they reveal the basis of a modern technique, recently set out in the harmonic elaboration of the *galant* era (Fux and counterpoint were material more for study in Vienna with Albrechtsberger). Among his resulting compositions, the *Cantata on the death of the Emperor Joseph II* (1790) stands out, with its precocious presentiment in the third section of a dream of happiness in the manner of the Ninth Symphony ('Then the men rose up to the light'), later appropriately re-used in the conclusion of *Fidelio*. Also sketched at Bonn were a few compositions published between 1795 and 1797 with an exceptional awareness that he was competing on the famous stage of Vienna; while Haydn, returning from his success in London, continued to be the city's best-known musician, Beethoven had a whole series of sociable works to be advertised, like the Serenade op. 8, the Trios for strings op. 9, the delicate song *Adelaide* and the Septet op. 20, besides a number of minuets, German dances and contredanses. They are less cheeky than Mozart's wind serenades, with more charming thematic writing that makes the Septet seem like a work for 'village musicians' who have moved to the city and rapidly become thorough *Kapellmeisters*. A natural gaiety inspired by Haydn which can scarcely be restrained shows itself in the finales of the Piano Trio op. 1 no. 1 and the Cello Sonata op. 5 no. 2 (written for the King of Prussia, whose passion for the cello had already inspired so much from Mozart and Boccherini), and above all in the rondos of the first two piano concertos. An episode from the First Concerto op. 15, which sounds as if it were overheard in some tavern or other, is presented as an up-dated version of the 'Turkish' or 'Hungarian' liberties that Mozart and Haydn had taken in similar situations.

Mixed up with these extrovert works that assured Beethoven's popularity in Vienna, however, are affirmations of a different type. Already the third of the Trios op. 1 no longer has much Haydn in it (a story, false but significant, had it that the elderly composer was against its publication), and it is fully orientated towards the most biting Mozartian C minor. But the field in which Beethoven meant to distinguish himself in the most decisive way from both Haydn and Mozart was that of piano music (he wrote twelve sonatas before 1800), continually leading the way with results that only later appeared in

other media. The three Sonatas op. 2 were published in 1796 with a
dedication to Haydn, but it would have been much more pertinent if
Muzio Clementi's name had appeared instead, especially at the head
of the third sonata in C major, with its mass of doubled notes,
arpeggios, broken octaves and trills in both hands, its virtuoso
gestures and its contrast between dense sonorities and light cantabile
writing, entirely based on Clementi's very anti-Mozartian piano
technique. The novelty of Clementi is tempered only in the finale,
with its recourse to the hybrid form of sonata-rondo, favoured by
the most sophisticated products of Haydn and Mozart's sonata style,
and to the chorale, introduced in a theme that recalls the voice of
northern tradition in catholic Vienna. An even greater polythematic
breadth, ideas drawn from Clementi and Dussek, and opportunities
for virtuoso outbursts are also evident in the Sonatas op. 7 and op.
22, which, like op. 2 no. 2, are concluded by charming Allegrettos;
these movements certainly have something Viennese in their easy
fluency, which was to appeal to the Weber of the Sonata in A flat,
deviating from the swift, categorical Haydn finale.

But a type of sonata which was in many ways new was already
beginning to appear; this type was in three movements, without
minuets or scherzos, and was concise, being polarized into thematic
areas that provided as much contrast as possible. The expressive C
minor category entered piano music; it was propounded in its
essential form in the first sonata of op. 10 and given an early, vast
summary in the *Sonata pathétique* op. 13 (1799). Contemporary with
the discovery of Cherubini's *Médée* and slightly later than Schiller's
essays on pathos (*Über die tragische Kunst* and *Über das Pathetische*,
written in 1792–3 during a period in which Schiller was reading
Kant), the work overflows with such vehemence that it loses its
overall balance, something that is not recovered by its rondo finale,
which sounds inadequate beside the preceding movements. The
sonorities dug up from the bass register by the opening Grave give
the first ten bars the aspect of a rock built out of harmonies, from
which untapped sources of energy inevitably spring forth, with
orchestral tremolos that are more exciting than similar examples by
Clementi and Mozart, and with syncopations and sforzatos of clearly
theatrical origin. A balance between this new essential element and
the breadth of the early sonatas is outlined in op. 10 no. 3, which has
its tragic epicentre in the Largo e mesto in D minor and contains a
reappearance of the minuet that represents an early look back to this
form from the past. In short, in the first twelve piano sonatas
Beethoven had already singled out all the paths that he was to follow

in the subsequent years (even the two Sonatas op. 14, which are quite easy to read, conceal the mixture of light and serious character that was to mature in future masterpieces); and in the year 1800 he also asserted himself in grander genres with the Third Piano Concerto, the First Symphony, the six Quartets op. 18, on which he worked for a long time, not without some reverential fear of Haydn and Mozart, and the 'heroic and allegorical' ballet *The Creatures of Prometheus* on a subject by the Neapolitan Salvatore Viganò, entirely devoted to extolling the educational virtues of the arts.

At the age of thirty, Beethoven felt an immense force within himself, and he provided evidence of it in the following decade with a dizzy course of creativity. The first step was made on the piano with a group of seven sonatas (op. 26, op. 27 nos. 1–2, op. 28 and op. 31 nos. 1–3) written between 1800 and 1802. To progress any further, thematic conflict and the tension of development were not enough; the sonata as an entity had to be considered, bearing in mind the risk of first movements overbalancing lightweight finales. This is what happens in op. 26, where, after opening with a charming theme with variations, the centre of gravity is found in the third movement, a 'marcia funebre' with rugged pianistic writing, placed between a scherzo and a restrained finale, the latter being the only one of the four movements that hints at sonata form. 'Quasi una fantasia' is the description written at the head of the two Sonatas op. 27 by a man who knew that he was infiltrating the most characteristic field of musical rationalism with new values. No sonata had ever opened with an Adagio sostenuto of such powerful suspense as op. 27 no. 2 in C sharp minor, which is in the mould of a great deal of literature dealing with night, and which became known through an irresistible tradition (one which stems from the Berlin writer Rellstab) as the 'Moonlight'. Both the Sonatas op. 27 are clearly weighted towards the finale, which in the second (Presto agitato) is presented on the largest scale undertaken by Beethoven up to this point, making use of all the technical possibilities, thick chords, an improvisatory cadenza and expanded cantabile writing under which the Alberti bass, driven forward with unusual rapidity, changes colour into a tremolo. The three Sonatas op. 31 readopt the traditional course, with the Allegro as the opening movement, but internally they display a variety of ideas and a flexibility of writing never before attempted on the piano. The first movement of the second sonata, in D minor, contains the most blatant assault on traditional Viennese sonata form, with a call to attention in the form of slow arpeggios, Clementian formulas translated into rattling lightness, themes of Gluckian geometry, and striking isolated recitatives. The whole movement represents a turmoil of unrefined material that Beethoven (like Prospero in Shakespeare's *The Tempest*, seeing that he himself authorized the comparison) whipped up with the very opening notes.

During this period only the oratorio *Christ on the Mount of Olives* (1803), in the wake of Haydn's great choral works, was in line with Viennese taste. In his chamber music, however, he moved away from this taste in the Sonata op. 47 for violin and piano (published with a dedication to Kreutzer), which seems to aim in a more topical direction with its autograph title, 'Sonata written in a very concertante ['brillante' is crossed out] style, almost like a concerto'; but by this time the definitive formulation of the great difference Beethoven was trying to affirm in comparison with Viennese precedents was also taking shape on a vast scale in the Third Symphony, the 'Eroica'.

Written for Napoleon Bonaparte and worked out over a length of time (1802–4) that was quite unusual for that period, the 'Eroica' is the synthesis of the aspiration towards the epic that was rediscovered in the revolutionary years, the supreme example of the desire to unite music and past events in rough and direct forms, in the *pièce à sauvetage*, the instrumental programme piece, the march and the hymn, which were revalued with grand expressive concepts. The dedication to Bonaparte, later removed in a fit of Plutarchan anger, remained indelible, not only literally, because it exists as a palimpsest, but also figuratively, since Beethoven, like Hegel, really thought he had seen 'the world-soul riding' in the person of the Corsican general.[45] The historical solemnity with which the 'Eroica' Symphony presents itself to today's listener should not, however, make us forget its actual character, which was perceived with some dismay by his contemporaries. The danger of the commonplace theme was not avoided, but deliberately explored. The first theme, which is related to a long family of E flat themes, is founded on the common chord and repeated countless times in statuesque isolation, intentionally revealing its points of origin; similarly the theme of the finale, already used by Beethoven in a contredanse, in the first episode of *The Creatures of Prometheus* and in a set of piano variations, appears as something conventional in order to make it easier to judge the new grand manner of the movement's construction.

The value of its grand scale and of the expansion to breaking-point of its formal framework is the first fact that can be safely acknowledged concerning the 'Eroica' – from its overall dimensions, surpassed only by the Ninth Symphony, to the size of its orchestra (with the use for the first time of three horns) and the frequent iterations of whole phrases or individual chords coloured by extraordinarily frequent sforzatos. The communion between its contemporary roots and its epic transfiguration is at its greatest in the 'Marcia funebre'; faced with timpani rolls and apocalyptic trumpet calls, the musicians of the *Garde Nationale* would have been able to recognize their prophet, though they would later have been amazed by the central fugato or the very gentle digression of the coda. Vicissitudes of musical language like these had never been heard before, in Vienna or elsewhere, and a further extension of them arrives in a third movement that invents completely from scratch the very swift and light type of scherzo which remained unaltered up to the Ninth Symphony and was also a distant source of Mendelssohn's overture for Shakespeare's *A Midsummer Night's Dream*, with its faint bubbling and its rapid running string passages at the point of the bow.

The compositional range of the 'Eroica', applied to a more immediate discursive style at a much lower level, appeared at the same time in the Piano Sonatas op. 53 and op. 57 (1803–5). In the imagination of their scheme of modulations and the daring of their juxtapositions of sound (due partly to a wide and adventurous use of the sustaining pedal) they went even further than the 'Eroica', while the overall form was completely reconsidered. If op. 31 no. 2, with its extremes of expression in the first movement, had once again had a weak counterbalance in the finale, Beethoven now turned to a sonata in two movements of equal importance separated by a slow interlude. An easy, neo-Haydnesque Andante was eliminated from op. 53 and replaced by twenty-eight bars of 'introduction', a dark, dense foundation from which the arrival of the finale again blazes out (this contrast has probably led to the work's present nickname in some countries, 'Dawn', though in England it is known as the 'Waldstein' Sonata). The Andante con moto of op. 57, with its three variations that already explore an amazing revaluation of this form, is again linked to the finale, even though it is more independent; a mirror of a tragically plastic sensibility like the 'Eroica', op. 57 (christened 'Appassionata' by the German publisher Cranz in 1838) sums up and marks a point of arrival for Beethoven the pianist, who wrote no more sonatas until 1809, when the publisher Breitkopf came forward with a request. 'I don't like spending much time composing sonatas for piano solo, but I promise to let you have a few'[46] was the reply from the composer who was going to choose a new area of experimentation, allowing opp. 53 and 57 clear supremacy.

In fact, in 1805, Beethoven was more than ever taken up with large-scale forms and was working simultaneously on a group of works; in the two years 1805–6 the completion of op. 57 coincided with the birth of the Fourth and Fifth Symphonies, the Fourth Piano Concerto, the Violin Concerto, the three Quartets op. 59 and *Fidelio*. The Fifth Symphony in C minor is rightly considered the paradigm of Beethoven's symphonies; the various alternatives to sonata form, explored in the piano works, are put to one side here in favour of the more rigorous example of Mozart, which is, however, raised to a superbly spectacular level. No piece had ever organized the principles of contrast and of the Schillerian 'pathetic' with such integration of metrical structure and thematic invention as does the first movement; the grand balancing of blocks of sound comes, as everyone knows, from a proverbial four-note idea, an idea unusable by others, and in that sense asocial, rather like the opening of *Coriolan* (1807), the overture for Collin's tragedy, with its powerful swelling unisons that explode into chords. In the second movement a few C major fanfares figure as some of the closest points of contact between Beethoven and the revolutionary *plein air*, and if the swift, tiptoeing type of scherzo had been born in the 'Eroica', the Fifth generates the ghostly type, one of the few ideas that Chopin was to accept from Beethoven. For the first time the device of linking the two final movements, already employed in the piano sonata, finally appeared in the symphony. Here the point at which they join is filled with a beam of blazing light which makes clear to everyone, whether or not they are experts, the great theme of Light triumphing over Darkness already treated in a cryptic way by Haydn and Mozart. The energy which fills the whole finale is compressed into fifty bars of motionless, traumatic tension; this movement is couched in the same language as the final chorus of *Fidelio*, and like it – indeed more so, in spite of the absence of words – is a celebration of the supreme and completely secular value of human dignity.

Within such symphonic unity the presence of the piano opened up new prospects, introducing a dreamy freedom and nuances not permitted by the forward momentum of the orchestra alone; this is what happens in the Fourth and Fifth Piano Concertos, which persevere beyond Mozart's greatest concertos in a way of which only Beethoven was capable. The second movement of the Fourth is still a violent contrast of moods between the piano and a Gluckian chorus of furies, and in the Fifth the solemnity of E flat is frequently presented in a programmatic fashion; but in both there is a common thread of gentleness comprising lyrical extrapolations over Alberti basses that are by now extended to a tenth, tunes stated but not developed (with complete disregard for the sonata principle), *pianissimo* paraphrases in the high register, and sometimes, over peaceful harmonies in the bass, magical sonorities reminiscent of the glockenspiel. His renunciation of the peremptory art of creation is also apparent in the single Violin Concerto, with its ideal of expressive intimacy, but it is greatest in the Fourth Piano Concerto, starting from its surprise beginning on the solo piano with a chord that was enough to enchant Schubert, with a pulsating rhythm identical to those of many sad passages in *Fidelio* (e.g. Leonore's 'und süssen Trost dir bringen')[47] or in the cycle *An die ferne Geliebte* ('Wo die Berge so blau'), and with the coming and going of simple and double scales whose external indifference prefigures the increase in ornamentation typical of the late works. This is the Beethoven furthest from the cult of Handel, the point of departure for pieces like the Violin Sonata op. 96 and the Piano Trio op. 97, the Beethoven who did not oppose, as he did in the Fifth Symphony and *Coriolan*, the front that had already been formed between Mozart and Schubert, but encouraged it from the peak of a language that remained famous.

But before continuing in that direction, this incredible two-year period (1805–6) included other events, above all the production of Beethoven's only opera *Fidelio*. Its expressive poles, at first sight, are the Fifth Symphony and the Fourth Piano Concerto, and the whole opera could be understood in instrumental terms, as a borderline case of the symphonic style that invaded the theatre in the early years of the century; and this impression seems to be confirmed by the four overtures that Beethoven wrote for it, each time unstitching and remaking a suit that seemed too tight for its contents. It was a labour in which the process started by Gluck of giving the overture significance by linking it to the plot reached its culmination. But awakening the gods of abstract music was a hazardous business; it rendered all the trappings of the theatre, from backdrops to costumes, superfluous. *Leonore* no. 3 (*Fidelio*'s third overture), just like the overtures to *Coriolan* and *Egmont*, acts in fact as a complete summary of the opera, a prelude to actions which no longer need to follow and to the raising of a curtain that is now superfluous.

This aspect of theatrical summary seems to be confirmed by the opera's initially mixed reception. At its first appearance, in November 1805 in a city which had been invaded a few days earlier by the

French, the opera did not last for more than three performances. It was revived in a different (shortened) version in March 1806 for two performances, and only in 1814, in a new edition which restored much of the first, was it to gain a firm hold on the German stage. Nevertheless, despite all its symphonic tributaries, *Fidelio*, precisely as theatre, is the greatest text of the realistic, adventurous vein that came to a head in the revolutionary decade. The opera has all the fingerprints of the French style, from arias with obbligato wind instruments to the type of ensemble that was favoured by Grétry in which the characters are confused, and from the opening of the second act, with the hero in a wretched state, to the figure of Rocco, a rough but good-hearted old man who harks back to Duni's *Le milicien*; and then there is Leonore, the virtuous and courageous woman who here receives her memorial. It is usual to put the blame for the opera's early failure on the public of French officers who did not understand German, but the Viennese would have looked, with even greater difficulty, for a Leonore from the light, capricious female gallery of their literary tradition; Beethoven's moralistic caution towards *Don Giovanni* produced in Leonore, in a positive way, a rock of determination and moral resolve whose ancestors go back to Rousseau's Julie. Even the opera's redundant opening (written in the language of *Doktor und Apotheker* and *Le nozze di Figaro*) can seem to be calculated to make its heroic climax, the dungeon scene comprising music and action combined as in great Mozartian theatre, stand out more. In the duet for Rocco and Leonore while they are digging the grave, with the funereal tone of the double bassoon, Beethoven introduces the grotesque note of *Galgenhumor* ('black humour') into musical theatre, and in the recognition duet 'O namenlose Freude' he concentrates an excitingly new intensity of passion. To the reviewer of the *Allgemeine musikalische Zeitung* (8 January 1806) this last duet sounded wrong because of its 'wild rejoicing' in place of a 'quiet feeling of deep sorrow';[48] but except for that initial explosion, it is really the romantic *Lied* that appears in the calm responses 'Ich bin/ Du bist', and it is the female sagas of Schumann that run through the continual interweaving of melodic curves. The newspaper correspondents of Leipzig and Berlin found more banality than excess: the trumpet call for the minister's providential arrival seemed a 'poor imitation' of a post horn; it was in fact a voice of reality, the result of various experiences which clashed with the prejudice of refined art and the ideal of beauty that was cultivated so carefully by eighteenth-century artistic theory.

Beethoven's rather unsuccessful theatrical venture pushed him back into instrumental work and the more intimate seclusion of the string quartet, with the three Quartets op. 59 linked with the name of Count Andrej Razumovsky, who requested them from the composer for his own domestic concerts. 'I am thinking of devoting myself almost entirely to this type of composition,' Beethoven wrote to Breitkopf in the summer of 1806, when the first quartet was already finished.[49] Nevertheless, in spite of such exclusiveness, the three Quartets op. 59 also show Beethoven's symphonic weight in the broad conception with which he settles into the chamber genre after a gap of five years, in the free extent of repetitions, and in the wide sweep of modulations. The whole sonata form was enlarged not with fits of violence or impatience, as in the piano sonatas, but by simply allowing the ideas to multiply by cross-fertilization: something clearly shown by the first movement of the first quartet, the third movement of the same work (where the symphonic aspect takes on the tone of a funeral march), and the Molto adagio of the second quartet. The strophic structure of sonata form is mixed up in a musical prose that bewildered the public of the time, who had even more preconceived ideas about chamber music than modern audiences.

This resolve to dedicate himself solely to the quartet was, however, distracted by the stream of symphonies which was still in full flow; closely following the Fifth Symphony, in fact, came its antithesis, the Sixth, the 'Pastoral', completed in 1807–8. Writing at the head of a description of the programme for the first violin part that it was 'more an expression of feeling than painting',[50] Beethoven kept his distance from the romantic vogue of the characteristic, picturesque piece by restricting the descriptive function of the titles attached to the movements ('Awakening of happy feelings on arriving in the country – By the brook – Joyous gathering of country folk – Storm – Shepherd's song; happy and thankful feelings after the storm'). A large proportion of the Sixth's rustic vocabulary is derived from Haydn's *The Seasons*; but Beethoven carries out a continuous metrical expansion, and this lengthening can be said to be the technical key to the composition, with phrases that normally straddle the barline, held notes, and repeated bars with a crescendo or diminuendo that accentuate the lack of movement and completely destroy the descriptive design. With its lengthy working out, the 'Pastoral' Symphony signals the end of the civic dominance that had had so much influence on the sonata style of the late eighteenth century. The picture of sonata form settled down into the most fascinating of spectacles; for Beethoven, living in a crowded city at the beginning of the industrial revolution, the country was not a place like any other, and certainly not as it had been for Mozart or Haydn, a place much worse than any other, but a physical and spiritual need, the symbol of an escape from everyday affairs and petty concerns, the right place for listening to superior and stronger realities. As a result, the wooded outskirts of Vienna were sacred, and a religious aura pervades the work, emerging especially in the finale, which contains the catchiest melody from this world, continually elevated by the tone of the chorale. Further evidence of this sacred character is found in the Mass in C major op. 86, written in the same year as the 'Pastoral' (1807) at the invitation of Nicolaus II Esterházy, who commissioned Haydn's Masses. Throughout the Mass there are instrumental parts, especially for the woodwind, of great melodic beauty, but at the Benedictus, in F major, an idea breaks out in the cellos that could easily come from the symphony; and this is still not enough, for at the end of the Agnus Dei oboe, clarinet and horn themes break up the formal equilibrium of the Mass which, as a result of its recollections of the countryside, is reluctant to finish, whereas earlier it had been so concise. Its commissioner could not make head or tail of it, and this was not surprising, since the walls of his chapel at Eisenstadt seemed to have been removed and he seemed to find himself in the open air.

Beethoven and early romanticism

Around 1809, the year of Haydn's death, Beethoven's career took a new turn: in the month of March the contract with the three Viennese noblemen confirmed the forty-year-old composer's enviable position. In May, Vienna was invaded for the second time by foreign troops, and the court and the nobility took refuge in Hungarian castles; Beethoven remained in the city, in his brother's cellar with his head between pillows so as not to hear the gunshots that were tormenting his afflicted ears. How the student of Rousseau had changed since 1794, when, with his Bonn friends, he spoke ironically about the pleasure-loving temperament of the Viennese! Now he railed against the war that was interrupting concert life and those social customs on which music depended so much. 'What a destructive, disorderly life I see and hear around me,' he wrote to Breitkopf in July; 'nothing but drums, cannons, and human misery in every form.'[51]

In the two years 1808–10 the common denominator of the symphony seemed to apply less to Beethoven's creativity. A division can be seen between two branches that were to grow further and further apart: one of 'grand' works, in which the symphonic surge of the years 1804–8 continued, the other of chamber works, with different characteristics. The Sonata op. 69 for cello and piano and the Trio op. 70 (1808) already offered a more divided picture of the sonata style, tending to include passages of marvellous contemplation, even if they are still worked out on a broad scale. But immediately afterwards a group of works with a fresher conception appeared, still eager for new ideas but without symphonic breadth or solemn affirmations: the Piano Sonatas op. 78 (in two movements) and op. 81a, *Das Lebewohl* (the 'Farewell'), which was written for Archduke Rudolph, who was leaving the city, and which was accompanied by precise subtitles ('The Farewell', 'The Absence' and 'The Return') in the manner of Dussek; the Quartets opp. 74 and 95, shorter and more 'chamber' than op. 59; the *Lieder* op. 75 and the attractive naturalness of 'Ich denke dein', by this time conscious of the tenderness poured out in Florestan's prison, in clear contrast to the ghostly *Vom Tode* of 1803, heir to the severity encapsulated in Gluck's *Klopstock Lieder*; and the Trio in B flat op. 97 (1811), Beethoven's last word in this field, which begins with an imposing phrase, but has a calm grandeur which excludes the martial aspect that is later denied on principle in explorations of ethereal timbres amid piano trills and string pizzicatos. And the trail continues with the Violin Sonata op. 96 (1812) and consolidates itself with another sonata in two movements, the Piano Sonata op. 90 (1814), whose finale lingers for a long time in the seclusion of domestic tenderness.

If with the 'Eroica', *Coriolan*, the Fifth Symphony and *Fidelio* Beethoven had embraced the revolutionary emphasis from the peak of his mastery of sonata style, in this series of works with more bourgeois and often charming features, he seemed to be trying out, still from a distance, the wider opportunities of the romantic movement, the minute instinct for construction, and the smoother thematic style. There was less hostility towards Vienna: the first movement of op. 78 is full of Schubertian ideas, and the finale of op. 90 offers an early example of Schubert's 'heavenly length'; in the scherzo of the Quartet op. 95 the rhythmic energy emits ghostly flashes like those of Schumann's *Kreisleriana*, while the finale opens with a pure theme in the style of a northern ballad. In op. 81a, the three notes that spell out 'Lebewohl' are superimposed on each other at the end of the first movement, tonic on dominant, fading away into delicate sonorities, like the coda of Schumann's *Papillons*.

This new sensibility, as is evident, can be fully traced in passages from instrumental chamber works; Beethoven's imperviousness to the romantic movement *en titre* is, however, apparent in his problematical relationship with musical theatre. The Beethoven of the first decade of the century had frequently expressed his dislike for magic, the central thread of the new German opera stemming from *Die Zauberflöte*, considering it boring in its argument and sentiments in comparison with the 'brilliant and attractive French operas'.[52] Meanwhile, however, Ferdinand Kauer had published *Das Donauweibchen* (1798), a source of future water sprites (or Rusalkas) for Pushkin and Dargomïzhsky; and on the Berlin stages Friedrich Himmel put on his opera *Die Sylphen* (1806) based on Gozzi's *La donna serpente*, and staged *Der Kobold* (1813) in Vienna, while Hoffmann competed with La Motte-Fouqué's *Undine* (1816). Now these examples of the new fashion, often filtering through literary friends and stirred up by the revival of *Fidelio* in 1814, reached Beethoven, who was intelligent enough to turn with a fervent interest to the new literary trends, but not enough to realize clearly that the only libretto suitable for his talent was that of sonata form; and so the problematic search for a good operatic plot began, turning up tragedies, legends and all kinds of texts. In 1809 he planned an 'Indian' *Singspiel* with the orientalist Hammer; in 1812 he asked Kotzebue for an opera 'whether it be romantic, quite serious, heroic, comic or sentimental', but specified a preference for a grand historical subject, particularly for one set in the 'dark ages', such as Attila.[53] In 1816 he planned a 'grand opera' for Berlin, the haunt of romanticism, and wrote to a friend about sounding out La Motte-Fouqué.[54] Later, around 1820, the name of Friedrich Kind, the librettist of *Der Freischütz*, appears in the conversation books, and the project of setting *Melusine* to music, with verses by Grillparzer, seemed to be taking shape;[55] other fairy-tale subjects, especially those of English origin, appear sporadically in the books and notes. Beethoven also took Ossian in hand, but the harp was the one instrument that had nothing to say to him; and the *Undine* type of woman, capricious and slightly neurotic, could not replace the only kind that interested him – Leonore, Rousseau's Julie and Goethe's Dorothea. Amid magic operas and Rossini he forgot about the theatre, and finally, in the face of the official romantics, he ended up proving a nuisance, as the old man Bach did before the Pietists.

To keep Beethoven busy there was, besides the themes of early romanticism, the other branch of composition, that of the large-scale works: the Fifth Piano Concerto dates from 1809 and the incidental music for Goethe's *Egmont* from 1810. (Setting *Faust* was a suggested project, but the actual meeting with the poet of the *Streben* occurred over his youthful text.) In the summer of 1811, for the inauguration of the German theatre in Pest, he hurriedly wrote incidental music to two celebratory stage works by the classicist Kotzebue, *King Stephen* and *The ruins of Athens*, and immediately afterwards began his Seventh Symphony, which, along with the Eighth, was completed in 1812 and was presented in a concert held in the assembly hall of the University of Vienna in aid of Austrian and Bavarian soldiers wounded in the Battle of Hanau (December 1813). As a result of German patriotism, the performance was a great success, probably because the 'Battle Symphony' was also in the programme, but the Seventh Symphony, too, had its direct share of the glory with the immediate encore of the Allegretto. In the Seventh the writing is less radical than in the Fifth, with greater opportunity to satisfy an overflowing imagination that seemed to his contemporaries (even to someone like Weber) to be bordering on extravagance: the linking of the introduction (Poco sostenuto) with the Vivace in the first movement (in which the possibility of a contrasting thematic area is not even considered), and the irony of the use of the term *allegretto* in the second movement for a canvas of enormous expressive proportions does indeed justify these first impressions of uninterrupted excess. The tone of a military epic is explicit in the trio of the scherzo, while the finale extends the possible combinations of the rondo to an orchestral virtuosity never before so conscious of its own brilliance. In the Eighth the minuet returns, like a glance back at the good old days, and the trio also preserves the memory of open-air serenades; after 1813 almost no more music of a purely symphonic type appeared for almost a decade.

In the years of the Congress of Vienna (1814–15) Beethoven was one of the glories of the German lands in the face of representatives from the whole of Europe. In the two years 1813–14, which were marked by the success of the 'Battle' and the Seventh Symphonies, the composer often appeared in public as a pianist (he did so again, for the last time, in January 1815), pushed into it by economic motives due to the devaluation of currency. A few works with a patriotic content date from this period, such as 'Germania' (1814) for chorus and orchestra (the final number of *Die gute Nachricht*, a *Singspiel* by Treitschke, including, among other things, music by Weigl and Hummel); King Stephen, too, full of prophetic frenzy, saw the heroes of Hungarian history galloping past – Ladislas, Andrew, Louis, Matthias Corvinus and finally the Austrian Emperor Francis I (an episode that seems to have been inspired by the imposing gallery of Hormayr's *Österreichischer Plutarch*, published in twenty volumes between 1807 and 1814). The most extensive example of this style, however, is *Der glorreiche Augenblick* (The glorious moment; 1814), an allegorical cantata for soloists, chorus and orchestra with which the composer of the 'Eroica' gave a restrained welcome to the Restoration.

After so much activity, the years 1814–16 were relatively meagre, especially 1815, which saw the two Cello Sonatas op. 102 as the only noteworthy works. On New Year's Eve 1814 Razumovsky's palace was burnt down, and Beethoven did not get another opportunity for social life. He fell in love for the last time in 1810; the letter to the 'Immortal Beloved', perhaps never sent and possibly a purely literary outlet, dates from 1812; in any case it is addressed to a woman who has remained unknown. After that point marital plans were set aside for ever, and from 1815 he began instead to take care of his nephew's education.

With the early years of the Restoration, then, Beethoven's life underwent profound changes, and his ideas on music also became open to new considerations. The approach towards romantic themes, unsuccessful in the theatrical field, re-emerged intermittently, and reached its peak of intensity around the years 1816–17, not only in works like the Piano Sonata op. 101, the song-cycle *An die ferne Geliebte* and the collections of Scottish folk songs and themes with variations opp. 105, 107 and 108, but also in his awareness on the theatrical level. Dating from this period is his rejection of Italian tempo indications, which he regarded as absurd and a heritage of the 'barbarous ages of music', as is recorded in a letter to the conductor von Mosel of 1817: *allegro, andante, adagio* and *presto* can serve at most to indicate the tempo, 'but the words describing the character of the composition [as do the directions in German in opp. 81a, 90, 101 and the cycle *An die ferne Geliebte*] are a different matter. We cannot give these up. Indeed the tempo is more like the body, but these certainly refer to the spirit of the composition.'[56] Tempo/character and body/spirit are really the romantic antitheses of which Beethoven gradually began to take notice, even if they ended up as merely intellectual ideas, passing reflections of a culture that was always close to the laborious aspect of composition.

The late works

After the circumspection of the years 1813–16, Beethoven's path moved in an entirely personal direction, with little interest in the romantic school, the result of an inner transformation that had taken account of the impossibility of continuing the great symphonic season. Beethoven's final creative period (1816–27) represents the decline of the sonata style based on the juxtaposition of thematic characters and the unification of events. The sonata declined because other forms became mixed in with it. These were not the brilliant pieces that flourished here and there, but historical, strict institutions, like variation and counterpoint, which were foreign in one way or another to the proper syntactical model of sonata form – not the ornamental variation of the late eighteenth century, but a new conception of transformation invented by Beethoven; and not academic fugue, nor even the fugato of Haydn and Mozart from the 1780s, but a new formal framework in which the principles of fugue sought to cross-fertilize with the contradictory but inevitably current principles of the sonata.

Late Beethoven witnesses a crisis of values, if by 'value' one means the theme in its position as protagonist/hero. Now themes tend to split up into fragments, little organisms which may lead anywhere, each one full of potential, or else they descend in rank and approach the popular; there is no longer that demiurgic spirit which takes over coarse material in order to build upon it. The man who had probed the sublime was now more tolerant towards the 'simple melody', and ideas typical of *Lieder*, ariettas, cavatinas and ariosos thus became transfigured in variations, but without violence, retaining something of their gentle source of origin. Syncopations and sforzatos are less common; in the harmonic field direct links between tonalities increase, augmented chords (already foreshadowed in the Sonata op. 81a) appear, and modal harmony, without leading notes, wins new room for itself. Ornamentation, especially on the piano, crystallizes in independent events, trills tending towards the high register, dazzling abstractions that are as important as the theme which they seek to envelop. Beethoven did not lose his head in the vacuum of grand ideals felt by post-Napoleonic Europe; his universe re-organized itself with a broad range, from the peak of compositional erudition to the most humble form, that was in a way a new positive testimony, even less restricted and richer in humanism than that contained in the great symphonic style of the early years of the century. The peak of eighteenth-century sonata form had proposed a structure in which tonal areas conditioned even the themes; now the discourse no longer accepted the directives of harmonic poles and was completely thematic in a very subtle way, without hierarchies or pre-established lines. In the end the sonata style of late Beethoven, in its formal freedom and its ability to follow every passing idea, shows links with the non-Viennese sonata, the alternative from Italy, Paris or London from Boccherini to Clementi; except that Beethoven arrived at this freedom only after he had tried out and fully exhausted the other path, the path of strict sonata writing. The greatness of late Beethoven really lies in its acceptance of the pregnancy of 'musical moments' and in its construction, in spite of this, of an organic whole.

The first step took place once again with the piano, in the last five sonatas (opp. 101, 106, 109, 110 and 111), written between 1816 and the early months of 1822. The typical three-movement form cannot be found in any of them, but it is utterly superfluous to resort to expressions like 'quasi una fantasia', because the dynamic is changed from within. Op. 101 opens with a theme like an 'Albumblatt' which returns as a backward glance before the finale and provides productive ideas in various episodes, but this climate is then jeopardized by the outburst of a march and the rustic vigour of a finale in which popular accompanimental figures go side by side with a grandiose fugato. Monumental dimensions are, however, associated above all with the following Sonata op. 106, conceived along with the early sketches for the Ninth Symphony and the *Missa solemnis*, and the project of a cantata for Archduke Rudolph, and also influenced in its grandiose conception by the gift of a six-octave piano which Thomas Broadwood delivered to the composer from London in 1818. With op. 106 Beethoven returned to the use of 'absurd' directions in Italian. He seemed to realize that many words (in the end all paraphrases of the term *Empfindung*, 'feeling') were more a hindrance than a help – better to rely on the superficialities of Italian; and so the opening tempo of the sonata, with its changes of colour from the communal energy of the chorale to solitary lyricism, in short all that a piano was capable of, is called, in a single word, 'allegro'. Although it is on a symphonic scale, there is no conflict, but the same ideas reappear in different lights. This scheme is even more apparent in the immense Adagio sostenuto, where the series of episodes leaves the impression of a set of variations, capable of linking the compactness of the chorale with the most open nocturne-like disintegration (with wide spacing in the left-hand chords well beyond the interval of a tenth in ways that were to become common only after Chopin). The closing fugue, also interrupted by an explicit, almost organ-like chorale, is preceded by a series of ideas (Largo – Un poco più vivace – Allegro – Tempo primo – Prestissimo), separate nuclei of energy and radical denials of sonata style, which were judged at first sight as oddities and incomprehensible whimsicalities.

The rejection of the fully dramatic vision is revealed by the gentle openings of the Sonatas opp. 109 and 110; nothing more remains of those lightning beginnings which in a few notes trace with clear outlines the play of forces within the entire sonata. The opening bars of op. 109 sound like an improvisation, and within a decade of such discretion the wonderful collections of short pieces by Chopin and Schumann were to be born. The cantabile style that is self-sufficient and not complementary to anything can be seen above all in op. 110, with soaring melodies in the right hand over an unobtrusive accompaniment in the left, with recitatives and ariosos of a pure singing quality. Op. 111 in C minor in fact opens with an unusual and almost quarrelsome aggressiveness, but there is no further trace of the inevitable metrical continuity of the Fifth Symphony; here the rhythmic fractures are continuous, open to the loose freedom of rubato and extemporary coloratura passages of touching sweetness. In the variations of opp. 109 and 111 Beethoven made all his new ideas about the old variation form quite clear: he preserves the theme's harmonic structure, but then for every variation invents a new theme which can in turn be varied, in a structure of concentric circles from which themes issue with the copiousness of flowing water. Beethoven does not demand originality from the theme of a Swiss, folk or characteristic song: his originality is entirely in thought and experimentation, and it is obvious why the sonata no longer interested him. The Beethoven of the 1820s could no longer imagine himself preparing a second theme or linking a recapitulation to the development; better a variation that uncovers themes at every bar and in the end envelops them, with a flood of light, in a single garland of trills. Within these sublime pages of everlasting circularity is fulfilled the dream of the whole of German culture (undertaken in a rather ambitious way in the second part of Goethe's *Faust*, and with disastrous existential consequences by Hölderlin, Tieck and Novalis), the dream of seeing directly into the world of pure forms, the realm of 'Mothers' and archetypes,[57] beyond the problems of reason and the conflict of the passions.

Variations, treated nevertheless in a direct and systematic way, also make up the final great work for piano, the *33 variations on a waltz by Diabelli* op. 120 (1819–23). Even in its external circumstances this work shows the distance which existed by this time between Beethoven and his contemporaries. The publisher and pianist Anton Diabelli had invited the most famous Viennese musicians to compose a variation each on one of his own waltzes, the dance most in fashion, whose extraordinary success was beginning to spread just at that time (Weber's rondo *Invitation to the dance* dates from 1819, and Schubert's *Valses sentimentales* were written not long after 1820). About fifty composers received the invitation, including Czerny, Hummel, Kalkbrenner, Moscheles and the eleven-year-old Liszt, as well as Schubert and others, and they all hurried to do it, while Beethoven slowly worked out his thirty-three variations, providing evidence of his great lack of self-restraint. They contain in fact a whole repertory of invention, paying court to the theme with its waltz rhythm and departing a very long way from it, here referring to Leporello's 'Notte e giorno faticar', there thickening the texture with mysterious harmonies, chorales, fughettas and a grand fugue in E flat which, along with the overture op. 124 for the inauguration of the Josephstadt theatre (*The consecration of the house*) and parts of the *Missa solemnis* and of the finale of the Ninth Symphony, is the most explicit proof of Beethoven's admiration for Handel. But the work ends with a minuet, even more disturbed than the one in the Eighth Symphony, a piece that, in its attachment to the past, might have inaugurated in the musical field, too, a 'Habsburg legend'.

After he had set down his new formal principles with the late piano sonatas, Beethoven brought the other category of composition, that of the large-scale works, to completion between 1822 and 1824 with the *Missa solemnis* and the Ninth Symphony. The external reason for the Mass was the election of Archduke Rudolph as Archbishop of Olmütz. Beethoven began work on it in the autumn of 1818, aiming to have it performed on 9 March 1820, the day of the solemn investiture. But the greatest musician of the new era was no longer a good workman and, as with the Diabelli Variations, he miscalculated and allowed the work to grow beyond the scale and time required until the early months of 1823. Even in the *Missa solemnis*, directly stimulated by the quality of the work of composition, there was a conflict between the historicism of the strict Palestrina style and the anxious religiousness of the modern harmonic *Lieder* style. There are many recurring similarities between the Gloria and the finale of the Ninth, based on a Handelian cheerfulness that becomes dishevelled in Bacchic joy, in a fusion of mythology and Christianity of which Beethoven was very conscious at this period. Some parts of the Gloria and Credo are dizzy with imitations, in contrast with the Kyrie and Agnus Dei, which are full of harmonic poetry, and above all with the Benedictus, where the solo violin, with appoggiaturas, tied notes and rising fourths that invite portamentos, ventures towards the supreme tenderness of the late piano sonatas.

The project of a new symphonic work, following the Seventh and the Eighth, cropped up as early as 1811 but remained dormant for a decade. Even in 1822 Beethoven had in mind two symphonies, one in D minor for the London Philharmonic Society and another using a chorus on a still unchosen German text, and only at the end of 1823 did the different ideas unite into one. The first performance of the symphony (and of three parts of the *Missa solemnis*) was on 7 May 1824 at the Kärntnertor theatre, Beethoven's last triumphant public appearance. On the notice advertising the event the adjective 'great' appeared everywhere: 'Grosse musikalische Akademie', opened by a 'grosse Ouverture' (op. 124), followed by three 'grosse Hymnen' (the Kyrie, Credo and Agnus Dei from the *Missa solemnis*) and finally the 'grosse Symphonie'. There were no doubts about its character as a solemn festival and a proud German affirmation against the growing success of Rossini. Although the composer had planned to present the symphony first at Berlin, it was given on that evening by the Beethoven circle in Vienna.

In the Ninth symphony there is indeed marvellous grandeur and an urge to summarize that subjugates and sums up everything; the encyclopaedic spirit of the nineteenth century, the replacement of the previous century's method of collaboration by one of systematic construction by a single person, and the cyclic vision that was to be so important in the novel, the music drama and the symphony of the late nineteenth century, have in the Ninth an early binding affirmation. The work begins *ab origine*, starting out from a numinous opening in which one seems to be present at the very birth of the theme, an unforgettable model for the late symphonic writing of composers like Bruckner and Mahler. The return to the vast field of the symphony brought back the tensions of sonata form, and vast areas of dramatic violence arise here and in the scherzo; but there is no longer the theorematic clarity of the Fifth Symphony, as an abundance of ideas, some of which are even in a shadowy, chamber style, was by now preferred to the transparency of the overall form. Certainly, compared with the late piano sonatas, the variations of the Adagio molto e cantabile seem to be worked out in a more scholastic way, but the crux, the link between the individual and the communal paths, is once again condensed into the introduction of the final section. The main themes of the three previous movements are recalled for the first time in the history of the symphony, like symbols evoked with great dramatic power, and are closely followed by fragments of instrumental recitative, until a human voice (an actual baritone voice) breaks the symphony's instrumental supremacy by singing in a broad fashion the words 'O friends, not these tones, but let us rather sing more pleasant and joyful ones'. This is the invitation to sing Schiller's ode *An die Freude* (1785), to abandon the instrumental metaphor for the comprehensible and sociable word. The use of Schiller's ode, which Beethoven had known and loved since his youth by the Rhine, with its celebration of the Joy that helps to overcome obstacles and its exhortation to brotherhood of a humanity that had never seemed so majestic, only served to clarify the ideological premise that is present in all Beethoven. The choice of the Ninth's finale was really an Enlightenment choice, a suitable point of arrival for a meditation on the relationship between music and words which had existed for decades: 'what custom has strictly separated', Joy's spells reunite. By restricting the intention, the 'strict separation' could also be that of music and poetry, to which linguistic theorists had devoted so much speculation and which now reunited in a clearly demonstrable communion that was more promising than ever.

After the memorable concert of May 1824, Beethoven's life became increasingly unvaried; the only salient events were his illness in the spring of 1825 that made him fear for his life, and his nephew's attempted suicide in 1826. In Vienna, which from 1823 worshipped Rossini, Beethoven, although noticed and admired, no longer stood out as he had done ten years earlier, in the days of the Congress. It took his death, on 26 March 1827, for the city to be shaken again and united in an impressive funeral ceremony.

In a state resembling inward soliloquizing, it fell to the late quartets to explore in a definitive way the regions uncovered by the late sonatas and to conclude Beethoven's artistic course in the three years 1824–6. There are five of them (opp. 127, 130, 131, 132 and 135), to which must be added the *Grosse Fuge*, conceived as the conclusion of op. 130 but later replaced by another finale and published separately as op. 133. The stimulus to return to this genre, after a gap of thirteen years, came from another Russian dilettante, Prince Nicolas Galitzin, who asked Beethoven for three quartets towards the end of 1822. Sketches for the first two (opp. 127 and 132) coincide with the final ones for the Ninth Symphony in 1824; here, too, as in the Diabelli Variations and the *Missa solemnis*, the dimensions of the commissioned product were exceeded. It was the work which made the decisions for the composer, and the three quartets that had been ordered (opp. 127, 132 and 130) were followed in 1826, as if by inertia, by opp. 131 and 135 which, with their predecessors, form a unique and complete record.

All the characteristics of Beethoven's late style, singled out above with regard to the piano sonatas, recur in the quartets, but as far as new ideas are concerned the quartets caused greater surprise than the sonatas because of the delay for the astonished customers and because of the more public scale of the chamber genre. The contrapuntal aspect was stimulated by the presence of four physically distinct instruments, and has its high points in the *Grosse Fuge* op. 133 and the first movement of op. 131 (with its old-fashioned aura of the ricercare); but polyphony penetrates everywhere as an internal expansion of an instrumental genre that, in Vienna since the 1780s, had become predominantly contrapuntal. On the opposite side, the ideal of song according to a commonplace model was given even more prominence by the cantabile nature of the string instrument. Pieces like the 'Cavatina' in the Quartet op. 130, the 'Holy song of thanksgiving to God by a convalescent, in the Lydian mode' in op. 132, the Adagio of op. 127 and the Lento assai cantante e tranquillo of op. 135 are the peaks of a transfiguration of instrumental song that had always been pursued by Beethoven; never, however, had the art of 'melodic consolation', through appoggiaturas and suspensions, managed to such an extent to make even the individual interval fruitful. In the strict context of the quartet, melodies of a popular character plumb the depths with their foreignness; in the second movement of op. 132 an unexpected musette, almost like a recollection of a Ländler played by bagpipes, sounds like the bells following the night of Faust or 'L'Innominato'.[58] Elsewhere there is also twilight, a detached wisdom that seems to have completely understood and even surpassed romanticism; these are the moments of Brahms-like solipsism, halfway through the Adagio of op. 127 or in the third and sixth of the Bagatelles for piano op. 126, in which the melodic style of a lullaby appears, as though out of the northern mists.

The medium of the quartet also increased the opportunities for an affectionate revisitation of Haydn, as in the new finale of op. 130, with its mixed rondo and sonata form, in the Vivace of op. 135 (with a theme fit for a Haydn finale), and in the rustic rondo structure with short juxtaposed sections. Ornamentation of thematic value and chains of trills recur as on the piano, but with a more feverish character compared with the transcendental purity of the percussive sound. Similarly recitative is present, explicit only in op. 132 but as a parlando style frequently adopted in detailed articulations where the voice seems to be pressing closely beneath a thin veil that is not, however, actually broken, as it was in the Ninth Symphony. The splitting up of the overall form is also more obvious than in the sonatas. The Quartets opp. 127 and 135 are still in four movements, but op. 130 has six, op. 131 seven, and op. 132 five, and internally the division of sections is continuous, determined bar by bar, and if anything enriched by cyclic attempts; for example, mysterious themes comprising four slow notes are common to the three Quartets opp. 130, 131 and 132, with an oracular character that recalls the mysterious nature of *Die Zauberflöte*. One no longer finds the titles 'Scherzo' and 'Variations'; there is a tendency towards forms that are completely open, a tendency which culminates in the *Grosse Fuge*, where fugue, sonata and variation attempt a dramatic collaboration. Late Beethoven does not seek to convince by preaching, but proceeds with a kind of narration that today we would call 'essayistic'. Going beyond sonata form did not mean collapse, a rhapsodic style or a pot-pourri, but greater formal mastery, a reduction of the contrast between different forms, both of his own era and of the past, to unity and continuity; hence it was yet another proof of strength, a confirmation by another, more convoluted path of the positiveness that returned to Beethoven.

Thus, from 1816 to 1826, concluding his work on the one hand with the *Missa solemnis* and the Ninth Symphony and on the other with the late sonatas and quartets, despite the infinite reciprocal relationships that can be found between these two categories, Beethoven had conditioned the two principal paths of nineteenth-century music: first, the orientation in grand works towards symphonic construction and encyclopaedic, systematic synthesis; and secondly, the cultivation of the infinitely small, of the analytical approach and of attention to the smallest entity and imperceptible movements. This was the direction in which the sonatas and quartets of the final decade moved, towards continuous thematicism and the autonomy of the fragment: a choice that in itself encouraged a suicidal tendency, as an end of the inner independent musical language, organized proportionately between tonal areas, themes and their development, cadences and modulations, that had been the great achievement of the last decades of the eighteenth century.

Late Beethoven remained for a long time a foreigner in the new century; for Berlioz, Mendelssohn and Schumann the influential Beethoven was that of the 'Eroica', the Fifth, the 'Pastoral' and the Sonatas opp. 53 and 57. Among his contemporaries the late works had a limited circulation. An exception, though it never became very widespread, was the Quartet op. 132, which presented the irresistible attraction of the 'Song of thanksgiving'; but other works were for the most part received with disappointment and embarrassment, even by those who admired the composer and put forward the excuse of his deafness: 'if only we knew what you were thinking about in your music!' Grillparzer confessed to him in 1823.[59] The *Grosse Fuge* is a typical case: after its first performance in March 1826 it was not heard again in Vienna for thirty-three years, a dead letter in concert life until well into the twentieth century.

In spite of all this, the prophetic work did find someone capable of understanding it, someone who looked at the score and studied it, copied it and transcribed it, namely Anton Halm, who was entrusted by Artaria with making a four-handed piano reduction of the *Grosse Fuge*. Beethoven did not like the result (he did it again himself), but the capable Halm passed in a month's work from pitch darkness to the light of comprehension, something which he expressed in an admiring letter to the composer. The aura of holy terror that the public of amateurs and connoisseurs felt around the late works could, then, be dissolved in the eyes of a professional. The good amateur, the pivot of the changes in music between the eighteenth and nineteenth centuries, people like van Swieten, Razumovsky and Galitzin, were not able to cope with late Beethoven; it needed the full-time professional. Yet, no longer writing music for the courts, for the princes or the archbishop, he had not intended to write for everyone, as it had seemed to the public in the stalls of the Kärntnertor theatre, raving over the Ninth, but only for a few, for musicians; and this was a dilemma that Beethoven bequeathed in its entirety to the new century.

33 New paths in the age of the Restoration

After the close of the Napoleonic epic, the restoration of the legitimate monarchy, and, in extreme cases, the attempt to resurrect the old regime, Europe's social structure around 1815 nevertheless remained middle class. Consequently no change of emphasis was introduced into the ordering of musical life; the ranks of Napoleonic officers were reduced, old officials were recalled from exile, Jesuits were readmitted almost everywhere, but the *maestro di cappella* and the castrato were not restored. No important musician devoted his energies any more to adding lustre to court life; his main concerns, as twenty years before, were the public concert, the publishing business and the private lesson, all opportunities that were increased after the peace by the growing means which the middle classes, the true commanders of the situation in spite of appearances, had at their disposal.

Beneath ephemeral returns to the past, the Restoration's true character lay in the discovery of values which transcended the action of the individual and of the hero. The *Streben*, the striving for unreachable goals under the thirst for adventure, was devalued in favour of an obligation that fitted in with a higher order and an effort at reconciling (but in reality subordinating) the individual to society. *L'Organisateur*, the periodical founded by Saint-Simon in 1819, and Heinrich Pestalozzi's last work, *Schwanengesang* (Swan Song), are based on the principle of the collective work and the social personality. The conviction that the hero no longer deserved so much celebration gained ground; perhaps he was only the product of a fortuitous fame that was notoriously unaware of the mass of fine actions performed daily in every social circumstance; perhaps other unknown men, perhaps the hero himself in private moments, had had to win more dangerous battles and reveal greater spiritual strength. A new interest surrounded common characters and situations: here are the humble, illiterate and peace-loving protagonists of Manzoni's *I promessi sposi*, and the domestic epics of the novels by Jane Austen (*Pride and prejudice*, rejected by the publisher Thomas Cadell in 1797, was published in 1813 by Thomas Egerton with extraordinary success). In Austria and Germany, in particular, this was the period that was later to be known as *Biedermeier*, after the name of an imaginary character, the worthy Papa Biedermeier, the embodiment of a mentality and a sentiment made up of domestic romance and resignation, not without a note of pedantry and anxiety against the background of Metternich's peace.

Not everyone, certainly, accepted the lack of action that followed Napoleon's fall or resigned themselves to the difference between past glory and present greyness of which Béranger's songs reminded the whole of Paris in the years around 1815. Many people no longer knew what to make of their own times; the drive to conquer and rule remained, but without any longer a broad, legitimate channel by which to develop it. The great characters of Stendhal's novels symbolize for everybody this state of mind: Fabrice del Dongo, who rushes off to Waterloo in the last hours of the battle, or Julien Sorel, who clambers up to lonely spots to read the *Memorial de Sainte-Hélène*. Like Dostoyevsky's Raskolnikov, they were always thinking of Napoleon and were stirred up by a continual urge to act in some direction or other, not excluding crime; for Armance, after his setback in private life, the way out was to go and fight for the freedom of Greece, like Byron and Santarosa. People were asocial; they brooded over a hatred that was deaf to order and the most important bourgeois virtue, that of renunciation.

Now, even though in a coded form, the person who had thoroughly explored this conflict between individual and society, between invention and formal institution, was the Beethoven of the final decade; the devaluation of the hero in a transcendental vision did not have, in any artistic manifestation of the time, a greater and more unfathomable interpreter. At the same time, no one had felt more strongly both the intoxication of anarchy and the reward of restraint on a higher intellectual plane. For no one, similarly, had the renunciation of conflict nevertheless meant a rise to a new positiveness rather than a refuge in the idyll or a defeat of reason. But there were also spiritual divisions, like the two souls of Schubert, one bourgeois and *Biedermeier* and the other sublime and demonic; and there was also someone who was the complete incarnation of the new era's desire for serenity and its rejection of extreme solutions: Gioacchino Rossini, whose star, which had risen when Napoleon was declining, shone throughout the Restoration. His particular musical innovations were opposed by the old supporters of Cimarosa and Paisiello and by other general purists who preferred Sacchini or Mayr, regarding Rossini as an unscrupulous extremist, but to the public at large his spiritual moderation sounded very cheerful and beneficial. Hegel recognized that his taste must have been corrupt because he preferred Rossini to Mozart, and Leopardi held that the reason for Rossini's universal success was his 'popular' melodies, considered as such because 'the people, hearing the beginning of them, guess their middle, their end and everything in between'.[60] In short, for the 'non-experts', who were by now in the majority, in Vienna, Paris and London not long after Waterloo, Rossini was the end of a nightmare; he was the guarantee that everything was continuing as before. On this ground not even Beethoven, still less Cherubini or Spontini, could challenge him.

With Rossini's appearance on the international stage, Italy returned to the forefront of music. Neither Cherubini nor Clementi had enabled it to do so, but *L'italiana in Algeri*, *Tancredi*, *Il barbiere di Siviglia* and *Otello* made people hear in an unequivocal way the voice of a nation that had known its last triumph with *Il matrimonio segreto* in 1792. Italy's artistic and cultural balance at the end of the Napoleonic wars was heavily in the red: Cimarosa had died in 1801, as had Casti and Alfieri in 1803; Foscolo was in exile; Cherubini was writing Requiem Masses and Canova was working on his own funeral monument; and mourning for the present state of a country whose greatness lay only in the past had already spread northwards with Mme de Staël's journey, *Corinne ou l'Italie* (1807). Now, in the great stagnation following the Congress of Vienna, Rossini again proposed to Europe values that had seemed to be extinct and reactivated strong antitheses between melody (reserved as the exclusive heritage of Italy) and harmony, between voice and orchestra, between bel canto and declamatory singing, and between the humanistic rationalism of feelings and northern fantasies, escapes into the supernatural; all the contrasts regained their strength because Rossini came on to the scene. He also caused a definite rise in the importance of the voice; after decades of instrumental experimentation and symphonic emphasis even in the theatre, the vocal instrument returned to prominence, and from Naples to Paris Isabella Colbran, Giuditta Pasta and Giovanni Battista Rubini wiped out in a short space of time the memory of the castratos.

If Rossini once again proposed grand vocal virtuosity, elsewhere the cult of simple, humble singing continued, a medium for teaching in the footsteps of J. A. Hiller's *Kinderlieder*. In Zurich Hans Georg Nägeli, along with the German singing-teacher Michael T. Pfeiffer, applied the bases of Pestalozzi's pedagogical method to the teaching of singing in a *Gesang-Bildungslehre* (1810). Singing tutors and anthologies of vocal pieces began to compete with the didactic instrumental output; choral societies became so numerous and active that the police suspected them of being secret societies. In Austria and Germany the *Lied* became a meeting place like the sonata and the quartet twenty years earlier; in 1809 Zelter founded the first *Liedertafel* in Berlin, a model for similar circles formed later on by Reichardt, Rellstab and Ludwig Berger, a pupil of Clementi who moved from the piano to the field of the *Lied*. In Paris the success of the romance and the vocal nocturne for the drawing room spread; hundreds of them were written by Giuseppe Blangini from Piedmont, who had studied counterpoint with a pupil of Padre Martini to become, during the Restoration, the most sought-after domestic singing-teacher in the capital. A relaxed style of melodic writing, without rhythmic tensions, made headway in every field. The theme designed for use in a sonata, a candidate for thematic working out, was fundamentally short; but with the decline of the sonata, variations and new dances like the Ländler and the waltz preferred long fluent melodies that were even adopted by Schubert and Weber in piano sonatas (and later chosen as typical 'themes of redemption' by Malvina in Marschner's *Der Vampyr* or Senta in Wagner's *The Flying Dutchman*). A regular melodic style spread from the peace of heaven or sleep through a wave of children's songs and carols, *Wiegenlieder* and *Krippenlieder* ('lullabies' and 'cradle songs'), devoutly composed by Nazarenes of vocal writing;[61] melodies which, as a result of their gentle mood, represent a kind of votive offering following the Napoleonic wars. Austria, especially the Tyrol, was a seminary for these songs, which can be summed up entirely in the famous *Stille Nacht* written by the organist Franz Xaver Gruber for two solo voices (in thirds or sixths), a small chorus and, originally, guitar, since even the organ, in the church at Oberndorf, was out of use on the night of 24 December 1818.

The innate religious component of this popular melodic trend led to the most striking musical aspect of the Restoration, the relaunching of sacred music. The religious reawakening that followed the fall of Napoleon had many aspects: from the restoration of formal and perhaps excessively devout aspects to the religious sentiment of Manzoni, Chateaubriand, de Lamennais and de Maistre, and the theosophical mysticism of Tsar Alexander, who formed a Holy Alliance and who was disliked even by the Pope on account of his suspicious orthodoxy. Conversion to Catholicism in a Protestant country was a phenomenon which grew with the speed of fashion, and certainly Catholicism had many points in its favour in the 1820s: it provided a word of immediate consolation, was closely linked with the life of the people, and had a romantic sympathy for the Middle Ages, the age of faith centred on its capital, Rome. But for intellectuals the strongest attraction was an aesthetic one, the fascination of a musical cult wrapped up in a mysterious remoteness. A holy terror, in the choirs of cherubim and seraphim, surrounds Kleist's *Die heilige Cäcilie, oder Die Gewalt der Musik* (St Cecilia, or the power of music); and even Hoffmann's dog Berganza, in Italy and Spain, had heard a kind of sacred music that, with its simple chord progressions, gave rise to sudden emotions of the kind experienced by the philosopher who 'raised his arms and fell to his knees, crying from the depths of his soul: "Sancta Cecilia, ora pro nobis!"'.[62]

On the calmer ground of the historical account, other writings by Hoffmann (*Alte und neue Kirchenmusik*, 1814) and the jurist Anton F. J. Thibaut (*Über Reinheit der Tonkunst*, 1824) accompanied the first editions of ancient sacred music. In Berlin in 1822 Zelter's work resulted in the foundation of the Königliches Institut für Kirchenmusik, one of the driving forces behind the rediscovery of Bach. In

Rome the priest Giuseppe Baini published his *Memorie storico-critiche* (1828) about Palestrina, and Thibaut founded a society in his own home for the performance of ancient music, in particular Palestrina; the legend of Palestrina as the inventor of music – the 'père de l'harmonie' as Hugo was to call him – grew up at this time.[63] All this fervour for ancient polyphony, however, had a cultural and historio-graphical aspect; in its directness, romantic religious feeling was not at ease with counterpoint and preferred the style of a simple song over a harmonic bass – the path shown by Mozart's *Ave verum* which returned in the grand Masses by Cherubini and Beethoven amid the web of imitative writing (the opening for solo voices of the Benedictus from Beethoven's Mass op. 86 could be straight out of Schubert's *Deutsche Messe*). Even in Bach's Passions and cantatas, after the revelation of the St Matthew Passion conducted by Mendelssohn in 1829, the element that impressed the most was the simple chorale harmonized in four parts, certainly not the solo arias, whose individual flights of fancy were subjected to heavy revisions.

The Restoration liked to distinguish between sacred and secular. In Vienna the police banned the performance of a Mass in a theatre in 1824, and the Kyrie, Credo and Agnus Dei of Beethoven's *Missa solemnis* had to be called 'hymns'; but they could not take the religious feeling away from the prisoners of *Fidelio* or deny Leonore, who breaks bread for her husband ('Da nim das Brot') in the gloomy dungeon, the ritual of a Christ at the Last Supper. Even in Italian opera monasteries, convents and religious choruses offered extremely fruitful opportunities for formal sacred production, which increas-ingly became a refuge for opera composers who had retreated from the battle of the theatres, a genre of composition in which to learn before moving on to other fields; and an indisputable sign of confusion was to appear in 1838 when Gregory XVI, in order to meet the complaints about the decadence of church music, invited Spon-tini, not Baini or a product of the Sistine Chapel, to draw up a report on the situation in Italy.

But the Italy of the 1830s identified itself precisely with opera; Rossini had ended his career in Paris in 1829, but the time for Donizetti and Bellini had already come, with *Anna Bolena* (1830) and *La sonnambula* (1831). Italy was again a leading figure, but only in a particular sense: it was no longer the land of music *par excellence*, but the home of one section of music – opera. In 1830 Chopin's Studies op. 10, Schumann's *Papillons* and Berlioz's *Symphonie fantastique* were distinctive voices, and although the interaction between the different spheres could be fruitful and sophisticated, Italy's common musical language, which had extended over the whole of Europe even at the time of Bach's death, was dead. Also finished, however, was the conception of a universal type of music based on the blood-relationship between vocal and instrumental, that universality of which Mozart had been the final great champion.

The intrusiveness of harmony and instrumental experimentation to the detriment of melody had been feared by the intellectuals of the late eighteenth century as the death of music; separated from nature and the mythical union with the word and pronunciation, music 'has already stopped speaking; soon it will no longer sing', as Rousseau had warned in his *Essai sur l'origine des langues*.[64] Now the moment seemed to have arrived, since Chopin's study certainly could not be found in nature. On the contrary, having overturned the accepted view, musicians now proceeded with an inventive vigour and a thirst for originality unknown to the generation born in the eighteenth century; there were to be more changes, not only in the field of harmony, but also in those of pianistic sonorities and structured, syntactical form, in the decade 1830–40 than in the entire half-century 1780–1830. The age of Mozart and Beethoven, with all the passions that had shaken it, had based its strength on convention and on formal codes that were firmly and very widely adopted, and was an age free from the maze of trials and experimentation for its own sake. In this sense the adjective 'classical', which generally goes with it, can be applied with justification.

READINGS

1 Carl Philipp Emanuel Bach

The *Versuch über die wahre Art das Clavier zu spielen*, or *Essay on the true art of playing keyboard instruments* (but in particular the harpsichord and clavichord), goes back to C. P. E. Bach's Berlin period and consists of two parts which appeared in Berlin in 1753 and 1762 respectively. The first part of the work is devoted mainly to problems of fingering and the realization of ornaments, the second to harmony, chords and the technique of accompaniment. The following extract is taken from the third chapter of the first part, entitled 'Performance', and reveals the importance of an emotional element in the performer as a significant virtue opposed to mere professionalism or superficial virtuosity. The importance given to the interpreter's autonomy, then, was not to disappear, but remained in a position to reveal ideas in the music being performed that were even beyond the composer's intentions. This translation is reprinted from *Essay on the True Art of Playing Keyboard Instruments by Carl Philipp Emanuel Bach*, translated and edited by William J. Mitchell, by permission of Ernst Eulenburg Ltd and by permission of W. W. Norton & Company, Inc. Copyright 1949 by W. W. Norton & Company Inc. Copyright renewed 1977 by Alice L. Mitchell.

1. Keyboardists whose chief asset is mere technique are clearly at a disadvantage. A performer may have the most agile fingers, be competent at single and double trills, master the art of fingering, read skillfully at sight regardless of the key, and transpose extemporaneously without the slightest difficulty; play tenths, even twelfths, or runs, cross the hands in every conceivable manner, and excel in other related matters; and yet he may be something less than a clear, pleasing, or stirring keyboardist. More often than not, one meets technicians, nimble keyboardists by profession, who possess all of these qualifications and indeed astound us with their prowess without ever touching our sensibilities. They overwhelm our

hearing without satisfying it and stun the mind without moving it. In writing this, I do not wish to discredit the praiseworthy skill of reading at sight. A commendable ability, I urge its practice on everyone. A mere technician, however, can lay no claim to the rewards of those who sway in gentle undulation the ear rather than the eye, the heart rather than the ear, and lead it where they will. Of course it is only rarely possible to reveal the true content and affect of a piece on its first reading. Even the most practiced orchestras often require more than one rehearsal of certain pieces which, to judge from the notes, are very easy. Most technicians do nothing more than play the notes. And how the continuity and flow of the melody suffer, even when the harmony remains unmolested! It is to the advantage of the keyboard that dexterity can be developed beyond the limits of other instruments. But finger velocity must never be misused. It should be reserved for those passages that call for it, without advancing the tempo of the piece as a whole. As proof that I do not disparage speed, nor scorn its usefulness and indispensability, I point to the Lessons in G and F minor [Sonata no. 2, third movement, and Sonata no. 6, first movement] and the runs in the C minor Fantasia [Sonata no, 6, third movement], all of which must be played as rapidly, but at the same time as distinctly as possible. In certain other countries there is a marked tendency to play adagios too fast and allegros too slow. The contradictions of such faulty playing need not be systematically stated. At the same time it must not be assumed that I condone those whose unwieldly fingers give us no choice but to slumber, whose cantabile is a pretense which hides their inability to enliven the instrument, whose performance, thanks to their lazy fingers, deserves far greater censure than that addressed to shallow fleetness. At least the technicians are subject to improvement; their fire can be damped by expressly checking their speed. The opposite remedy is either not at all or only partially applicable to the hypochondriac disposition which is disclosed, to our greater misery, by flabby fingers. Both, however, perform only mechanically; but a stirring performance depends on an alert mind which is willing to follow reasonable precepts in order to reveal the content of compositions.

2. What comprises good performance? The ability through singing or playing to make the ear conscious of the true content and affect of a composition. Any passage can be so radically changed by modifying its performance that it will be scarcely recognizable.

3. The subject matter of performance is the loudness and softness of tones, touch, the snap, legato and staccato execution, the vibrato, arpeggiation, the holding of tones, the retard and accelerando ['Stärcke und Schwäche der Töne, ihr Druck, Schnellen, Ziehen, Stossen, Beben, Brechen, Halten, Schleppen und Fortgehen']. Lack of these elements or inept use of them makes a poor performance. [. . .]

5. In general the briskness of allegros is expressed by detached notes and the tenderness of adagios by broad, slurred notes. The performer must keep in mind that these characteristic features of allegros and adagios are to be given consideration even when a composition is not so marked, as well as when the performer has not yet gained an adequate understanding of the affect of a work. I use the expression, 'in general', advisedly, for I am well aware that all kinds of execution may appear in any tempo.

6. There are many who play stickily, as if they had glue between their fingers. Their touch is lethargic; they hold notes too long. Others, in an attempt to correct this, leave the keys too soon, as if they burned. Both are wrong. Midway between these extremes is best. Here again I speak in general, for every kind of touch has its use.

7. The keyboard lacks the power to sustain long notes and to decrease or increase the volume of a tone or, to borrow an apt expression from painting, to shade. These conditions make it no small task to give a singing performance of an adagio without creating too much empty space and a consequent monotony due to a lack of sonority; or without making a silly caricature of it through an excessive use of rapid notes. However, singers and performers on instruments which are not defective in this respect also do not dare to deliver an undecorated long note for fear of eliciting only bored yawns. Moreover, the deficiencies of the keyboard can be concealed under various expedients such as broken chords. Also, the ear accepts more movement from the keyboard than from other instruments. Hence, satisfactory and successful examples of the art of performance can be presented to all but those who bear a strong prejudice against keyboard instruments. A golden mean is difficult but not impossible to discover, particularly in view of the fact that our most usual sustaining devices, such as the trill and the mordent, are also well known to other instruments and the voice. Such embellishments must be full and so performed that the listener will believe that he is hearing only the original note. This requires a freedom of performance that rules out everything slavish and mechanical. Play from the soul, not like a trained bird! A keyboardist of such stamp deserves more praise than other musicians. And these latter should be more censured than keyboardists for bizarre performance. [...]

12. As a means of learning the essentials of good performance it is advisable to listen to accomplished musicians... Above all, lose no opportunity to hear artistic singing. In so doing, the keyboardist will learn to think in terms of song. Indeed, it is a good practice to sing instrumental melodies in order to reach an understanding of their correct performance. This way of learning is of far greater value than the reading of voluminous tomes or listening to learned discourses. In these one meets such terms as Nature, Taste, Song, and Melody, although their authors are often incapable of putting together as many as two natural, tasteful, singing, melodic tones, for they dispense their alms and endowments with a completely unhappy arbitrariness.*

13. A musician cannot move others unless he too is moved. He must of necessity feel all of the affects that he hopes to arouse in his audience, for the revealing of his own humor will stimulate a like humor in the listener. In languishing, sad passages, the performer must languish and grow sad. Thus will the expression of the piece be more clearly perceived by the audience. Here, however, the error of a sluggish, dragging performance must be

---

* Two specimens appeared serially in Marpurg's *Der Critische Musicus an der Spree.* Both were translations from the French. The first, *Grandvall's Essay on Good Taste in Music,* started on June 3, 1749. Later, starting December 2, 1749, an *Essay on the Decline of Good Taste in Music* by Bollioud de Mermet began. Both contain terms similar to those mentioned here and are marked by 'a completely unhappy arbitrariness'.

avoided, caused by an excess of affect and melancholy [this sentence appeared as a footnote in the 1787 edn]. Similarly, in lively, joyous passages, the executant must again put himself into the appropriate mood. And so, constantly varying the passions, he will barely quiet one before he rouses another. Above all, he must discharge this office in a piece which is highly expressive by nature, whether it be by him or someone else. In the latter case he must make certain that he assumes the emotion which the composer intended in writing it. It is principally in improvisations or fantasias that the keyboardist can best master the feelings of his audience. Those who maintain that all of this can be accomplished without gesture will retract their words when, owing to their own insensibility, they find themselves obliged to sit like a statue before their instrument.* Ugly grimaces are, of course, inappropriate and harmful; but fitting expressions help the listener to understand our meaning. Those opposed to this stand are often incapable of doing justice, despite their technique, to their own otherwise worthy compositions. Unable to bring out the content of their works, they remain ignorant of it. But let someone else play these, a person of delicate, sensitive insight who knows the meaning of good performance, and the composer will learn to his astonishment that there is more in his music than he had ever known or believed. Good performance can, in fact, improve and gain praise for even an average composition.

2   Jean-Jacques Rousseau

In the epistolary novel *Julie ou la nouvelle Héloïse* (1761), Rousseau (1712–78) returns to some of his ideas on contemporary music, which he had already expounded in particular in the *Lettre sur la musique françoise* (1753). In the forty-eighth letter of the first part of the novel (Saint-Preux to Julie), the old *querelle* between Italian and French music takes on a passionate tone in which the literary man surpasses the musician in imagining a type of music directly linked to the passions (drawing abundantly, moreover, in the realism of some of the images, on *An essay on musical expression*, published by Charles Avison in 1752). The translation is by Philip Yarrow.

Ah! my Julie! what did I hear? What touching sounds! what music! what a delicious source of emotion and pleasure! Waste not a moment; gather carefully together your operas, your cantatas, your French music, light a great fire, and when it is burning well, throw all this lumber on it, and poke it carefully so that all that ice may burn on it and give out heat at least once. Make this propitiatory sacrifice to the god of taste, in order to atone for your

---

* Marpurg (*op. cit.*, Sept. 9, 1749) in covering similar material writes, 'I know a great composer [Bach?] on whose face one can see depicted everything that his music expresses as he plays it at the keyboard.'

crime and mine of having prostituted your voice to this heavy psalmody and of having for so long mistaken a noise that merely deafens the ear for the language of the heart. Oh, how right your worthy brother was! In what a strange error I have hitherto lived concerning the productions of this charming art! I felt their ineffectiveness, and I attributed it to its weakness. I said: music is only an empty sound which can flatter the ear and acts only indirectly and slightly on the soul; the impression made by the chords is purely mechanical and physical; what has it to do with feeling, and why should I hope to be more keenly moved by a beautiful harmony than by a beautiful blend of colours? In the accents of the tune applied to those of the language, I did not perceive the powerful and secret link between passion and sound; I did not see that the imitation of the various tones with which the feelings animate the speaking voice gives the singing voice in its turn the power of agitating hearts and that the forceful representation of the movements of the soul of him who is making himself heard is what constitutes the true charm for those who are listening to him.

This is what my Lord's singer, who, for a musician, speaks pretty well about his art, pointed out to me. 'Harmony', he said to me, 'is only a remote accessory in imitative music; in harmony in the strict sense, there is no principle of imitation. True, it reinforces the intonations, it testifies to their accuracy; and, by making the modulations more perceptible, it adds energy to the expression and grace to the singing. But it is from melody alone that the invincible power of passionate accents springs; from it is derived all the power of music over the soul. If you form the most skilful sequences of chords without any admixture of melody, you will be bored after a quarter of an hour. Beautiful songs without any harmony are long proof against boredom. If the accent of feeling animates the simplest airs, they will be interesting. On the other hand, a melody that does not speak always sings badly, and mere harmony has never been able to say anything to the heart.' [. . .]

Then, having recited some Italian scenes without singing them, he made me aware of the connection between music and words in the recitative, between music and feeling in the arias, and everywhere of the force that exact time and the choice of chords add to the expression. Finally, having added to my knowledge of the language the best idea within my reach of the rhetorical and pathetic accent, that is to say of the art of speaking to ear and heart in a language without articulating words, I proceeded to listen to this enchanting music, and I soon felt, from the emotions it aroused in me, that this art had greater power than I had imagined. An indefinable voluptuous sensation gradually stole over me. It was no longer an empty succession of sounds, as in our recitatives. At every phrase, some image entered my brain or some feeling my heart; the pleasure did not stop at the ear, but penetrated to the very soul; the execution flowed effortlessly, with charming felicity; all the performers seemed to be animated by the same spirit; the singer, in perfect control of his voice, readily drew from it everything that the melody and the words required of him; and it was above all a great relief to me to feel neither the heavy cadences, nor the painful vocal effects, nor the constraint that, with us, is imposed on the musician by the perpetual conflict between song and time, which, being unable ever to agree, weary the hearer no less than the performer.

But when, after a series of agreeable arias, they came to those great expressive pieces that can arouse and describe the disorder of violent passions, I forgot at every moment the notion of music, singing, and imitation; I seemed to hear the voice of grief, wrath, and despair; I seemed to see mothers in tears, deceived lovers, enraged tyrants; and in the emotions I was compelled to experience, I had difficulty in remaining in my chair. I understood then why this same music that had formerly bored me now excited me till I was quite carried away; for I had begun to understand it, and as soon as it could affect me at all, it affected me with all its force. No, Julie, one is not half-receptive to such impressions: they are excessive or non-existent, never weak or mediocre; one must remain insensible or allow oneself to be moved beyond measure; either it is the empty noise of a language one does not understand, or it is an impetuosity of feeling that carries one away, and that the soul cannot resist.

I had only one regret, but it did not desert me; namely, that someone other than you formed sounds by which I was touched, and that I had to see the tenderest expressions of love come from the mouth of a vile castrato! O my Julie! is it not for us to lay claim to everything that pertains to that emotion? Who shall feel, who shall say better than we what a loving soul must say and feel? Who shall be able to utter 'cor mio' and 'idolo amato' in a more loving tone? Ah! how the heart will give force to art if ever we sing together one of those charming duets that cause such delicious tears to flow!

3 The orchestra at Mannheim

From among the numerous reports concerning the skill and organic unity that were characteristic of the orchestra established at Mannheim by the Elector Carl Theodor of the Palatinate, here is the evidence of the historian, composer and organist Charles Burney (1726–1814), published in *The present state of music in Germany, the Netherlands, and United Provinces* (London, 1773), i, 92–7 (modern edition in *Dr Burney's musical tours in Europe*, ed. P. A. Scholes (London, 1959), 2 vols.)

I cannot quit this article, without doing justice to the orchestra of his electoral highness, so deservedly celebrated throughout Europe. I found it to be indeed all that its fame had made me expect: power will naturally arise from a great number of hands; but the judicious use of this power, on all occasions, must be the consequence of good discipline; indeed there are more solo players, and good composers in this, than perhaps in any other orchestra in Europe; it is an army of generals, equally fit to plan a battle, as to fight it.

But it has not been merely at the Elector's great opera that instrumental music has been so much cultivated and refined, but at his *concerts*, where this extraordinary band has 'ample room and verge enough,' to display all its powers, and to produce great effects without the impropriety of destroying the greater and more delicate beauties, peculiar to vocal music; it was here that Stamitz first surpassed the bounds of common opera overtures, which had hitherto only served in the theatre as a kind of court cryer, with an 'O Yes!' in order to awaken attention, and bespeak silence, at the entrance of the singers. Since the discovery which the genius of Stamitz first made, every effect has been tried which such an aggregate of sound can produce; it was here that the *Crescendo* and *Diminuendo* had birth; and the *Piano*, which was before chiefly used as an echo, with which it was generally synonimous, as well as the *Forte*, were found to be musical *colours* which had their *shades*, as much as red or blue in painting.

I found, however, an imperfection in this band, common to all others, that I have ever yet heard, but which I was in hopes would be removed by men so attentive and so able; the defect, I mean, is the want of truth in the wind instruments. I know it is natural to those instruments to be out of tune, but some of that art and diligence which these great performers have manifested in vanquishing difficulties of other kinds, would surely be well employed in correcting this leaven, which so much sours and corrupts all harmony. This was too plainly the case to-night, with the bassoons and hautbois, which were rather too sharp, at the beginning, and continued growing sharper to the end of the opera.

My ears were unable to discover any other imperfection in the orchestra, throughout the whole performance; and this imperfection is so common to orchestras, in general, that the censure will not be very severe upon this, or afford much matter for triumph to the performers of any other orchestra in Europe.

The Elector, who is himself a very good performer on the German flute, and who can, occasionally, play his part upon the violoncello, has a concert in his palace every evening, when there is no public exhibition at his theatre; but when that happens, not only his own subjects, but all foreigners have admission gratis.

The going out from the opera at Schwetzingen, during summer, into the electoral gardens, which, in the French style, are extremely beautiful, affords one of the gayest and most splendid sights imaginable; the country here is flat, and naked, and therefore would be less favourable to the free and open manner of laying out grounds in English horticulture, than to that which has been adopted. The orangery is larger than that at Versailles, and perhaps than any other in Europe.

His electoral highness's suite at Schwetzingen, during summer, amounts to fifteen hundred persons, who are all lodged in this little village, at his expence.

To any one walking through the streets of Schwetzingen, during summer, this place must seem to be inhabited only by a colony of musicians, who are constantly exercising their profession: at one house a fine player on the violin is heard; at another, a German flute; here an excellent hautbois; there a bassoon, a clarinet, a violoncello, or a concert of several instruments together. Music seems to be the chief and most constant of his Electoral highness's amusements; and the operas, and concerts, to which all his subjects have admission, forms the judgment, and establishes a taste for music, throughout the electorate.

4 Francesco Algarotti

Francesco Algarotti (1712–64), who became famous in Europe with a popular little work on the optical laws of Newton (*Neutonianismo per le dame*), was one of the most typical representatives of eighteenth-century culture orientated towards the accumulation of information and exchange of ideas in the most varied fields. Present at Paris, at Cirey in the salons of Madame du Châtelet and Voltaire, at Berlin at the court of Frederick the Great, at the Saxon court of Augustus III, and at Parma with du Tillot, Algarotti took an active part in the debate on the reform of opera, summarizing these themes in the successful *Saggio sopra l'opera in musica* (published in 1755, with additions in 1762, and translated into English, German and French between 1767 and 1773). Taken from the third part of the *Saggio* (Essay), the following passage confirms two of the fundamental points, repeated by the theorists, of a 'literary' opera: the excellence of the recitative, as an ideal place for a dramatic kind of music, and the subordinate position that the instruments should occupy in relation to the voice. This translation is reprinted from *Source Readings in Music History*, compiled and edited by Oliver Strunk, by permission of Faber and Faber Ltd and by permission of W. W. Norton & Company, Inc. Copyright 1950 by W. W. Norton & Company, Inc. Copyright renewed 1978 by Oliver Strunk.

After the overture, the next article that presents itself to our consideration is the recitative; and as it is wont to be the most noisy part of an opera, so is it the least attended to and the most neglected. It seems as if our musical composers were of opinion that the recitative is not of consequence enough to deserve their attention, they deeming it incapable of exciting any great delight. But the ancient masters thought in a quite different manner. There needs no stronger proof than to read what Jacopo Peri, who may be justly callèd the inventor of the recitative, wrote in his preface to *Euridice*. When he had applied himself to an investigation of that species of musical imitation which would the readiest lend itself to theatric exhibitions, he directed his tasteful researches to discover the manner which had been employed by the ancient Greeks on similar occasions. He carefully observed the Italian words which are capable of intonation or consonance and those which are not. He was very exact in minuting down our several modes of pronunciation, as well as the different accents of grief, of joy, and of all the other affections incident to the human frame, and that in order to make the bass move a timing attendance to them, now with more energy, now with less, according to the nature of each. So nicely scrupulous was he in his course of vocal experiments that he scrutinized intimately the very nature of the Italian language; on which account, in order to be more accurate, he frequently consulted with several gentlemen not less remarkable for the delicacy of their ears, than for their being uncommonly skilled both in the arts of music and poetry.

The final conclusion of his ingenious inquiry was that the groundwork of all such imitation should be an harmony chastely following nature step by step; a something between common speaking and melody; a well-combined system between that kind of performance which the ancients called the *diastematica* ['Diastematic' implies, according to the sense of the ancients, a simple interval, in opposition to a compound one, by them called a system. (Note from translator's glossary)], as if held in and suspended, and the other, called the *continuata* ['Continuata', in vocal music, means to continue or hold on a sound with an equal strength or manner, or to continue a movement in an equal degree of time all the way. (Note from translator's glossary)]. Such were the studies of the musical composers in former times. They proceeded in the improvement of their art with the utmost care and attention; and the effect proved that they did not lose their time in the pursuit of unprofitable subtleties.

The recitative in their time was made to vary with the subject and assume a complection suitable to the spirit of the words. It sometimes moved with a rapidity equal to that of the text and at others with an attendant slowness; but never failed to mark, in a conspicuous manner, those inflections and sallies which the violence of our passions can transfuse into the expression of them. All musical compositions finished in so masterly a manner were heard with delight. Numbers now living must remember how certain passages of simple recitative have affected the minds of an audience to a degree that no modern air is able to produce.

However, the recitative, all disregarded as it may be, has been known to excite emotions in an audience when it was of the *obbligato* kind, as the artists term it, that is, when strictly accompanied with instruments.* Perhaps it would not be improper to employ it oftener than is now the custom. What a kindly warmth might be communicated to the recitative if, where a passion exerts itself, it were to be enforced by the united orchestra! By so doing, the heart and mind at once would be stormed, as it were, by all the powers of music. A more evincing instance of such an effect cannot be quoted than the greater part of the last act of *Didone*, set to music by Vinci, which is executed in the taste recommended here; and no doubt but Virgil's self would be pleased to hear a composition so animating and so terrible.

Another good purpose which must be derived from such a practice is that then would not appear to us so enormous the great variety and disproportion now observable in the *andamento* of the recitative and that of the airs; but, on the contrary, a more friendly agreement among the several parts of an

---

* For Metastasio's views, see his letter to Hasse, published by Burney in his *Memoirs of the Life and Writings of the Abate Metastasio* (London, 1796), i 315–30.

opera would be the result. The connoisseurs have often been displeased with those sudden transitions where, from a recitative in the *andantissimo* and gentlest movement, the performers are made to skip off and bound away into ariettas of the briskest execution, which is to the full as absurd as if a person, when soberly walking, should all on the sudden set to leaping and capering.

The surest method to bring about a better understanding among the several constituent parts of an opera would be not to crowd so much art into the airs and to curb the instrumental part more than is now the custom. In every period of the opera these two formed the most brilliant parts of it; and, in proportion as the musical composition has been more and more refined, so have they received still greater heightenings. They were naked formerly in comparison of what we see them now and were in as absolute a state of simplicity as they had been at their origin, insomuch that, either in point of melody or accompaniments, they did not rise above recitative.

Old Scarlatti was the first who infused life, movement, and spirit in them. It was he who clothed their nakedness with the splendid attire of noble accompaniments, but they were dealt out by him in a sober and judicious manner. They were by no means intricate or obscure, but open and obvious; highly finished, yet free from all the minuteness of affectation; and that not so much on account of the vastness of the theatres, by means of which many of the minor excellencies in musical performances may be lost, as in regard to the voices, to which alone they should be made subservient.

But unwarrantable changes have happened, since that great master's time down to ours, in which all the bounds of discretion are wantonly overleapt. The airs now are whelmed under and disfigured by crowded ornaments with which unnatural method the rage of novelty labors to embellish them. How tediously prolix are those *ritornelli* that precede them; nay, and are often superfluous! For can anything be more improbable than that, in an air expressive of wrath, an actor should calmly wait with his hand stuck in his sword-belt until the *ritornello* be over to give vent to a passion that is supposed to be boiling in his breast? And after the *ritornello* then comes on the part to be sung, but the multitude of fiddles, etc., that accompany it in general produce no better an effect than to astonish the faculty of hearing and to drown the voice of a singer. Why is there not more use made of the basses, and why not increase the number of bass viols, which are the shades of music? Where is the necessity for so many fiddles, with which our orchestras are now thronged? Fewer would do, for they prove in this case like too many hands on board of a ship which, instead of being assistant, are a great impediment to its navigation. Why are not lutes and harps allowed a place? With their lights and piercing notes they would give a sprightliness to the *ripienos*. Why is the *violetta* excluded from our orchestras, since from its institution it was intended to act a middle part between the fiddles and the basses in order that harmony might thence ensue?

But one of the most favorite practices now, and which indeed makes our theatres to resound with peals of applause, is, in an air, to form a contest between the voice and a hautboy or between the voice and a trumpet so as to exhibit, as it were, a kind of musical tilting-match with the utmost exertion on either side. But such a skirmishing of voices and instruments is very displeasing to the judicious part of the audience, who, on the contrary, would receive the greatest delight from the airs being accompanied by instruments differently qualified from the presen⁺ in use, and perhaps even by the organ, as hath been formerly practiced. [In the orchestra of the theatre in the famous villa of Cataio an organ is now to be seen.] The consequence then would be that the respective qualities of instruments would be properly adapted to the nature of the words which they are intended to accompany and that they would aptly glide into those parts where a due expression of the passion should stand most in need of them. Then the accompaniment would be of service to the singer's voice by enforcing the pathetic affections of the song and would prove not unlike to the numbers of elegant and harmonious prose, which, according to the maxim of a learned sage, ought to be like the beating on an anvil by smiths, at once both musical and skilfully labored.

5 In praise of Metastasio

From among the affirmations of the lasting glory of the dramatic poet Metastasio, this is one by an author certainly not suspected of weakness towards eighteenth-century conventions, Giuseppe Baretti (1719–89). The article, which appeared in no. iii (1 November 1763) of *La Frusta letteraria* as a review of a Venetian edition of Metastasio's *Opere drammatiche*, far from restricting itself to praising the clarity and musicality of Metastasio's librettos, recognizes the autonomy of a literary genre (the *dramma per musica* defined by its numerous connections with the music. From G. Baretti: *La Frusta letteraria*, ed. L. Piccioni (Bari, 1932). The translation is by Eric Cross.

The clarity, as I said, and precision by which the works of this poet are supremely characterized, are such that it takes very little to memorize entire scenes from them. And of all the thousands of people who can, among other sections of his poetry, repeat from memory the whole of the aforementioned *Canzonetta a Nice*, there are perhaps not five in every hundred for whom learning it from memory may have taken more effort than reading it two or three times. There are few poetry readers who can recite from memory long passages of some other poet, when they have not set out with the firm intention of learning them deliberately; but Metastasio's verses find their way into the reader's memory without his realizing it, because his poetry is clearer and more precise than any other, that is to say much more natural than all the rest of our poetry, although among this poetry Italy claims the most natural. I shall say even more: that in many Englishmen I have come across, some, though not very well versed in our language, could still repeat the whole of the aforementioned *Canzonetta a Nice* from memory, without being able to repeat afterwards a single verse of the three translations of the same canzonetta which are printed in *A collection of poems* published in London in six volumes by Robert Dodsley; and yet in each of those translations the thoughts and order of their original are faithfully preserved; but the clear, precise expression is not preserved, nor, in my opinion, can it be preserved; and likewise in France many know this poem by heart, but very few know that Voltaire himself, besides many others, has turned it into French with one of his translations, because Voltaire has taken it from Metastasio, and has not taken it from the centre of his own heart, as one can say that Metastasio has done. Yet to the readers of Metastasio, and especially to those who are or who have been in love, it seems that they would have had to make little effort to express their thoughts, and especially their thoughts of love, as Metastasio has expressed his, and that they would also have been able to express them very easily with exactly the same words, too, which Metastasio used; nor can one suspect almost at first sight that speaking in verse with the same ease with which Metastasio has spoken is something extremely difficult. From the attempt, however, that so very many have made to do it, all without exception have been convinced that appearances are deceptive, and that to say easily even the easiest things to say is something that is anything but easy, indeed one of the most difficult things of all.

However, the reader must not believe that with this long-winded dwelling of mine on Metastasio's clarity, precision and incomparable facility for versifying, I mean that his poetic merit consists solely in these three things. No indeed, this is not my intention. Metastasio has in fact very many other fine qualities, which make him a poet on many other counts, and one of the greatest poets in the world. Metastasio is so sweet, so very polished and so very *galant* in expressing amorous feelings, that in many of his dramas he is able to touch all the remotest fibres of your heart and move you to tears; and whoever is not a Vandal or a Turk must weep whether he wants to or not when reading especially his *La clemenza di Tito* or his *Giuseppe riconosciuto*. Metastasio is sublimely elevated in very many places, and Italy has no piece of noble poetry that surpasses certain of the speeches of Cleonice, Demetrio, Temistocle, Tito, Regolo and other of his heroes and heroines; and even more sublime than those speeches are many whole scenes and many choruses in his oratorios and cantatas. And these cantatas, incidentally, even more than his oratorios and his dramas, reveal him as a poet with such a fertile imagination that no matter how hard we may exert ourselves in this area, that is to say in invention, he does not leave anyone with the slightest shadow of hope of approaching him and matching him, let alone exceeding him. [. . .]

And another of the very highest qualities of this great poet is that great experience and most profound knowledge that he has of inner man, or, as others put it, metaphysical man. A countless number of feelings and affections, that Locke and Addison were scarcely able to express in prose, a world of almost imperceptible emotions of our mind, and of ideas as good as hidden from the very people that conceive them, and of thoughts and desires sometimes scarcely shaded from our heart, have been set by him with an extreme and amazing skill and clarity in verses and rhyme; and any expert knows what an obstacle verses and rhyme may be to the free and passionate outpouring of our ideas clothed in clear and precise words.

Not that the difficulty of expression in verse and rhyme was the only innate difficulty invariably skilfully conquered and overcome by Metastasio. He also conquered and overcame other equally great difficulties which are peculiar to his type of poetry. The fine effect of a drama, as everyone knows, depends largely on the music, in the service of which, as every drama is principally destined, it is necessary that the poet, wanting to obtain that effect, should consider the music and its restricted capacity, perhaps more than is fitting to his own dignity. So that the capabilities of music, then, can expand as much as their nature allows, it is necessary that every drama should not exceed a certain number of verses, and that it be divided into only three acts, and not into five, as the rules of Aristotle would require. It is necessary that each scene should end with an aria. It is necessary that an aria should not come directly after another from the mouth of the same character. It is necessary that all the recitatives be short, and very much broken up by alternating speeches from those who are appearing on the stage. It is necessary that two arias in the same mood should not follow on immediately, even if sung by two different voices, and that the cheerful, for example, should not follow on the heels of the cheerful, or the pathetic on the pathetic. It is necessary that the first and second acts end with an aria of greater commitment than the others scattered here and there within these acts. It is necessary that in the second and third acts two appropriate niches be found, one for placing a noisy recitative followed by a bustling aria, and the other for placing a duet or trio, without forgetting that the duet must always be sung by the two principals, the hero and the heroine. These and a few other dramatic laws seem ridiculous to the common sense of any type of poetry; but whoever wants to abide by the individual reasoning of dramas destined to be sung has to submit to all these laws, as firm as they are strange, and has to take care over them even more than over the actual intrinsic beauties of the poetry. Let us add to these rules also the other most hard and fast rule concerning decorations, for which the poet has to provide the opportunity to the painter to display his wider talents. Tell me now whether the intellectual efforts that are boasted about so much of the gentlemen who imitate Petrarch and Berni, and in addition the whole crowd of sonnetists, canzonists and capitolists [the *capitolo* was a burlesque poetical composition in terza rima] of Italy are comparable with a thousandth of the intellectual effort of a writer of musical dramas; I mean whether they can with a clear conscience continue to compare themselves, as many of them impudently do, with someone who not only has written so many almost perfect tragedies, subordinating himself to the many rules, but who was in fact the author of these various very strict rules, having been aware for some time that without them there would never have been a way of rendering universal the delight of a musical drama?

6   Christoph Willibald Gluck

In the famous preface (very probably drawn up in conjunction with Calzabigi) to the first edition of *Alceste*, published in Vienna in 1769 by Trattnern with a dedication to the Grand Duke of Tuscany (the future Emperor Leopold II), Gluck sets out his ideas on the reform of *opera seria* in a fundamental, illuminating summary. Translated by Eric Blom in A. Einstein: *Gluck* (London: Dent, 1964), 98–100.

YOUR ROYAL HIGHNESS

When I undertook to write the music for *Alceste*, I resolved to divest it entirely of all those abuses, introduced into it either by the mistaken vanity of singers or by the too great complaisance of composers, which have so long disfigured Italian opera and made of the most splendid and most beautiful of spectacles the most ridiculous and wearisome. I have striven to restrict music to its true office of serving poetry by means of expression and by following the situations of the story, without interrupting the action or stifling it with a useless superfluity of ornaments; and I believed that it should do this in the same way as telling colours affect a correct and well-ordered drawing, by a well-assorted contrast of light and shade, which serves to animate the figures without altering their contours. Thus I did not wish to arrest an actor in the greatest heat of dialogue in order to wait for a tiresome *ritornello*, nor to hold him up in the middle of a word on a vowel favourable to his voice, nor to make display of the agility of his fine voice in some long-drawn passage, nor to wait while the orchestra gives him time to recover his breath for a cadenza. I did not think it my duty to pass quickly over the second section of an aria of which the words are perhaps the most impassioned and important, in order to repeat regularly four times over those of the first part, and to finish the aria where its sense may perhaps not end for the convenience of the singer who wishes to show that he can capriciously vary a passage in a number of guises; in short, I have sought to abolish all the abuses against which good sense and reason have long cried out in vain.

I have felt that the overture ought to apprise the spectators of the nature of the action that is to be represented and to form, so to speak, its argument; that the concerted instruments should be introduced in proportion to the interest and the intensity of the words, and not leave that sharp contrast between the aria and the recitative in the dialogue, so as not to break a period unreasonably nor wantonly disturb the force and heat of the action.

Furthermore, I believed that my greatest labour should be devoted to seeking a beautiful simplicity, and I have avoided making displays of difficulty at the expense of clearness; nor did I judge it desirable to discover novelties if it was not naturally suggested by the situation and the expression; and there is no rule which I have not thought it right to set aside willingly for the sake of an intended effect.

Such are my principles. By good fortune my designs were wonderfully furthered by the libretto, in which the celebrated author, devising a new dramatic scheme, had substituted for florid descriptions, unnatural paragons and sententious, cold morality, heartfelt language, strong passions, interesting situations and an endlessly varied spectacle. The success of the work justified my maxims, and the universal approbation of so enlightened a city has made it clearly evident that simplicity, truth and naturalness are the great principles of beauty in all artistic manifestations. For all that, in spite of repeated urgings on the part of some most eminent persons to decide upon the publication of this opera of mine in print, I was well aware of all the risk run in combating such firmly and profoundly rooted prejudices, and I thus felt the necessity of fortifying myself with the most powerful patronage of YOUR ROYAL HIGHNESS, whose August Name I beg you may have the grace to prefix to this my opera, a name which with so much justice enjoys the suffrages of an enlightened Europe. The great protector of the fine arts, who reigns over a nation that had the glory of making them arise again from universal oppression and which itself has produced the greatest models, in a city that was always the first to shake off the yoke of vulgar prejudices in order to clear a path for perfection, may alone undertake the reform of that noble spectacle in which all the fine arts take so great a share. If this should succeed, the glory of having moved the first stone will remain for me, and in this public testimonial of Your Highness's furtherance of the same I have the honour to subscribe myself, with the most humble respect,

Your Royal Highness's

Most humble, most devoted and most obliged servant,

CHRISTOFORO GLUCK.

7 A description of sonata form

Francesco Galeazzi (1758–1819), the composer, violinist and theorist from Turin, published the two volumes of *Elementi teorico-pratici di Musica, con un saggio sopra l'arte di suonare il violino analizzata e a dimostrabili principi ridotta* in Rome in 1791 and 1796. In the second volume, Part IV, Section II, Article III, entitled 'Of melody in particular, and of its parts, members and rules', the author sets out the principles of sonata form, some of which are reproduced here, with particular regard to the three regular sections – exposition, development and recapitulation. (The entire description, with a full introduction and with musical examples chosen by Galeazzi, has been published in Italian and English by B. Churgin: 'Francesco Galeazzi's description (1796) of sonata form', *Journal of the American Musicological Society*, xxi (1968), 181–99, whence this translation is taken.)

23. To find a motive, to continue it even for a few measures is indeed the work of a beginner, but not that of the perfect composer. In the larger pieces of music, such as arias, or other pieces of theatrical or church music, and in instrumental [music], such as symphonies, trios, quartets, concertos, etc., when the motive has been written, nothing has yet been accomplished. This much is certainly true, that the best composers do not make any choice of motives; to them they are all equally good. But let us not anticipate that which we must discuss shortly. The art, then, of the perfect composer does not consist in the discovery of galant motives, [or] of agreeable passages, but consists in the exact conduct of an entire piece of music. It is principally here that one recognizes the ability and knowledge of a great master, since any most mediocre motive can, [if] well developed, make an excellent composition.

24. Therefore, having to discuss here the most interesting aspect of modern music, that is, the manner one must follow in laying out the melodies, we shall advise our reader first to learn from compositions by others how well to discern and distinguish their parts and members which we shall here enumerate and explain in all detail. Every well-conducted melody is divided into two parts, either connected, or separated in the middle by a repeat sign. The first part is usually composed of the following members: 1. Introduction, 2. Principal Motive, 3. Second Motive, 4. Departure to the most closely related keys, 5. Characteristic Passage or Intermediate Passage, 6. Cadential Period, and 7. Coda. The second part is then composed of these members: 1. Motive, 2. Modulation, 3. Reprise, 4. Repetition of the Characteristic Passage, 5. Repetition of the Cadential Period, and 6. Repetition of the Coda. [...]

26. The Introduction is nothing but a preparation for the true Motive of a composition. It is not always used, but the composer may use it at will ... It is then possible, sometimes, instead of beginning with the true motive, to present first a section of cantilena preparatory for it; this, if it is suitable and connected in a natural way to the motive, makes an excellent effect, provided that it makes a cadence, either formal or implied, at the moment when the motive begins. It is good practice that the Introduction (if there is one) be sometimes recalled in the course of the melody, so that it should not seem a detached section and be entirely separated from the rest, since the fundamental rule for the conduct [of the composition] consists of the *unity of ideas*.

27. The Motive, then, is nothing but the principal idea of the melody, the subject, the theme, one might say, of the musical discourse, and the whole composition must revolve upon it. The Introduction is permitted to begin on any note, and even outside the key, but the Motive must infallibly begin with the notes constituting the key, that is, with its first, third, or fifth [degree]. In addition, it must be well rounded and lucid, for, being the theme of the discourse, if it is not well understood neither will the following discourse be understood. The Motive should always terminate with a cadence in either the principal key, or on its 5th or 4th. In duets, terzets, and quartets, vocal as well as instrumental, the period is often repeated twice in different voices ... The Motive, then, is a most essential member of every melody. It is characteristic of beginners to rack their brains to select a beautiful Motive for their compositions without reflecting that every good

composition must always grow in effect from the beginning to the end. Now, if one selects a wonderful Motive, it will be very difficult for the composition to grow [in interest]; on the contrary, indeed, it will considerably decline. This will totally discredit the composition in spite of the most beautiful Motive. If, on the contrary, one will use a mediocre Motive, well conducted according to the precepts which we will now give, the composition will keep increasing its effect, and this will render it [i.e. the composition] more and more interesting and agreeable to the audience at every moment, and earn more than usual applause. And this precisely we see to be the practice of the most classical writers; whence it usually comes that an excellent Motive is in most cases the mark of a poor composition, [for] the latter's merit consists, as has already been said, in the conduct and not the Motive.

28. I call the Second Motive what is named the countersubject in the fugue; that is, an idea which is either derived from the first or entirely new, but which, well connected with the first, immediately succeeds the period of the Motive, and also sometimes serves to lead out of the key, terminating in the dominant of the key, or the relative major of minor keys. In most cases, if the Motive has ended its period in the fifth of the key, the Second Motive will begin in this same key; but if the Motive has cadenced in the principal key, then the Second Motive will begin in this key, leading then, as has been said, to the fifth or the fourth, etc. This period only occurs in very long pieces; in short pieces it is omitted, so that it is not essential. [...]

32. After making the final cadence, which concludes the last cadential period, it is not unusual that instead of ending the first part here, a new period, called a Coda, is elegantly added. It is an addition or prolongation of the cadence, and therefore not an essential period, but it serves very well to link the ideas which end the first part with those with which the second part begins, as we intend to point out. And this is its principal function ...

33. It is well to know here that in all pieces of music, of whatever kind or style, whether divided in the middle by a repeat sign or continuous, the first part always closes in the dominant of the principal key, rarely in the subdominant, and often in the relative major of minor keys.

34. The second part then also begins with its motive, which it can do in four different ways: 1. Beginning it with an Introduction, either analogous to the first part, if there is one, and transposed to the fifth of the key, or modulating in diverse ways. This method, however, is tedious and little practiced by good composers. 2. Beginning the second part with the same motive as the first, transposed to the fifth of the key. This method is also in disuse, as is the former, since it does not introduce any variety in compositions, which is always the purpose of all the skills of genius. But the following two are the most commendable methods: 3. One may begin the second part with some passages freely taken from the first, and especially from the Coda (if there was one), but in the same key in which the first part ends ... 4. The last method finally is to begin the second part with an idea that is quite new and foreign. However, in such a case it is not good to present it in the key in which the first part ends, but rather, for greatest surprise, it should be in some related key, but separated and unexpected. This period is always essential. [...]

36. The Reprise succeeds the Modulation. However remote the Modu-

lation is from the main key of the composition, it must draw closer little by little, until the Reprise, that is, the first Motive of Part I in the proper natural key in which it was originally written, falls in quite naturally and regularly. If the piece is a long one, the true Motive in the principal key is taken up again, as it has been said, but if one does not want to make the composition too long, then it shall be enough to repeat instead the Characteristic Passage transposed to the same fundamental key ... In such a case, it is necessary that the motive itself be conducted gradually to the subdominant of the key ... Or if the second method has been used – that is, the reprise of the Characteristic Passage – then the Modulation shall be ended on the dominant of the key, in order to start then the Characteristic Passage in the main key; and also in this case it is good practice to touch upon somewhere, though slightly, the modulation to the subdominant of the key.

8   Wolfgang Amadeus Mozart

During the composition of *Die Entführung aus dem Serail* (produced at the Burgtheater, Vienna on 16 July 1782), Mozart (1756–91) wrote two letters to his father, dated 26 September and 13 October 1781, in which he outlines, even if in a fragmentary and colloquial way, his 'poetics' of musical theatre. Clearly emerging from these letters, besides the feverish delight with which Mozart worked on *Die Entführung*, are the pre-eminence of the music over the poetry (the opposite of Gluck and Calzabigi) and Mozart's practice of writing the characters' roles bearing in mind the precise physical characteristics of the voices that would be singing them. The rejection of any intellectual position is evident later on in the final section of the second letter. This translation is taken from *The letters of Mozart and his family*, trans. and ed. E. Anderson (London, rev. 2/1966, ed. A. H. King and M. Carolan), ii, 768–73, by permission of Macmillan, London and Basingstoke.

MON TRÈS CHER PÈRE!

VIENNA, *26 September 1781*

Forgive me for having made you pay an extra heavy postage fee the other day. But I happened to have nothing important to tell you and thought that it would afford you pleasure if I gave you some idea of my opera. As the original text [by C. F. Bretzner] began with a monologue, I asked Herr Stephanie* to make a little arietta out of it – and then to put in a duet instead

---

* Gottlieb Stephanie (1741–1800): Austrian dramatist and actor. He succeeded J. H. F. Müller as director of the National-Singspiel, arranged the text for *Die Entführung*, and wrote the libretto of *Der Schauspieldirektor* (1786).

of making the two chatter together after Osmin's short song.* As we have given the part of Osmin to Herr Fischer, who certainly has an excellent bass voice (in spite of the fact that the Archbishop told me that he sang too low for a bass and that I assured him that he would sing higher next time), we must take advantage of it, particularly as he has the whole Viennese public on his side. But in the original libretto Osmin has only this short song and nothing else to sing, except in the trio and the finale; so he has been given an aria in Act I, and he is to have another in Act II. I have explained to Stephanie the words I require for this aria – indeed I had finished composing most of the music for it before Stephanie knew anything whatever about it. I am enclosing only the beginning and the end, which is bound to have a good effect. Osmin's rage is rendered comical by the use of the Turkish music. In working out the aria I have (in spite of our Salzburg Midas [the Archbishop]) allowed Fischer's beautiful deep notes to glow. The passage 'Drum beim Barte des Propheten' is indeed in the same time, but with quick notes; but as Osmin's rage gradually increases, there comes (just when the aria seems to be at an end) the allegro assai, which is in a totally different tempo and in a different key; this is bound to be very effective. For just as a man in such a towering rage oversteps all the bounds of order, moderation and propriety and completely forgets himself, so must the music too forget itself. But since passions, whether violent or not, must never be expressed to the point of exciting disgust, and as music, even in the most terrible situations, must never offend the ear, but must please the listener, or in other words must never cease to be *music*, so I have not chosen a key remote from F (in which the aria is written) but one related to it – not the nearest, D minor, but the more remote A minor. Let me now turn to Belmonte's aria in A major, 'O wie ängstlich, o wie feurig'. Would you like to know how I have expressed it – and even indicated his throbbing heart? By the two violins playing octaves. This is the favourite aria of all those who have heard it, and it is mine also. I wrote it expressly to suit Adamberger's voice. You feel the trembling – the faltering – you see how his throbbing breast begins to swell; this I have expressed by a crescendo. You hear the whispering and the sighing – which I have indicated by the first violins with mutes and a flute playing in unison.

The Janissary chorus is, as such, all that can be desired, that is, short, lively and written to please the Viennese. I have sacrificed Constanze's aria a little to the flexible throat of Mlle Cavalieri, 'Trennung war mein banges Los und nun schwimmt mein Aug' in Tränen'. I have tried to express her feelings, as far as an Italian bravura aria will allow it. I have changed the 'Hui' to 'schnell', so it now runs thus – 'Doch wie schnell schwand meine Freude'. I really don't know what our German poets are thinking of. Even if they do not understand the theatre, or at all events operas, yet they should not make their characters talk as if they were addressing a herd of swine. Hui, sow!

Now for the trio at the close of Act I. Pedrillo has passed off his master as

---

* It is worthy of note that the part of Osmin, which in Bretzner's libretto is negligible, was transformed by Mozart in collaboration with Stephanie into the towering figure of *Die Entführung*. Possibly Mozart was encouraged to do this as he was composing for a magnificent singer.

an architect – to give him an opportunity of meeting his Constanze in the garden. Bassa Selim has taken him into his service. Osmin, the steward, knows nothing of this, and being a rude churl and a sworn foe to all strangers, is impertinent and refuses to let them into the garden. It opens quite abruptly – and because the words lend themselves to it, I have made it a fairly respectable piece of real three-part writing. Then the major key begins at once pianissimo – it must go very quickly – and wind up with a great deal of noise, which is always appropriate at the end of an act. The more noise the better, and the shorter the better, so that the audience may not have time to cool down with their applause.

I have sent you only fourteen bars of the overture, which is very short with alternate fortes and pianos, the Turkish music always coming in at the fortes. The overture modulates through different keys; and I doubt whether anyone, even if his previous night has been a sleepless one, could go to sleep over it. Now comes the rub! The first act was finished more than three weeks ago, as was also one aria in Act II and the drunken duet [between Pedrillo and Osmin; 'Vivat Bacchus, Bacchus lebe'] (*per i signori viennesi*) which consists entirely of *my Turkish tattoo*. But I cannot compose any more, because the whole story is being altered – and, to tell the truth, at my own request. At the beginning of Act III there is a charming quintet or rather finale, but I should prefer to have it at the end of Act II. [This is the quartet at the end of Act II.] In order to make this practicable, great changes must be made, in fact an entirely new plot must be introduced – and Stephanie is up to the eyes in other work. [. . .]

VIENNA, 13 October 1781

Now as to the libretto of the opera. You are quite right so far as Stephanie's work is concerned. Still, the poetry is perfectly in keeping with the character of stupid, surly, malicious Osmin. I am well aware that the verse is not of the best, but it fitted in and it agreed so well with the musical ideas which already were buzzing in my head, that it could not fail to please me; and I would like to wager that when it is performed, no deficiencies will be found. As for the poetry which was there originally, I really have nothing to say against it. Belmonte's aria 'O wie ängstlich' could hardly be better written for music. Except for 'Hui' and 'Kummer ruht in meinem Schoss' (for sorrow – cannot rest), the aria too is not bad, particularly the first part. Besides, I should say that in the opera the poetry must be altogether the obedient daughter of the music. Why do Italian comic operas please everywhere – in spite of their miserable libretti – even in Paris, where I myself witnessed their success? Just because there the music reigns supreme and when one listens to it all else is forgotten. Why, an opera is sure of success when the plot is well worked out, the words written solely for the music and not shoved in here and there to suit some miserable rhyme (which, God knows, never enhances the value of any theatrical performance, be it what it may, but rather detracts from it) – I mean, words or even entire verses which ruin the composer's whole idea. Verses are indeed the most indispensable element for music – but rhymes – solely for the sake of rhyming – the most detrimental. Those high and mighty people who set to work in this pedantic fashion will always come to grief, both they and their music. The best thing of all is when a good composer, who understands the stage and is talented enough to make sound suggestions, meets an able poet, that true phoenix; in that case no fears need be entertained as to the applause even of the ignorant. Poets almost remind me of trumpeters with their professional tricks! If we composers were always to stick so faithfully to our rules (which were very good at a time when no one knew better), we should be concocting music as unpalatable as their libretti.

Well, I think I have chattered enough nonsense to you; so I must now enquire about what interests me most of all, and that is, your health, my most beloved father! In my last letter I suggested two remedies for giddiness, which, if you do not know them, you will probably not think any good.

9 A hymn for 14 July

To celebrate the first anniversary of the storming of the Bastille on 14 July 1790, the *Journal de la municipalité* (Paris, 6 June 1790) proposed the following form for the ceremony: the singing of the Te Deum, a civic oath, and the singing of a hymn to liberty set to music by a famous composer. In the issue for 24 June, the *Chronique de Paris* published a long letter by an anonymous correspondent, here quoted in part, which demands a French hymn instead of the Te Deum; the aesthetic value openly took second place in comparison with the symbolic value of the new hymn. Taken from C. Pierre: *Les hymnes et chansons de la Révolution* (Paris, 1904), 199. The translation is by Philip Yarrow.

I know that when the oath is taken, the cannon will roar; the flags of liberty will be raised; a forest of pikes, sabres, and bayonets will be agitated; I well know that I shall shed tears as I grip my rifle; but what shall I say to the Eternal? When I am full of Him, full of liberty, overcome by the enthusiasm that she inspires, do you think that you can satisfy me by making me bawl this Te Deum which I do not understand?

First, why speak Latin on the day of the festival of the French? [. . .]

The Te Deum? but tyrants have had it sung, and it was sung for the birth of Charles IX and for that of Louis XIV; it has been sung for crimes, it has been sung for trivialities; and I certainly do not want to hear what was fit for all these things on the Fourteenth of July.

The Te Deum? It is sung when one wins, sometimes when one is beaten, always when one does wrong, when country districts have been ravaged and towns burnt, when thousands of poor wretches put there only to kill or be killed have been slaughtered! Ah! that is not the hymn for the Fourteenth of July. [. . .]

After crossing the Red Sea, Moses composed a canticle which is unworthy of the miracle, but which, made for the event, is far better than this widely sung Te Deum, the child of a Bishop of Africa . . . Horace would have made himself immortal, had he written nothing but his *Carmen seculare*.

What the Jews could do, what the proud Romans did, the free French will do.

Jean–Baptiste [Rousseau] is dead, it is true; Piron [Alexis, poet and playwright], more virile than he, is no more; granted, we shall not have a masterpiece.

I am not asking for one; it would be unjust to demand that; but I am asking for a French hymn which shall merely be superior to the Te Deum. Our young poets, to be sure, need not be afraid of measuring themselves against St Augustine . . . Why should the author of *Charles IX* [Marie-Joseph Chénier?] not enter the lists? This young poet is not altogether a prodigy; but neither is the Bishop of Africa a Horace. Ah! if the Breton who composed the address and the oath of our brothers of Pontivy would write verse, my mind would be at rest; he would soon write a canticle, simple and forceful like the oath, majestic and great like the Fourteenth of July.

Let the execution be simple! Relaxed young boys and girls artless as liberty herself . . . will sing the hymn to the god of liberty. A refrain will be taken up by the chorus, by a chorus of twenty-four million men . . .

10 Ludwig van Beethoven

Beethoven (1770–1827) did not leave any significant comments, descriptions or technical indications concerning his works. Nevertheless, his letters contain a good deal of evidence about his ideas on music, his varied interests, and the social position of a musician in the new era. The letters here are from *The letters of Beethoven*, trans. and ed. E. Anderson (London, 1961), pp. 47–9, 1351–4 and 272–4, and are quoted by permission of Macmillan, London and Basingstoke.

(a) Letter to the publisher F. A. Hoffmeister, Leipzig
Emerging plainly from this letter, besides the enthusiasm for the rediscovery of J. S. Bach, is the aspect of the 'businessman' which the modern composer was in the process of assuming. Every work is given a considered monetary value, and there is the utopian idea of a 'market for art' at which the composer should aim for his economic security.

VIENNA, *January 15 (or thereabouts), 1801*
I have read your letter with very great pleasure, my most beloved and worthy brother and friend. I thank you most warmly for the good opinion you have formed of me and my works, and I only hope that I shall be able

fully to deserve it. Please convey too to Herr K[ühnel]* my dutiful thanks for his courteous and friendly remarks about me – I am delighted also to hear of your undertakings and I hope that if works of art can produce any profit, the latter will fall to the lot of genuine and true artists rather than to that of mere tradesmen – Your desire to publish *the works of Sebastian Bach* is something that really warms my heart which beats sincerely for the sublime and magnificent art of that first father of harmony ['Urvater der Harmonie']. I trust that I shall soon see this plan fully launched and I hope that as soon as we hear the announcement of our golden age of peace [The Peace of Lunéville, 9 February 1801] I myself shall be able even from Vienna to contribute something to this scheme when you are collecting subscriptions for it† – Well, as to our own business matters, since you now desire such an arrangement, I am prepared to serve you. And for the time being I am offering you the following compositions: a septet [Op. 20] (about which I have already told you, and which could be arranged for the pianoforte also, with a view to its wider distribution and to our greater profit) 20 ducats – a symphony [Op. 21] 20 ducats – a concerto [Op. 19] 10 ducats – a grand solo sonata (Allegro, Adagio, Minuetto, Rondo) [Op. 22] 20 ducats. (This sonata is a first-rate composition, most beloved and worthy brother.) Now for a fuller elucidation. Perhaps you will be surprised that in this case I make no distinction between sonata, septet and symphony. The reason is that I find that a septet or a symphony does not sell as well as a sonata. That is the reason why I do this, although a symphony should undoubtedly be worth more (NB. The septet consists of a short introductory Adagio, then Allegro, Adagio, Minuetto, Andante with variations, Minuetto, another short introductory Adagio and then Presto)‡ – I am valuing the concerto at only 10 ducats because, as I have already told you, I do not consider it to be one of my best concertos – If you treat all the works as one item you will not, I believe, find my demand excessive. At least I have endeavoured to make the prices as moderate for you as possible – As to the draft, since you give me the option, you may send it to Geimüller or Schuller [Johann Heinrich Geymüller and Adam Schuller were Viennese bankers] – The total sum for all four works would thus be 70 ducats. The only currency I can cope with is Viennese ducats. How much that sum amounts to in your thalers and gulden does not concern me, because I am really an incompetent business man who is bad at arithmetic –

Well, that tiresome business has now been settled. I call it tiresome because I should like such matters to be differently ordered in this world. There ought to be in the world a *market for art* where the artist would only have to bring his works and take as much money as he needed. But, as it is, an artist has to be to a certain extent a business man as well, and how can he manage to be that – Good Heavens – again I call it a *tiresome business* – As to

---

* Ambros Kühnel (1770–1813), Court Organist at Leipzig, joined F. A. Hoffmeister in founding in December, 1800, the music publishing firm called Bureau de Musique, later C. F. Peters Verlag.

† Hoffmeister & Kühnel began in 1801, and continued until about 1806, to publish a number of J. S. Bach's keyboard works. These publications were subsequently taken over by C. F. Peters.

‡ In the published version the second minuet was called Scherzo, and the second short introductory Adagio became Andante con moto alla marcia.

the Leipzig r[eviewers], just let them talk; by means of their chatter they will certainly never make anyone immortal, nor will they ever take immortality from anyone upon whom Apollo has bestowed it [This sentence about the Leipzig reviewers does not appear in the facsimile of the letter from which this edition was produced.] –

Now may Heaven preserve you and *your partner*. For some time I have not been well; and so it is a little difficult for me even to write down notes and, still less, letters of the alphabet. I hope that we shall often have an opportunity of assuring ourselves how much you are my friends and how much I am

> your brother and friend
>
> L. V. BEETHOVEN

I am expecting an early reply – Adieu.

(b) From the Heiligenstadt Testament

This famous document, retrieved from Beethoven's papers after his death, was published for the first time in the *Allgemeine musikalische Zeitung* of 17 October 1827. Apart from its aspect as a direct confession, the text reflects Beethoven's eighteenth-century upbringing, with his ideas on the supremacy of virtue, the value of struggle, and the missionary character assigned to art. The mention of misanthropy, too, must be interpreted in the light of eighteenth-century *Geselligkeit* (sociability) rather than that of romantic solipsism. For the eighteenth-century man, 'misanthropic' meant 'lacking virtue'.

HEILIGENSTADT, *October 6, 1802*

FOR MY BROTHERS CARL AND [JOHANN] BEETHOVEN*

O my fellow men, who consider me, or describe me as, unfriendly, peevish or even misanthropic, how greatly do you wrong me. For you do not know the secret reason why I appear to you to be so. Ever since my childhood my heart and soul have been imbued with the tender feeling of goodwill; and I have always been ready to perform even great actions. But just think, for the last six years I have been afflicted with an incurable complaint which has been made worse by incompetent doctors. From year to year my hopes of being cured have gradually been shattered and finally I have been forced to accept the prospect of a *permanent infirmity* (the curing of which may perhaps take years or may even prove to be impossible). Though endowed with a passionate and lively temperament and even fond of the distractions offered by society I was soon obliged to seclude myself and live in solitude. If at times I decided just to ignore my infirmity, alas! how cruelly was I then driven back by the intensified sad experience of my poor hearing. Yet I could not bring myself to say to people: 'Speak up, shout, for I am deaf'. Alas! how could I possibly refer to the impairing *of a sense* which in me should be more perfectly developed than in other people, a sense which at one time I possessed in the greatest perfection, even to a degree of

---

* In the autograph the name of Beethoven's youngest brother, Johann, is omitted.

perfection such as assuredly few in my profession possess or have ever possessed – Oh, I cannot do it; so forgive me, if you ever see me withdrawing from your company which I used to enjoy. Moreover my misfortune pains me doubly, inasmuch as it leads to my being misjudged. For me there can be no relaxation in human society, no refined conversations, no mutual confidences. I must live quite alone and may creep into society only as often as sheer necessity demands; I must live like an outcast. If I appear in company I am overcome by a burning anxiety, a fear that I am running the risk of letting people notice my condition – And that has been my experience during the last six months which I have spent in the country.* My sensible doctor by suggesting that I should spare my hearing as much as possible has more or less encouraged my present natural inclination, though indeed when carried away now and then by my instinctive desire for human society, I have let myself be tempted to seek it. But how humiliated I have felt if somebody standing beside me heard the sound of a flute in the distance and *I heard nothing*, or if somebody heard *a shepherd sing* and again I heard nothing† – Such experiences almost made me despair, and I was on the point of putting an end to my life – The only thing that held me back was *my art*. For indeed it seemed to me impossible to leave this world before I had produced all the works that I felt the urge to compose; and thus I have dragged on this miserable existence – a truly miserable existence, seeing that I have such a sensitive body that any fairly sudden change can plunge me from the best spirits into the worst of humours – *Patience* – that is the virtue, I am told, which I must now choose for my guide; and I now possess it – I hope that I shall persist in my resolve to endure to the end, until it pleases the inexorable Parcae to cut the thread; perhaps my condition will improve, perhaps not; at any rate I am now resigned – At the early age of 28 I was obliged to become a philosopher, though this was not easy; for indeed this is more difficult for an artist than for anyone else – Almighty God, who look down into my innermost soul, you see into my heart and you know that it is filled with love for humanity and a desire to do good. Oh my fellow men, when some day you read this statement, remember that you have done me wrong; and let some unfortunate man derive comfort from the thought that he has found another equally unfortunate who, notwithstanding all the obstacles imposed by nature, yet did everything in his power to be raised to the rank of noble artists and human beings. – And you, my brothers Carl and [Johann], when I am dead, request on my behalf Professor Schmidt, if he is still living, to describe my disease, and attach this written document to his record, so that after my death at any rate the world and I may be reconciled as far as possible – [. . .] My wish is that you should have a better and more carefree existence than I have had. Urge your children to be *virtuous*, for virtue alone can make a man happy. Money cannot do this. I speak from experience. It was virtue that sustained me in my misery. It was

---

* Evidently Beethoven had moved to Heiligenstadt early in April. In his day it was a small village with sulphur springs. He stayed there also during the summers of 1807, 1808 and 1817.

† For Ferdinand Ries's moving account of Beethoven's gradual loss of hearing see F. G. Wegeler and F. Ries: *Biographische Notizen über Ludwig van Beethoven* (Koblenz, 1838, suppl. Bonn, 1845, both R1972), 117–18.

thanks to virtue and also to my art that I did not put an end to my life by
suicide – Farewell and love one another – [...] Well, that is all – Joyfully I
go to meet Death – should it come before I have had an opportunity of
developing all my artistic gifts, then in spite of my hard fate it would still
come too soon, and no doubt I would like it to postpone its coming – Yet
even so I should be content, for would it not free me from a condition of
continual suffering? Come then, Death, *whenever* you like, and with courage
I will go to meet you – Farewell; and when I am dead, do not wholly forget
me. I deserve to be remembered by you, since during my lifetime I have
often thought of you and tried to make you happy – Be happy –

LUDWIG VAN BEETHOVEN

(c) Letter to Therese Malfatti, Mödling (near Vienna)

Writing to Therese Malfatti in a rare inner moment of leisure,
Beethoven declares his educational conception of music (bound up
with Platonic ideas: beauty is the perceptible aspect of goodness)
and his passion for country life. Literary culture and gallantry come
together in his question about new literature and in the quotation
from Goethe's *Egmont*.

[VIENNA, *May, 1810*]

In this letter, beloved Therese, you are receiving what I promised you
[possibly the piano piece *Für Elise*]. And indeed, if the most powerful
obstacles had not prevented me, you would be receiving still more, if only to
show you that I always *do more for my friends than I promise* – I trust, and
have no doubt about it, that your pursuits are just as delightful as your
entertainment is pleasant – yet the latter must not be excessively pleasant, so
that we too may be remembered – No doubt I should be counting too much
on you or valuing my worth too highly if I were to apply to you the saying
'People are united not only when they are together; even the distant one, the
absent one too is present with us' [Egmont to Ferdinand, from Goethe's
Egmont, Act v]. Who would apply such a saying to our volatile T[herese]
who treats so lightheartedly all the affairs of life? – In connexion with your
pursuits be sure not to forget the pianoforte or, in general, music as a whole.
You have such a splendid gift for music, why don't you cultivate it
seriously? You who have so much feeling for all that is beautiful and good,
why will you not direct it to discerning in such a glorious art what is fine and
perfect, a quality which in its turn ever radiates beauty upon us? – I am
leading a very lonely and quiet life. Although here and there certain lights
would like to awaken me, yet since you all left Vienna, I feel within me a
void which cannot be filled and which even my art, which is usually so
faithful to me, has not yet been able to make me forget – Your pianoforte
has been ordered and you will soon have it – I wonder what difference you
will have found in the treatment of a theme which was invented one evening
and the way in which I have recently written it down for you. Work it out
for yourself, but please do not take punch *to help you*.

How fortunate you are to be able to go into the country so soon. I cannot
enjoy this happiness until the 8th, but I look forward to it with childish

excitement. How delighted I shall be to ramble for a while through bushes, woods, under trees, through grass and around rocks. No one can love the country as much as I do. For surely woods, trees and rocks produce the echo which man desires to hear* –

You will soon receive a few other compositions of mine; and in these you will not have to complain too much about difficulties – *Have you read Goethe's Wilhelm Meister and Shakespeare in Schlegel's translation?* One has so much leisure in the country. Perhaps you would like me to send you these works – [. . .]

Well, all good wishes, beloved T[herese]. I would like you to have everything that is good and beautiful in life. Remember me and do so with pleasure – Forget my mad behaviour – Rest assured that nobody can wish you a gayer and happier life than I and that I desire it even if you take no interest whatever

in your most devoted servant and friend

BEETHOVEN

NB. It would be very nice of you if you were to tell me in a few lines how I can be of service to you here in Vienna? –

11 Ernst Theodor Amadeus (Wilhelm) Hoffmann

E. T. A. Hoffmann (1776–1822), who changed his third Christian name to Amadeus in homage to Mozart, was the greatest witness to the lasting connection between music, poetry and literature typical of early German romanticism. In Berlin (1807–8) he associated with the romantics Fichte, Schleiermacher and Chamisso; at Bamberg (1808–13) he became a music critic, collaborating in particular on the *Allgemeine musikalische Zeitung*. He composed music in every genre, theatrical (*Undine*, 1816), symphonic and chamber. He identified himself with the figure of Johannes Kreisler, the tormented musician, hostile to professionalism and despised by the bourgeois Philistines, the protagonist of *Kreisleriana*, one of the *Fantasiestücke in Callots Manier* (Berlin, 1814–15). The trio of Haydn, Mozart and Beethoven, like three complementary moments of a unique creative stream, probably had its most authoritative documentation in these pages. With regard to the Fifth Symphony,

* At this point in the autograph four lines have been deleted, but can be deciphered. The passage runs as follows: 'Kindly give your dear sister Nanette the song ("Lied") arranged for guitar. The song ("Gesang") too would have been copied out, but I had too little time.'

the inspiration of the literary writing is counterbalanced by the continual reference to the organic unity of the work, the product of a 'high self-possession'. The extract also contains significant and prophetic praise of the piano as an instrument privileged to sound the sea of harmony and, in general, of instrumental music as an independent and superior means of expression. Thus the scorn of Enlightenment culture for abstract instrumental music as an insignificant and inferior genre became relegated to the archives. From E. T. A. Hoffmann: *Kreisleriana*, no. 4 of the *Fantasiestücke in Callots Manier*; partial translation from Strunk: *Source readings*, 777–81, with additional sections translated by Elizabeth Skinner.

BEETHOVEN'S INSTRUMENTAL MUSIC

Romantic taste is rare, romantic talent still rarer, and this is doubtless why there are so few to strike that lyre whose sound discloses the wondrous realm of the romantic.

Haydn grasps romantically what is human in human life; he is more commensurable, more comprehensible for the majority.

Mozart calls rather for the superhuman, the wondrous element that abides in inner being.

Beethoven's music sets in motion the lever of fear, of awe, of horror, of suffering, and wakens just that infinite longing which is the essence of romanticism. He is accordingly a completely romantic composer, and is not this perhaps the reason why he has less success with vocal music, which excludes the character of indefinite longing, merely representing emotions defined by words as emotions experienced in the realm of the infinite?

The musical rabble is oppressed by Beethoven's powerful genius; it seeks in vain to oppose it. But knowing critics, looking about them with a superior air, assure us that we may take their word for it as men of great intellect and deep insight that, while the excellent Beethoven can scarcely be denied a very fertile and lively imagination, he does not know how to bridle it! Thus, they say, he no longer bothers at all to select or to shape his ideas, but, following the so-called daemonic method, he dashes everything off exactly as his ardently active imagination dictates it to him. Yet how does the matter stand if it is *your* feeble observation alone that the deep inner continuity of Beethoven's every composition eludes? If it is *your* fault alone that you do not understand the master's language as the initiated understand it, that the portals of the innermost sanctuary remain closed to you? The truth is that, as regards self-possession, Beethoven stands quite on a par with Haydn and Mozart and that, separating his ego from the inner realm of harmony, he rules over it as an absolute monarch. In Shakespeare, our knights of the aesthetic measuring rod have often bewailed the utter lack of inner unity and inner continuity, although for those who look more deeply there springs forth, issuing from a single bud, a beautiful tree, with leaves, flowers, and fruit; thus, with Beethoven, it is only after a searching investigation of his instrumental music that the high self-possession inseparable from true genius and nourished by the study of the art stands revealed.

Can there be any work of Beethoven's that confirms all this to a higher degree than his indescribably profound, magnificent symphony in C minor? How this wonderful composition, in a climax that climbs on and on, leads the listener imperiously forward into the spirit world of the infinite! Nothing can be more simple than the two bars of the main idea of the first Allegro, which in unison at the opening does not even tell the listener what the key is. The melodious secondary theme only offsets even more clearly the character of the anxious, restless longing which this movement carries within itself! The breast oppressed and disquieted by the presentiment of something monstrous, of something which threatens to destroy, seems to want to give vent to its feelings violently with sharp sounds, but soon a friendly figure passes by, radiant, and illuminates the deep terrible night (the charming theme in G major which was first broached by the horn in E flat major). How simple – let it be said once again – is the theme which the master laid as the foundation to the whole, but how marvellously all the secondary and transitional ideas are linked to it through their rhythmic relationship, so that they serve only to develop more and more the character of the Allegro which that main theme had only suggested. All the phrases are short, nearly all of them consisting of only two or three bars, and in addition distributed in a constant exchange between wind and string instruments; one would think that out of such elements only something which was disjointed and incomprehensible could emerge, but instead it is precisely that arrangement of the whole, as well as the constant successive repetition of phrases and single chords, which intensifies the feeling of an unutterable longing to the highest degree. Quite apart from the fact that the contrapuntal treatment is evidence of the deep study of the art, the transitional ideas and the constant allusions to the main theme also demonstrate how the great master conceived and thought through the whole with all its passionate features. Does the charming theme of the Andante con moto in A flat major not sound like a blessed voice of the spirit, which fills our breast with hope and comfort? But here too the dreadful spirit which seized and worried the soul steps threateningly out of the stormcloud into which it disappeared, and the friendly figures which surround us flee before its flashes of lightning. What should I say about the Minuet? Listen to its original modulations, the cadences on the dominant major chord which the bass takes up as the tonic for the following theme in the minor – the theme itself which is continually expanding by a few bars! Does that restless, unutterable longing, that sense of the wonderful realm of the spirit in which the master reigns not seize you again? But the magnificent theme of the final movement shines like blinding sunlight in the exulting jubilation of the whole orchestra. What marvelous contrapuntal interlacing joins itself here again to the whole. No doubt the whole rushes like an ingenious rhapsody past many a man, but the soul of each thoughtful listener is assuredly stirred, deeply and intimately, by a feeling that is none other than that unutterable portentous longing, and until the final chord – indeed, even in the moments that follow it – he will be powerless to step out of that wondrous spirit realm where grief and joy embrace him in the form of sound. The internal structure of the movements, their execution, their instrumentation, the way in which they follow one another – everything contributes to a single end; above all, it is the intimate interrelationship among the themes that engenders that unity which alone has the power to hold the listener when he overhears it in the connecting of two movements or discovers it in the fundamental bass they have in common; a deeper relationship which does not reveal itself in this way speaks at other times only from mind to mind, and it is precisely this relationship that prevails between sections of the two Allegros and the Minuet and which imperiously proclaims the self possession of the master's genius.

How deeply thy magnificent compositions for the piano have impressed themselves upon my soul, thou sublime master; how shallow and insignificant now all seems to me that is not thine, or by the gifted Mozart or that mighty genius, Sebastian Bach! With what joy I received thy seventieth work, the two glorious trios, for I knew full well that after a little practice I should soon hear them in truly splendid style. And in truth, this evening things went so well with me that even now, like a man who wanders in the mazes of a fantastic park, woven about with all manner of exotic trees and plants and marvelous flowers, and who is drawn further and further in, I am powerless to find my way out of the marvelous turns and windings of thy trios. The lovely siren voices of these movements of thine, resplendent in their many-hued variety, lure me on and on. The gifted lady who indeed honored me, Capellmeister Kreisler, by playing today the first trio in such splendid style, the gifted lady before whose piano I still sit and write, has made me realize quite clearly that only what the mind produces calls for respect and that all else is out of place.

Just now I have repeated at the piano from memory certain striking transitions from the two trios. It is indeed true that the grand piano (pianoforte) remains an instrument which is of more use for harmony than for melody. The finest expression of which the instrument is capable does not give the melody that vibrant life in a thousand shadings which the bow of a violinist, the breath of a wind-player is capable of effecting. The player struggles in vain with the insuperable difficulty presented to him by the mechanism which makes the strings vibrate and resound through a blow. On the other hand there is probably no other instrument (leaving aside the harp, which is still more limited) like the piano which embraces the realm of harmony in full chords and which unfolds its treasures in the most wonderful forms and shapes to the expert. If the fantasy of the master has been seized by a complete tone-painting with rich groups, bright lights and deep shadows, then he can realize this on the piano so that it emerges from the inner world vivid and sparkling. The full score, this real musical magic book which guards in its notes all the wonder of music, the mysterious choir of the most varied instruments, becomes alive under the hands of the master at the piano, and a passage from the score which is played well and completely in this way could be compared with the successful copper engraving taken from a large painting. Thus the piano is most admirably suited to improvisation, to playing from the score, for individual sonatas, chords, etc., just as trios, quartets, quintets, etc., where the usual string instruments are added, fully belong to the realm of piano compositions, because if they are composed in the true art (i.e. really in four, five or more parts) then it is a matter of harmonic composition which excludes of itself the emergence of single instruments in brilliant passages.

I have a real aversion to all the actual piano concertos. (Those of Mozart and Beethoven are not only concertos but also symphonies with piano obbligato.) Here the virtuosity of the soloist should be allowed to display itself in passagework and in the expression of the melody; however, the best player on the most beautiful instrument strives in vain for that which for example the violinist achieves with little effort.

After the full tutti of violins and wind, every solo sounds stiff and dull, and one admires such things as the dexterity of the fingers without any real impact being made on the soul.

How well the master has understood the specific character of the instrument and fostered it in the way best suited to it!

A simple but fruitful theme, songlike, susceptible to the most varied contrapuntal treatments, curtailments, and so forth, forms the basis of each movement; all remaining subsidiary themes and figures are intimately related to the main idea in such a way that the details all interweave, arranging themselves among the instruments in highest unity. Such is the structure of the whole, yet in this artful structure there alternate in restless flight the most marvelous pictures in which joy and grief, melancholy and ecstasy, come side by side or intermingled to the fore. Strange figures begin a merry dance, now floating off into a point of light, now splitting apart, flashing and sparkling, evading and pursuing one another in various combinations, and at the center of the spirit realm thus disclosed the intoxicated soul gives ear to the unfamiliar language and understands the most mysterious premonitions that have stirred it.

That composer alone has truly mastered the secrets of harmony who knows how, by their means, to work upon the human soul; for him, numerical proportions, which to the dull grammarian are no more than cold, lifeless problems in arithmetic, become magical compounds from which to conjure up a magic world.

Despite the good nature that prevails, especially in the first trio, not even excepting the melancholy Largo, Beethoven's genius is in the last analysis serious and solemn. It is as though the master thought that, in speaking of deep mysterious things – even when the spirit, intimately familiar with them, feels itself joyously and gladly uplifted – one may not use an ordinary language, only a sublime and glorious one; the dance of the priests of Isis can be only an exultant hymn. Where instrumental music is to produce its effect simply through itself as music and is by no means to serve a definite dramatic purpose, it must avoid all trivial facetiousness, all frivolous *lazzi*. A deep temperament seeks for the intimations of that joy which, an import from an unknown land, more glorious and more beautiful than here in our constricted world, enkindles an inner, blissful life within our breasts, a higher expression that can be given to it by mere words, proper only to our circumscribed earthly air. This seriousness, in all of Beethoven's works for instruments and for the piano, is in itself enough to forbid all those breakneck passages up and down for the two hands which fill our piano music in the latest style, all the queer leaps, the farcical capriccios, the notes towering high above the staff on their five- and six-line scaffolds.

On the side of mere digital dexterity, Beethoven's compositions for the piano really present no special difficulty, for every player must be presumed to have in his fingers the few runs, triplet figures, and whatever else is called for; nevertheless, their performance is on the whole quite difficult. Many a so-called virtuoso condemns this music, objecting that it is 'very difficult' and into the bargain 'very ungrateful'.

Now, as regards difficulty, the correct and fitting performance of a work of Beethoven's asks nothing more than that one should understand him, that one should enter deeply into his being, that – conscious of one's own consecration – one should boldly dare to step into the circle of the magical phenomena that his powerful spell has evoked. He who is not conscious of this consecration, who regards sacred Music as a mere game, as a mere entertainment for an idle hour, as a momentary stimulus for dull ears, or as a means of self-ostentation – let him leave Beethoven's music alone. Only to such a man, moreover, does the objection 'most ungrateful' apply. The true artist lives only in the work that he has understood as the composer meant it and that he then performs. He is above putting his own personality forward in any way, and all his endeavors are directed towards a single end – that all the wonderful enchanting pictures and apparitions that the composer has sealed into his work with magic power may be called into active life, shining in a thousand colors, and that they may surround mankind in luminous sparkling circles and, enkindling its imagination, its innermost soul, may bear it in rapid flight into the faraway spirit realm of sound.

Notes

Part I. Instrumental music

1 In the foreword to the *Geistliche Chormusik* of 1648. H. Schütz: *Neue Ausgabe sämtlicher Werke*, v, ed. W. Kamlah (Kassel and Basle, 1955), p. vi; 'der rechten Musicalischen hohen Schule ...'

2 From 1734 to 1743 Goldoni was employed by the theatre-owning Grimani family to provide *opera seria* librettos, the most famous of these being his arrangement of Zeno's *Griselda* for Vivaldi in 1735. See P. Weiss: 'Goldoni poeta d'opere serie per musica', *Studi Goldoniani*, iii (1973), 7–40.

3 The section describing Vienna is in Part I, Chapter 7; see Mme de Staël: *Oeuvres complètes* (Paris, 1861/R1967), ii, 16.

4 For a translation of part of this criticism see H. T. David and A. Mendel: *The Bach Reader* (New York, 1945, rev.2/1966), 238–51.

5 D. Diderot and J. Le Rond D'Alembert: *Encyclopédie ou Dictionnaire raisonné des sciences, des arts et des métiers*, vii (Paris, 1757), 360.

6 'Quadrivium' was the name given to the four branches of mathematics in medieval education: arithmetic, geometry, astronomy and music.

7 Quoted in W. S. Newman: *The sonata in the classic era* (Chapel Hill, 1963), 46.

8 In his *De oratore* (55 B.C.) Cicero expounded a 'middle style' of oratory, midway between the mannered and esoteric style of the Asianic school and the severe austerity of the Atticists.

9 Johann Kirnberger, a great admirer of Bach, wrote several theoretical works, his most important being *Die Kunst des reinen Satzes* (1771–9). Heinrich Koch is best known for his *Versuch einer Anleitung zur Composition* (1782–93) and his *Musikalisches Lexikon* (1802).

10 C. F. D. Schubart: *Ideen zu einer Ästhetik der Tonkunst* (Vienna, 1806), 202, quoted in Newman: *Sonata*, 709.

11 *Aus meinem Leben. Dichtung und Wahrheit*, Part I, Book 4. *Goethes Werke*, ix, ed. E. Trunz and L. Blumenthal (Hamburg, 1955), 123; 'in einem Frauenzimmerlichen Stil, mit lauter Punkten und in kurzen Sätzen'.

12 J. J. Rousseau: *Julie ou la Nouvelle Héloïse* (Paris, 1761), Part II, fragments attached to Letter 2; Eng. trans. J. H. McDowell (London, 1968), 164.

13 Letter of 18 August 1771, in *The letters of Mozart and his family*, trans. and ed. E. Anderson (London, rev.2/1966), i, 192.

14 C. P. E. Bach: *Essay on the true art of playing keyboard instruments*, trans. W. J. Mitchell (New York, 2/1951), 160; the chapter entitled 'Performance', paragraph 28.

15 C. Burney: *The present state of music in Germany, the Netherlands, and United Provinces* (London, 1773), ii, 269.

16 For Burney's discussion of Müthel as a composer see Ibid, 328–9.

17 Newman: *Sonata*, 634.

18 Under the entry 'Adagio'.

19 Quoted in R. Giazotto: 'Il sinfonismo preromantico in Europa', *Rassegna Musicale Curci*, xix bis/2.

20 See H. C. R. Landon: *Haydn: chronicle and works*, i, *Haydn: the early years 1732–1765* (London, 1980), 61.

21 Quoted in R. Würtz: 'Mannheim', *The new Grove dictionary of music and musicians*, ed. S. Sadie (London, 1980), xi, 625.

22 Letter of 29 June 1778; see Anderson: *Letters of Mozart*, ii, 556.

Part II. Vocal music

1 *La Cecchina ossia La buona figliola*, Act II, scene 6; 'Come, come with me, you who happily come to war, and provide many kinds of diversion.'

2 4 October 1746.

3 From *Wilhelm Meisters Treatralische Sendung*, Book II, Chapter 8, in *J. W. Goethe Gedenkausgabe der Werke, Briefe und Gespräche* (Zurich, 1949), 636; 'die Scharen rühriger Menschen, die wie Ströme die ganze Welt durchkreuzen, wegführen und zurückbringen'.

4 See F. Venturi: *Settecento riformatore* (Turin, 1969), 668.

5 *La buona figliola*, Act I, scene 12; 'I shall leave ... I shall go and look for love, poor little Cecchina'.

6 *La buona figliola*, Act I, scene 5; 'poor little girl, I have to work so hard the whole day long'.

7 Galiani's letter to Tanucci is in G. R. Ansaldi: 'Le testimonianze dell' Abate Galiani sulla formazione del gusto neoclassico', *La Rassegna Italiana*, xxiv (1941), no.283.

8 *The autobiographies of Edward Gibbon*, ed. J. Murray (London, 1897), 405.

9 Verse 12 of *L'Infinito*, in G. Leopardi: *Canti*, ed. J. H. Whitfield (Manchester, 1967), 63.

10 From the section 'Von dem Wesentlichen der Kunst', in J. Winckelmann: *Sämtliche Werke*, iv (Donaueschingen, 1825), 42–81.

11 A. Manzoni: *I promessi sposi*, ed. A. Momigliano (Florence, 1951), 801; this passage from the end of Chapter 37 is an ironic dig at Metastasian poetry.

12 *Iphigenie auf Tauris*, Act I, scene 1, line 12, in *Goethes Werke*, v, ed. J. Kunz (Hamburg, 1952), 7; 'Das Land der Griechen mit der Seele suchend'.

13 From the first part of 'Dissertation sur la tragédie', the preface to *Sémiramis*, in *Oeuvres complètes de Voltaire*, 'Théatre', iii (Paris, 1877),

492; 'dignes de Corneille quand il n'est pas déclamateur, et de Racine quand il n'est pas faible'.

14 F. J. Chastellux: *Essai sur l'union de la poésie et de la musique* (Paris, 1765/*R*1970), 41; 'quel charme inexprimable l'orielle éprouve lorsqu'après avoir erré dans les phrases irrégulières et dans les modulations variées du récit, elle entend commencer cette période musicale dont elle conçoit sur le champ le plan et la structure'.

15 Quoted in T. Gotti: 'Bologna musicale del '700 e Cristoforo Gluck', *Due secoli di vita musicale, storia del Teatro Comunale di Bologna* (Bologna, 1966), i, 77.

16 A. Einstein: *Gluck*, trans. E. Blom (London, 1936), 99. See Reading no. 6, p. 274.

17 From the first letter of J. G. Noverre: *Lettres sur la danse, et sur les ballets* (Lyons, 1760; Vienna, 1767), 8.

18 See Cicero's *Orator, De oratore, Rhetorica ad Herennium*, III, 12–14, and *De natura deorum*, II, 58.

19 See J. J. Rousseau: *Essai sur l'origine des langues*, ed. C. Porset (Paris, 1970), 143 (Chapter XII).

20 E. B. de Condillac: *Essai sur l'origine des connaissances humaines* (1746), Part II, section I, Chapter 2, paragraph 14; ed. C. Porset (Artigues-près-Bourdeaux, 1793), 201: 'Dans l'origine des langues, la manière de prononcer admettoit donc les inflexions de voix si distinctes, qu'un musicien eût pu la noter ...'

21 Rousseau: *Essai*, 159 (Chapter XIV); 'La mélodie en imitant les inflexions de la voix exprime les plaintes, les cris de douleur ou de joye, les menaces, les gémissemens; tous les signes vocaux des passions sont de son ressort.'

22 *Voltaire's correspondence*, ed. T. Bestermann, lxvii (Geneva, 1961), 235; 'en suivant ses nottes, et en adoucissant seulement les intonations.'

23 C. Batteaux: *Les beaux-arts réduits à un seul principe* (Paris, 1773/*R*1969), 340 (Section II, Chapter I).

24 Quoted in E. Newman: *Gluck and the opera* (London, 1895), 191.

25 J. J. Rousseau: *Écrits sur la musique*, ed. C. Kintzler ([Paris], 1838/*R*1979), 397; 'Persuadé que la langue françoise, destituée de tout accent, n'est nullement propre à la musique et principalement au récitatif, j'ai imaginé un genre de drame dans lequel les paroles et la musique, au lieu de marcher ensemble, se font entendre successivement, et où la phrase parlée est en quelque sorte annoncée et preparée par la phrase musicale.'

26 Letter of 12 November 1778, in *The letters of Mozart and his family*, trans. and ed. E. Anderson (London, rev.2/1966), ii, 631.

27 Paisiello's letter to Galiani is quoted in A. della Corte: *Settecento italiano: Paisiello – L'estetica musicale di P. Metastasio* (Turin, 1922), 60.

28 G. Tani: 'Angiolini, Gasparo', *Enciclopedia dello Spettacolo* (Rome, 1954), 621–2.

29 From the chorus in Act III of the Italian version of *Alceste*.

30 *Journal de Paris*, 19 May 1779, quoted in *Mémoires pour servir à l'histoire de la révolution opérée dans la musique par M. le Chevalier Gluck*, ed. G. M. Leblond (Naples [Paris], 1781/*R*1967).

31 See G. C. Ballola: 'Accademismo e classicismo', *Storia dell'Opera*, ed. G. Barblan and A. Basso (Turin, 1977), I, ii, 114.

32 See J. F. Marmontel: *Essai sur les révolutions de la musique en France* (Paris, 1777), reprinted with notes by Leblond in *Mémoires pour servir à l'histoire.*

33 See *The Age of Enlightenment, 1745–1790*, vol. vii of *The New Oxford History of Music*, ed. E. Wellesz and F. Sternfeld (London, 1973), 240.

34 From Bertoni's preface to *Orfeo*, published in 1776, reproduced in G. Gaspari: *Catalogo della Biblioteca del Liceo Musicale di Bologna* (Bologna, 1890–1905), iii, 291.

35 *Arvire et Evelina*, Act I, scene 5.

36 Einstein: *Gluck*, 99. See Reading no. 6, p. 274.

37 See J. Rushton: 'Salieri's "Les Horaces": a study of an operatic failure', *Music Review*, xxxvii (1976), 266.

38 See Einstein: *Gluck*, 182.

39 See M. F. Robinson: *Naples and Neapolitan opera* (Oxford, 1972), 192 n32.

40 *Socrate*, Act II, scene 10.

41 O. E. Deutsch: *Mozart: a documentary biography*, trans. E. Blom, P. Branscombe and J. Noble (London, 1965), 274.

42 For a discussion of the differences of opinion between Bach and Johann August Ernesti see K. Geiringer: *The Bach family: seven generations of creative genius* (New York, 1954/R1981), 185–7.

43 For Benedict XIV's encyclical see *Magnum Bullarium Romanum*, xviii: *Constitutiones Benedicti XIV ab Anno 1748 usque ad Annum 1752* (Luxemburg, 1754), 13.

Part III. Haydn and Mozart

1 *Goethes Werke*, vi, ed. E. Trunz (Hamburg, 1951), 9.

2 Ibid, 66.

3 Ibid, 47.

4 Ibid, 99.

5 From Mozart's *Così fan tutte*, Act I, scene 5.

6 See F. Venturi: *Settecento riformatore* (Turin, 1969), 665.

7 C. P. E. Bach: *Essay on the true art of playing keyboard instruments*, trans. W. J. Mitchell (New York, 2/1951), 152; 'a musician cannot move others unless he too is moved' (Part I, chapter 3, paragraph 13). See Reading no. 1, p. 263.

8 See Mozart's letter of 17 October 1777, in *The letters of Mozart and his family*, trans. and ed. E. Anderson (London, rev.2/1966), i, 329.

9 Quoted in *The Age of Enlightenment*, vol. vii of *The New Oxford History of Music*, ed. E. Wellesz and F. Sternfeld (London, 1973), p. xx; 'vier vernünftige Leute sich untereinander unterhalten'.

10 G. J. Vogel: *Betrachtungen der Mannheimer Tonschule* (Mannheim, 1779–80/R1974), ii, 62; quoted in W. S. Newman: *The sonata in the classic era* (Chapel Hill, 1963), 34.

11 See H. C. R. Landon: *Haydn: chronicle and works*, ii, *Haydn at Esterháza 1766–1790* (London, 1978), 633.

12 Haydn describes them as being 'auf eine gantz neue besonderer Art' in letters to several patrons; see Ibid, 454–5.

13 J. J. Rousseau: *Dictionnaire de musique* (Paris, 1768), entry under 'Sonate'. See also Newman: *Sonata*, 36.

14 Letter to P. C. Kayser, Frankfurt am Main, 29 December 1779; J. W. Goethe: *Briefe der Jahre 1764–1786* (Zurich, 1951), 472–3.
15 R. Hughes: *Haydn* (London, 1950), 47.
16 For Boccherini's letter see Landon: *Haydn at Esterháza*, 447.
17 See K. Geiringer: *Haydn: a creative life in music* (London, rev.2/1964), 106.
18 For some of these criticisms see Landon: *Haydn at Esterháza*, 154, 161, 169 and 174.
19 For these two letters see Ibid, 447 and 702.
20 The *Fantasiestücke in Callots Manier* (Capriccios in the style of Callot) by E. T. A. Hoffmann were published in Berlin in 1814–15. They include *Kreisleriana*, an extract from which appears as Reading no. 11.
21 Landon: *Haydn at Esterháza*, 593.
22 'Tag vor dem Tage, göttlich werde du verehrt!
Denn aller Fleiss, der männlich schätzenswerte,
Ist morgendlich.'
Quoted in T. Mann: 'Goethe als Repräsentant des bürgerlichen Zeitalters', *Leiden und Grösse der Meister*, part of Mann's *Werke* (Berlin, 1935).
23 *Goethes Werke*, ii, ed. E. Trunz (Hamburg, 1952), 460; 'Denn ein geschäftiges Weib tut keine Schritte vergebens.'
24 M. Kelly: *Reminiscences* (London, 1826/R1968), ii, 237.
25 See G. de Rothschild: *Luigi Boccherini: his life and work*, trans. A. Mayor (London, 1965), 19.
26 Ibid, 99.
27 F. M. Grimm: *Correspondance littéraire, philosophique et critique*, ed. M. Tourneux (Paris, 1877–82), vii, 81–3; trans. in O. E. Deutsch: *Mozart: a documentary biography*, trans. E. Blom, P. Branscombe and J. Noble (London, 1966), 56–7, and in P. Nettl: *The book of musical documents* (New York, 1948/R1969), 147.
28 Deutsch: *Mozart*, 138.
29 Letter of 4 September 1776, trans. in Anderson: *Letters of Mozart*, i,266.
30 See the letters from Leopold Mozart dated 16 and 23 February 1778; Ibid, i, 483–4 and 489–93.
31 Letter of 4 April 1781; Ibid, ii, 720.
32 Letter of Leopold Mozart of 16 February 1785; Ibid, ii, 886.
33 See Deutsch: *Mozart*, 278.
34 Ibid, 274.
35 See *The autobiography of Karl von Dittersdorf*, trans. A. D. Coleridge (London, 1896/R1970), 252.
36 Ibid, 253.
37 Letter of Leopold Mozart of 28 October 1772, trans. in Anderson: *Letters of Mozart*, i, 213.
38 Letter of 4 September 1776; Ibid, i, 266.
39 See L. Magnani: 'Goethe e Mozart', in *Goethe, Beethoven e il demonico* (Turin, 1976), 99.
40 Letter of 13 October 1781, trans. in Anderson: *Letters of Mozart*, ii, 772–3; see Reading no. 8.
41 Mozart's postscript to Maria Anna Mozart's letter of 8 November 1777 to her husband; trans. in Anderson: *Letters of Mozart*, i, 362.
42 Quoted in B. Paumgartner: *Mozart* (Zurich, 3/1945), 298; 'in seinem

künstlerischen und wirklich schönen Satz, nur ein neuer Schöpfer zu werden, zu hoch versteigt ... wobei freilich Empfindung und Herz wenig gewinnen'.

43 This is a reference to the 'Mothers' in Goethe's *Faust*, Part II, Act I, scene 5 (in the 'Finstere Galerie'), who represent a dimension beyond time and space, an area beyond human knowledge.

44 L. Da Ponte: *Memoire e altri scritti*, ed. C. Pagnini (Milan, 1971), 147.

45 *Ganymed*, in *Goethes Werke*, i, ed. E. Trunz (Hamburg, 1952), 47; 'Ich komme! Ich komme!/Wohin? Ach, wohin?'

46 From the finale to Act IV of *Le nozze di Figaro*; 'it makes me tingle with excitement', 'how my hand tingles' and 'how my heart falters'.

47 *Don Giovanni*, Act I, scene 13; 'those last words, which the wicked man spoke, his whole voice recalled in my heart that disgrace which in my apartment ...'.

48 Deutsch: *Mozart*, 394.

49 *Le nozze di Figaro*, Act IV, finale; 'Ah, let's hurry, my love, and let pleasure make up for the pains.'

50 *Don Giovanni*, Act I, scene 9; 'Let's go, let's go, my love, to make up for the pains.'

51 *Die Zauberflöte*, Act II, finale; 'Yes, yes, that is Pamina's voice! Be happy, now she can go with you, no fate will ever be able to separate you.'

52 J. W. Goethe: *Faust, Part I*, trans. R. Jarrell (New York, 1976), 7.

Part IV. Beethoven

1 De la Chevardière, quoted in H. Riemann: *Musik-Lexicon*, ed. W. Gurlitt and H. H. Eggebrecht, 'Sachteil' (Mainz, 12/1967), 722.

2 Quoted by H. Radiguer: 'La musique française de 1789 à 1815', in A. Lavignac: *Encyclopédie de la Musique et Dictionnaire du Conservatoire*, first part, *Histoire de la musique: France, Belgique, Angleterre* (Paris, 1914), col. 1563; 'une révolution parmi les artistes musiciens, qui a précédé de peu la grande révolution politique. Oui, je m'en souviens, les musiciens, que l'opinion maltraitait, se sont levés à tout à coup et ont repoussé l'humiliation dont on les accablait.'

3 G. W. F. Hegel: *Aesthetik*, in *Sämtliche Werke*, ed. H. Glockner (Stuttgart, 1953), xii, 31–2; trans. T. M. Knox in *Aesthetics* (Oxford, 1975), 10–11.

4 'Heliopolis, im letzten Jahre der alten Finsterniss' is the fictitious place of publication of the first edition of 1793.

5 'Man, your grandeur on the earth does not belong to your state; it belongs to your character.'

6 The motion of the Convention was reported in the *Moniteur* of 2 August 1793; see A. Pougin: *L'Opéra-comique pendant la Révolution* (Paris, 1891), 81–2.

7 Quoted in A. Coy: *Die Musik der französischen Revolution* (Munich, 1978).

8 Germinal was the seventh month of the French revolutionary calendar, from 21 March to 19 April.

9 Fructidor was the twelfth month of the French revolutionary calendar, from 18 August to 16 September.

10 F. Schlegel: 'Gespräch über die Poesie', *Athenäum*, iii (Berlin, 1800),

fascicle I, 58–128 and fascicle II, 169–87; reprinted in F. Schlegel: 'Charakteristiken und Kritiken I (1796–1801)', *Kritische Ausgabe*, ii, ed. H. Eichner (Munich, 1967), 297; 'der heilige Stifter und Vater der modernen Poesie'.

11 From the essay 'Über Dante in philosophischer Beziehung' of 1803, in F. W. J. Schelling: *Sämmtliche Werke*, v (Stuttgart and Augsburg, 1859), 156; 'jedesmal einzig, eine Welt für sich'.

12 From the introduction to the first chapter of Part I, Book I; F. R. Chateaubriand: *Oeuvres complètes*, ii (Paris, 1860), 9; 'la plus poétique, la plus humaine, la plus favorable à la liberté, aux arts et aux lettres'.

13 J. N. Bouilly: *Mes récapitulations* (Paris, 1836–7), ii, 64.

14 See section 6, 'Klio', of *Hermann und Dorothea*, in *Goethes Werke*, ii, ed. E. Trunz (Hamburg, 1952), 482.

15 See F. Venturi: *L'Italia fuori d'Italia*, VI, 3, in *Dal primo Settecento all'unità*, vol. 3 of *Storia d'Italia* (Turin, 1973), 1200–02.

16 Paër's *Camilla*, Act I, scene 7.

17 See G. Carpani: *Le Rossiniane* (Padua, 1824), and also C. Botta: the final 'Dissertazione' of *Storia d'Italia continuata da quella di Guicciardini sino al 1789* (Paris, 1832) and *Scritti musicali, linguistici e letterati*, ed. G. Guidetti (Reggio Emilia, 1914).

18 J. J. Rousseau: *Dictionnaire de musique* (Paris, 1768), entry under 'Sonate'.

19 See Mozart's letters of 12 January 1782 and 7 June 1783, in *The letters of Mozart and his family*, trans. and ed. E. Anderson (London, rev.2/1966), ii, 792 and 850.

20 See L. Plantinga: *Clementi: his life and music* (London, New York, Toronto, 1977), 193, 223 and 303.

21 R. Schumann: *Gesammelte Schriften über Musik und Musiker* (Leipzig, 1914), i, 339; 'die trauliche Muttersprache'.

22 See Mozart's letter of 26 November 1777, in Anderson: *Letters of Mozart*, i, 391.

23 *Thayer's life of Beethoven*, rev. E. Forbes (Princeton, rev.2/1967), 115.

24 *Goethe's Werke*, vi, ed. E. Trunz (Hamburg, 1951), 43; 'Sie sind fürchterlich, wenn Sie so lustig sind.'

25 *Thayer's life of Beethoven*, 537.

26 Letter of 2 August 1794, in *The letters of Beethoven*, trans. and ed. E. Anderson (London, 1961), i, 18.

27 Letter of 29 June 1801; Ibid, i, 58.

28 Letter of 6 July 1804; Ibid, i, 109.

29 Letter of February 1808; Ibid, i, 186.

30 Letter of 28 January 1812; Ibid, i, 355.

31 This Schillerian phrase (which would not be out of place coming from the Marquis of Posa in *Don Carlos*) appears in the letter to Joseph Sonnleithner dated March 1804; Ibid, i, 107.

32 Letter of 8 August 1809; Ibid, i, 241–2.

33 Letter of May 1810; Ibid, i, 273. See Reading no. 10(c), p. 287.

34 A. W. Ambros: *Die Grenzen der Musik und Poesie: eine Studie zur Ästhetik der Tonkunst* (Leipzig, [1855]/R1976), 'Vorrede', p. ii.

35 In G. A. Villoteau: *Recherches sur l'analogie de la musique avec les arts qui ont pour objet l'imitation du langage* (Paris, 1807/R1971).

36 Letter of 26 July 1809, in Anderson: *Letters of Beethoven*, i, 235.

37 *Schillers Werke*, x, ed. S. Seidel (Weimar, 1980), 7.

38 *Auslegung deutsch des Vater unnser fuer dye einfeltigen leyen* (Leipzig, 1519), in *D. Martin Luthers Werke: Kritische Gesammtausgabe*, ii (Weimar, 1884), 101; 'nur ein wille unnd nith zwene willen widder eynander'.

39 Book v of J. J. Rousseau: *Émile ou de l'éducation* (Paris, 1764), 605; 'mais n'ayant rien à combattre pour suivre ses penchants ...'

40 *Wilhelm Meisters Lehrjahre*, Book I, Chapter 14, in *Goethes Werke*, vii, ed. E. Trunz (Hamburg, 1950), 54.

41 Letter to J. A. Streicher from Vienna in 1796, in Anderson: *Letters of Beethoven*, i, 25–6.

42 Letter of 26 September 1781, in Anderson: *Letters of Mozart*, ii, 769; see Reading no. 8.

43 Carpani: *Le Rossiniane*, 78; 'un canto che non è canto, ma voglia interrotta di canto'.

44 In A. Schering: *Beethoven und die Dichtung* (Berlin, 1936/R1973).

45 Hegel used this phrase in writing to a friend the day before the battle at Jena in 1806. See *Briefe von und an Hegel*, ed. J. Hoffmeister, i (Hamburg, 1952), 120; 'diese Weltseele ... hinausreiten'.

46 Letter of 19 September 1809, trans. in Anderson: *Letters of Beethoven*, i, 244.

47 *Fidelio*, Act I, scene 6.

48 Quoted in *Thayer's life of Beethoven*, 387.

49 Letter of 5 July 1806, in Anderson: *Letters of Beethoven*, i, 150.

50 G. Nottebohm: *Zweite Beethoveniana* (Leipzig, 1887/R1970), 378; 'mehr Ausdruck der Empfindung als Mahlerei'.

51 Letter of 26 July 1809, in Anderson: *Letters of Beethoven*, i, 234.

52 Letter of 4 January 1804; Ibid, i, 105.

53 Letter of 28 January 1812; Ibid, i, 353.

54 See letter of 6 January 1816; Ibid, ii, 549.

55 See letter of 17 September 1823; Ibid, iii, 1089.

56 Ibid, ii, 727.

57 See note 43 to Part III.

58 'L'Innominato' ('The Unnamed') is a character in Manzoni's *I promessi sposi*.

59 From the beginning of May 1823, in J.-G. Prod'homme: *Les cahiers de conversation 1819–1827* (Paris, 1946), 269; 'Si l'on savait ce que vous pensez dans votre musique!'

60 *Tutte le opere di G. Leopardi* (Milan, 1938), ii: *Zibaldone di Pensieri*, 322–3 (nos. 3208–10); 'il popolo, udendone il principio, ne indovina il mezzo e il fine e tutto l'andamento'.

61 The Nazarenes were a group of German painters who, in the early nineteenth century, tried to restore the quality of religious art (see p. 184).

62 From *Nachricht von den neuesten Schicksalen des Hundes Berganza*, no. 5 of the *Fantasiestücke in Callots Manier*, in E. T. A. Hoffmann: *Fantasie- und Nachtstücke* (Darmstadt, 1979), 118; 'sank der Philosoph mit emporgehobenen Händen auf die Knie, indem er tief aus dem Innersten heraus rief: "Santa Caecilia, ora pro nobis!"'

63 V. Hugo: *Les rayons et les ombres*, XXXV, iii, in *Oeuvres complètes de Victor Hugo*, ed. J. Cornuz, xviii (Berne, 1968), 385.

64 J. J. Rousseau: *Essai sur l'origine des langues*, ed. C. Porset (Paris, 1970), 179; 'Elle a déja cessé de parler; bientôt elle ne chantera plus.'

Essential bibliography

Abbreviations

AcM   Acta musicologica
JAMS   Journal of the American Musicological Society
MJ   Mozart-Jahrbuch
ML   Music and Letters
MQ   The Musical Quarterly
MR   Music Review
NRMI   Nuova Rivista Musicale Italiana
PRMA Proceedings of the Royal Musical Association.

Part I. 1-3

General
E. Bücken: *Die Musik des Rokokos und der Klassik* (Potsdam, 1927)
P. H. Lang: *Music in western civilization* (New York, 1941), chaps. 12-15
R. G. Pauly: *Music in the classic period* (Englewood Cliffs, New Jersey, 1973)
E. Wellesz and F. Sternfeld, eds: *The New Oxford History of Music*, vii, *The Age of Enlightenment, 1745-1790* (London, 1973). This includes an extensive bibliography. See also reviews by M. Mila in *NRMI*, viii (1974), 300 and W. S. Newman in *JAMS*, xxviii (1975), 384

For a cultural history
R. Wellek: *A history of modern criticism*, i (Yale University Press, 1955)

Replacing numerous earlier studies of the 'galant' style
D. A. Sheldon: 'The galant style revisited and re-evaluated', *AcM*, xlvii (1975), 240

For the development and success of sonata form
W. S. Newman: *The sonata in the classic era* (Chapel Hill, 1963; rev. 2/1972)
C. Rosen: *Sonata forms* (New York, 1980)

Bibliography

Important for other particular aspects

L. G. Ratner: 'Harmonic aspects of classic form', *JAMS*, ii (1949), 159
: 'Eighteenth-century theories of musical period structure', *MQ*, xlii (1956), 439

W. Mellers: *The sonata principle from c. 1750* (London, 1957) = vol iii of *Man and his music* by A. Harman, A. Milner and W. Mellers

G. Lazarevich: 'The Neapolitan intermezzo and its influence on the symphonic idiom', *MQ*, lvii (1971), 294

Rousseau and music

J. Tiersot: *Jean-Jacques Rousseau, un maître de la musique* (Paris, 1912/R1977)

4–8

Indispensable starting points for the Italian harpsichordists

F. Torrefranca: *Le origini italiane del romanticismo musicale* (Turin, 1930)
:*Giovanni Benedetto Platti e la sonata moderna* (Milan, 1963)

C. P. E. Bach

P. Barford: *The keyboard music of C. P. E. Bach* (London, 1965)

C. P. E. Bach: *Essay on the true art of playing keyboard instruments*, tr. W. J. Mitchell (New York, 1949): a translation of the *Versuch*

The origins of the symphony

G. Cucuel: *La Pouplinière et la musique de chambre au XVIIIᵉ siècle* (Paris, 1913/R1971)

B. S. Brook: *La symphonie française dans la seconde moitié du XVIIIᵉ siècle* (Paris, 1962), 3 vols.

The Mannheim school

H. Riemann: 'Die Mannheimer Schule', in *Denkmäler der Tonkunst in Bayern*, III/i (Leipzig, 1902)

E. K. & J. K. Wolf: 'A newly identified complex of manuscripts from Mannheim', *JAMS*, xxvii (1974), 371

For a basic history of the string quartet

L. Finscher: *Studien zur Geschichte des Streichquartetts* (Kassel, 1974); see also the review by J. Webster in *JAMS*, xxviii (1975), 543

Individual composers

B. Churgin: *The symphonies of Sammartini* (diss., Harvard Univ., 1963)

P. Gradenwitz: 'The symphonies of Johann Stamitz', *MR*, i (1940), 354

E. K. Wolf: *The symphonies of Johann Stamitz: authenticity, chronology, and style* (New York, 1972)

C. S. Terry: *Johann Christian Bach* (London, 1929; rev.2/1967)

Part II. 9–15

General

A. Lowenberg: *Annals of opera 1597–1950* (Geneva, 2/1955)

D. J. Grout: *A short history of opera* (New York, 2/1965)

G. Barblan & A. Basso, eds: *Storia dell'Opera* (Turin, 1977), 3 vols.

Bibliography

A. A. Abert: 'Die Oper zwischen Barock und Romantik', *AcM*, xlix (1977), 137. A basic bibliographical survey since the Second World War

The 'querelle des bouffons'
D. Launay, ed: *La Querelle des Bouffons: texte des pamphlets avec introduction, commentaires et index* (Geneva, 1973), 3 vols.
E. Surian: *A checklist of writings on 18th-century French and Italian opera (excluding Mozart)* (Hackensack, 1970)
A. M. Whittall: *La Querelle des Bouffons* (diss., Univ. of Cambridge, 1963)
O. Strunk: *Source readings in music history* (London, 1952), with English translations of selected passages

On the significance of the debate in relation to French philosophy
E. Fubini: *Gli enciclopedisti e la musica* (Turin, 1971)

More detailed aspects
F. Fido: *Guide a Goldoni. Teatro e società nel Settecento* (Turin, 1977), includes a chapter devoted to Goldoni as a librettist
W. Bollert: *Die Buffoopern Baldassare Galuppis* (diss., Univ. of Berlin, 1935)
A. Chiuminatto: *The liturgical works of Baldassare Galuppi* (diss., Northwestern Univ. 1958)
A della Corte: *Piccinni: settecento italiano* (Bari, 1928)
H. Abert: 'Piccinni als Buffokomponist', *Gesammelte Schriften und Vorträge* (Halle, 1929)
J. G. Rushton: *Music and drama at the Académie Royale de Musique, Paris, 1774–1789* (diss., Univ. of Oxford, 1970)
B. Cagli: 'La buona figliola e la nascità dell'opera semiseria', *Chigiana*, xxxii (1977), 265

The rediscovery of classical antiquity
G. Highet: *The classical tradition. Greek and Roman influences on western literature* (Oxford, 1949)

Metastasio
Tutte le opere, ed. B. Brunelli (Milan, 1947–54), 5 vols; vols. iii, iv and v include his letters
F. Gavezzeni: 'Introduzione' to P. Metastasio: *Opere scelte* (Turin, 1968)

Melodrama
J. van der Veen: *Le mélodrame musical de Rousseau au Romantisme* (The Hague, 1955)
E. Vogl Garret: 'Georg Benda, the pioneer of the melodrama', *Studies in eighteenth-century music: a tribute to Karl Geiringer* (London, 1970), 236

The courts at Parma and Stuttgart as centres of theatrical reform
A. Yorke–Long: *Music at court: four eighteenth-century studies* (London, 1954)
D. Heartz: 'Operatic reform at Parma: "Ippolito ed Aricia" ', *Convegno sul Settecento parmense nel 2° centenario della morte di C. I. Frugoni* (Parma, 1968), 271

303

Bibliography

Individual composers

H. Abert: *Niccolò Jommelli als Opernkomponist, mit einer Biographie* (Halle, 1908)

H. Goldschmidt: 'Traettas Leben und Werke', in *Denkmäler der Tonkunst in Bayern*, XIV/I (Leipzig, 1913)

H. Bloch: 'Tommaso Traetta's contribution to the reform of Italian opera', *Collectanea Historiae Musicae*, iii (1963), 5

M. Cyr: 'Rameau e Traetta', *NRMI*, xii (1978), 166

D. di Chiera: *The life and operas of Gian Francesco de Majo* (diss., Univ of California, Los Angeles, 1962)

P. Donati: *Lineamenti dell'arte di Gian Francesco de Majo* (diss., Univ. of Rome, 1966)

F. Lippmann: 'Über Cimarosas "opere serie" ', in *Sviluppi stilistici della musica italiana fra il 1770 e il 1830*, Analecta musicologica, xxi (forthcoming)

J. E. Johnson: *Domenico Cimarosa (1749–1801)* (diss., Univ. College, Cardiff, 1976)

16–18
Gluck

K. Hortschansky: *Parodie und Entlehnung im Schaffen Christoph Willibald Glucks*, Analecta musicologica, xiii (Cologne, 1973), includes a general and a detailed bibliography

Christoph Willibald Gluck. Sämtliche Werke (Kassel, 1951–), with introductions and critical commentaries to individual works

A. Carse: *The history of orchestration* (New York, 1964), on his instrumentation

'Gluck e la cultura italiana nella Vienna del suo tempo', conference papers published in *Chigiana*, xxix–xxx (1975)

The problems of the 'reform'

P. Howard: *Gluck and the birth of modern opera* (London, 1963)

P. Gallarati: *Gluck e Mozart* (Turin, 1975)

Gasparo Angiolini

L. Tozzi: *Il balletto pantomimo del Settecento: Gasparo Angiolini* (L'Aquila, 1972)

Piccinni and Salieri in Paris

G. M. Leblond, ed.: *Mémoires pour servir à l'histoire de la révolution opérée dans la musique par M. le Chevalier Gluck* (Naples [Paris], 1781/R1967)

F. Degrada: 'Due volti di Ifigenia' and 'Le due Ifigenie e la Querelle Gluck-Piccinni', *Chigiana*, xxxii (1975), 165

J. Rushton: 'Salieri's "Les Horaces": a study of an operatic failure', *MR*, xxxvii (1976), 266

:' "Iphigénie en Tauride": the operas of Gluck and Piccinni', *ML*, liii (1972), 411

19–20
Eighteenth-century opera buffa in general

M. Scherillo: *L'opera buffa napoletana durante il Settecento. Storia letteraria* (Milan, 2/1917)

Bibliography

A. della Corte: *L'opera comica italiana del '700* (Bari, 1923), 2 vols.

M. Robinson: *Naples and Neapolitan opera* (Oxford, 1972)

R. A. Mooser: *Annales de la musique et des musiciens en Russie au XVIIIe siècle* (Geneva, 1949–51), 3 vols.

Paisiello

H. Abert: 'Paisiellos Buffokunst und ihre Beziehungen zu Mozart', *Gesammelte Schriften und Vorträge* (Halle, 1929) and *Archiv für Musikwissenschaft*, i (1918/19), 402

A. della Corte: *Paisiello* (Turin, 1922)

A. Einstein: 'A "King Theodore" opera', *Essays on Music* (New York, 1956; rev.2/1958), 195

Da Ponte's memoirs

C. Pagnini, ed: *Memorie e altri scritti* (Milan, 1971); English translations by L. A. Sheppard (London, 1929) and A. Livingston and E. Abbott (Philadelphia, 1929/R1967)

Comic opera outside Italy

S. Clercx: *Grétry, 1741–1813* (Brussels, 1944)

G. Calmus: *Die ersten deutschen Singspiele von Standfuss und Hiller* (Leipzig, 1908)

R. Pröpper: *Die Bühnenwerke Johann Friedrich Reichardts: ein Beitrag zur Geschichte der Oper in der Zeit des Stilwandels zwischen Klassik und Romantik* (Bonn, 1965)

E. W. White: *The rise of English opera* (New York, 1951/R1972)

R. Fiske: *English theatre music in the eighteenth century* (London, 1973)

J. Subirá: *La tonadilla escénica* (Madrid, 1928–30), 3 vols.

21

General

O. Ursprung: *Die katholische Kirchenmusik* (Potsdam, 1931)

F. Blume: *Geschichte der evangelischen Kirchenmusik* (Kassel, 1965); trans., enlarged, as *Protestant church music : a history* (New York, 1974)

E. Olleson: 'Church music and oratorio', *The New Oxford History of Music*, vii (London, 1973), chap. 4

R. G. Pauly: 'The reforms of church music under Joseph II', *MQ*, xliii (1957), 372

M. Chusid: 'Some observations on liturgy, text and structure in Haydn's late masses', *Studies in eighteenth-century music: a tribute to Karl Geiringer* (London, 1970), 125

Part III. 22–3

The 'Sturm und Drang'

L. Mittner: *Storia della letteratura tedesca: dal pietismo al romanticismo (1700–1820)*, part 3 (Turin, 1964)

R. Pascal: *The German Sturm and Drang* (Manchester, 1953)

Bibliography

G. Baioni: *Classicismo e rivoluzione: Goethe e la Rivoluzione francese* (Naples, 1969)

B. S. Brook: 'Sturm und Drang and the romantic period in music', *Studies in romanticism*, ix (1970), 269

'Viennese classical style' and its links with sonata form

R. H. Rowen: 'Some 18th-century classifications of musical style', *MQ*, xxxiii (1947), 90

T. G. Georgiades: 'Zur Musiksprache der Wiener Klassiker', *MJ*, 1951 (Salzburg, 1953), 50

L. Finscher: 'Zum Begriff der Klassik in der Musik', *Deutsches Jahrbuch der Muskwissenschaft*, xi (1966), 9

J. P. Larsen: 'Some observations on the development and characteristics of Vienna classical instrumental music', *Studia Musicologica*, ix (1967), 115

F. Ritzel: *Die Entwicklung der 'Sonatenform' im musiktheoretischen Schriftum des 18. und 19. Jahrhunderts* (Wiesbaden, 1968)

H. C. R. Landon: *Essays on the Viennese classical style* (London, 1970)

C. Rosen: *The classical style: Haydn, Mozart, Beethoven* (London, 1971; rev.2/1973)

H. H. Eggebrecht: *Versuch über die Wiener Klassik. Die Tanzszene in Mozarts "Don Giovanni"*, Beihefte zum Archiv für Musikwissenschaft, xii (Wiesbaden, 1972); see also the review by L. Bianconi in NRMI, vii (1973), 134

R. Barret-Ayres: *Joseph Haydn and the string quartet* (London, 1974)

J. R. Stevens: 'Theme, harmony, and texture in classic–romantic description of concerto first-movement form', *JAMS*, xxvii (1974), 25

J. Webster: 'Towards a history of Viennese chamber music in the early classical period', *JAMS*, xvii (1974), 212

C. Dahlhaus: 'Storia europea della musica nell'età del classicismo viennese', *NRMI*, xii (1978), 499

24

Haydn – major works

A. van Hoboken: *Joseph Haydn: thematisch-bibliographisches Werkverzeichnis* (Mainz, 1957–78), 3 vols, the main catalogue of his works

H. C. R. Landon, ed: *The collected correspondence and London notebooks of Joseph Haydn* (London, 1959)

D. Bartha and H. C. R. Landon, eds: *Joseph Haydns gesammelte Briefe und Aufzeichnungen* (Kassel, 1965)

H. C. R. Landon: *Haydn: chronicle and works* (London, 1976–80), 5 vols. (*Haydn: the early years 1732–1765*; *Haydn at Esterháza 1766–1790*; *Haydn in England 1791–1795*; *Haydn: the years of "The Creation" 1796–1800*; and *Haydn: the late years 1801–1809*)

Earlier Haydn bibliography

K. Geiringer: *Joseph Haydn* (Potsdam, 1932)

 :*Haydn: a creative life in music* (New York, 1946; enlarged 2/1963/R1968)

J. P. Larsen: *Die Haydn-Überlieferung* (Copenhagen, 1939)

Bibliography

D. F. Tovey: 'Haydn's chamber music', *Essays and lectures on music* (London, 1943), I
R. Hughes: *Haydn* (London, Master Musicians series, 1950, 5/1975)
H. C. R. Landon: *The symphonies of Joseph Haydn* (London, 1955); with supplement (1961)

25

Boccherini
Y. Gérard: *Thematic, bibliographical and critical catalogue of the works of Luigi Boccherini* (London, 1969)
G. de Rothschild: *Luigi Boccherini: sa vie, son oeuvre* (Paris, 1962); trans. A. Mayor as *Luigi Boccherini: his life and work* (London, 1965); contains an appendix of letters from the years 1780–1800

Dittersdorf
Lebensbeschreibung, seinem Sohne in die Feder diktiert (Leipzig, 1801), published in a modern edition, ed. E. Schmitz (Regensburg, 1940); trans. A. D. Coleridge as *The autobiography of Karl von Dittersdorf* (London, 1896/R1970)

Cambini and the Parisian quartet
L. Trimpert: *Die Quatuors concertants von Giuseppe Cambini* (Tutzing, 1967)

26

Mozart
Main Bibliography
L. von Köchel: *Chronologisch-thematisches Verzeichnis sämtlicher Tonwerke Wolfgang Amade Mozarts* (Leipzig, 1862; 7th ed. Wiesbaden, 1965)
W. A. Bauer, O. E. Deutsch and J. H. Eibl, eds: *Mozart: Briefe und Aufzeichnungen: Gesamtausgabe* (Kassel, etc., 1962–75), 6 vols; trans. and ed. E. Anderson as *The letters of Mozart and his family* (London, 1938; rev.2/1966, ed. A. H. King and M. Carolan), 2 vols.
O. E. Deutsch: *Mozart: die Dokumente seines Lebens* (Kassel, 1961); trans. E. Blom, P. Branscombe and J. Noble as *Mozart: a documentary biography* (London, 1965, 2/1966; supplement 1978)
Mozart-Jahrbuch, founded by H. Abert in 1923 and from 1950 published by the Internationale Stiftung Mozarteum, Salzburg, gives a guide to Mozart studies
W. A. Mozart: Neue Ausgabe sämtlicher Werke (Kassel, etc., 1955–), for introductions and critical commentaries to individual works

For lists of recent publications
R. Angermüller and O. Schneider: 'Mozart-Bibliographie (bis 1970)', *MJ* (1975)
: *Mozart-Bibliographie 1971–1975 mit Nachträgen bis 1970* (Kassel, 1978)

Classics of the Mozart bibliography
H. Abert: *W. A. Mozart*, 5th revised edn of O. Jahn's biography (Leipzig,

Bibliography

1919–21 in 2 vols; 7/1955–6 in 3 vols.); trans. (Cambridge, forthcoming)

T. de Wyzewa and G. de Saint-Foix: *Wolfgang Amédée Mozart: sa vie musicale et son oeuvre* (Paris, 1912–46), 5 vols.

B. Paumgartner: *Mozart* (Berlin, 1927; enlarged 6/1967)

A. Einstein: *Mozart: his character, his work* (New York, 1945; German orig. 1947, 4/1960)

Mozart's operas

E. J. Dent: *Mozart's operas: a critical study* (London, 1913; 2/1947)

W. Mann: *The operas of Mozart* (London, 1977)

C. Osborne: *The complete operas of Mozart* (London, 1978)

W. Ruf: *Die Rezeption von Mozarts "Le nozze di Figaro"*, Beihefte zum Archiv fur Musikwissenschaft, xvi (Wiesbaden, 1977), on the history of musical theatre at Vienna in the decade 1780–90

Mozart und Italien, Analecta musicologica, xviii (Cologne, 1978); papers from a conference held in Rome in 1974

H. Abert: *Mozart's "Don Giovanni"* (London, 1976; German orig. 1919–21)

M. Mila: *Lettura della "Nozze di Figaro"* (Turin, 1979), from a university course 1969–70

J. Rushton: *W. A. Mozart: "Don Giovanni"* (Cambridge, 1981)

Part IV. 27

The development of the public concert

S. J. Sadie: 'Concert life in eighteenth-century England', *PRMA*, lxxxv (1958–9), 17

H. Raynor: *A social history of music* (London, 1972), chap. 18

C. Pierre: *Histoire du Concert spirituel 1725–1790* (Paris, 1975)

L. Finscher: 'Zur Sozialgeschichte des klassischen Streichquartetts', *Bericht über den Internationalen Musikwissenschaftlichen Kongress* (Kassel, 1963)

J. Tick: 'Musician and Mécène: some observations on patronage in late 18th-century France', *International Review of the Aesthetics and Sociology of Music*, iv (1973), 245

The origins of modern music historiography

E. Hegar: *Die Anfänge der neueren Musikgeschichtsschreibung um 1770 bei Gerbert, Burney und Hawkins* (Leipzig, Strasbourg and Zurich, 1932)

P. A. Scholes: *The great Dr. Burney* (London, New York and Toronto, 1948), 2 vols.

28

Music and the French Revolution

C. Pierre: *Les hymnes et chansons de la Révolution* (Paris, 1904)

J. Gallay, ed: *Un inventaire sous la Terreur. État des instruments de musique relevé chez les émigrés et condamnés par A. Bruni* (Paris, 1890)

G. Knepler: *Musikgeschichte des 19. Jahrhunderts* (Berlin, 1961), 2 vols.

A. Coy: *Die Musik der französischen Revolution (zur Funktionbestimmung von Lied und Hymne)* (Munich, 1978); the most comprehensive work

Bibliography

T. Fleischman: *Napoléon et la musique* (Brussels and Paris, 1965); a more general study

29

Romanticism – general
M. Praz: *La carne, la morte e il diavolo nella letteratura romantica* (Turin, 1942), opening chapters
C. Magris: *Il mito asburgico nella letteratura austriaca moderna* (Turin, 1963)
F. Antal: 'Reflections on Classicism and Romanticism', *The Burlington Magazine*, lxvi (1935), 159
F. B. Artz: *From the Renaissance to Romanticism* (Chicago, 1962)

Musical
F. Blume: *Classic and romantic music* (London, 1970); a collection of earlier essays
A. Forchert: ' "Klassisch" und "romantisch" in der Musikliteratur des frühen 19. Jahrhunderts', *Die Musikforschung*, xxxi (1978), 405

30

General
A. Pougin: *L'Opéra-comique pendant la Révolution* (Paris, 1891)
:*Un directeur d'opéra au dix-huitième siècle* (Paris, 1914)
E. J. Dent: *The rise of romantic opera*, lectures from 1937–8 ed. W. Dean (Cambridge, 1976)
A. Einstein: *Music in the romantic era* (New York, 1947), in particular the section on 'Antecedents of the romantic opera' (p. 104)
R. M. Longyear: 'Notes on the rescue opera', *MQ*, xlv (1959), 49
N. Demuth: *French opera: its development to the Revolution* (London, 1964)
W. Dean: 'Opera under the French Revolution', *PRMA*, xciv (1967–68), 77
A. L. Ringer: 'Cherubini's "Médée" and the spirit of French revolutionary opera', *Essays in Musicology in Honor of Dragan Plamenac* (Pittsburgh, 1969/R1977), 281

Individual composers
C. Schroeder: *Chronologisches Verzeichnis der Werke Luigi Cherubinis* (Berlin, 1962)
B. Deane: *Cherubini* (London, 1965)
G. Confalonieri: *Cherubini* ([Milan], rev.2/1978)
A. Pougin: *Méhul* (Paris, 1889; 2/1893)
G. Gaetti and M. Spontini, eds: *Espistolario familiare e documenti vari dal 1774 al 1851 di Gaspare Spontini* (Maiolati, 1974)
P. Fragapane: *Spontini* (Bologna, 1954), with a catalogue of printed and manuscript works to be found in Italian libraries
L. Ronga: 'Gaspare Spontini', in *Arte e gusto nella Musica* (Milan and Naples, 1956)
J. Freeman: 'J. S. Mayr and his "Ifigenia in Aulide" ', *MQ*, lvii (1971), 187

Bibliography

31

Clementi

A. Tyson, ed: *Thematic catalogue of the works of Muzio Clementi* (Tutzing, 1967)

R. Allorto: *Le sonate per pianoforte di Muzio Clementi: studio critico e catalogo tematico* (Florence, 1959)

L. Plantinga: *Muzio Clementi: his life and music* (London, 1976)

The London piano school

E. Blom: *Classics: major and minor* (London, 1958)

A. L. Ringer: 'Beethoven and the London pianoforte school', *MQ*, lvi (1970), 742

Chamber music and the symphony

H. Unverricht: *Geschichte der Streichtrios* (Tutzing, 1969)

A. L. Ringer: 'A French symphonist at the time of Beethoven: Étienne Nicolas Méhul', *MQ*, xxxvii (1951), 543

Viotti

R. Giazotto: *Giovan Battista Viotti* (Milan, 1956)

C. White: *G. B. Viotti and his violin concertos* (diss., Princeton Univ., 1957)

32–3

Beethoven – main bibliography

G. Kinsky and H. Halm: *Das Werk Beethovens: thematisch-bibliographisches Verzeichnis seiner sämtlichen vollendeten Kompositionen* (Munich and Duisburg, 1955)

Beethoven-Jahrbuch published by the Beethovenhaus in Bonn (1953–)

Ludwig van Beethoven: Werke: neue Ausgabe sämtlicher Werke (Henle, Munich, 1961–), edited by the Beethoven-Archiv in Bonn; so far over twenty volumes have appeared

Ludwig van Beethovens sämtliche Briefe, ed. E. Kastner (Leipzig, 1910), rev. and enlarged J. Kapp (Leipzig, 1923)

The letters of Beethoven, trans. and ed. E. Anderson (London, 1961), 3 vols.

G.Schünemann, ed: *Ludwig van Beethovens Konversationshefte* (Berlin, 1941–3), 3 vols; followed by volumes from VEB–Deutscher Verlag für Musik, ed. K. H. Köhler, G. Herre and H. Schöny (Leipzig, 1968–), so far four volumes numbered iv–vii have appeared

Classics of the Beethoven bibliography

A. W. Thayer: *Ludwig van Beethovens Leben*, i–iii, ed. H. Dieters (Berlin, 1866–79); iv–v, ed. H. Riemann (Leipzig, 1907–8); trans. H. E. Krehbiel as *The life of Ludwig van Beethoven* (New York, 1921), 3 vols., rev. E. Forbes as *Thayer's life of Beethoven* (Princeton, 1964, 2/1967)

P. Bekker: *Beethoven* (Berlin, 1911; trans. 1925)

A. Sandberger: *Beethoven-Aufsätze* (Munich, 1924)

R. Rolland: *Beethoven, les grandes époques créatrices* (Paris, 1928–49), 6 vols; vol. i trans. E. Newman as *Beethoven the creator* (London, 1929)

W. Hess: *Beethoven* (Zurich, 1956, enlarged 2/1976)

M. Solomon: *Beethoven* (New York, 1977)

Bibliography

J. Kerman: 'Tovey's Beethoven', *Beethoven Studies 2*, ed. A. Tyson (Oxford and New York, 1977), lists numerous studies by D. F. Tovey

H. Schenker: *Beethovens Neunte Sinfonie* (Vienna, 1912, 2/1969); see also Schenker's annotated edition of the last five piano sonatas (Vienna, 1913–21), and the analysis of the 'Eroica' Symphony, 'Beethovens Dritte Sinfonie', *Das Meisterwerk in der Musik*, iii (Munich, 1930/R1974), 29

More recent publications
J. Kerman: *The Beethoven quartets* (New York, 1967)

M. Cooper: *Beethoven: the last decade* (London, 1970)

D. Arnold and N. Fortune, eds: *The Beethoven Companion* (London, 1971)

L. Magnani: *Beethoven nei suoi quaderni di conversazione* (Bari, 1970; 2/Turin, 1975, with an appendix 'Beethoven e l'Inghilterra')

The Musical Quarterly, lvi/4 (1970)

Beethoven-Studien: Festgabe der Österreichischen Akademie der Wissenschaft (Vienna, 1970)

'La fortuna di Beethoven nella vita musicale italiana di ieri', *NRMI*, iv/6 (1970) and following numbers

H. H. Eggebrecht: 'Zur Geschichte der Beethoven-Rezeption', *Beethoven 1970* (Wiesbaden, 1972), for the characteristics of the German literature on Beethoven

H. Unverricht: 'Beethovens Leben and Werk. Ein Bericht über den heutigen Stand der Forschung', *Die Musikforschung*, xxxi (1978), 38; an examination of the main directions of current research, which can be brought up to date by consulting the individual volumes of the *Beethoven-Jahrbuch.*

Important contributions to the up-dating and exploration of new trends in research
Beethoven-Studien I (Leipzig, 1974)

A. Tyson, ed: *Beethoven Studies* (New York, 1973)

: *Beethoven Studies 2* (Oxford and New York, 1977)

: *Beethoven Studies 3* (Cambridge, 1982)

Studies of the sketchbooks
P. Gossett: 'Beethoven's Sixth Symphony: sketches for the first movement', *JAMS*, xxvii (1974), 248, refers to the nineteenth-century work of G. Nottebohm (the pioneer in this field) and recent contributions from H. Schmidt, D. Johnson, A. Tyson and J. Kerman which have given a great impetus to this area of research

D. Johnson: 'Beethoven scholars and Beethoven's sketches', *19th Century Music*, ii (1978–9), 3

Index

Index

Index

Index

Index

316

Index

Index

Kotzebue, August Friedrich Ferdinand von, 163, 242, 243
Koželuh, Leopold Antonin, 207, 208
Kreutzer, Rodolphe, 188, 210, 212, 234

La Motte-Fouqué, see Fouqué, Friedrich Heinrich Karl de la Motte
Ländler, 182, 251, 256
language and music, 59–64, 250
La Pouplinière, J. J. Le Riche de, 34, 129, 169
Laserna, Blas de, 94
Latilla, Gaetano, 46
Lavater, Johann Kaspar, 101, 107, 174, 175
Lechantre, Mme, 172
Le Duc, Simon, 129, 171
Léger, 177
Leipzig, concert life in, 169–70
Lemoyne, Jean-Baptiste, 84
Lenz, Jakob, 101, 102, 103
Leo, Leonardo, 46, 48
Leopold II, Emperor of Austria, 92, 142, 145, 146, 220
Lessing, Gotthold Ephraim, 9, 10, 23, 43, 58, 75–6, 114, 152, 163
Lesueur, Jean-François, 194–5, 216
    La caverne, 194
    Ossian, 183, 195, 196
Lichnowsky, Prince Carl von, 170, 220
Lied, 23, 76, 95, 100, 164, 186, 197, 199, 208, 238, 248, 256
lira organizzata, 115, 116
Liszt, Franz, 84, 186–7, 215, 248
Lobkowitz, Ferdinand, 167
Lobkowitz, Prince Franz Joseph, 220
Locatelli, Giovanni Battista, 5, 49
Lolli, Antonio, 65
London: and Haydn, 116, 122–4
    musical life in, 38–9, 169
Lorenzi, Giovanni Battista, 87, 88, 120
Lully, Jean-Baptiste, 45, 58, 61, 66

Maelzel, Johann Nepomuk, 217
Malfatti, Therese, 221, 223, 286–7
Manfredi, Filippo, 131, 132
Mannheim, court orchestra at, 33, 266–8
Mannheim symphonists, 3, 5, 31, 35, 63, 66, 104, 119, 129, 141, 151, 170
Manzoni, Alessandro, 51, 251, 254, 257
Marcello, Benedetto, 56, 70
Maria Theresa, Empress of Austria, 3, 36, 73, 114, 140, 143, 146
Marmontel, Jean-François, 56, 80, 104, 186
Marpurg, Friedrich Wilhelm, 7, 8–9, 11, 25, 27, 106, 146, 207, 263n, 264n
Marschner, Heinrich August, 163, 200, 257
Martini, Giovanni Battista ('Padre

Martini'), 1, 32, 37, 38, 97–8, 140, 141, 150, 173, 174, 189, 207, 215, 256
▸ Martín y Soler, Vicente, 90, 132, 145
    Una cosa rara, 90, 146
'Masonic music', 55, 165, 180, 189
Mass, 98–9, 258
Mattei, Saverio, 65, 88
Mattei, Stanislao, 200, 215
Mattheson, Johann, 8, 231
Mayr, Johannes Simon, 108, 188, 201–2, 203, 255
    Medea in Corinto, 202
Mazzolà, Caterino, 163
Méhul, Étienne-Nicolas, 176, 180, 196, 197, 198, 201, 203, 213
    operas, 183, 185, 195
    symphonies, 212–13
melodrama, 62–4, 137, 190, 200
melody: and the imitation of language, 61–2
    and the sonata, 109
Mendelssohn-Bartholdy, Felix, 194, 195, 213, 235, 252, 258
Mercadante, Giuseppe Saverio, 186
Metastasian opera, 56–9
Metastasio, Pietro, 41, 47, 51, 66, 69, 70, 71, 72, 73, 89, 113, 120, 139, 149, 162, 163, 269n, 271–4
metronome, 217, 230
Meyerbeer, Giacomo, 84, 129, 198
Milan, musical life in, 32
Mingotti, Angelo and Pietro, 69, 71
minuet: 7, 8, 30, 122, 182
    and Beethoven, 231, 243, 248
    and Boccherini, 135, 150
    and Mozart, 145, 148, 150
    position in the symphony of, 16–17, 29, 34, 110–11, 148
    in the sonata, 21, 24, 27, 28, 110–11
Misón, Luis, 94
Mizler von Kolof, Lorenz Christoph, 14
Molière (Jean-Baptiste Poquelin), 73, 78
monferrina, 207
Monsigny, Pierre-Alexander, 94, 187, 195
Moore, Thomas, 182, 199
Mörike, Eduard, 165, 166, 216
Morlacchi, Francesco, 200
Moscheles, Ignaz, 207, 248
Mozart, Leopold, 7, 21, 32, 34, 35, 138, 139, 141, 149, 151
Mozart, Maria Anna (Nannerl), 139
Mozart, Wolfgang Amadeus, 13, 64, 76, 87, 92, 105, 111, 112, 122, 129, 134, 136–66, 170, 203, 214, 216, 217, 219, 225, 229, 230, 232, 259
    and J. C. Bach, 40, 139, 141–2, 148, 161
    and Beethoven, 163, 217, 224, 226–7, 228, 233
    career of, 138–48
    and Clementi, 147, 204, 207–8

318

Index

early influences on, 21, 28, 32, 69,
    148-9
and Freemasonry, 144, 154, 165
and Haydn, 120, 124, 125, 140-1,
    144, 149, 155
influences on other composers of, 70,
    90, 128, 130, 186, 192, 197, 202,
    211, 215
musical language of, 165-6
operatic finales of, 109, 158-9, 208
and patronage, 140, 142-4, 145, 147-8
Abendempfindung K 523, 76
chamber works with piano, 157
Clarinet Concerto in A K 622, 165
Divertimento K 247, 150
Ein musikalischer Spass K 522, 158
Fugue for two pianos in C minor
    K 426, 155
Das Lied der Trennung K 519, 76
operas, 149, 152-3, 157-61, 162-3
    Apollo et Hyacinthus, 149
    Ascanio in Alba, 140
    Bastien und Bastienne, 149
    La clemenza di Tito, 145, 162, 163
    Così fan tutte, 145, 162
    Don Giovanni, 90, 112, 120, 145,
        153, 157, 158-61, 162, 165, 176,
        180, 191, 224, 226, 227, 238, 248
    Die Entführung aus dem Serail, 96,
        144, 154-5, 159, 161, 162, 164,
        278-81
    La finta giardiniera, 86, 96, 137,
        141, 150
    La finta semplice, 149
    Idomeneo, 143, 152-3, 159, 227
    Lucio Silla, 140, 149
    Mitridate, 140
    Le nozze di Figaro, 89, 90, 110, 120,
        137, 144, 145, 146, 157-61,
        162-3, 165, 176, 191, 226, 238
    L'oca del Cairo, 157
    Il rè pastore, 150
    Der Schauspieldirektor, 157, 279n
    Lo sposo deluso, 157
    Die Zauberflöte, 49, 55, 83, 146,
        151, 155, 163-5, 180, 186, 193,
        197, 226, 242, 252
piano concertos, 144, 151, 156-7, 182
    K 271 in E flat, 137, 140, 151, 156,
        161
    K 466 in D minor, 157, 191, 227
    K 491 in C minor, 156, 157
    K 503 in C, 156, 157
    other works, 156
piano sonatas: K 279 in C, 40
    K 280 in F, 40
    K 282 in E flat, 150
    K 284 in D, 105, 150
    K 310 in A minor, 105, 151
    K 331 in D, 151
    K 332 in F, 151
    K 457 in C minor, 157
    K 576 in D, 155, 162

quartets, 155-6
    K 156-60, 149
    K 168-72, 149
    K 173 in D minor, 104, 149
    six quartets dedicated to Haydn
        (K 387, 421, 428, 458, 464 &
        465), 125, 144, 155, 161
quintets, 149, 162
sacred works, 99, 150-1, 152
    Ave verum K 618, 164, 165, 258
    Kyrie K 341, 152
    Masses, 150-1, 152, 155
    Requiem K 626, 145, 155, 165, 191,
        194, 207
    Die Schuldigkeit des ersten Gebots
        K 35, 149
    Vesperae solennes de confessore K 339,
        152
serenades, 150, 154, 231
Sinfonia concertante in E flat for wind
    K Anh. 9 (297b), 152
Sinfonia concertante for violin and
    viola in E flat K 364, 152
symphonies, 161
    K 16, K 19, K 22, K 43, K 45 & K 48,
        148
    K 183 in G minor, 40, 104, 140, 149,
        150, 151, 204
    K 200 in C, 149
    K 201 in A, 149, 150
    K 297 in D ('Paris'), 151-2
    K 338 in C, 152
    K 385 in D ('Haffner'), 161
    K 425 in C ('Linz'), 161
    K 504 in D ('Prague'), 161
    K 543 in E flat, 161
    K 550 in G minor, 161, 202
    K 551 in C ('Jupiter'), 123, 124, 155,
        161, 162, 192, 223
violin concertos, 151
violin sonatas, 151
Müller, Wenzel, 186
Müthel, Johann Gottfried, 26, 104
music printing and publishing, *see*
    printing of music
Mysliveček, Josef, 32, 69

Naderman, François-Joseph, 216
Nägeli, Hans Georg, 256
Naples: and comic opera, 87-93
    and operatic reform, 65-70
Napoleon Bonaparte, 93, 117, 147, 182,
    185, 193, 196, 197, 198, 201, 210,
    221, 234, 254, 255, 257
Nardini, Pietro, 65, 131, 140
Neefe, Christian Gottlob, 27, 63, 95, 219
Nichelmann, Christoph, 7
Noverre, Jean-Georges, 56, 58, 59, 65,
    73, 140, 141
    Lettres sur la danse, 57, 73

opera: act finales in, 43, 47, 49, 109,
    158-9, 280

Index

Index

Index

Index

court theatre in, 41
and the early symphony, 36–7
musical life in, 3, 72, 105–6, 129, 170, 186, 258
and sacred music, 97, 99
and *Singspiel*, 96
Viganò, Salvatore, 233
Villoteau, Guillaume André, 61, 223
Vinci, Leonardo, 269
Viotti, Giovanni Battista, 5, 171, 189, 210–11, 212
Vivaldi, Antonio, 4, 16, 26, 30, 31, 35, 37, 40, 118, 129, 133
  Le quattro stagioni, 117–18
Vogel, Johann Christoph, 84, 179, 231
Vogler, Abbé Georg Joseph, 107, 129
Voltaire, François-Marie Aronet, 33, 43, 57, 58, 61, 89, 199, 268, 272
  Lettres philosophiques, 10, 46

Wagenseil, Georg Christoph, 36, 40, 98, 116, 128, 136, 139, 148, 151
Wagner, Richard, 79, 185, 187, 200
  The Flying Dutchman, 55–6, 257
Waldstein, Count Ferdinand, 218, 219
Walsh, John, 31, 171

waltz, 182, 200, 207, 210, 247–8, 256
Weber, Aloysia, 141, 142, 144, 152
Weber, Costanza, 144
Weber, Carl Maria von, 62, 123, 129, 163, 164, 185, 200, 232, 243, 256, 257
  Der Freischütz, 64, 127, 197, 199, 242
  Invitation to the dance, 248
  Preziosa, 64
Weigl, Joseph, 186–7, 230, 243
Wendling, Dorothea, 152
Werner, Gregor, 114, 118, 127
Wieland, Christoph, 55, 85–6, 95, 163, 222
Winckelmann, Johann Joachim, 50–1, 197
Wolf, Ernst Wilhelm, 27

Zelter, Carl Friedrich, 174, 256, 257
Zeno, Apostolo, 69
Zingarelli, Nicola Antonio, 185–6, 200, 215
Zinzendorf, Count Nikolaus Ludwig, 146
Zmeskáll, Count Nikolaus Paul, 220, 223

323